Dedication

This book is dedicated to the men and women of the United States
Navy and to the People of Hawai`i.

Acknowledgements

These fine people, their associates, and many others too numerous to
list, went out of their way to help us. They were gracious, informative,
candid, and most friendly. They made our work a joy.

Washington DC
    National Archives
        Rick Peuser, Archivist

D0010632

Naval Historical Center
    Glen Helm, Chief Librarian

Annapolis
    United States Naval Academy
        John Cummings, Associate Librarian
        Barbara Parker, Associate Librarian
        Alice Creighton, Archivist
        Mary Rose Catalfano, Archivist
        Gary LaValley, Archivist

United States Naval Instititute
    Ann Hasinger, Librarian

California
    US Naval Postgraduate School, Monterey
        Commander Rich Grahlman, USN
        Michaele Lee Huygen, Reference Librarian

National Archives, San Bruno
    Kathleen O'Conner, Archivist

Hawaii
Camp H M Smith
Admiral Joseph Prueher, USN
Vice Admiral Timothy Beard, USN
Captain Kevin Wensing, USN
Lieutenant Commander Gil Mendez, USN
Colonel Thomas Boyd, USAF
Thomas Gordon, Historian

Pearl Harbor
Navy Base
Rear Admiral W.G. Sutton, USN
Rear Admiral R.T. Reimann, USN (Ret.)
Rear Admiral W.A. Retz, USN (Ret)
Captain W Rigby, USN
Captain J Shrewsbury, USN
Commander Mary Ann Duff, USN
Lieutenant Commander Rod Gibbons, USN
Agnes Tauyan, Deputy PAO

Sub Base/Naval Station
Captain G Covington, USN

FISC
Jim Murray, Deputy PAO

Shipyard
Commander Kelley Spellman, USN
Marshall Fukuki, Editor, LOG
Frances Abbatuan, Librarian
Pat Yornes, Librarian

PACDIV
Jeff Dodge, Historic Preservationist

USS Arizona
Dan Martinez, Park Historian
Edean Saito, Business Manager

USS Missouri
Vice Admiral Robert Kihune, USN (Ret), President
Roy Yee, Past-President, Memorial Association
Tom Manuel, Vice President, Mem'l Assoc.
Adrianne Greenlees, Executive Assistant

USS Bowfin
Captain Gerald Hofwolt, USN (Ret)
Bob Burt, Assistant Director
Charles Hinman, Archivist

Bishop Museum
Betty Lou Kam, Archives Chairman
Stephen Coles, PhD, Zoologist
DeSoto Brown, Archvist

University of Hawai`i
Henry Iwasa, Executive Secretary, Committee for the Preservation
and Study of Hawaiian Language, Art and Culture

Hong Kong
The American Club
Pat Eden, Librarian

Singapore
National Archives
Pitt Kuan Weh, Assistant Director

National University
Brian Farrell, Chairman, Military History Department

Research Assistants
Heidi Maisl
Michael Landauer
Vincent Travens

Table of Contents

Introduction i

1   Discovery and Settlement 1

2   Two Captains and a King 9

3   Rise and Fall of the American Navy 23

4   Birth of the United States Navy 31

5   Round the Horn to Whyteetee 39

6   Years of Crisis 47

7   Foreigners Try to 'Save' Hawaii 55

8   'Mad Jack' Percival & ap Catesby Jones 65

9   Discontent and Paulet's Folly 79

10   The Great Mahele 95

11   Politics and Sugar 101

12   Worth its Weight in Sugar 109

13   An Election Surprise 119

14   1887: A Bad Year for Kalakaua 127

15   Ruthless Politics 135

16   Monarchy is *pau* 143

17   Confluence 153

18   The New Territory 161

19   Acquisition of Pearl Harbor 169

20   The Marines Land 179

21   Territorial Years 189

22   Two New Weapons 197

23   The Territory Matures 209

24   Too Much *Pilikia* 219

25   Another Drawdown 241

26   The Ominous Thirties 249

27   The Attack 261

28   War 271

29   Statehood 291

30   Challenges 303

31   Changes 311

32   Memorials 323

33   A New Century 331

PANINA 349

Table of Contents (continued)

APPENDICES 351

    I   Rulers

    II   Governors

    III   SECNAVs

    IV   CNOs

    V   PACRONs

    VI   NAVSTA, 1899 - 1915

    VII   14th ND, 1916 - 1979

    VIII   NAVBASE, 1980 - Present

    IX   NAVSTA, 1955 - 1998

    X   NAVBASE, 1945 - 1950

    XI   YARD

    XII   SUPPLY

    XIII   SUBASE

    XIV   USMC

    XV   PWC

    XV   NAVBASE Organization

ABBREVIATIONS 373

ENDNOTES 375

BIBLIOGRAPHY 399

INDEX 407

INTRODUCTION

If there is any task historical research forces upon the researcher, it is the answering of questions. But the questions must first be formulated. And one element which makes research so fascinating is that many answers lead to more questions.

Our goal was to follow two streams of history: that of the People of Hawaii and that of the United States Navy and the relationships of these two great segments of society after they came together. Our initial direction was determined by such questions as: Who are (were) these people who called themselves "The United States Navy"?; By whom were they greeted in Hawaii?; What was the nature of their reception?; What cultural conflicts occurred, and what were the results? And, of course, why did they come together in the first place?

The search for the answers to these (and many more) questions formed the basis of our quest. We followed the sometimes bizarre, sometimes tragic, interaction between these two groups of people. The relationship between the United States Navy and the Hawaiian People is as alive and vibrant today as it ever has been. Emphases have changed. Missions have changed. The political climate has changed. Our story seeks the origins and traces the people through their amazing history to the end of the twentieth century.

The name Pearl Harbor evokes different images in the minds of different people. To some it is a place to visit on a trip to Hawaii. To others it is a location where people once fished, sought pearls, and planted Taro. There are those who view it as the strategic defensive focus of the American west coast. But the most vivid feelings are in the minds of those alive during the sudden, deadly, and devastating attack on December 7, 1941. The first question most Americans asked each other that day in the halls of Washington, the streets of Dallas, or the restaurants of San Francisco was, "Where the hell is Pearl Harbor?" Most had never heard of it and many did not even know the location of the Hawaiian Islands. They soon found out and images of death and destruction became all too vivid in a war that lasted four grueling years.

The lagoon, or estuary, now called Pearl Harbor existed long before the "date that will live in infamy"[1] and still does. It is a place of military activity, industry, recreation, and a refuge from the sea. Its original inhabitants sustained themselves on the most remote islands in the world for centuries. When the estuary was acquired by the United States Navy it became a Supply Center, Shipyard, and Naval Station, as well as a place of uneasy cooperation between disparate cultures.

A comment about orthography is in order here. We have eschewed an attempt to ascribe the appropriate diacritical marks to each Hawaiian word used in our text. The macron (mekona) and the glottal stop ('okina) are extensively used in current printed Hawaiian literature. However since our opening chapters are simply an overview of the culture that evolved, we felt that several Hawaiian words and expressions were proper to use. We have used the apostrophe in place of the proper glottal stop mark as an indication of the pronunciation for readers unfamiliar with current Hawaiian usage. To ascribe all the proper marks would require the work of linguists with more experience than we have. To convey the wonderful flavor of the Hawaiian language is our goal.

Also, although our text has been reviewed by people from the US Navy, the University of Hawaii, the National Park Service and several historians, the opinions expressed herein are those of the authors.

We trace the historic changes in the lagoon and the uses of this unique place by the earliest inhabitants as well as the first European and American settlers. We discuss the varied and sometimes incredible events that occurred between 'discovery' and acquisition by the United States. The role of this unique place in peacetime and war will be a major focus as will recent changes and plans for its future.

The event that brought Pearl Harbor to the attention of the world in 1941 was cataclysmic, but in the larger picture it was only one event in the flow of its historical existence.

1 Franklin D Roosevelt address to joint session of Congress, December 8, 1941.

Chapter 1 - Discovery and Settlement

The islands of Hawaii, *Na Moku Hawai'i*, are a chain of mountain tops rising in the middle of the Pacific Ocean more remote from land than any other place on earth. They are over two thousand miles from both the west coast of the United States and the east coast of Japan. Created by volcanic action, the internal fires that created these islands continue to change its contours, create new land and extend the reach of the archipelago.

These islands were unknown in the west until encountered by sea-going Europeans in the 18th century. By then what we now call Pearl Harbor, on the island of Oahu, was already occupied, used and enjoyed by a culture soon to be discovered by the rest of the world.

The early settlement of the Hawaiian Islands is shrouded in mist. No one knows who the first human being was who saw Hawaii. There may have been people who came only to perish in the islands and there may have been others who saw the islands but could not reach them. One group came to this remote place from the southern ocean in the first millennium of the present era. Little evidence of their tenure exists other than a few artifacts. There are also many stories and legends told by ancestors of living Hawaiians to their descendants. The date for this early discovery is vague and may never be known. It has been postulated that the first landing occurred in the first century of the present era. Some believe that this occurred in the fourth century and others believe it was in the eighth century. All agree that some centuries later there was another group which found the islands independently, probably in the 12th or 13th century. The first group probably came from the Marquesas, the second from Tahiti in the Society Islands. This is based on a major cultural shift that occurred at this time. The origins of the Hawaiians are still unclear. What is known is based partly on language, since the Hawaiian language has an eighty percent agreement with the Tahitian language. These origins are also based on archaeological evidence, local legends, chants, rituals and racial similarities and differences.

One remarkable feature of the arrival of the Hawaiians is the fact that they reached these remote islands at all. Two theories exist concerning how these early people came to Hawaii. One is that they found the islands accidentally. The other is that they came intentionally.[1] If the discovery was accidental, then they did not need great navigational skills to get there. They did, however' need sea-going vessels if they were to survive the trip. Such vessels existed. Polynesians had traveled long distances among the islands of the South Pacific Sea for many centuries. They had perfected the building and handling of canoes with outriggers, sails and even large double canoes before they left those islands.

It is difficult to imagine these great voyages as accidental because the people who made them were more than familiar with the sea; they lived in it, on it and ate the bounty from it every day. They must have been skilled navigators to find their way among far flung islands. Anyone who has traveled in a small craft away from the shore knows the baffling anonymity of waves and the endless expanse of sky. In such emptiness, with no landmarks, position is difficult to assess and frustration is high when a noon sight on a cloudy day is impossible. They had no navigational instruments such as sextant, chronometer or compass. Imagine the skill of an ancient seafarer who could find his way without such aids. It was a daunting, formidable task, yet they did it.

They built canoes, lashed two hulls together to make double canoes connected by a platform. Some of these are reported to have been sixty feet long and others, especially those used for long voyages, up to one hundred feet long. Made of hollowed out trees, they were bound together with bark and fibers, the sails woven of pandanus leaves or other local materials. These vessels were sturdy enough to survive immersion in salt water for long periods and endure the endless pounding of waves. Wear on parts and connections must have been fierce.

They carried several kinds of material and staples with them and repaired worn parts as they went along. Whenever encountered, fish and birds were caught for food. Thirty men and women, maybe more, might travel aboard a single vessel. If it were an extensive trip, they would bring animals, food and water, images and gods. Even today, such a voyage would be intimidating. Yet they did it.

And what of the people themselves? All those who sail today know the strain a long voyage can have on compatibility, under the best of modern circumstances. What did they do about sickness or injury? How did the master navigator stay awake? How did they settle differences? It took men and women of great courage and stamina. Yet they did it.

These intrepid voyagers had vast knowledge and experience of the sea, the weather, and the sky. Genealogies and legends corroborate that voyages over prodigious distances did take place.[2] Star charts made of twigs and shells have been found which may have been used as memory joggers for navigators. They were not the primary instrument nor were they necessary. Wayfinding was the responsibility of one group with special knowledge. In the 1970s anthropologists located men on Pacific Islands who had been trained in the wayfinding system that was used by their ancestors. They had not forgotten the skill.

The technique includes knowing the night sky and the position of each star at each hour of the night at each latitude. It was also necessary to know and read the direction of waves by day, and be familiar with wind direction. This difficult responsibility was re-created by Nainoa Thompson, with the help of native 'wayfinders' and modern astronomers. In 1980 *Hokule'a*, a sixty-five foot fiberglass replica of a double canoe headed to Tahiti with no motor and no modern navigational instrument. A dozen people made that trip. Besides steering the boat, they cooked, mended and repaired parts that wore out. The most vital member of the crew, however, was Nainoa. With the help of a native wayfinder from the island of Satawal, in the Carolines, Micronesia, he navigated the entire way. The trip was an experiment, a test of this ancient navigation system as well as of boat construction. It strongly suggested that it could have been done centuries earlier.[3] This successful trip of six thousand miles each way, doesn't prove that it was originally done that way, but it was now clear that it was possible.

One last question is vital. How did the first seamen to reach Hawaii know it was there? According to legend, they studied wind patterns, clouds, birds and the abundant sea life. They knew oral tales of many islands seen by their ancestors on the long journey east from Asia into Polynesia. They had learned to recognize the signs. It is reasonable to assume that they kept searching until they found this fertile, spacious and salubrious land.

Imagine the joy they felt when they sighted islands in the distance shimmering under the clouds. Picture the exhausted, parched natives stumbling to the shore to see endless white sand beaches, crystal clear streams and emerald green water in many lagoons and coves. All of it backed by sharp, craggy mountains and everything covered with a panoply of lush green vegetation.

In the 20th century, the voyage of *Hokule'a* helped to spark a revival of interest in early culture by Hawaiians and academics alike. This was the first modern demonstration that man could, with intention and determination, travel over thousands of miles of empty sea to reach these islands.

Based on these data and deductions from legends, two things are clear. Polynesians, from the Marquesas and Society Islands, used astounding seafaring skills to travel prodigious distances over the huge, empty sea to reach Hawaii. Second, beyond frequent voyages to the nearby visible islands and a diminishing number of journeys back to Tahiti, their long distance navigational skills were allowed to fade away when they no longer were needed. These remarkable people had found a place that was safe from invaders, with enough water, natural vegetation, fertile land and space to allow them to survive. Of necessity they turned their energies to agriculture, aquaculture and living according to the demands of their many gods.

Early writers about the Hawaiian people suggested that the first wave of Polynesians who came to these islands were conquered and exterminated by the second. Recently, it was suggested that the first group became commoners and the second became *ali'i* or the ruling class.[4] This speculation has not been corroborated.

There was a major cultural shift around the 12th century, anthropologists say. This conclusion is based on new dating techniques and archaeological evidence as well as comparison with other cultures and oral tradition. There was a new migration from the south which brought changes in food production, new religious idols and customs, including a new War God named *Ku*, and the initiation of human sacrifice as well as an increase in the size of the heiau or temple.[5]

When Europeans first met them, Hawaiians could recite genealogies that covered ninety-nine generations[6]. By Hawaiian reckoning that would be about three thousand years. Accurate or not, it shows the existence of a very long oral tradition. One modern writer bases her history on genealogies because they are the Hawaiian concept of time and are therefore the history of the Hawaiian people.[7] Even though these genealogies pertain only to the *ali'i nui*, or ruling class, she says they are the history of all because rulers were collective ancestors of all the people.

The culture that evolved on the Hawaiian islands over the centuries was based on Polynesian ideas and practices. Its major features include a social structure based on blood ties, the belief that ruling chiefs are directly descended from creator gods, and that the world is controlled by forces to be mollified and manipulated.[8] It was a primitive culture not unlike other cultures in similar situations and conditions elsewhere in the world.

Major features of this culture were subsistence, power, the ownership or control of land and the *kapu*, or taboo as Europeans often call it. They lived off the land and were dependent on it for food, clothing, shelter, rituals and customs. Originally, the land was divided in triangular segments, called *ahupua'a* that ran from *mauka*, the mountains, to *makai*, the sea. Thus a section could provide different resources at each level. Their leaders limited fishing to specific seasons. They irrigated fields and kept the production of crops under strict control. To maintain this rigid culture, chiefs had power over all, based on their family and how much land they controlled. *Ali'i*, the name for the Hawaiian high born class, were interpreters of the will of the Gods and tradition bearers.[9] Chiefs became increasingly land hungry and were willing to go to war to control an entire island and even neighbor islands. The more land they controlled, the richer and more powerful they became.

The ruling order was complex and stratified, among the most stratified of all Polynesian cultures. The chiefs ruled over an elaborate organization of lesser chiefs and aides that was similar in structure to European systems, a fact which later led to the emulation of European royalty by Hawaiian leaders.

Kapu was a system of regulations that covered every aspect of Hawaiian life and was overseen by the most exalted chief. It was a rigid moral code designed to direct the lives of the people. Much of it dealt with food. The sexes were strictly forbidden to eat together. Women were not allowed to consume some foods at all, such as turtle, banana or pork. Food of men and women had to be cooked in separate ovens in separate huts, even for a husband and wife living in the same place. Violating these rigid rules of kapu brought immediate death.

The culture that existed on Kauai, Oahu, Molokai, Maui and Hawaii was no more static than any other culture. It tended to change more slowly, as subsistence cultures do, but it did change. All we really know of it from its inception are the facts that the legends and genealogies tell us and the reports that the Europeans produced when they visited in the 18th century. One writer estimated that there were about 300,000 Hawaiians living on the five major islands when Captain Cook arrived, though other estimates place the number as high as 800,000. The island of Hawaii had the largest population, around 120,000, and Oahu had about 65,000 people.[10] The figures are estimates and vary widely among historians.

Much has been written about the pre-contact Hawaiians, but much as we yearn to, we will never really know what their lives were like. Some areas they inhabited have been studied and oral histories are being recorded. Songs, dances, clothing, chants and prayers are still being reconstructed and elaborated upon. Much has changed in the past two centuries and 20th century Hawaiians cannot be sure that the Hawaiian culture they are reconstructing is like the original at all. However, at this distance, it is all that exists.

One of the major areas in which Hawaiians lived, worked and played was a lagoon or estuary on the south shore that we call Pearl Harbor. They did not call it that and no consistent evidence exists to show what they did call it. It is possible that it had no name and they referred to it by the name of each river that flowed into it or by a nearby peninsula or both. Two names are mentioned most often; *Pu'uloa*, which means long hill, and *Waimomi*, which means pearl river. Each is often cited as the name of the inlet, a feature of it or the surrounding area.

Waimomi, on the south shore of Oahu, is a series of drowned river valleys which started as a bay and was filled with silt from inflowing rivers. When the land sank, the area was drowned until the ice ages began and the sea level fell drastically. When the ice melted, the water rose again and filled in the low areas.[11] Each loch or finger within the estuary is the drowned mouth of a valley created by a stream. One if its major characteristics, which leads to a unique ecosystem, is the mixing of fresh and salt water.[12] It has been called an inlet, a lagoon, an estuary and even a lake. The land is flat and marshy, some of it fertile, some dry. Rainfall in the area is 15 and 40 inches a year. The Ko'olau Range of mountains is to the east, the Waianae Mountains to the west, and higher ground to the north from whence flow the rivers. Lava flowing toward the sea from volcanoes long ago is now the bedrock of the island and permeable to water. Oahu contains the largest coastal plain of all the major Hawaiian islands. Its thickness forms a caprock which helps create and retain artesian water on which the island depends.[13] A large coral reef, several hundred feet thick, grew around the south coast of the island. It helps retain the artesian water under the harbor.

The first people to occupy Oahu and use the area now called Pearl Harbor are lost in the mists of time. But when it was first described by Europeans, it was an active place. There were many *lokos*, fish ponds or traps, near the water's edge and crops grew on peninsulas and islands in the inlet. Fishing was a vital source of food and the seas around the islands teemed with fish. An early chief, Keaunui of Ewa, the area around the inlet, was reported to have cut a shallow channel near the opening to make the estuary accessible by boat. It must have been an arduous task, considering the tools available to the men who did the work. This could have taken place thirteen generations ago or twenty-six, according to legend.[14] Modem researchers believe that this may have happened in the 11th or 12th century.

The new channel brought fish into the harbor in greater numbers than before. To catch them, the inhabitants constructed ponds, sometimes called weirs, taking note of swift incoming and slower outgoing tides. Made of wooden stakes or large stones, with at least one side built into the land, the fish ponds were oval or circular in shape.

The place called Pu'uloa, Waimomi or the Pearl River, and now Pearl Harbor, was a very active fishing place. When it was first studied by archaeologists in the 20th century, there were signs or remnants of some thirty ancient ponds. Some of them were thirty acres, some three acres, some only a few feet across.[15]

The ponds were originally owned by chiefs and probably built by commoners. One site is at least two hundred and fifty years old, built by a line of commoners who took lava stones from a mile away and passed them from hand to hand to the site of the pond wall. The traps were under water at high tide. Fish entered the pond at that time and were caught when the water receded.

Several species of fish regularly visited the harbor. One very important one was the shark. This area was known as the home of *aumakua*, the benevolent shark god, a helper to all fishermen. '*Unihipili*, another shark god would do one's bidding for evil, but he was not so visible.[16] Mackerel, bonito, mullet and goat fish were also caught in the lagoons along with many other species.

In this area the first breadfruit was planted by Kahai, one of the chiefs who brought it from Samoa.[17] The date is not certain. It may have been a successful transplant, but it is seldom mentioned as a staple of the Hawaiian diet.

Clams, crabs and several species of oysters were also found in the estuary. Many fossil oysters were found in the 1840s and pearl bearing oysters were still reported in the area in the 19th century. One early European reported that pearls of good quality and size were often collected in this area.[18] There are a number of legends about this, one of which recounts the wrath of a god to explain why pearls disappeared from the harbor. By the 1820s, a number of divers were employed in taking them from the harbor.[19] Drainage from farms and silt from the rivers were clouding the water, and by the end of the 19th century pearl oysters disappeared from the estuary. The reasons are not difficult to assess.

This area is known in legends as the "many harbored sea of Pu'uloa"[20]. The name is now used for a residential area on the west, or Ewa, side of the entrance channel. Some sources cite Pu'uloa as the name for the entire harbor so it may have been called that at one time. One citation of 1910 lists Pu'uloa as a town, and a legend recorded in 1899 says fishermen lived there. In a book written in 1878, there is a reference to the "present Pu'uloa saltworks and the great estuary of Pearl River".[21]

Another name for the area is spelled many different ways. Wy Momi, Waimomi or Wymumme, which is also given as a synonym of the Pearl River.[22] Described as an inlet that extends ten miles up country and contains pearls, there is no doubt that it is the same place. Some of these observations come from European visitors who knew neither the local language nor the territory so it is understandable that the spelling and definition of the place differ so widely.

The major island in the largest finger of this extensive inlet was called *Moku'ume'ume* by early inhabitants. It was covered with Kiawe trees used for firewood. Crops were also grown there as well as watermelon and *pili* grass used for thatching roofs. The island was originally without natural water, so irrigation of the melon fields was necessary and extensive.

The first inhabitants of this area are not known, but many historians believe that fishermen lived there and much later chiefs and kings made homes on the shores of the inlet. The separate inlets are now called West, Middle and East Loch. Each peninsula that separated the lochs had a specific name. Waiau, Waimalu & Kalauao, Waipio & Waiawa and Halawa are names still found on the peninsulas or in the settled areas of Ewa.

Invasions of Oahu by neighboring chiefs often came by way of this inlet for its entrance was easily negotiated by canoe. In the 14th century, according to legend, the harbor became the path to a bloody battle farther inland but the harbor inhabitants were not involved in the carnage.[23]

When the first Europeans landed on these islands, Hawaiian life changed forever and the consequences have endured.

Chapter 2 - Two Captains and a King

Near the end of the eighteenth century, two different cultures were poised to collide. The Hawaiian people were about to be propelled into the modern world.

The first European to see these islands was reputed to be Juan Caetano, captain of a Spanish Galleon in 1555. A chart found in 1765 in the Spanish Hydrographic Office notes the "Islas de Mesa" near the location of Hawaii.[1] There were rumors of visits of foreign ships landing in the islands before Captain Cook, but none are confirmed. In 1743, Lord Anson of the ship *Centurian* captured a Spanish Galleon and found a chart which showed these islands as being a thousand miles east of Hawaii's real location.[2] There is no indication that Caetano landed on the islands, but if he did he did not linger. The islands were not publicized or claimed by the Spanish. If indeed, they knew of these islands, they had good reason to keep their location secret. Manila Galleons like Caetano's traveled across the Pacific carrying enormously valuable cargoes from the orient to Navidad on the west coast of Mexico, bound eventually for Spain. The Spanish did not want their route known by other nations.

In 1778, Captain James Cook, with the ships *Resolution* and *Discovery*, was on his third voyage of exploration in the Pacific Ocean. On his way to North America to try to find the legendary passage through that continent, several islands appeared in the vicinity of 22° north latitude, and 150° west longitude.

Cook's arrival in Hawaii is germane to our story for two reasons. He was the first European known to land on Hawaiian soil and then introduce the splendors of the islands to the rest of the world. Secondly, three Americans were with this expedition, John Gore, Simon Woodruff, and John Ledyard. Captain Gore was born in Virginia and elected to remain loyal to King George and Great Britain. Woodruff served as a Gunner's Mate on *Resolution*[3]. John Ledyard, an American adventurer, was an enlisted Marine and an American citizen. He can arguably be considered the first American military seaman to land in Hawaii. Some writers say he was the first American military seaman in Honolulu as well, but he did not land there. His chart of Cook's voyage, which he continued after Cook's death, clearly shows *Resolution* reaching from Karakakoa (Kealakokua) Bay north past Mowee (Maui), Ranai (Lanai) and Morotai (Molokai). Then the ship tacked west to the north shore of Woahoo (Oahu) and anchored on February 25 of 1779. From there *Resolution* sailed to Atooi (Kauai) and home to England. Ledyard, therefore, did not come close to the Honolulu area. He was however, the first American military man in Hawaiian waters.[4]

When Cook first sighted these islands, the ships anchored on the southern coast of Kauai, the westernmost of the major islands. After a stay of ten days, during which they restocked the ships with water and food, the ships headed again for the Northern Pacific and their search for the Northwest Passage. After many discouraging months of searching in this icy world, no northwest passage was found and Cook ordered both ships back to Hawaii for the winter. This time, wind and sea drove the ships to the west coast of the biggest of the islands, Hawaii.

It was a fateful event for the Hawaiians, for James Cook and for the world. Cook selected an interesting name for his newly discovered islands. His patron, the man in charge of the Royal Navy during the "War of the Rebellion", whose title was First Lord of the Admiralty, was John Montagu, the fourth Earl of Sandwich. To honor him, Cook named the lovely chain of islands we now know as Hawai'i, the Sandwich Islands.

Unknown to the outside world for centuries, these islands, home of the Hawaiian people, were unknown no longer. Cook was impressed with the natives for they "have never once attempted to cheat us and understand trading as well as most people."[5] The Expedition stayed in the islands for two months. The most important aspect of this meeting for the history of Hawaii is that the Englishmen were intensely interested in the natives, closely observed them and recorded everything they saw. They drew pictures of men, women and children, their weapons, boats, music, dance, ritual objects and houses of worship. They wrote descriptions of events and commented on their customs, activities, food, behavior and the character of the Hawaiians. They remarked on and described everyday clothing, and drew pictures of the native's ceremonial raiment, their masks, spectacular headdresses, skirts and feather capes. Much that is now known of early Hawaiians comes from these records.

Amasa Delano, who traveled to Hawaii in 1802, observed the natives at work and play. He described the clothing of the common people at their daily activities.

"The women commonly wear a square piece wrapped round their waist, in the same manner that a blanket is put round an infant in this country, which reaches from their hips to the calves of their legs. They sometimes wear a piece over their shoulders, similar to a handkerchief, or shawl; but they most commonly go without this. The males wear a very narrow strip round their loins."[6]

The men often wore spectacular headdresses, cloaks and feathered capes, especially at ceremonial functions. Some European accounts from later ships are full of admiration and high praise, some derogatory and uncomplimentary. In their extensive travels in the Pacific Ocean, the men with Cook had seen similar cultures before they saw Hawaiian life and had some experience on which to base their assessments. A great deal of the culture was a mystery to them because they did not know the language, although they did have an English speaking Tahitian interpreter on board.

There are two important aspects of the logs, notes, diaries, letters and drawings in which these observations are found. One is that they are the first recorded description of Hawaiian culture. The other is that this record was made before this unique culture was radically changed by European culture and technology.

When Cook's ships, *Resolution* and *Discovery* came to anchor in what they called Kearaharoora (now Kealakekua) Bay in January of 1779, they were greeted with a tumultuous outpouring of welcome from the natives. They were surrounded by native canoes, colorful costumes, shouting and singing. They soon learned that they had arrived just as a local celebration called *makahiki* was getting under way. Captain Cook was hailed as the god named Lono, who, according to legend, had left and was now returning. One problem arose immediately. Cook's Tahitian interpreter had died before they reached Hawaii and all communication was in sign language.[7]

When the celebrations were over, culture clashes ensued which led to many misunderstandings. Most were quelled or smoothed over until a fateful day, the 13th of February, 1779. That morning, when Cook found that a cutter had been stolen from *Discovery*, he was furious and wanted to teach the natives a lesson. Cook went ashore with six marines, one of whom was the American Marine, Corporal Ledyard. On shore, he was intent on taking one of the leaders of the island hostage.[8] Word and deed led to violence. Captain Cook and four marines were killed. From then on, the shore was lined with natives, watching, menacing, no longer welcoming the newcomers.

As the English fled to their ships, sporadic fighting broke out and continued through the night and an uneasy few days ensued. They tried unsuccessfully to retrieve the Captain's body, but parts of it were returned several days later. Captain James Cook was revered by his men and respected by the world. After his death, and after a fruitless assault on a native village, the crews sadly turned to the business of getting underway. The men of *Resolution* and *Discovery* heaved on the capstan bars until the anchors were secured at the catheads, unfurled the sails, caught the wind and set their course. They made for Maui, then rounded the north shore of Oahu and finally reached their original Hawaiian anchorage on Kauai. There they remained for some weeks restocking the ships with food and water. They finally weighed anchor and stood for home on March 15, 1779.[9]

As with every place on the globe that Europeans discovered, once the Sandwich Isles were known to the world, they became a golden prize to be used, acquired, possessed and manipulated, often under the guise of 'protection'. After the first visits by Spanish and English, they were visited, explored, and often claimed by Spaniards, Frenchmen, Englishmen, Russians, Americans and even a small band of Californians.

Remote though the islands are, they are the closest place in the Pacific Ocean to the American west coast. To Americans, having an English, Spanish or French possession so close to their shores was intolerable, but it was fifty years after the discovery of the Hawaiian Islands before the United States could turn its attention to the Pacific Ocean. And then the islands were not conquered but colonized and christianized by American missionaries.

The first westerners we know of who landed on the island of Oahu were Captains Clerke and Gore of *Resolution* and *Discovery*. After Cook's death, they sailed these ships along the southeast shore of Maui, across the Kaiwi Channel and along the windward shore of Oahu. They stopped briefly at Waimea on the north shore before they sailed for Kanai.

Two English ships, under the command of a Captain Nathaniel Portlock, came to the island of Oahu in 1786. Low on water, he landed some of his small boats between Makapu'u Point and Koko Head on the east shore in search of a fresh stream or waterfall. Finding the only available water too far away to carry to the ship, they continued west. When the ships rounded what is now called Diamond Head, the men saw a large bay on the south shore. They became the first westerners to see the south shore that today stretches between Diamond Head and Barber's Point and the first to anchor in what was to become Honolulu Bay. There the natives brought them water in calabash gourds. Neither the amount they paid nor the medium of exchange is given, nor do they mention Pearl Harbor.[10]

Over the next forty years, the inlet west of Honolulu remained undisturbed by newcomers. Access to the area from the sea was limited to shallow draft canoes and boats because a large reef created shoal water just outside the entrance channel. European deep draft vessels could not enter. In spite of that, newcomers did board small boats and sometimes took overland hikes from Honolulu to see, survey, enjoy and take some of the fish from the lagoon. Peter Corney describes the inlet in 1819 and says that provisions that can be bought from the natives here are cheap and plentiful. He also reports that a man named Manning owns the island in the center.[11] This man was a Spanish physician named Marin who owned the island and later was called in to treat King Kamehameha in his last illness.

Levi Chamberlain, an early visitor, and a small group rode in a canoe to a place where oysters are abundant. The year was 1822. He did not identify it by name, but since this estuary was the only place on the south shore where pearl bearing mollusks existed in such abundance, it had to be *Waimomi* (or Pu'uloa). When Chamberlain's canoe arrived, the native handling the canoe showed them where a large group of inhabitants were diving to retrieve pearls for sale. Chamberlain reports that he saw the divers collect a "couple of calabashes of oysters."[12]

Many stories and legends are told about the fishermen, the fish, and especially about the sharks of Pu'uloa. Some fishermen lived in caves on the edge of the land, or used these caves for processing the fish. The natives used the land around and in the lagoon for many purposes other than farming or fishing. One tale is told about a sexual game or sport called *Ume* that was played occasionally on the island of *Moku'ume'ume*. The game was played by the common people, not chiefs or *ali'i*. It also shows that the area was one in which the common people lived, worked and played. This island was also called Rabbit Island, Poka 'Aliana,[13] Ford's and later Ford Island.

No one knows the first European or American who went into the inlet we call Pearl Harbor. Early explorers were drawn there by the provisions they could purchase, especially fresh fish. Others were intrigued by the pearls or by the need to explore, survey and record. They may have been ordinary sailors or early traders. They were probably not leaders of expeditions or major foreign leaders because no such discovery or exploration is mentioned in their journals.

Fate, coincidence or inevitability decreed that the status quo in the islands was destined to change internally just as they were being discovered, coveted and exploited by Europeans.

The individual who would make these changes was Kamehameha, a remarkable man born somewhere around 1750 in the Kohala region of Hawaii, easternmost of the major islands. He was an *ali'i*, the island equivalent of an aristocrat, educated to rule by his uncle, chief Kalaniopu'u, who controlled the largest island, Hawaii, as well as the southern part of Maui. Later Kamehameha was given the high honor of having the responsibility for protecting the statue of the war god, *Ku*. He had to make sure the large wooden statue was safe and was with the High Chief whenever he entered battle. Trusted by the chief, Kamehameha was soon made his heir.

An incident occurred during the visit of the first English ships to the Big Island in 1778 that was to have a profound affect on Kamehameha and his people. While the noisy festivities were going on, Kalaniopu'u, chief of the island on which Kealakekua Bay is situated, took his retinue in a large canoe to visit Captain Cook aboard *Resolution*. Aside from the usual ceremonial greetings, gift giving, rituals, and professions of friendship, the important aspect of the visit for posterity was that Kamehameha was a member of this party. He was about twenty-five years old.

Kamehameha was impressed with everything about the ship and the men he met as well as the muskets, cannon, steel knives, brass buttons, and gunpowder. They were so superior to anything he had that he coveted them all. He was not involved a few weeks later in the death of Captain Cook, but is reputed to have taken control of the chaos that resulted and brought order after the killing. Peace was restored. Cook was dead, his bones were delivered to the ship for burial and the English ships departed. But they left behind ideas and objects that the Hawaiians had never seen before and never even dreamed existed. The experience made a vivid impression on Kamehameha, the man who was to become ruler of this island realm.

Kamehameha fought many battles as a trusted aide and warrior beside Kalaniopu'u. In 1782, three years after Cook's visit, when Kalaniopu'u died, Kamehameha was accepted as ruler of the big island of Hawaii. In 1790, he launched a campaign to subdue, control and rule all of the islands.

One reason for Kamehameha's eventual success, besides innate ability and superior knowledge, was that he used new tactics that he had learned and weapons that he had obtained from western advisors who were men who had been left on the beach by circumstance. Soon he had another visitor.

In 1790, Princess Royal from the west coast of North America, anchored in Hawaii. She was a prize which had been seized from the British by a Spaniard named Quimper. He had come to these islands to investigate the possibility of creating a Spanish settlement in Hawaii. He was the first of many to have this idea. Quimper's purpose was to create a replenishment stop for Spanish ships coming from the orient. His plan was not acted upon by the Spanish government, but his 1790 report is valuable because he recorded that sixteen ships had visited the islands since Captain Cook discovered them eleven years earlier.

One of the first merchant ships to come to Hawaii anchored in Kealakekua Bay on the island of Hawaii in 1790. She was *Eleanora*, a two masted, square rigged vessel with her mainsail on a trysail mast instead of on the main like a brigantine, a configuration which was called a Snow.[14] Commanded by Simon Metcalfe, she was from Boston bound for China with a load of furs when she stopped at the islands.[15] The crew spent its time re-stocking the ship with water, vegetables, meat and firewood. According to one contemporary writer[16], Captain Metcalfe was the first to realize the value of the wood his men were gathering. It was colorful and had a sweet aroma when burned or dried. It was sandalwood, a prized material in the orient, used for making boxes, chests and also as incense. Others give the honor of this discovery to Captain John Kendrick of *Lady Washington*.[17]

Eleanora stayed longer than originally intended while the crew gathered as much sandalwood as the ship could carry. Metcalfe would trade it in Canton along with the furs in his holds. When other traders discovered the value of this crop, sandalwood became a premier trade item, controlled and regulated by King Kamehameha, sole ruler of the islands by then. This discovery by Europeans was the first step in the utter destruction of Hawaiian sandalwood forests. The forests were stripped and denuded so fast that Hawaiian sandalwood was exterminated and the trade was finished just thirty years later. After decades of extinction, the sandalwood forests are back now, reintroduced and bolstered by new trees imported from India. It is reported growing well on all of the islands.[18]

Uncompromising in his rigid discipline, Captain Metcalfe of *Eleanora* had trouble in Maui. His brutal treatment of the natives resulted in mortal danger for him and his crew. His misfortunes and violent relationship with his hosts began on the west shore of Hawaii where he first landed. He struck a visiting chief for some transgression and had him thrown off the ship. The next incident happened on Maui near the town and port of Lahaina. A group of natives stole a boat from *Eleanora* and killed a sailor. To punish them, the captain ordered their village burned. When he learned that the thieves had actually come from another village, Olowalu, down the coast, he lay in wait for them.

A number of natives in canoes left the shore, armed with rocks, clubs, and spears. Hopelessly underarmed, they approached Metcalfe's ship. From the main deck of the *Eleanora*, the captain aimed his deck guns and muskets at the slowly moving canoes and opened fire. His grape shot and rifle balls mercilessly tore through the canoes and natives. The lagoon fell silent, except for the empty, bobbing canoes. When the smoke cleared, over one hundred natives had been slaughtered.

This clash between European culture and natives hastened Metcalfe's departure and would have dire results for the next visiting ship.

Shortly after *Eleanora* left the shore of Maui the trader *Fair American* arrived, captained by Thomas Metcalfe, son of Simon. No one on the ship was aware of the events that preceded them and it is doubtful that the natives knew the relationship of the captain to *Eleanora's* captain. Revenge was a way of life in the islands and Thomas had shown up at the wrong time. By night, the natives boarded *Fair American*. Thomas Metcalfe and his crew were beaten to death and thrown overboard.[19]

The two ships involved in these tragedies inadvertently brought some good to the islands. They supplied Kamehameha with two of his most trusted advisors, John Young and Isaac Davis.

Isaac Davis was an American crewman of the merchant ship *Fair American*. When his ship was attacked, he was seized by natives and tossed overboard. Though beaten severely, he managed to survive and swim ashore only to be taken prisoner by Kamehameha's men.

John Young, also an American, was boatswain on the merchant ship *Eleanora*. Young, who went ashore to look for members of his crew, was taken prisoner and put in a cell with Davis. Young was left behind by *Eleanora* because Captain Simon Metcalfe, thinking he was dead or had deserted, left without him when *Eleanora* stood out to sea.[20] There are reports that the captain did try to find his boatswain, but the natives would no longer tolerate his presence on the island. Young and Davis soon became friends in prison.

Kamehameha took the opportunity to learn from the two men. He released them, offered them positions in his service and consistently treated them with respect. They were given land and servants, wives were chosen for them and they remained in his service as long as they lived.

Because Young and Davis were westerners who had knowledge of military tactics, Kamehameha was eager to learn about technology and weapons from them. In knowledge of how to sail and how to use ships of war, western style, the influence of the two men was even more valuable. They taught the Hawaiians how to use the weapons and ships that Kamehameha purchased. They advised him on foreign ideas, dress, customs and the value of trading with Europeans. Kamehameha also learned a great deal from them about Europeans in relation to the maintenance of power. He saw many benefits of adopting western ideas for Hawaiians.

The fateful visits of English, and later American, ships to the shores of Hawaii brought more than new ideas, weapons, foods and disease. They brought new and different concepts of power and new ways to govern, tactical uses of weapons, strategic use of armies, intrigue and the desire for power. Internal power struggles in the islands had existed long before Europeans came, of course, but had been based on the ownership of land. Other factors in these disputes were chiefs, the system of *kapu*, the rule of the gods and legends interpreted by the priests and *kahunas*, Hawaiian priest leaders.

In 1792, another *Discovery* appeared in a bay on the island of Hawaii thirteen years after the first one. It was not Captain Cook's old ship, but a new one built for this voyage. In command was Captain George Vancouver who was on a new exploring voyage for the British King George III. Vancouver had been a midshipman aboard Cook's ship on his fatal voyage and was acquainted with the islands, the people and their characteristics. By this time, the islands were overrun with British and American traders, brawling seamen and pirates of many nationalities. They disdained island customs, brought disease, brawled in the streets and sold rum and guns to anyone who had the asking price in trade or women.

Not the least of the problem was the Hawaiian himself. Tales of other lands had reached him along with knowledge of technology that was superior to his. And he saw the untold wealth that all newcomers lavishly displayed. Much knowledge of the Americas and Europe came from young Hawaiians who had been hired on foreign ships as crewmen. They were called 'kanakas', a word that simply means 'man' in Hawaiian, and soon earned a reputation as excellent sailors. When they came back home, they were full of tales about the wonders of the world. By this time, contact with Europeans had brought affluence to some, discontent, disillusion and the beginning of distrust to others. It also accelerated the already declining faith in island religion and customs.

While the Hawaiians were learning European customs, they were exhibiting Hawaiian ideas that startled their new acquaintances. Amasa Delano, in his journal, told of a young man who chose to ship aboard an English ship in 1802. Delano noticed the boy's mother "making a great lamentation for her son". He described her cries as ones he could never forget, and that he was accused of taking her only son to sea where she would never see him again. Delano, moved by her tears and distress, called for a canoe to return the lad to his mother. Delano reported, "He said he could not go back, as it would be unmanly, that it would redound [sic] very much to his dishonor to have it said that he had relinquished a design of such importance, for no other reason than his mother cried about it, that she was nothing but a woman and she would forget it by tomorrow and be well enough".[21] Delano was persuaded by the boy and accepted him as part of his crew on the voyage to Canton.

Early in 1793, Captain Vancouver wrote in his journal,

> "With a pleasant breeze from westward on Sunday morning the 24th, we plied to the windward, along the south side of Woahoo, until [sic] the afternoon, when we anchored abreast the western most opening or lagoon, mentioned in our former visit to this island, called by the natives O-poo-ro-ah [Pu'uloa] and which since has been reported to us, by the natives, as capable of admitting vessels by warping into it."[22]

The natives were probably unaware of the draft (depth in the water) of English ships. Although the lochs in the inlet we call Pearl Harbor are six to seven fathoms in many places, not even warping (maneuvering a ship by the use of lines) would have enabled the deep draft ships to pass the reef which was later determined to allow only 6' or 7' of clear water.

Vancouver's men did enter this lagoon in a small boat, but soon determined that it was not usable as an anchorage. Vancouver, as British explorers had for decades, recorded the names of native sites as he heard them. For instance, for Pu'uloa he wrote O-poo-roo-ah, Honolulu became

Honoonoono, Kamehameha was written Tomohomoho, Waikiki was recorded as Whyteetee. Vancouver was not alone in writing names in such a way. A few years later, in 1806, the log of the US frigate *Pearl* recorded this: "At 6 a.m., got under way and towed into the harbor of Ounanoou, the harbor of Whyteete Bay."[23]

The interesting characteristics of the Hawaiian language were noted in a humorous way in a local magazine article in 1915. The writer said that the American press was having a good time poking fun at the names of places in European war news. He went on,

"We smile at the mention of Przsansyz or Przemysl, for instance, but what would Moiliili or Laupahoehoe sound like, (or look like) to an unsuspecting Russian in his home town? It would seem that there has been a misdeal of the alphabet - the Slavs have all the consonants while the vowels were spilled in the lap of the Pacific."[24]

Vancouver was different from many other explorers. He stepped onto these unpredictable shores with a strength of character and a message for peace. On his first visit he met Kamehameha, the man who would soon be ruler of all the Hawaiian islands. They talked frequently and formed a friendly liaison between their two worlds. Vancouver wanted to settle the unrest in the islands so Great Britain could make favorable trading agreements with the king. On his part Kamehameha used his friendship with the powerful British explorer to help conquer and control the islands. Since their first meeting, he carried a British flag with him wherever he went. This could be where the use of the Union Jack as part of the Hawaiian flag began.

Vancouver, determined to preserve friendly relations with the natives, carefully promoted his own image as benevolent father to Hawaiians, agent of His Britannic Majesty's government and a non-combatant. He refused to issue, sell or trade arms with any one.

He visited Hawaii three times, stopping to replenish water and provisions before heading east to explore the northwest coast of North America. He visited in March, 1792, February, 1793 and January, 1794. His last stay was extended to March of 1794. In spite of the fact that he was not in constant residence in the islands, he did help to maintain a period of peace in Hawaii between residents and visitors.

During his third visit in 1794, Vancouver and Kamehameha made an agreement, the nature of which is now vague. Many writers have reported simply that at this meeting Kamehameha ceded Hawaii to England.[25] Early reports said that the agreement consisted of a comment Kamehameha made to Vancouver, "When you return, tell the king of Britain to take care of this land of ours."[26] This implies that he had no intention of giving his land to Great Britain or anyone else, nor that he was even asking for immediate protection. His subsequent action in extending his rule over all the islands make this interpretation a reasonable one. No one knows his true intention.

Vancouver says that he and Kamehameha created an agreement in which Kamehameha made a voluntary cession of the islands to Great Britain. The two men had discussed the subject on Vancouver's earlier visits and "during my absence the subject had been most seriously discussed by the chiefs of the island."[27]

In order to obtain the protection they required, Vancouver says that it was important that Tamaahmaah (Kamehameha) should surrender formally to him, Vancouver, on behalf of His Majesty, the King of Great Britain. He thinks the Hawaiians were stimulated to do this because of the treatment they had received from other visiting strangers. There was no dispute, Vancouver was sure, over the claim that Great Britain had to the Sandwich Islands.[28]

There was a public ceremony with all the chiefs on the island of Hawaii attending. They were "highly sensible of the advantages they had derived from us", so Vancouver wrote, "and seemed to comprehend the nature of the business". Speeches were made and the assembled chiefs declared their consent by saying they were "no longer Tanata no Owhyhee (i.e. people of Hawaii) but Tanata no Britanee."

After the formalities, Vancouver turned to one of his subordinates, Peter Puget, the man after whom the sound in northwest America was named, and ordered him ashore with several other officers to display the British flag and take formal possession of the island of Hawaii.[29] This was done in the usual European custom, in the name of His Britannic Majesty George III.[30]

Since Kamehameha did not control all of the islands yet, it is possible that he meant to cede only the island of Hawaii, not all of the Hawaiian Islands, to the British. Or perhaps he simply intended to allow Vancouver and other British captains to anchor in the harbor. The interpretation of the word 'cession' was certainly understood by the British, but its complete implications may not have been grasped by the Hawaiians. Another interpretation cites letters between Kamehameha and George III in concluding that the Hawaiian king was sure this cession was merely an alliance.[31]

No formal piece of paper was created or signed to establish the agreement, at least none has yet been found, but Vancouver says that an inscription was made on copper and presented to Kamehamaha.[32]

After this, his third visit to Hawaii, Vancouver sailed away and never returned. When he reached Great Britain, King George was ill and a great furor rose against Vancouver concerning events far from Hawaii, mainly his alleged flogging of a titled member of his crew. No more is heard of this agreement between Kamehameha and Vancouver and the latter died two years later. The implication has always been made that if the king of England had known about the agreement, he would have made Hawaii a protectorate of Great Britain. Vancouver certainly wanted to, but died before he could make it happen. It's a moot point now, but interpretations and inferences often exceed or replace reality.

Kamehameha learned much about power, integrity and proper British behavior from Vancouver. Kamehameha's dealings with a certain Captain Henry Barber of the American snow *Arthur* may owe much to the Englishman. Barber arrived in Honolulu in 1796 to do some trading. There is a story that Barber was caught trying to cheat Kamehameha in a deal over rum, but no punishment was meted out to him. He left Honolulu in a storm in late October and his ship was wrecked on the southwestern point of Oahu, known as Kalaeloa. Barber survived and this area has been called Barber's Point ever since.[33] Some years later, Barber returned to Hawaii. When he discovered that divers working for Kamehameha had retrieved the guns from his ship, he demanded that they be returned to him. The guns had been refurbished and set up to guard the port of Lahaina. They remained where they were.[34]

Kamehameha had conquered all of the islands, except Kauai and Ni'ihau, by about 1795. Though he tried mightily, he could not control or subdue the ruler of the island of Kauai. By 1810, he had made an agreement which allowed the Kauaian chief to continue to rule his domain as a dependent kingdom, owing his allegiance to Kamehameha. It has been said that if Kamehameha had not united these islands under his strong rule when he did, they would have been swiftly grabbed and partitioned by foreign, mainly European, nations or individuals.[35]

Kamehameha then ruled all Hawaii, and brought the *ali'i* to dwell at his capital, which was wherever he chose to reside at the moment. He retained a man who acted as a prime minister to deal with foreigners. The man chosen for the job was Kalanimoku. He was so effective with foreigners that he began to dress like an Englishman and soon he was being called William Pitt, after England's first Prime Minister. This name was used more often than Kalanimoku, though islanders and visitors soon shortened it to "Billy Pitt".

Kamehameha also created a Hawaiian Navy that was unique in the Pacific and rare for a native chief. When George Vancouver was in Hawaii in 1792-4, his carpenters, assisted by John Young, Isaac Davis and James Boyd, a shipwright, built a warship for Kamehameha in Kealakokua Bay. Kamehameha wanted his people to learn to build boats and small vessels for themselves. This first European style vessel built in the islands was twenty-nine feet long[36] and was to be called Britannia. She became the first ship of Kamehameha's navy.[37]

By 1794, Kamehameha had a navy yard at Kawaihae, a bay on the west coast of the island of Hawaii fifty or sixty miles north of Kealakokua Bay. John Young was its director. By the following year, Kamehameha owned twenty vessels of twenty to forty tons. Working for him also was Archibald Campbell, a former sailmaker aboard a British trading schooner. By 1804, Kamehameha had many vessels. Some displaced up to seventy five tons and their bottoms were sheathed with copper. He was now ready to take his trade to foreign lands. Under the direction of James Harbottle, a Hawaiian who had great knowledge and admiration for the British and their seafaring expertise,[38] his ships were captained by men skilled in navigation by the most up-to-date instruments, including the compass, sextant and perhaps even the new chronometer.

The assessment of one modern writer is that Kamehameha had the largest naval force in the entire Pacific Ocean at the time, 1794 - 1819.[39] He acquired Fair American and also purchased the largest of his vessels, the 175 ton Lelia Bird, from an American. This vessel became his flagship. Even though he had many traditional double canoes, tied together with a platform on which he was often seen at the steering oar, he was also proud of his European ships. He even had one of the canoes fitted with western sails. By 1791, he had thirty ships at Waikiki, where he resided, and a dozen more in Honolulu Harbor several miles to the west.[40]

This fleet of ships may have been accumulated by Kamehameha in order to protect his domain from foreigners, to trade with them or to expand his realm. He was astute enough to see that he needed ships for all three purposes to secure and enhance his kingdom. Kamehameha's first priority was the entire Hawaiian island chain, and he was certainly aware of its importance to many other nations. Because of his interest and the many foreign visitors he had entertained, such as Vancouver, Kamehameha had learned how strategic Hawaii was in the Pacific Ocean. He was determined to deal with foreigners as equals, learn from them and trade with them without letting them dominate him.

When Archibald Campbell, the sailmaker, had first come to Hawaii in 1810, he was struck by the appearance of the king of the island. Kamehameha greeted the ship in a large double canoe, he wrote, dressed as a European in a blue coat and gray pantaloons.[41] He apparently felt it was polite to do so. Another traveler, Amasa Delano offers another view of the great king,

"Tomahammaha, the present king, is very well disposed towards the white people who stop at these islands; but should some one of the chiefs be invested with the reins of the government, on the death of the present king, I do not think it would be safe for small vessels to stop there"[42]

Kamehameha had been fortunate in his dealings with Cook and Vancouver and he was careful with others. He was a cautious, but forward looking man in many ways, yet unsophisticated in others. The only time he affected western dress was on ceremonial occasions when British, French or American presence required that courtesy. Still, though he ruled his kingdom like a monarchy, similar to those of Europe, he remained true to his own culture. He upheld construction of new heiau, and rigidly supported ancient and oppressive kapu to control his people. No matter how onerous and brutal these laws were, he was beloved by his people. Other 'Kamehamehas' followed him, creating the kingdom of Hawaii, but none ever lived up to his character or standards or displayed his wisdom.

Chapter 3 - The Rise and Fall of the American Navy

Before there was a 'Pearl Harbor' there was an American Navy, but long before there was an American Navy, there was a lagoon called, *Pu 'uloa* or *Waimomi*.

In 1775, three years before Captain Cook arrived in the Sandwich Islands, men in the British colonies on the east coast of America decided that British rule was intolerable. Their protests having failed, they concluded that more forceful means were needed to achieve their goals of independence and freedom. That required an army and a navy.

A young Virginia planter named George Washington was quietly active in colonial politics. He had military experience in the French and Indian wars of 1763, albeit meager, but it set him apart from other colonists at the time of the rebellion against Great Britain. This experience plus his stature and bearing at the meetings, emphasized by the wearing of his uniform, made him the choice to command the irregulars known as the Continental Army. When the British made their famous march to Lexington to seize rebel munitions and search for two 'troublemakers' (John Hancock and Samuel Adams), they were met and opposed by determined citizen farmers near the town of Lexington and then at Concord. Shots rang out and men fell. The Revolutionary War had begun.

Among many other problems, Washington had two that directly related to maritime commerce. He needed arms for his troops and he needed to stop the steady flow of seabourne supplies from Europe to the British. While his troops could acquire foodstuffs and weapons from the local farmers and craftsmen, the British were totally dependent on supplies from England. Washington needed a navy.

Washington's assessment of the situation was not shared by all of his colleagues. There were those who did not trust such power in the hands of a central government. They felt that if they authorized the protection of merchant shipping from harassment by foreign forces, it would lead to conflicts and wars that the country was ill able to finance.

While the Continental Congress debated the need for a navy versus its expense, General Washington, on his own initiative, ordered eight small, swift schooners to be built for the purpose of harassing British ships. Congress formed a Maritime Committee (ominously on Friday the 13th of October[1]), but by then Washington had already done the administrative work required to form the flotilla.[2] It was not until December of 1775 that the nucleus of the new Navy, the 200 ton frigate Alfred was commissioned in Philadelphia. A converted merchantman built in Philadelphia in 1774, she was launched with the name *Black Prince*. Her Captain was a young lieutenant named John Paul Jones.[3]

Washington's authority for ordering ships built was found in the vague language of Congress' instructions, "destroy or make prisoners" of anyone who "shall appear in arms against the good people of the United Colonies". He acted in hopes of making a "fortunate capture of an Ordnance Ship."[4] There were many young men in Washington's army who had spent time at sea. Life in the fields and camps, while never pleasant, was particularly galling to these young sailors. Infantry activities were dull, hot, dirty, and, worst of all, far from the sea with which they were so familiar. The men who served on Washington's first ships are unheralded, but they can certainly claim the title of the first American seamen at war.

Some small coastal vessels had challenged the British, unsuccessfully, to follow them into fortified inlets, but while Washington appreciated the spontaneous efforts, he needed a more organized activity to harass British shipping. Hence he chose eight expertly crafted schooners from Marblehead shipyards. These swift, 50-80 ton schooners could tack and come about far easier than the 400 ton square-rigged British ships of the line. The Americans had little fear of being outgunned, or outmanned, because of their consummate knowledge of local waters. In fact, they were able to capture 13 ships, 18 brigs, 11 schooners, and 13 sloops.[5]

Unfortunately, the major American ships were commanded by men appointed for political reasons or those who purchased their commissions. These men did not fare well upon the sea. Washington was disappointed that General Esek Hopkins, who unfortunately had neither maritime experience nor knowledge, was appointed by the Maritime Committee to command the newly formed, ill-fated American fleet that replaced the original small flotilla of schooners.

Washington accomplished his goal of harassing the British fleet in sufficient measure to contribute to his successful land war. By the end of the war, however, the American Navy ceased to exist, having been swept from the sea by the skill, experience, firepower, and tonnage of the British Fleet. The last remaining squadron of the Continental Navy was captured on May 12, 1780, attempting to defend the city of Charleston, South Carolina.[6]

During the war, the mutually cordial attitude of the new United States with France had become strained. In order to avoid total severance of relations, President Adams sent a three-man commission to Paris. They were met in October of 1797 by crafty Charles Maurice de Talleyrand-Perigord who demanded a $250,000 bribe plus a large 'loan' to the French government. The Americans quickly and angrily cast aside the overture and answered, "No! No! Not a sixpence!" This bitter refusal has been euphemistically changed to "Millions for defense, but not one cent for tribute!".[7]

Sometimes, however, occasional bits of cordiality were observed. In 1779, the year that John Paul Jones, commanding *Bon Homme Richard*, captured Serapis, his friend Benjamin Franklin advised the commanding officers of American armed ships not to treat "that most celebrated navigator and discoverer, Captain Cook," as an enemy. The news of Cook's death in the Sandwich Islands had not yet reached Europe. Therefore Franklin wrote from Paris on March 10, 1779, that the Cook Expedition was soon to arrive in England on its return from "discoveries of new countries in unknown seas". He also urged American captains and their crews to "treat the said Captain Cook and his people with all civility and kindness, affording them assistance as common friends to mankind".[8] The American Congress did not disapprove of this remarkable courtesy and did not censure Franklin.

The war drew slowly to its successful conclusion and the debate flared anew concerning the need for a navy. Bearing heavily on the discussion was the fact that the new nation was close to bankruptcy. Also there were two major threats to the country. One was a possible conflict with Canada, and therefore the British, since they still owned it. The other threat to consider was the constant proximity of Indians. Even when some of our seamen were captured by an arrogant Algerine pirate in the summer of 1785, the focus of Congress' reaction was how to raise and pay the ransom rather than how to build a fleet to prevent such further acts.[9] The Constitutional Convention in 1787 proposed giving Congress power to raise sufficient money to "provide and maintain a navy". The proposal was not greeted with enthusiasm. The Secretary of State, Thomas Jefferson, argued for the formation of a Mediterranean squadron with the comment, "a domestic naval force can never endanger our liberties"[10]. His efforts, unfortunately, produced meager results. Congress voted additional funds for the ransom of the captured United States sailors and promised to build a fleet when it could afford it.

In December 1787, Captain John Paul Jones wrote, referring to America, "The creation of a Marine Force will necessarily be among the first objects of her policy".[11] However, by the time of his death in 1792, the only organized naval force the United States had was the Revenue Cutter Service, a predecessor of today's Coast Guard. Perhaps Congress was influenced, and thought no US Navy was necessary, because of successful activities of the merchantmen who sailed under Letters of Marque or 'Sea Letters' representing the new nation. The letters served to introduce and identify a captain and implied authorization of his actions. The guns aboard their ships and the new Stars and Stripes Banner at their mastheads did not go unnoticed by the people of the lands they visited.

It was John Kendrick, one of these daring captains, whose audacious acts tied the United States Navy to events some 6000 miles away in a small harbor in the Sandwich Islands.

Before whaling lured American seamen into the Pacific Ocean, the China trade had been established. China offered silk, tea, and other exotic products for sale or trade, and since the newly formed United States was almost bankrupt, trade was the solution. But what did the new nation have to trade? The answer was found along the Pacific Northwest coast of America. In his report on the successful fur trade of the Russians, John Ledyard attracted the attention of merchant ship owners. These ships sailed for their own profit, and displayed the American flag prominently around the world. The engagement of these ships in the China trade was fortuitous both for the owners and for the country. Six American businessmen from Boston and New York underwrote a voyage for the ship Columbia Rediviva and the sloop *Lady Washington* to inaugurate trade with the Chinese, using as currency the rich, soft beaver furs, often called "soft gold".

A young shipmaster from Wareham, Massachusetts, John Kendrick, was chosen to command the expedition. His flagship was Columbia. She was a stout ship, 85' long and 212 tons burden, built at Hobart's Landing on the North River, Massachusetts in 1773. Her tender, *Lady Washington*, a 170 ton sloop was commanded by Robert Gray.

The purpose of the expedition was far more ambitious than a single business venture. The owners envisioned establishing permanent factories and stations in the Northwest under the aegis of the United States, similar to the successful Hudson's Bay Company. Therefore part of Kendrick's commission was to purchase land for the location of these proposed buildings. He was the Commodore of a tiny fleet, captain of his own ship, businessman, explorer, and trader, but never an admiral. That rank was not used in the US Navy until 1862.[12] Until then the highest grade that was attainable by commanders of ships was Captain. Often, when one man commanded a squadron of ships, he assumed the unofficial title and uniform of Commodore. Although Kendrick was commander of the two-ship squadron, he maintained the title of Captain.

Due to the disbanding of the Continental Navy, Kendrick and his ships, as well as fellow merchantmen and their ships, were the closest thing the new nation had to a regular navy on the seas.

Lady Washington (Gray) and *Columbia* (Kendrick) stood out of Boston Harbor on September 30, 1787. The voyage went well and they succeeded in April of 1788 in becoming the first American vessels to round Cape Horn. Their activities along the Northwest coast went efficiently as planned, and on October 1, 1788 they celebrated the anniversary of their departure from Boston. As his guests, Kendrick entertained two British captains, Douglas and Funter at a fine dinner aboard the *Lady*. The men under his command continued to trap, hunt, and trade to increase their inventory of furs. All ancillary activities, e.g. killing; skinning, dressing and tanning of the beaver, when added to the necessary maintenance of the ships, kept his crews busy for several months.

Finally the day of departure came. On July 30, 1789, Captain Kendrick ordered the collected furs stowed aboard Columbia and, with Gray in command, dispatched her to China via the recently discovered Sandwich Islands. Kendrick followed in a similarly laden *Lady Washington*. While in the islands, Kendrick took on a small amount of sandalwood, as the cruel Captain Metcalfe had four years earlier. Kendrick later found the fragrant wood to be in great demand in Canton. Sandalwood was so plentiful in Hawaii that some people in China years later, referred to the islands as "Tan Heong Shan" or Sandalwood Fragrant Mountains.[13]

This innovative addition to the fur trade was indicative of Kendrick's initiative. He also used the facilities of an abandoned sugar mill on Kanai to make molasses. The Indians, whose friendship he had cultivated in the Northwest, loved the sweet liquid more than anything foreign traders offered. Kendrick's astute business acumen was evident and many furs were acquired in trade for the molasses. While in China, Kendrick had *Lady Washington* rerigged as a brig.

Some 52 years before Commodore Perry made his historic voyage to Japan, Kendrick entered a southern Japanese port in company with *Grace* (Douglas) and attempted to establish trade with the Japanese. He was unsuccessful, but despite this failure he was successful at his other ventures. He managed the fur trade so well that it flourished for the next several years.

One of the places Kendrick had anchored was off the southern coast of Oahu, west (or Ewa) of Diamond Head. This spectacular southeastern tip of Oahu had been named "Point Rose" by Captain Nathaniel Portlock in 1786 in honor of George Rose, his patron, who was First Lord of the British Treasury.[14] Behind the point was a large hill and the caldera of an extinct volcano. Portlock called it Diamond Hill for the glittering bits of quartz his men found on the hillside. He explored "a fine, deep bay running well to the northward" in an area which appears to be west of Honolulu Harbor. It was probably the first description of what we call Pearl Harbor and the natives called *Pu'uloa* or *Waimomi*.

On December 3, 1794, Kendrick's ship lay at anchor in Honolulu Roads alongside two British ships, *Jackal* (Brown) and *Prince Lee Boo* (Gordon). Honolulu, at that time a small village, was called *Honoonoono* by Vancouver, "Fair Haven" by Americans and Europeans and *Ke Awa o Kau* by Hawaiians.[15] The anchorage to seaward of the harbor was called Honolulu Roadstead or simply Honolulu Roads. Roads or roadstead is the customary name used where there is no enclosed harbor, only open anchorage. It was here the first recorded event occurred that concerned an American naval force and the people of Hawaii.

The chief, or *ali'i nui* of Oahu was Kalanikupule. He was struggling with his half-brother, Kaeokulani, for supremacy of the island. Kaeokulani's forces were advancing and Kalanikupule's situation had become desperate. The question of cession of land in exchange for military assistance arose.

Citing the precedents of Kamehameha and other island chiefs, Kalanikupule offered Captain William Brown of *Jackal* 400 pigs and Oahu for his military help. Brown's journal indicates the offer was complete cession of the entire island. What Kalanikupule meant can never be determined. Perhaps it was only use of the anchorage in Honolulu Harbor. To make the agreement official in British eyes, Brown had some of his officers draw up a contract which they and he signed along with the marks of Kalanikupule and four of his chiefs. The contract, as written, "most formally ceded Woahoo [sic] to Mr. Brown" and added four islands to windward for extra measure. It further stated that one James Coleman was appointed as resident in charge of the archipelago. The ambitious Captain Brown accepted the incredible offer and dispatched from his crew nine sailors to side with Kalanikupule to fulfill his part of the bargain. Brown's aid, however, was ineffective. The king was at the threshold of defeat at the battle of Punahawale in Ewa, just west of Pu'uloa, or Pearl Harbor. In the battle several British sailors were slain or wounded and Brown withdrew his support to reassess the situation.

Into the void stepped Captain John Kendrick. He had watched from his ship and been advised of the proceedings. When he learned of Brown's withdrawal, Kendrick offered his military expertise and assets to Kalanikupule. With the aid of the Americans the tide of battle quickly turned and Kalanikupule emerged victorious. The battle of Kalauao, also in Ewa, was decisive. The chief retained his island and his head. The would-be usurper, Kaeokulani, ran through the lush, green vegetation in his *ahu'ula*, a stunningly brilliant coat made of red and yellow feathers. Some of Kendrick's men were in a small boat in what is now called East Loch of Pearl Harbor. They fired on the fleeing Kaeokulani locating him for Kalanikupule. The ambitious would-be king was easily found, and disposed of by Kalanikupule's men. Victory belonged to the chief of Oahu and his allies, the Americans. John Bolt's account of December 6, 1794, states that,

> "On the 6th. of ye same month in consequence of a long quarrel between the Chiefs of Whahooa & Atooi [Kauai] a battle was fought & victory was gain'd by the King of Whahooa, by the assistance of Capt. Kendrick"[16].

That was the first time the flag of the newly constituted United States of America flew over the waters of Pearl Harbor.

There is no available record of what Kendrick's reward might have been. Tragically, this remarkable man met his death by what is reported to be an accident. Captain John Bolt of the sloop Union, wrote Kendrick "inform'd Captain Brown that on the morrow he shuld cause the Flag of the United States to be hoisted and fire a federal salute, which he beg'd might be answer'd by the two Englishmen"[17].

Brown agreed and ordered three guns to be emptied of shot. Only the powder was to remain for the salute. Bolt's journal continued,

"The gunner of Brown's ship, on coming to the 3'd gun it was discovered not to be prim'd. So the Apron of the 4th Gun was taken of[f], which was fir'd, & being shoted with round & Grape Shot, it pierced the topside of the Lady Washington & kill'd Capt. Kendrick as he sat at his table".[18]

The body of the late Captain Kendrick was taken to a small grove of trees *mauka*, toward the mountains, of Honolulu and laid to rest. His clerk, John Howell, a onetime clergyman, read the burial service. The observing islanders thought the prayer and invocation were pleas to the *haole* god to effect the death of Captain Brown.[19] This, as with other legends, can be scoffed at, but in fact, on New Year's Day in 1795 Captains Brown and Gordon were alone aboard their ships when a party of Oahuans crept aboard and slew them both.

Later Amasa Delano, an American, wrote,

"Captain Kendrick was the first American that burst forth in the world and traversed those distant regions which were before but little known to the inhabitants of this part of the globe. He taught many of his countrymen the way to wealth, and the method of navigating distant seas with ease and safety. I wish to impress it strongly on the minds of every American, not to let his rare merits be forgotten, and to cast a veil over his faults, they being but few compared with his amiable qualities"[20]

Thus ended the life of this remarkable man. He was innovative as a businessman, intrepid as an adventurer, more than able as the Commanding Officer of a ship and, as will be seen, the first of several American seamen who displayed the presence of the United States in the Hawaiian Islands to counter other foreign powers, particularly in the Pearl Harbor area. All this was accomplished while Congress still pondered the idea of a Navy for the country. Soon events would force a decision.

Chapter 4 - The Birth of the United States Navy

The year Captain Kendrick was killed, 1794, was a significant one for naval affairs in United States. Late in 1793 Portugal withdrew her protection of ships in the Mediterranean and signed a truce with Algiers. To the United States that meant that Portugal would no longer attempt to restrain the Algerine pirates from preying on American ships in the Mediterranean. At the end of the year over 100 American seamen were being kept somewhere in the miserable prisons of Algerian North Africa. There was no US Navy to argue the issue. By this time, Congress, out of patience with the effrontery of these pirates, was warming to the idea of an official United States Naval Force. President Washington, who had always promoted the idea of a strong force at sea, appealed to Congress in these words, "If we desire to avoid insult, we must be able to repel it; if we desire to secure peace...., it must be known, that we are at all times ready for War".[1] Soon afterward, January 2, 1794, a House resolution stated that a naval force adequate to the protection of the commerce of the United States against Algerine corsairs, ought to be provided. So important was the Algerine threat that the resolution specifically mentioned them. Eighteen days later another resolution recommended construction of six frigates.

Impetus was given the movement toward the formation of a United States Navy when the alarming news was received that Great Britain had instituted a policy of prohibiting any neutral trade with the French West Indies. This outrageous affront to the new country, and abrogation by England of the Treaty of Paris in waters near the US, was enough to effect the passage of an act authorizing the President to acquire six frigates; four of forty-four guns each and two of thirty-six guns. The act passed both houses of congress and was signed into law by the President, March 27, 1794.

The United States Navy was born. At least on paper.

The selection of this type of ship, a frigate, was a wise one. A 'ship of the line' was large and powerful, but not very maneuverable. A sloop (the three masted, square-rigged type) was too small to carry sufficient arms and too slightly built to withstand the onslaught of naval cannon. The frigate had the best qualities and characteristics of both.

These first six frigates were no ordinary ships. Armed with this authorization, President Washington acted quickly. Since no Navy Department had been established, he turned to his Secretary of War Henry Knox (and later Secretaries Pickering and McHenry) for action. The decision was made to build new ships rather than attempt to convert existing merchantmen to military use. On April 15, 1794, Knox's recommendations were accepted enthusiastically by Washington and the search for designers, yards, materials, and builders began.

To direct the design team, Joshua Humphreys, a Philadelphia designer and builder of note was selected. Humphreys' eleven acre shipyard was later (180 1) purchased by the government for $38,636 and was renamed the Federal Street Navy Yard.[2] The selection of Humphreys was a fortuitous one. He had long been recommending to the government (located then in his city, Philadelphia) a radical new design which would produce the most advanced ships the world had seen. A brief description of an existing nautical problem and his innovative solution is in order.

As long as large square-rigged ships had been sailing, an inescapable problem had vexed designers. A ship is built somewhat similar to the upper skeletal torso of a human, in that there is a 'backbone' or keel, and ribs. If a person can be visualized as lying on his back with weights applied to his face and pelvis, the strain on his back can easily be understood. The farther a ship's hull reaches down into the water, the more the upward displacement pressure increases. That means that while the tonnage of both ship and cargo is evenly distributed, the resistance of the seawater is not. The ocean 'pushes' up at the center of a ship much more than at her bow and stem. This distortion of a ship's keel (upward in the center) stole precious speed from the hull as the vessel aged. Called 'hogging', it is evident on many a salvaged vessel of the late 18th century.[3]

Ships could only overcome this deficiency by oversizing the keel, slowing her speed, or making the ship longer and lighter. This made her faster, but weaker and more vulnerable to enemy firepower. Military ships were particularly susceptible to this phenomenon because, unlike merchantmen that carried their cargoes deep in the hold, thereby supporting the keel, cannon were always distributed along the gun deck high above the keel. Countless new designs were tried to no avail until Joshua Humphreys pondered the construction of a gate on his farm. The gate had a diagonal member which transferred much of the weight of the gate back up to the hinge. Parallel boards could move and sag, but the diagonal board would not change length by tension (stretching) or compression (squeezing). This restriction maintained the original rectangular shape of the gate. He was convinced that the introduction of diagonal members, which he called 'riders', would prevent the hogging of his hulls.

The use of these diagonal riders was not Humphreys' only innovation. Heavy guns, which weighed up to three tons, exerted an enormous force on the gundeck and its connections to the hull. He supported these connections with heavy knees, L shaped wood braces that connect deck boards to planks in the hull, and strakes which are long wood planks that extend from bow to stem. These two members were rabbetted together and ran the full length of the ship. In order to have a sense of the size and strength of these parts, it may help to know that the riders were one foot thick by two feet wide in cross section. They were heavy, dense live oak weighing several tons each. The additional tonnage was acceptable because the riders supported and maintained the original shape and sailing characteristics of every ship on which they were installed.

The hull was also impressively designed. Thick planks rode over mighty ribs both inboard and outboard. In some places the hulls for these six new frigates were solid live oak almost two feet thick. Live oak was in great demand the world over for its strength to weight ratio and, with marvelous fortuity for the new US Navy, it was found only in America. Later the flagship of this small but mighty fleet was to exhibit such resistance to cannon fire that the thundering missiles of destruction would literally bounce off of her topsides. Hence the name that has lasted over two hundred years, "OLD IRONSIDES".

To distribute the financial rewards of such a large building program, existing boatyards were selected. Baltimore, Boston, Gosport Virginia, New York, Philadelphia, and Portsmouth New Hampshire were the fortunate six.[4] This act evoked much public support in these well populated, maritime-oriented cities. The local yard superintendents worked closely with ex-Continental Navy Captains who served as technical advisers. Later these experienced mariners became commissioned as Captains in the embryonic United States Navy.

President Washington, delighted with the progress of his new navy, requested Secretary of War Timothy Pickering to submit names for the new ships. During construction their designations were A, B, C, D, E, & F. The names chosen were *Chesapeake, Constellation, Congress, President, United States* and *Constitution*, which was the flagship of the fleet.

Then, suddenly, in March of 1796, word was received that a truce had been negotiated with Algiers. That meant, by a provision in the act that authorized building the six frigates, construction on the new ships should cease. The terms of the agreement stunned the maritime people of the country, especially those involved with building the new fleet. A ransom of over one million dollars was paid for the release of captive American seamen. And, incredibly, the terms included the construction of a 32 gun frigate, *Crescent*, for the recent long-time enemy.

Washington's powers of persuasion were so formidable that he was able to convince Congress to finish three of the six frigates. *United States* was launched at Philadelphia on May 10, 1797, then *Constellation* from Baltimore on September 7, and on October 21, 1797, the magnificent flagship of the fleet, *Constitution*, slid down the ways at Boston. At the risk of committing a historic pun, the ships were not just evolutionary, they were revolutionary.

The flagship measured 175' at the waterline, 204' overall, with a beam of 43.5' and towering masts probing 220' into the sky. These ships were a formidable sight indeed. They would strike fearinto the hearts of knowledgeable enemies and stir the hearts of all Americans who were lucky enough to see them. They displaced over 2,000 tons, and carried 40,000 square feet of sail, depending on how each was rigged for wind and sea. They could achieve 14 knots, which was faster than any other warship in the world at the time. Their main batteries of 32 '24 pounder' long guns could demolish any other frigates, and with their speed they could outmaneuver a ship-of-the line which might be foolish enough to challenge them .5 These superb ships were joined in 1799 by the three other super frigates whose construction had been temporarily halted. The names of the captains of these mighty ships are now well known in United States Naval history; Edward Preble, William Bainbridge, Stephen Decatur, Isaac Hull, Charles Stewart, and Thomas Truxtun. The last named will appear in this history a few years later in Hawaii.

Lest we tend to think of the battles these ships fought as being just off the shores of the new United States, we should remember that Stephen Decatur, commanding United States, captured Macedonian (Carden) off the Canary Islands on October 25,1812. On December 2g the same year, William Bainbridge of Const~tution, sank Java off the coast of Brazil, and on February 24th of 1813, Captain James Lawrence, sailing in command of *Hornet*, captured the brig Peacock near the coast of the country now called Guyana. All these significant victories were achieved in engagements hundreds, and sometimes thousands, of miles from home.

The flagship of the fleet of new frigates, USS *Constitution*, after 36 engagements including over 20 captures, was retired in 1881 looking forward to a short period at a dock and then to the breakers. She was saved, however, by strong sentiment and action by citizens of the country she had served so well. Some of her riders were found to be rotted and removed by people who had no idea of their purpose. The ship remained in commission as a museum with occasional trips to sea. In the late 1980s restoration was begun. Exhaustive design studies uncovered much of what had been forgotten. Because of the removal of the riders, the keel had 'hogged' 14 inches and her decks were soft and weak. Rigging was unsafe and the sails were either nonexistent or unusable. The riders were replaced, soft wood was renewed, her eight miles of rigging were redone, new sails were crafted, and the ship is, today, in as good or better shape than she has ever been. A short sail under her own power in July of 1997 displayed the magnificent result of the work of thousands of people who had contributed totherestoration.

During her first war (1812) there was no lack of patriotic sentiment among the citizens of the new country. One poster proudly (and accurately) acclaimed,

"Huzza for our Navy! Another 15 minutes Job. Being
the 8th Naval Victory in which John Bull has been obliged
to douce his flag, to the invincible skill of American Tars."[6]

In the period after the revolution, several incidents at sea involved
the new country's aging ships. Except for the new frigates, US vessels were
over twenty years old. New construction was hampered by fiscal restraints
and shipbuilders turned their attention to more lucrative and dependable
contracts from private merchants who wanted new ships. Apprehension was
rising in Washington concerning the ineffective administration of our meager
naval force, governed at that time by a small detail in the War Department.
Congress became so aware of the need for a strong naval management unit,
that when an act was introduced in the senate to establish a Department of
the Navy, it passed easily and quickly. After some wrangling, an amended
version passed the house and President John Adams signed the bill on April
30, 1798. The first Secretary of the Navy was Benjamin Stoddart. The United
States Navy was born again.[7]
        A large part of the new navy consisted of armed merchantmen sailing
with Sea Letters to authorize their activities. In August of 1798 one of these
American armed merchantman Neptune (Greene) anchored in Honolulu
Roadstead. On board was Ebenezer Townsend, Jr. who kept a journal of his
visit to the islands. He wrote that the harbor of Honolulu was a good one, but
rather narrow to enter. He described pearl oysters in a river about three or
four miles from where his ship anchored. Although the area had been visited
by previous sailors, this is the first American reference explicitly mentioning
the Pearl River and its estuary.
        Americans were not the only foreigners with an interest in Hawaii.
Russians were already operating an extensive fur trade in Alaska by the 1790s
and needed to make connections with the best market for fur. To accomplish
this, they wanted to establish trade with China and try to open trade with
Japan.[8] Hawaii was a vital stopover for any ship sailing across the huge
Pacific Ocean so they began to plan to build a settlement in the islands as
early as 1809.
        Russian knowledge of the discovery of the Sandwich Islands came
from British reports and Russian visits to the islands in 1804. A few years
later, a Russian voyage of exploration headed around the world commanded
by Lt. Captain Hagemeister. He sent a report to the directors of the Russian American
Fur Company in 1809 from the ship Neva. He said that
Kamehameha did not allow his subjects to engage in trade, but handled it all
himself and was not willing to sell his goods at a reasonable price. The Russian
was aware of the antagonism between Kamehameha and Kaumuali'i of Kauai

and felt that Kauai held good possibilities for Russian settlement. The natives are not as advanced as those on Hawaii, he said, and suffer from a lack of organization.

Another possibility Hagemeister suggested would be the island of Molokai which is more fertile than the others. He extolled its virtues and ended with "The inhabitants are lazy by nature but, if enlightened by faith, they could learn to lead better lives and improve their habits".[10] This is a rare mention of religion in the Russian documents detailing their plans for Hawaii. He remarked that Oahu may be the best of the islands because it has moderate climate and an excellent harbor. However the opportunities for establishing a settlement there were not propitious.

He was sure a settlement in Hawaii, specifically Kauai, could grow enough food to take care of the entire population of Asiatic Russia. Rice, taro, Sugar cane, for use in making rum, and other farm crops were the focus of his attention. He also suggested that they might buy land from the king or just occupy it and start growing crops. It would be wise to send two ships, two cannon, twenty men to farm and twenty for defense, he wrote. Russians were sure that the English owned the island of Hawaii, and that is the reason they stayed away from it. The report was filed, but no one acted on the plan.

Among the first recorded references to the Pearl Harbor area by Americans was one made by Lieutenant Jonathan Thorn, the first US Naval Officer to reach the Sandwich Islands. An officer aboard USS *Constitution*, he requested a leave of absence, as many sailors did in the pre-war period, to command an expedition ship, the Tonquin, for John Jacob Aster and his Pacific Fur Company. He sailed from New York on September 8, 1810, reaching the Sandwich Islands off Waikiki on February 21, 1841. His observations concerning both Honolulu Harbor and the inlet a few miles to the West stated that each, or both, if dredged, would be excellent harbors for US Navy ships and would even justify the establishment of a Naval Station. This early recognition of the Hawaiian Islands as a strategic location was far-sighted indeed. Thom was not thinking of a coaling station, although that soon became one reason for a US Naval Station in the island, nor could he have foreseen the long-distance threat of carriers and aircraft. Their invention and use would corroborate his opinion over a century later.

Another tie between the United States and Hawaii was created when George Tamoree, son of Kaumuali'i, a descendant of Kaeokulani and king of Kauai, served in the War of 1812 in Stephen Decatur's squadron in the campaign against the Algerines and again aboard *Thaddeus* in 1820.

Most naval activities of the early 19th century took place in oceans other than the Pacific and are therefore outside our purview. There were, however, many heroic and extraordinary events which occurred in the Pacific, particularly in the Honolulu/Pearl Harbor area. We will meet one seafarer who commanded the first United States warship to round Cape Horn and enter the Pacific Ocean, Captain David Porter USN. The man who commanded the first US Warship to round up and heave to in the Honolulu/Pearl Harbor area was the leader of Porter's Marine detachment, Lieutenant John Marshall Gamble, USMC.

Chapter 5 - Round the Horn to Whyteetee

Captain David Porter, USN, saw action in the early part of the War of 1812 and was acclaimed by his peers and by the public. He captured six prizes, and was so adept at maneuvering his ship that with a single broadside from his ship the frigate USS *Essex*, he took the British ship HBMS *Alert*, bearing 20 guns and 98 men.[1] *Essex* bore a figurehead indicative of the spirit of her captain and the events soon to be encountered. At her launching in the Salem Yard in 1799, the figure of an "Indian holding a tomahawk in an upraised arm and grasping a scalping knife in the other hand"[2] was fitted under her bowsprit. The adventurous frigate carried 32 guns peering out through a yellow ochre gun stripe, rather than the usual white stripe. Economy was the reason. White paint was in short supply and difficult to obtain at the time, so yellow had to be substituted. The flag that flew from the gaff of the mizzenmast had fifteen stripes. Congress did not decide on thirteen stripes for the national flag until 19 years later.[3]

Porter hated having 'carronades' rather than 'long guns' in his ship's main battery. He complained bitterly and often in his letters to the Secretary of the Navy Paul Hamilton. Carronades were first built at the Carron Iron Works in Scotland and were short, large caliber guns which could be devastating at short range. However, American gunners preferred long range guns and felt their skill and accuracy would prevail in long-distance encounters. They were proven correct in engagements between *Constitution* and *Guerriere*, as well as against *Java*, and by *United States* in a battle with *Macedonian*. In all, the American ships were victorious, thanks in large part to the skill of American gunners and their ordnance.

The following is a letter written by Porter to the Secretary of the Navy on 12 October 1811, during the commerce raiding cruise of Essex, near Crany Island in the South Pacific [4]

"Sir:
Considering as I do that Carronades are merely an experiment in modern warfare and that their character is by no means established I do not conceive it proper to entrust the honor of the flag entirely to them. Was this ship to be disabled in her rigging in the early part of an engagement, a ship much inferior to her in sailing and force, armed with long Guns, could take a position beyond the reach of our Carronades, and cut us to pieces with out our being able to do her any injury. Long Guns are well known to be effective and the management of them familiar to seamen. I have therefore required of Capt. Evans four long eighteen

pounders to mount on the gun deck and shall on the receipt
of them, send on shore some defective Carronades.
    I hope Sir the reasons I have given will in your opinion
justify the change.
    I have the honor to be With great respect
    Your Obt Servt   D. Porter."[5]

    Later, however, Porter would find the smaller guns essential for use
in various actions against natives in the South Pacific.
    Essex was assigned to the Atlantic squadron under the command of
William Bainbridge. The other two frigates in the flotilla were USS
Constitution and USS *Hornet*. These two ships left port in the summer of
1812, but Porter's ship was undergoing overhaul and fitting-out. He was not
ready to leave the yard until October of that year. When he sailed, he had
aboard an 18 year old midshipman named David Farragut.[6] Because Porter
missed the rendezvous with the other two ships, he had the choice of harassing
British shipping in the South Atlantic or rounding Cape Horn into the Pacific.
Unfortunately for the British whaling fleet, he chose to head around the Horn.
Thus *Essex* became the first United States Warship into the Pacific Ocean.[7]
Earlier, Kendrick and others, had done so as armed American merchantmen.
    After reprovisioning in Valparaiso, Chile, he made for the Galapagos
Islands where he fell upon the unsuspecting British like an Avenging Angel.
He captured almost a dozen British whale ships, which was a remarkable
feat considering that once his devastating actions had begun, the British could
have united to present a credible defense. They did not, however, and Porter
captured the lot. His single ship became a 12 ship flotilla.
    Two of these prizes were HBMS *Seringapatam* and *Greenwich*, both
of which were soon to be involved in the life of John Gamble, the young
Marine lieutenant on Porter's ship. Porter experienced little difficulty and
suffered no losses in these engagements. The ships he captured were well
armed and loaded with provisions. Until the arrival of Porter, the British had
enforced their will upon local American whalers.
    Porter's success in the Galapagos Islands was threefold. He eliminated
the British presence off the West Coast of both North and South America,
captured several British ships, and freed some American sailors and
whaleships to practice their industry without hindrance from foreign powers.
One British prize, *Atlantic*, was fitted out as a fighting ship and renamed
Essex, Junior; not an elegant name, but appropriate. One could say that for
almost a year, Porter controlled the entire Pacific Ocean.

    Once the British fleet had been subdued, he sailed South to the lovely
island of Nuku Hiva in the Marquesas. There he ordered his little frigate
careened, that is, pulled up onto the beach at ebb tide and laid on her side.

Thereupon, crewmen and natives who were hired for the job, used knives and coconut shells to scrape the exposed hull and remove the barnacles and other sealife which cling to the hulls of ocean-going vessels. They turned the ship to the other side and did the job again. When the task was finished, they set controlled, smoldering fires below decks to get rid of pests and contaminants. Over fifteen hundred rats scrambled from the smoke onto the beach, thus bringing a new species of pest to Nuku Hiva. Impervious to the smoke which had expelled the rats were thousands of cockroaches which took up residence on board. This exchange of pests was of dubious value to either side.

During the stay, native girls and sailors found a means of communication and mutual gratification. As Porter observed in his journal, it was "helter-skelter and promiscuous intercourse, every girl the wife of every man."[8] Captain Porter did not look with approval on this behavior but neither did he forbid it. Concerning the liaison between one of his officers and a native woman, he wrote,

> "Yet this lady, like the rest of the women of the island,
> soon followed the dictates of her own interests, and formed
> a connection with one of the officers, which lasted with but
> little fidelity on her part, as long as we remained, showing
> herself on the whole a most notorious jilt."[9]

English reviewers of these published journals, men who were jealous of Porter's naval success in the Pacific, singled out this passage, and several others, branding Porter a "hoary, proficient in swinish sensualism ".[10] His revised journal, published in 1822, was toned down considerably. So incensed were the British at Porter's naval triumphs that they ignored the events in the Galapagos and dwelled on his illicit association with natives. These journalists, William Gifford in particular, overlooked the brilliance of Porter's campaign and became obsessed with his sometimes lurid prose. According to them, Porter represented the rude, vulgar American people. Gifford wrote,

> "We cannot pollute [sic] our pages with the description
> which Captain Porter gives of his transactions with these
> people. His language and his ideas are so gross and indelicate,
> so utterly unfit for this hemisphere, that we must leave the
> undivided enjoyment of this part of his book to his own
> countrymen"[11]

Encouraged by the friendly reception of the native girls, Porter understandably attempted to make friends with the natives, but that proved to be difficult. Various groups were at war with each other and each group solicited his powerful military help. The difficulty was that the opposing sides in the conflicts kept changing, and anyone whom he had not befriended that day was his enemy. The difference lay in the concept of 'war' the natives had, compared with Porter's. The rule among natives was to frighten or wound, but not to kill. When Porter and his Marines killed a half dozen natives, four thousand on both sides surrendered and offered fruit and pigs as atonement. This military skirmish, ironically, brought peace to that area of the island.

It was at Nuku Hiva in 1813 that the first overseas US Naval Station was established. Porter named it Madisonville in honor of his President. To accomplish the building of docks and sheds, he used his own sailors and Marines, several English prisoners from the Galapagos, as well as native islanders. His efforts were not noted with much enthusiasm in Washington because the War of 1812 was going badly. In fact, so little attention was paid to the acquisition of this group of islands, that when the French, a few years later, declared the Marquesas to be theirs, no opposition was heard from the US government.

While cruising and charting the Marquesas, Porter encountered the British frigate *Sir Andrew Hammond* sailing under a Letter-of-Marque. As he explained the engagement, "..at 4 o'clock we were within gun shot, when, after firing 6 or 8 shot at her, she bore down under our lee, and struck her colours."[12] *Sir Andrew Hammond* was a rewarding prize. She was loaded with whale blubber worth two to three thousand dollars. Perhaps worth more at the time was the cargo of fresh vegetables and "two puncheons of choice Jamaica spirits".[13] The ex-British ship was 390 tons with a 16' draught.[14] Porter placed his chaplain, Mr. Adams, in command of the captured vessel with orders to sail her to Rendezvous Bay in the Marquesas where the other prize ships were anchored.

On the 13th of December, 1813, Captain Porter with *Essex* and *Essex Junior* put to sea and set a course for Valparaiso where he calculated he could meet and engage newly-arrived British ships. He left young Lieutenant John Marshall Gamble, USMC, in command of the Marquesas site. Porter said he would return in five months. If Gamble had not been there, he would have left a letter buried in a bottle at a well-marked site for the intended recipient, as he had done before.

Lt. Gamble had three ships under his command, *Greenwich, Sir Andrew Hammond,* and *Seringapatam.* He had three officers, twenty men, and six prisoners of war. His main activity while waiting for Porter's return was the repair and maintenance of the ships One recurring problem was the parting of anchor rodes and cables. The constant wearing of the hawser in its chock as the ship wore back and forth and circled with the tides and currents caused constant vigilance and frequent repair. If the line went unobserved for any length of time, the danger of parting arose. When the anchor line parted, the anchor was lost, as no means of reaching it was available. That is, not until a native volunteered to dive to the sunken anchor, attach a line, and let the men raise it by means of the capstan. Gamble's men were incredulous of the offer since the lost anchor lay in over six and a half fathoms of water.[15] The native dove, attached his line and the anchor was pulled up to the deck. The native was rewarded with a shark's tooth. He so enjoyed his prize that he volunteered to dive and retrieve other 'lost' anchors. Lest it be overlooked, six and a half fathoms is almost 40' of sea water!

On May 4th, 1814, while most of his officers and men were working ashore or aboard *Greenwich* or *Sir Andrew Hammond*, Lt. Gamble learned of a potential mutiny among the English prisoners on board *Seringapatam*. He took two midshipmen and went to the ship to investigate. He arrived too late. "One of them drew a large knife from his bosom, and desired his accomplices to lay hold of Lieut. Gamble."[16] Gamble and his two companions were bound, beaten, and thrust into the run, a small space 'tween decks. Later, for no apparent reason, one of the mutineers shot Gamble through his left ankle. Gamble, in great pain, was placed in a small boat and set adrift. There was little reason for the mutineers to expect the small party to survive. While the mutineers made off with the *Seringapatam*, Lt. Gamble and his companions, thanks to their Herculean efforts at the oars, overcame the tidal current to reach the *Greenwich*.

Instead of relief, however, Gamble found natives plundering the ship. In severe pain from his leg wound, Gamble ran from gun to gun, loading, ramming, and firing each gun. With this action he was temporarily able to repel the canoes coming from shore. Then he ordered his remaining men to set a torch to Greenwich. She was in poor condition and he had hardly enough men left to crew *Sir Andrew Hammond*, his only remaining ship. Leaving the burning derelict ablaze, he and his men bent their backs into the oars of the small boat and made for the *Sir Andrew Hammond*. They barely got aboard, fleeing attacking natives. With a powerful swing of an ax the crippled crew cut the anchor cable, set the mizzen top sail and jibs and worked out of the harbor into deeper water. Bending on as much sail as the old girl would stand, the young Marine Lieutenant decided not to try for Valparaiso to find Porter because mutineers had stolen his compass, charts, and other navigational gear.[17]

At this point he made the incredible decision to stand for the Sandwich Islands. To realize his desperate situation, consider his crew:

"Himself - severely wounded in the heel
Midshipman Clapp - In good health
Bispham - do
Caddington - wounded in the head
Worth - a fractured leg
Sansbury -Rheumatism
Burnham - an old man, just cured of the scurvy
Pettenger - a cripple"[18]

It did not add to their peace of mind that he had only six cartridges aboard. With amazing modesty, Gamble reported, "Nothing material occurred until we reached the island of Owyhee on the 23rd"[19] He was met there by friendly natives bearing much appreciated gifts of swine, poultry, fruit, and vegetables. On the afternoon of the 31st of May, 1814 he "came to off Whyateetee Bay on the S.W. side of the island of Waohoo"[20]

Thus, *Sir Andrew Hammond*, although a captured British ship, was the first US warship to anchor in the Honolulu/Pearl Harbor area.

A Hawaiian-American named James Harbottle piloted *Hammond* into the harbor of Honolulu where Gamble met Captain Nathaniel Winship who helped restore and reprovision the battered, leaking, anchorless ship. It was on July 4th, 1814, that the first Independence Day was celebrated in the islands. Aging Kamehameha attended the festivities with captains of three merchant ships which were in the harbor, *Albatross* (Nathan Winship), *Isabella* (Davis) and *O. Kane*, (Jonathan Winship).

Later, as Lt. Gamble sailed his re-supplied, but defenseless ship to Chile to meet Porter, *Sir Andrew Hammond* was recaptured by the British ship Cherub (Tucker). Gamble returned to the United States and served in several posts. Because of his old wound, his later commands were all shoreside. Brevet Lieutenant Colonel John Marshall Gamble died on September 11, 1836 in New York.[21] He will forever retain the honor of being the first man to command a United States warship into the waters of Honolulu.

The magnificent square rigged wooden ships of the 18th and 19th centuries were nearing the end of their reign. They had served the United States well from the beginning when it was a weak, fledgling nation, concentrated on the East Coast of America. These splendid ships had carried the American flag into the Atlantic Ocean, the Mediterranean, the Indian Ocean, around Cape Horn and into the Pacific Ocean. They ran before the wind, tacked and often courageously sailed into danger. They had triumphed both economically and militarily. Their gallant crews set sail in the still, stifling heat of the tropics, and lay aloft to trim sails when the sheets and shrouds were frozen like iron rods and the canvas was stiff as carved Carolina Oak. They bravely carried the flag of the United States to all ports of the world, but their lives and livelihood were about to change.

On February 7, 1815, at the urging of Secretary of the Navy Benjamin Crowninshield, a Board of Commissioners was formed to centralize all U.S. Naval policy decisions. The Board lasted until it was abolished on August 31, 1842.

During this period, two monumental inventions were made which would toll the death knell of these magnificent ships.

One was the first operating steam-driven engine and the other was the invention of explosive shells. Together, they would force the end of these beautiful sailing ships. But before the end of the age of sail, a number of naval events took place in the far off Sandwich Islands. Some of these activities were funny, some tragic, and some downright bizarre. All of them changed forever the relationship between the Hawaiian people and the United States Navy.

Chapter 6 - Years of Crisis

The arrival of Captain Cook in 1778 in the Hawaiian Islands was the signal that many changes were coming to these islands. The changes came slowly at first, but soon foreign ships were anchored in many Hawaiian harbors and roadsteads. Besides their major goals of exploring or trading, the men from these ships were observing and recording the ways of the people. Merchants saw opportunities for lucrative trade and the value of the islands as a stopover on the China trade. Forty years after the world first heard of the Sandwich Isles, and after the sojourn of Lt. Gamble there, events occurred that had momentous and far-reaching effects on Hawaii's people.

By about 1790 or 1795, Kamehameha ruled all the Hawaiian islands except Kanai. Kaumuali'i, the high chief of Kauai, pledged allegiance to him and remained its chief. Sometime after he was acknowledged as ruler of all Hawaii, an event with no firm date but which fell between 1795 and 1810, Kamehameha moved to Waikiki on Oahu. At that point he decreed that there would be no more war. This had a profound effect on his people because it changed their way of life from within. As with the atrophy of the remarkable navigational skills they once had, this edict led to the withering of the skills of Hawaiian warriors.

Kamehameha continued to enforce the *kapu*. It was the only law that existed in the islands and it curbed, if not controlled, the worst abuses that human beings bring on each other. Violation of the religious and civil laws was always punished by death. The transgressors were killed in a variety of ways, some by ritual sacrifice on an altar of a *heiau* or temple. The methods employed were clubbing, strangling or burying the violator alive. Killings were done by priests, not warriors.[1] The skills of a warrior were no longer necessary for survival. Now warriors only existed for the protection of the ruler and their costumes for display in ceremonies.

It was a time of peace, if not peacefulness, and yet it was also a time of radical change. When Kamehameha moved to Oahu, its main settlement of Honolulu became the first real town in Hawaii and the favorite port of call for foreign ships.[2] During the 1780s, a steady stream of ships brought traders and explorers from many nations to the islands.

While Kamehameha and his successors were trying to consolidate their hegemony over the islands, their sovereignty was challenged by several European powers. Among the first groups to visit and make inroads into the islands, though they seldom tried to take land, were explorers, traders and whalers. French explorer Jean La Perouse visited Maui in 1786 to map and survey possibilities for trade and to study the resources available. The islands became a regular stop on the Boston to China fur trade route and stopover for the long voyages of whalers.

Beginning in 1791, hundreds of American whaleships visited ports in the Hawaiian Islands. *Hope* out of Boston, with Captain Ingraham in command,[3] was the first American whaling ship to call at that port. *Lady Washington* had been there in 1789 carrying on the fur trade. When Captain Ingraham arrived, he was handed a note warning him to take care, for it was known that the natives would steal foreign ships, though the practice was discouraged by Kamehameha.[4] It was still a chancy thing, in the 1780s and 1790s, to spend time in outlying ports of these islands.

Whalers came to Hawaii in a steady stream for nearly a hundred years, eventually stopping at all the islands. They first appeared at Hawaii, Oahu and Maui. Later in the 1830s to 1860s they are reported at Kauai, Lanai and Molokai. Often a ship would visit a number of ports many times in one trip and frequently move from island to island. At first they sought Sperm whales, which abound in all oceans. Later, when this species became scarce, they began to pursue Humpbacks which still gather off Maui's west coast every winter. The crews worked at whaling and then relaxed in the towns of Honolulu and Lahaina. The ships stocked up on water and food at every island.

The gathering of whales around the islands, the fish, fresh fruits, sandalwood, coconuts and other products made the islands a potential gold mine for traders.

It has often been noted that the British displayed admirable restraint in not acquiring Hawaii for themselves in the early years of the 19th century. Later they did make several attempts, but at the time, they were distracted from overseas adventures by the Peninsular wars against Napoleon in Spain.

Other foreign nationals attempted to lay claim to Hawaii in the early years of the century. Such incursions would probably not have been attempted while Kamehameha the Great was alive. None of his successors on the throne of Hawaii had the intelligence, the power, or the charisma to protect the realm from more powerful nations.

When he was about seventy years old, in 1818, Kamehameha became ill and was taken back to Kailua on the big island. The Kahunas and other high chiefs did as much for him as they could, but prayers and incantations were useless. Kamehameha called for a European resident of the islands who had been his trusted advisor and confidante. Don Francisco de Paulo y Marin owned and worked agricultural lands, raised goats, had vineyards and sugar cane fields. He also owned a large island in the center of Pearl Harbor called Moku'ume tume, now Ford or Ford's Island.[5] He was reputed to have had some medical knowledge and was ordered to accompany Kamehameha when he moved back to the island of Hawaii. Though he remained by Kamehameha's side, there is no evidence that he improved the great leader's condition in any way.[6] Hawaii's first and greatest ruler died on May 18, 1819.

This crucial event in the history of the islands led to a number of radical changes. Kamehameha did not cause the changes that would come with his death, but some would not have happened if he had still been alive, others he could not have stopped.

The first significant event after the death of Kamehameha took place in May of 1819 and would not have happened, at least not at this particular time, if he had been alive. When the old unifier of the islands died, so did old Hawaii. Kamehameha had always upheld the kapu and other traditions of his ancestors. He kept order and stability during the years when these idyllic islands were being encroached upon by covetous foreigners. Yet he also brought in new ideas, tools and skills as he unified the islands under his rule. He had been the rock on which his people had depended for twenty-five years.

Now he was gone. In his place was his son, Liholiho, later called Kamehameha II, whose mother was a high ranking chiefess. Liholiho had been declared the heir to the throne of Kamehameha when he was only five years old. Protected, revered and spoiled, he grew up in very different circumstances from his father.

Twenty-two years of age when his father died, Liholiho was not prepared for the turbulent times in which he had to assume the responsibilities of the throne. Fortunately for him, and also for Hawaii, a woman was standing by who was prepared and eager to help. Ka'ahumanu was the favorite wife of Kamehameha, though she was not Liholiho's mother. She was politically astute and knew ways to wield power. After Kamehameha died, it was revealed by Ka'ahumanu that he had bestowed upon her the power of *kuhina nui*, or executive officer, regent, advisor to the new king. Whether he actually did this or it was her idea is unknown. She said he told her this, but no written communication ever passed between leaders of this Hawaiian world so there is no record. Whatever the truth, she is reported to have consulted with Liholiho who agreed to allow her to advise him as king. Ka'ahumanu oversaw all coronation ceremonies.

Ka'ahumanu sat in traditional dress beside the new king all during the coronation. Amid a sea of native dress worn by the chiefs and *ali'i*, women with voluminous flower leis around their necks, holding towering staffs topped with colorful feathers, flowers and greenery, surrounded by drums, song and dance, sat Liholiho. He wore the king's tall Hawaiian headdress, held his staff and his shoulders were draped in a resplendent yellow and red feathered cloak. Underneath all the native Hawaiian splendor, he wore a red suit trimmed with gold lace cut like that of a 19th century Englishman.[7] Around his neck, he also wore a large, gold medallion in the British style.[8] He chose to become a king like the European monarchs. He also chose to be called Kamehameha II.[9]

After all the rituals had been observed, Ka'ahumanu called for the attention of the most powerful chiefs, the ali'i and the common people. Then she declared that she and Liholiho would rule together.

The scene is significant, more so than is apparent at first. Liholiho was not an ideal king. He was often described as a playboy, a wastrel and gambler with an affinity for European alcoholic spirits. While he did enjoy these diversions, he was also interested in anything British. He adored the pomp, the gold braid and glorious trappings of British Navy uniforms and royalty. Soon, he made it clear that he was more interested in his plan to visit England than in problems in his own realm. It appeared to every eye that mattered, he needed Ka'ahumanu's help in all aspects of his reign.

Liholiho was king from 1819 to 1824. Ka'ahumanu positioned herself in the right place to affect future policy and Liholiho allowed her to do so. She was determined to change the old ways and was in the right place at the right time to take the lead in achieving the next major change: abolishing the *kapu*.

It is not easy for westerners to understand the hold the *kapu* system had on the Hawaiian people. It was oppressive, rigid and brutal. It was a Polynesian cultural system that the natives had brought with them from Tahiti and was not unique to Hawaii. At the same time it was still practiced throughout Polynesia in varying degrees. But, because of its oppressive and seemingly arbitrary nature, it was also collapsing at about the same time all around the Pacific. This was due to its own specifics as well as to the disruption of native life caused by Europeans and their new ideas and sensibilities.

> "(*Kapu*) covered every part of the life of the Hawaiian of the olden time with its vast and intricate network of regulations... Death was the penalty for any violation of these rules."[10]

Besides the rigid restrictions about food, there were many aspects of the kapu system that made no sense to Europeans. One was the untouchability of the *ali'i* by anyone of lesser power. It was supposed to damage the high-born severely, though it was not apparent what was the nature of the damage.

In 1819, it was determined by Ka'ahumanu and a few of her high ranking confederates that the system no longer had any merit and was out of date. She saw that white men did not have such an oppressive system and they were not struck dead by the gods for violating its rules. A moral creed can be broken by an individual every day, but it is not laid aside by an entire people without thought, reason or resistance. Still, many were now disbelievers in the system and it had begun to crumble. It could not be destroyed until after Kamehameha died, though a wide range of ideas on ways to terminate the practices had apparently been discussed for some time.

The overthrow of the system was led by four very prominent people in the Hawaiian hierarchy: Ka'ahumanu, advisor to the king, Kalanimoku, Kamehameha's 'prime minister', Keopuolani, the mother of Liholiho and a high priest or *Kahuna* named Hewahewa. Inroads were made for a number of months and the final act took place during a feast held in late 1819, over six months after Kamehameha the Great died. The event was secretly planned for some time and the venue carefully chosen. The reason was that the *kapu* most galling to women, and most easily broken, was the prohibition against men and women eating together.

The two prominent women ate coconuts and pork, both forbidden by the *kapu*, in full view of the guests and were not destroyed by the gods. Then Liholiho came to walk around several of the women's tables and then sat to eat with them. He was reluctant, clearly being prodded by his mother and Ka'ahumanu, but he did it. Not everyone accepted the changes, of course, but enough did to create a severe questioning and weakening of the old, traditional laws.

The *kapu* system was the greatest barrier to change in this culture.[11] Its destruction demolished the structure of the religion that had prevailed for five hundred years. The highest chiefs could no longer rule in the traditional ways.[12] The loss of the system left a vacuum in the lives of many natives when the old beliefs were gone because they felt that their gods had failed them. They did not know that, coincidentally, a group of people who were heading for the islands at that very time, would attempt to install a new, and even more oppressive, religion in place of the old.

There was a Christian living in Hawaii before the arrival of Presbyterian missionaries. John Howell had come to the islands as a clerk on *Lady Washington* and was reported to be a clergyman of the Church of England.[13] There are reports that his license had been withdrawn by the church. He himself had certainly fled from European society. He arrived in 1793 and went about his secular business as a clerk. After he learned the Hawaiian language, he began to discuss God with ordinary people and with the king. He became acquainted with Kamehameha in the course of his duties and one of their interviews was reported by another early visitor to the islands. He said that when Howell made his first attempt to talk to Kamehameha about God, the king told him to throw himself over the nearest *pali*, a steep, jagged cliff. If he survived the fall, Kamehameha would believe him.[14] No report survives as to Howell's subsequent action.

Howell was the only Christian minister available to officiate when John Young and Isaac Davis were wed to native women. He did so on Kamehameha's orders. Howell did not proselytize for his religion among Hawaiians, perhaps because of his failure with Kamehameha, and soon left to become a business agent or broker in China.

The group that was at sea on the way to Hawaii when the old religion was toppled in 1819 were members of a missionary society of Congregationalists and Presbyterians. Several native Hawaiians, who had been educated in the United States at theological schools, spoke to church groups and missionary societies asking help for their native land. After several talks by these native Hawaiians in Boston, the society decided to send a mission to the Hawaiian Islands. They departed from Boston in October of 1819 aboard the small ship Thaddeus and arrived in the islands on March 30, 1820 after an arduous journey of almost six months. They had came to civilize and convert the natives of Hawaii to Christianity. They also intended to teach the word to the godless traders and whalers who stopped there, if they could.

After extended negotiations, several American missionaries came ashore at Kailua on the island of Hawaii on April 10, 1820. There were six men and their wives plus five children. For almost six months, traveling across two seemingly endless oceans, they had been preparing themselves for the conditions in the islands, but despite that, they were amazed and shocked at what they found.

> "The appearance of destitution, degradation and barbarism among the chattering, and almost naked savages, whose heads and feet, and much of their sunburnt, swarthy skins was bare, was appalling. Some of the newcomers exclaimed, 'Can these be human beings?'"[15]

They asked to see King Liholiho and requested to be allowed to remain in the islands and teach Christianity to the people. The king gave them one year. A few would stay at Kailua on the big island of Hawaii and the rest would set up a mission in Honolulu. Later two of them went to Kanai. The newcomers had been shocked at the naked condition of the heathen, of course, but they were even more shocked at the fact that they seemed to do no work. They lolled about, played games, swam or rode the surf naked on great long boards, apparently enjoying themselves shamelessly.

The natives in their turn were curious about the layers and layers of clothes, often black, that both men and women wore in spite of hot sun and humidity. They watched the women work and, while they showed up to hear the men preach, through interpreters, it was mainly out of curiosity.

Conversions were few and the work was slow. Restraints that were required by the new religion did not go over well in Hawaii. For instance, to get the King to convert, the Christians knew they would have to convince him to give up four of his wives as well as the spirits that he liked so much. He would not.

One basic tenant of Christianity that was difficult, if not impossible, to teach to the islanders was a sense of sin. Anything which gives pleasure was good in the eyes of the early Hawaiians and while the missionaries tried to teach them about the Christian ideas of spiritual transgression, they did not understand. It was not surprising that they were not receptive to it. Eventually, a number of Hawaiians converted to Christianity, including Ka'ahumanu, many of the *ali'i*, and commoners as well. Yet the basic belief of the Christian faith that all men are sinners never was totally accepted in Hawaii.

Another problem was communication. Hawaiians had to learn English because only a few of the first missionaries or their wives had taken the effort to learn to speak Hawaiian. Those missionaries who did also created a written form of the language a few years later. Since pronunciation could vary from island to island, and group to group on each island, dealing with the language was frustrating, though rewarding. When they were finally able to communicate in both languages, schools were established in which bible studies and spoken English were taught, as well as reading and writing in both languages.

The turning point in the effort to teach Christianity to the Hawaiians came because of Ka'ahumanu. When she became ill, Sybil Bingham, wife of missionary Hiram Bingham, nursed her back to health. While Ka'ahumanu was recovering, she learned about the new religion from the missionary's wife. Because she was a strong and respected leader, her acceptance of the new religion led chiefs and *ali'i* to convert also.

The death of Kamehameha, the breaking of the *kapu* and the arrival of the missionaries, all occurring in 1819 or 1820, were critical. Kings also now followed European rather than Hawaiian patterns of leadership. The repudiation of the kapu destroyed much of the belief structure of the ancient Hawaiian culture. Missionaries muzzled Hawaiian songs, dances and behavior that the natives had always enjoyed. In two years, 1819 and 1820, Hawaii had changed more than at any other time since the Hawaiians arrived from the southern hemisphere hundreds of years before.

Chapter 7 - Foreigners Try To 'Save' Hawaii

The missionaries changed Hawaiian life in ways the Hawaiians could never have imagined. They were not the only source of the transformations that were to come, but they were one of the first and most rigid in demanding change. Natives were taught English so they could read the Bible. As they learned the new religion, they learned that alcohol and promiscuousness were evil in the eyes of the keepers of the new religion. They were forbidden to practice the old ways and were constantly harangued about the degradation of sloth and pleasure. Their attire, or lack of it, was considered immoral and corrupt. The missionaries wanted to rid them of their traditions, change their way of life and direct and control their beliefs. Many natives refused to listen to the fussy, strict newcomers who were bent on shaming them.

In April of 1823, another group of missionaries came from America and concentrated their efforts on the islands of Hawaii and Maui. They were welcomed as old friends by the original group of missionaries who had already toiled in the islands for three years. The task was not easy nor were living conditions pleasant for any of these dedicated people, most of whom had grown up in cities on the east coast of the United States. They disliked much of what they saw, thought it shameful and set about immediately trying to change the Hawaiians, that is, to civilize them.

American missionaries were neither the first nor the only ones to treat native people as if they were no better than animals or ignorant children, deride their mores and their customs and destroy their religion. It had happened and was happening in other parts of the world, including both North and South America. From the time they began exploring the rest of the world, Europeans were convinced that the culture they had created was the best in the world, verified by the one true God of Christianity, and all people would benefit from it. At the time, it was considered noble and selfless to wade into a primitive culture, throw out anything incommensurate with their convictions and introduce their own ideas. It was not wrong to the men of the 19th century These facts do not make their actions right, but it helps to understand the motive behind these actions.

The charge that Christian missionaries came to Hawaii to save souls and stayed to become rich and powerful is not far from the truth.[1] However, in the beginning that was not the motivating force for their being in Hawaii.

The first thing they attacked was the nudity of the natives. They banned women from wearing the *pa'u*, a short tapa skirt and the *kihei*, a cape worn over their shoulders which exposed their breasts. This attire was inappropriate if not scandalous to the missionaries. They first tried to clothe natives in American style garments donated by mainland churches. This did not work Natives would wear the top of a dress or jacket without the bottom or put inappropriate pieces together. Then a simple garment for the women called a Mother Hubbard was devised, an ankle length gown made of cotton that covered them from neck to toe. One question always arises: why did native women agree to wear these garments? The answer may lie in the material of which it was made, cotton. The natives had never felt anything like cotton against their skin and enjoyed the new colors and styles.[2] This may be just trying to put a positive spin on a painful subject, and it will not please those who believe all missionary acts destructive, but the fact is that the native women did wear and adapt this garment. Today, it has evolved into the graceful, varicolored *muu muu*, the *holoku* and other styles. It is elegant, colorful attire, and a source of pride and identification.

The missionaries tried to encourage and teach the domestic arts and proper decorum to the women, wipe out gambling, drinking and indolence among the men. To accomplish this, the missionaries encouraged the natives to learn western ideals, arts and building techniques.[3]

The fact that these forced changes were often arbitrary and overbearing is indisputable. But why did natives comply? Even the queens wore the new foreign dress or a variation of it.[4] Perhaps they did so because the missionaries did not allow them to enter the new religion unless they agreed to the church rules.

When Hiram Bingham and other missionaries saw the suggestive and sensual dance called the hula, they were horrified. Bingham also complains of the "noisy hula",[5] referring to the accompanying drums. They set about immediately to ban these shameful displays which they felt "were designed to promote lasciviousness."

> "Nowhere in Polynesia are these dances vulgar save in
> Hawaii, and only here because white men from whaling ships
> have corrupted it by the desire to see suggestive dancing."[7]

Clearly, Americans did not understand or take the time to learn what the dance was all about. They learned that an ingrained and important part of Hawaiian culture could not be eliminated so easily. Participation of natives in hula displays are reported in 1825[8] and picnics with women in the old traditional topless costume were still taking place as late as 1895. By 1875, the hula was being performed in the open again, though the dancers were clad in blouses where before they had worn only flower leis. Photographs show them wearing far more clothes than any of Cook's artists depicted, but the dance had not changed significantly.

An aversion to work was deeply ingrained in Hawaiian society, according to the missionaries. They tried to imbue the Hawaiians with an American sense of accomplishment and ambition. They made little headway in these areas because they didn't understand the island version of work. When it was necessary, Hawaiians could work extremely hard to build a *heiau*, a fish pond or a dwelling for a chief. They simply did it on a different time scale than the one understood by Americans.

Promiscuity and the sanctioning of marriage between close relatives was even more difficult to curb. This kind of conduct had been common for centuries and no sense of shame accompanied either practice in island society. It was a sensitive area the missionaries found hard to understand.

It has been said that the missionaries banned the use of the Hawaiian language altogether, but few sources confirm this. The written language they devised, with a character for every sound, could be expressed by seven consonants and five vowels. Therefore twelve Latin letters represented the Hawaiian language. According to a missionary involved in this task, their system could express every sound in pure Hawaiian dialect.[9]

They made little effort to include all the phonetic indications and diacritical marks that would be necessary to ensure the precise pronunciation of Hawaiian words. Many words have double vowels and stresses are not easy to indicate in the English system.

The first people to encounter this unusual language spelled words and names so strangely that it is sometimes difficult to recognize the word. At least twenty five different spellings of Honolulu have been collected: Honoruru, Hanarura and Onorourou, to note a few. The new system standardized the use of consonants that did away with the confusion between K and T, R and L, B and P. It was arbitrary and wasn't perfect, but it sufficed. The language could then be written in a standardized form.[10] Most important for the missionaries, the Bible could be translated into Hawaiian.

The missionaries then set about with a vengeance to ban any kind of work on Sunday. Natives were even prohibited from building fires or cooking food on that sacred day. This was extreme even for Calvinists and Puritans, but they felt that extreme measures were the only ones that would work. They tried to turn savages into saints, as one author put it. In truth, it was too much too soon and little attempt was made to explain why such restrictions were necessary. Hawaiians had lived with their own inflexible system of *kapu* and they understood its requirements. They did not understand the unexplained and rigid Calvinist restrictions.

The original missionaries never won the complete victory they coveted for their religion. A few native Hawaiian clergymen were trained and admitted to the church beginning in 1863. But by 1870, the Episcopalian, Mormon and Roman Catholic churches in the islands offered the natives several other avenues of worship.[12]

The original missionaries are now often derided in the islands, blamed for many of today's ills and the loss of so much of Hawaiian culture. Some groups, such as the Mormons of Brigham Young University and their Polynesian Cultural Center, the University of Hawaii, the National Park Service, the Bishop Museum, and others, have made a point of trying to restore some of the losses. The Christian religion, in its many denominations, thrives in Hawaii, but is now no more rigid than anywhere else in the country.

King Liholiho, Kamehameha's son, ruled Hawaii for five years during the changes brought about by the destruction of the *kapu* system, the radical changes imposed by the missionaries, and the incursions of foreigners. From 1819 to 1824, he was acknowledged king, with all the pomp and ceremony he desired, but he was not solely in control. His advisor, the *Kuhina nui*, Kamehameha's wife Ka'ahumanu, and his mother Keopuolani, controlled his official actions rigidly and stood as buffers between the king and the chiefs. The latter still had a great deal of power and were able to wrest control of the sandalwood trade from Liholiho and reap the benefits themselves until overcutting led to the trade's demise. For the time being, the king was able to maintain control over the lands which had been owned by his father.[13]

It was the rigid control of his personal life that caused Liholiho to rebel. He did a great deal of drinking and carousing to avoid his duties. Liholiho wanted to see the outside world and yearned to visit his 'friend' George the IV, king of England. The trip was made and as a result, he was gone for at least two of the five years he was nominal ruler. Because of his father's affection for Captain George Vancouver and faith in the British, Liholiho thought that in England he would find out how to rule and how to deal with chiefs as well as foreigners. Merchants, traders and entrepreneurs were uncontrolled, he thought, especially Americans, French and Russians. He was also aware that the missionaries were interfering with everything. It is significant that he did not search for answers among the elders, wise men or chiefs of his own people.

There is no specific time that one can define as the date Hawaiians generally embraced the new religion. Ka'ahumanu had accepted Christianity after a severe illness in 1822 and many followed her lead. In the spring of 1823, Liholiho's mother, Keopuolani, became ill. Like Ka'ahumanu, she found time then listen to the message of the new religion. As she was dying, she converted and was baptized in the Christian faith. Keopuolani died in September of 1823.

Late the same year, Liholiho's trip to Europe began. He was accompanied in Europe by Kamamalu, his favorite wife, and a large retinue which included Boki, governor of Oahu and his wife, Lilihia. After he consolidated his rule in all of the islands, the first Kamehameha had created the post of governor to administer each island. Governors were appointed by the king and ruled under his jurisdiction.

While Liholiho, now called King Kamehameha II, was absent in Europe, the realm was technically in the hands of his younger brother, Kauikeaouli who was only nine years old. So Ka'ahumanu, first wife of Kamehameha the Great, was regent. Billy Pitt, native advisor to Kamehameha and skilled at dealing with foreigners, remained as 'prime minister'.

Liholiho and the royal party were stricken on their European tour with measles against which they had no immunity. The king and his wife died two weeks later. King George gave orders for HBMS *Blonde*, a British frigate of forty guns under the command of Captain George Anson, Lord Byron, cousin of the famed British poet, to take the coffins and the royal party to Hawaii. Boki and his wife, both of whom recovered from the disease, took charge of seeing that the king was given the proper royal ceremony. The ship arrived May 6, 1825, bringing the king home two years after he sailed away. Boki was baptized into the Christian religion before the ship reached Honolulu.

The funerals of the king and his wife were as full of pomp and ceremony as Liholiho could have wished. *Blonde* delivered a 21 gun salute which was echoed by two forts ashore, one at the harbor and one on the hill called Punchbowl, *mauka* of Honolulu. Anchored in the harbor, was an American ship which joined in the solemn, reverberating salute. The funeral procession wound solemnly from the harbor between lines of native soldiers, standing naked except for a loin cloth "with rusty arms reversed".[14] A few of these men wore Russian military jackets and some wore the towering feathered ceremonial headdresses. *Blonde* sent a marine band to play ceremonial marches and accompany the procession.[15]

The age-old mourning practices of the Hawaiians that followed shocked and disgusted the foreigners who witnessed them. They could understand the wailing in an emotional primitive people, but they did not understand why they defaced themselves, knocked out their own teeth or hacked off their hair. It seemed barbaric to missionaries and sailors alike. No one recorded the native point of view.

The death of the king and queen, who were not baptized when they caught the dread disease, propelled many a Hawaiian, commoner and chief alike, to turn toward the new church.[16] Hawaiians could understand a direct relation with the gods and many concluded that the king and queen had died because they had not accepted the new religion.

While the crew of *Blonde* was in the islands, they took time to visit places of interest and explore the back country. One crew member, horticulturist James Macrae, reported that he and a number of others took a trip from Honolulu to the Pearl River or Harbor. The party embarked around noon on May 17, 1825 in several small sailing vessels. They sailed along the coast and then entered the Pearl River, which he describes as a river divided into several branches forming two islands. One, now Ford Island, was called Rabbit Island for the many rabbits on it. The other island was Kuahua, now a peninsula, near the mouth of Halawa Stream. After exploring the area, they found a shack on the larger of the islands in which they spent the night. It was not possible to go back the same day as it was a good ten miles to Honolulu against the wind and there were no convenient roads on the island. They saw the hut on the island,

> "..and with the help of canoes, all including the ladies, were able to land. The ladies were somewhat discontented, but after a good dinner partaken sitting on mats spread on the grass, harmony was restored."[17]

The Pearl River, Macrae noted, is seven miles to the west of Hanarura, his version of Honolulu. It is improperly called a river for it is an estuary fed by several small streams that ends in a series of inlets from the sea. It branches into three parts, now called East, Middle and West Lochs. Macrae said that these names were given to the inlets by a Scottish surveyor from *Blonde*. The country behind the harbor was extensive where farms were enclosed with rock walls four to six feet high. There was much forest and uncultivated land beyond the harbor as well.

Another naturalist, Andrew Bloxam, was on the same expedition and described the hazards of sailing through the coral reefs into Pearl. He remarked that it would be an excellent harbor, except for this treacherous approach. He was convinced that the deep water inside had enough room to float the entire British navy.[18]

Macrae asked Billy Pitt, the king's prime minister, to help him organize a collecting tour in the back country of Oahu. Macrae wanted to find as many unusual plants as he could. After preparations were made, the party left a few days later. He described sugar cane fields, potato crops and how the natives approached him without the least timidity. He concluded that this was because they have a greater familiarity with foreigners than natives he met on other islands. That evening a group of players performed music and dances, which include songs with graceful movements of arms and body. The fact that the hula was being openly performed shows that either it was not yet banned or that the ban was ineffective. In his opinion, the vocals he heard hadn't the least resemblance to music.[19]

To illustrate the society he found in Honolulu in 1825, Macrae relates a story that brings Englishmen, missionaries and natives, into conflict. It concerns a magic lantern show that the king requested be put on by Lord Byron, captain of the *Blonde*. No details are given of this 'magic lantern', but it might have been pictures lit by whale oil light projected onto a screen. Just as the show was about to begin, "owing to the religious fanaticism of the American Methodists"[20] the king was prevented from attending this show. The reason for this zealotry is not explained by Macrae, nor is the content of the pictures. The furor seems to have subsided for nothing further was made of it.

While *Blonde* and her crew tended to their diplomatic duties, Royal Navy Lt. C. R. Malden made a survey of the south shore of Oahu which included Honolulu and Pearl Harbor. He produced a chart of the entrance channel and all three lochs. It includes Rabbit Island (now Ford Island) and the water depths inside the harbor and out. This chart was included in a map of the Sandwich Islands published in England in 1843.[21] Malden also surveyed Hilo harbor and one of his colleagues surveyed other ports. Malden may be the surveyor that Macrae says gave the name loch, Scottish for lake or arm of the sea, to the fingers of the Pearl Harbor inlets.

The visit of the *Blonde* brought a great many Englishmen into contact with Hawaiians on all levels and the natives continued to look up to the British. The king's appointment of Lord Richard Charlton as British Consul in Honolulu was supposed to continue that feeling. One of Charlton's main tasks was to encourage trade with Great Britain.[22] He was hostile to the United States in general and hated American Commercial Agent, John Coffin Jones, in particular. While there was always tension between them, they had one view in common. They both hated missionaries. They despised the influence missionaries had on Hawaiians and did not support their work. Charlton was not an upstanding Englishman, as has been sometimes reported. He damaged the esteem in which most of the Hawaiians held the English. He reportedly threatened natives, and in one instance he even horsewhipped a newsman.[23] The British government was either oblivious to his behavior or chose to ignore it, and let him stay in the islands for twenty years. Finally the Hawaiian government had endured enough. They removed him and sent him back to England.

Governing Hawaii was never smooth. Every new visitor seemed to know what was right, what would help the Hawaiians and how it should be done. There was a meeting in 1825 held at Billy Pitt's house. Attending were Pitt, all the upper echelon chiefs and Lord Byron, captain of the *Blonde*. The subject of the meeting was to discuss a slate of laws that should be established in the islands. The idea seems to have been to elicit from the English lord and sea captain suggestions for further action. This meeting had no official standing. The king was not there, nor was the regent. Boki, the governor of Oahu did attend, however, and he gave a speech praising what he had seen in England. He urged that they establish laws on British patterns. No action or conclusion is noted.[24] Boki made a request that natives be allowed to have fires in their houses and cook on Sunday. The missionary ban on Sunday work was being carried too far, in his opinion. If any changes resulted from this meeting, they were not noted.

Near the end of their stay at Honolulu, officers of *Blonde* went ashore, found an appropriate place and created the first cricket ground in Hawaii. They proceeded to demonstrate the game to the Hawaiians and to while away their time playing endless games until the ship was ready for departure. Fijians, Tongans and Samoans loved the game, but cricket never caught on in Hawaii.[25]

While Hawaiians watched the British play cricket, Macrae was watching the Hawaiians. He noted that the sea shore was seldom empty of natives swimming or lolling in the sand. They swam with perfect ease, he remarked, as if they were a species of aquatic creature.

Americans have been in the islands for many years, Macrae observed, but none possess land of their own.[26] He overlooked, or did not know of the land Kamehameha had given the American John Young. Macrae was convinced that Americans cared only for the sandalwood trade and had not improved the morals of the natives at all. Whether he was referring to all Americans or only to missionaries is not clear. He castigates Americans, too, for neglecting to teach the natives about farming, beyond what they already knew. This may have been a biased assessment, but it does show little change had occurred in the years since the missionaries came, in spite of their five year long effort.

The two naturalists, MacCrae and Bloxom, made voluminous observations of local flora and fauna. They wrote anthropologic and sociologic records of native behavior. When their work was done, they returned to the ship and prepared to leave. The crew of the Blonde bade warm farewells to their new friends and left for Tahiti on July 14, 1825.

After the funeral ceremonies and rituals for Kamehameha II and his wife, and the courtesies attendant to the service the British ship *Blonde* had given to Hawaii in bringing the bodies home, a national council met to name the next king. The choice was inevitable, though Kauikeaouli was only nine years old. Since the kingdom followed the precepts of European royalty, the European policy of primogeniture was made the law of the land.

Kauikeaouli, second son of Kamehameha the Great, was declared Kamehameha III and king of all Hawaii, with Ka'ahumanu as regent. The education of Kamehameha III had been strongly influenced by American missionaries and British visitors. He wore British style uniforms on state occasions and is seldom if ever pictured in traditional Hawaiian dress. He appeared at formal occasions in a uniform or a suit always cut in European style. Occasionally a feathered cloak and perhaps a native headdress were donned, but underneath was always European style clothing. Handsome and tall, he loved drinking, gambling and women as had the recently deceased King Liholiho, his older brother, in spite of his missionary education.

He also loved display and coveted all things British. Traders met with Hawaiian officials with an eye to getting access to the sandalwood forests. Often they brought new vessels for them to see and perhaps to buy. One of them, made of fir, had a showy cabin with mirrors and sofas covered in red morocco cushions. It was called "Cleopatra's Barge" and was coveted by the new king. Later he signed a contract with a trader to pay ninety thousand dollars in sandalwood for it.

Ka'ahumanu was *de facto* ruler of Hawaii until her death in 1832, though technically she was never the Queen. She was regent, or *kahina nui*, and wielded a great deal of power. When the king, Kamehameha 111, was eighteen years old, Ka'ahumanu died. He decided the regency was now over. The council of chiefs had been waiting for this opportunity as much as the king had but for the opposite reason. The council overruled the king and immediately appointed another kahina nui for him, his half-sister, Kinau, daughter of Kamehameha the Great and one of the wives of his dead brother, Liholiho. Though they issued a statement declaring joint leadership, the king was reportedly annoyed when she took the major role. She also became governor of Oahu.

The king rebelled and began to indulge his love of drinking and carousing, as his brother had done. He defied his Christian teachings and his royal duty. He declared that penalties against adultery were lifted and rescinded as many other restrictions that were offensive to Hawaiians as he could. He and a number of friends sought out students and members of churches, encouraging them to spend their days surfing, gambling and dancing the hula as in the old days. This defied Christian bans on these activities. In such pursuits, he was supported by Liliha, wife of Boki, and many who yearned for a return to the ways of old Hawaii.

In the early 1800s, trade was increasing and the number of ships visiting Hawaii each year was growing rapidly. U.S. warships USS *Cyane* (Finch) and USS *Vincennes* (Dupont) are among notable visitors. Trade in sandalwood had increased so much by 1826 that it was necessary to build a wharf in Honolulu Harbor. Using the sunken hulk of a boat as the base, the dock was built on top of it. This was removed ten years later and a real wharf constructed. To enlarge and improve the harbor, Nu'uanu stream was diverted as it was filling the area with silt. In 1848, the Hawaiian government built a breakwater to direct the stream away from the harbor on the west side .[27]

The sandalwood trade was extremely active by 1811, but was over by 1830. Avaricious and short sighted businessmen and traders had demanded so much that the Hawaiians had stripped the forests until there was no more sandalwood to fell. Unfortunately, even the chiefs had sold their remaining sandalwood forests. When the trees were gone, so was the trade. None of the Hawaiians benefited substantially from this trade.

Another industry, whaling, was just around the corner, though this one proved to be even more detrimental to native Hawaiians in the long run. Since discovery of the use of whale oil as light and lubrication, oil from the sperm whale had become highly prized. The whaling industry had grown slowly and steadily. Both British and American whalers were roaming the seven seas by the 1830s in search of whales. The sperm whale, in demand for its fine oil, is found in every sea. Hawaiian ports were as open and welcoming for whalers as they had been for explorers and traders. At times harbors and roadsteads were forests of masts. The Lahaina anchorage off Maui was especially active due to the proximity of humpback whales as the area was, and still is, the animals' winter calving ground.

Unfortunately, the whalers from all countries brought disease, barbarism, and alcohol. Hawaiian natives were not immune to the temptations, and for many, they found the 'recreations' of the new visitors to be fatal.

Americans began to look at other harbors in the islands that might be useful to them, especially the nearly inaccessible Pearl River area. Because of America's growth and size, it had to depend more and more on its merchant fleet as well as its Navy. By mid-century Commodore Matthew Perry would negotiate a treaty with Japan and, because of trouble looming with Great Britain in the Oregon area, national attention would turn again to the Pacific.

Chapter 8 - 'Mad Jack' and ap Catesby Jones

By the year 1814, the United States Navy feared no other. Her ships were magnificently designed and built, powerfully armed, and capable of extraordinary speed. Her men were experienced, more than able, and acclaimed as the best, most accurate gunners in the world. The political momentum the Navy had gained during the War of 1812 led to the establishment of a Board of Navy Commissioners by Congress. The board was a prestigious one in that the original three officers were Captains Isaac Hull, David Porter, and John Rogers. The next member to join the Board was Stephen Decatur. Their high profiles in social circles of the day, combined with their splendid records as seamen gave the Board more credibility than any equivalent unit in Washington. It was a good thing for the US Navy that these men were so admired because shortly after the fleet sailed for the Mediterranean to quell the recurring Algerine problems, some members of Congress yet again looked for and found ways to trim the national budget. They cut funds for what they considered to be the unnecessarily powerful and expensive ships at sea.

In addition to a fleet in the Mediterranean, the United States had squadrons in every ocean of the world. When the ships returned home, alas, they were greeted with indifference. The attention of the country had turned to the newly developing West, and merchants felt that no other country's ships would, or could, challenge our merchant ships. As happened in 1783, and would happen again, the people ashore apparently thought that the reputation won by the Navy in the last war would deter any aggression that might occur. The years 1815 and 1816 were not the last time this philosophy would sweep the country and its Congress.

"In 1815 a Board of Navy Commissioners was established to assist the secretary' and it was under the direction of this board that the fleet was first divided into permanent squadrons on a number of stations. Although detachments of vessels had been called squadrons before 1815, they were organized on an ad hoc basis to carry out a specific mission. Upon completion of that mission, the squadron ceased to exist.

The six earliest squadrons established on a permanent basis, on the order of establishment were: Mediterranean Squadron, West India Squadron, Pacific Squadron, Brazil Squadron, East India Squadron and the Home Squadron."[1]

Although many major US Navy ships were decommissioned and construction was temporarily suspended on planned replacements, there was still an active force in the Pacific. Captain David Porter, before his appointment to the new Navy Board, demonstrated a remarkably independent existence during his voyages. His 1813 - 1814 journey into the Pacific did not once receive supplies or money from mainland United States. He landed at distant lands for food, water, and recreation. He repaired his ships on the beaches of remote islands and still emerged victorious as a fighting seaman. This independence was a characteristic of the captains in the Pacific. For the next few years, the innovations brought by steam-driven engines and explosive shells were not a part of the Pacific Theater. However foreign incursions were.

It was during this time that the Hawaiian Islands suffered yet another group of foreign intrusions.

In 1815 the Russians made a second foray into the islands when Alexander Baranov, director of the Russian-American Company in Alaska, sent a group of ships to Honolulu. Their advertised object was to investigate the natural life of the islands. This is the story Dr. George Scheffer, Baranov's representative, was instructed to tell anyone who asked. The real reason was to win the favor of the Hawaiian king and get him to grant the Russians land and trading concessions. When Scheffer, who was a linguist and a naturalist, finally saw the chief of the island of Kauai, he demanded payment for the loss of the Russian ship *Bering*, which had been wrecked on Kauai some years before. All the cargo, copper sheathing, bolts and nails had been taken by the Hawaiians and the Russians wanted restoration of the cargo or payment for it. He did not reveal to the chief that his main goal was to get a foothold for the Russians in the islands.

While he waited for answers, Scheffer explored and surveyed Kauai and planned the future Russian settlement. He also set about renaming everything, an exercise that early Europeans simply could not resist. His choices were ill advised at best. Who would want to use the name "Schefferthal" when the area was already called "Hanalei"?

Once Scheffer's claims were settled to the satisfaction of all, he brought up the subject of the sandalwood trade. Baranov had instructed him to get trading concessions similar to those the Americans had. It was a thinly disguised attempt to establish a military presence in the islands. The terms had to be profitable for Russia and the Russian-American Trading Company of Alaska.' Baranov admitted his ignorance of sandalwood and he did not know whether Hawaiians sold it by weight or amount.[4] Scheffer was instructed to find out. Baranov did know sandalwood had recently sold in Canton for nine dollars a picul, a measure of weight extensively used in the Orient. A picul weighed between 130 and 140 pounds and since that was where the sandalwood market was, the measure was also used in Hawaii.

Dr. Scheffer was told to make friends with Kamehameha's chief minister, Kalanimoku, the man known as Billy Pitt, because he was a shrewd business man. He was also cautioned to pay homage to the wives of the king for they were all very influential.

Leaders of expeditions are often arrogant, independent and jealous of others in the same business. They frequently act far beyond the orders they've been given. Sometimes these orders clash with others from their own countries. Such was the case with the Russians. Otto von Kotzebue appeared in Honolulu with a Russian Naval expedition to Hawaii in 1816. He ignored Scheffer and called him insane for attempting to pit the king of Kauai against Kamehameha in the hopes of annexing land for the empire of Russia.[5] He disavowed Scheffer to Kamehameha and undid all the Doctor had done.

Scheffer, who believed he had an agreement with the chief of Kauai, had already built forts on that island and was prepared to complete his settlement. When Kotzebue appeared, Scheffer knew he was doomed. Shortly after Kotzebue left, Scheffer was forcibly detained, put on a boat in full view of a large crowd of Hawaiians and foreigners, and told to leave the island of Kauai. Some of his misfortune came at the hands of American traders, some was brought on by his own arrogance, but most of it originated with Kotzebue. The Russian adventure had come to naught.[6]

The Hawaiians were still very wary of foreigners. Louis de Bouganville had landed on Tahiti in 1768, claiming it for France. Later explorers added the Tuamotu Archipelago, the rest of the Society Islands and the Marquesas, all in the South Pacific. Soon Catholic missionaries from France arrived to convert Tahitian natives to Catholicism. This was the first step in their projected hegemony over the Pacific Ocean.

The Frenchman La Perouse came to the Hawaiian Islands in 1786, but did not claim them for his country. The end of the 18th century was a turbulent time in France. The kingdom was wracked by revolution, war, failing governments and a search for survival.

It was twenty years later, when life in France was peaceful again and Napoleon was just a memory, that the French once more turned their attention to Hawaii. Louis de Freycinet came to Hawaii on board the ship *Uranie* and made a survey in 1816 .[7] Ten years later in 1826, Jean Rives, a resident of Hawaii, tried to get the English and the French to join in backing his plan to establish a large commercial, colonial venture in the islands. His reason, like those of men from other countries with eyes on possessing the islands, was trade for his country. A secondary reason, but also important, was to gain prestige for himself by establishing such an important colony. The idea of spreading the French flag was tantalizing.

Rives' project was to include a private commercial venture, a permanent colony and a religious mission to convert the heathen. It was to be headed by Monsieur de Morineau, emigre and lawyer. The backers saw the enterprise as one that would eventually cover all Oceania, that is the islands of the Pacific, to support and protect all of France's commercial ventures. The expedition that was ordered in 1826 by the king of France was to go aboard *Comete*, sail around South America, stopping at various Spanish ports and plant the French flag on an island in Oceania.

The Comete arrived in Honolulu Harbor on July 7, 1827 with great expectations. They planted a French flag, but soon found that Rives had fallen from whatever favor he had gained with the king and his ministers. The native government hesitated to allow the Frenchmen to disembark. The islanders had heard tales of abuse of the natives by the French in their Pacific colonies and had been warned that the French were coming. While they were friendly enough, they were not disposed to treat the Frenchmen with much deference.[9] American missionaries, who had been in Honolulu for six years by then, were polite but did not welcome Catholics into what had so far been their Protestant domain.

The French colonists eventually were allowed to land and to rent three cabins. They explored Honolulu, a village of about five thousand souls at that time. They met residents who were American, English, German, Dutch, and Spanish. The Europeans accounted for about two hundred people all told. Natives outnumbered all.

No French trading house existed in Honolulu and the captain of *Comete* was told that he could not sell his cargo without that connection. He did not trust the Americans to make the deal he wanted, and since he could not buy sandalwood to take to China without the proceeds from the sale, he had to leave. When the French ship left, one of the leading chiefs told the French who were ensconced in rented houses, that they should depart also. Because of gifts given, the order was reversed and expulsion postponed.

The would-be French colonists stayed in their rented places for about three months. Then they were granted a tract of land near town on which to build a permanent church. Some sources say the grant was in writing, but it has never been found. Disputes arose over whether the grant was to be given to an individual, the leader de Morineau, or to the mission. Before the disputes could be settled, a group of chiefs met to decide on the continuing presence of these "papists", a curiously Protestant and European word to use. They remained four more years.

By 1828, the colony was even smaller than when it began. It lost its friends at the French court as well as the influence it had in Hawaii. Also there was a native group that believed the community in Honolulu was too small to support rival religions. In December of 1831, the two Catholic missionaries were put aboard the brig *Waverly* and sent to California. The French venture seemed to be at an end. But it wasn't.

This and similar incursions in the Pacific, prompted requests for assistance from the meager US Naval forces which were trying to protect American interests in the entire eastern Pacific. In response to requests, Secretary of the Navy Benjamin Crowninshield dispatched a small flotilla. In 1818, the Sloop-of-War *Ontario* (Biddle), and schooners *Franklin* and *Dolphin* followed Porter's charts around Cape Horn and up the West Coast. Their purpose was to claim the lands adjacent to the mouth of the Columbia River in the Oregon Territory. They were beseeched by merchants along their route to protect them from Spanish and Latin American ships. The first and principal Pacific industry at the time was whaling, and it is reported that over a hundred American whaleships were operating in the Pacific by 1827. One reason was the search for new sources of their quarry as many Atlantic whaling grounds had already become depleted.[10]

A few years earlier, in 1821, the Pacific Squadron of the US Navy was formed. The new organization was not the result of the pleas of a few merchants alone; almost 200 New England merchants and shipowners lobbied President Monroe and his successor, John Quincy Adams, to create an American Naval Force in the Pacific. It was feared that marooned American seamen in Hawaii and other islands "naked and destitute might become a nest of pirates and murderers". There was a saying at the time that "There's no law around the Horn", which some found fully justified.[12] Monroe and Congress were convinced; from that time forward, an American presence in the Pacific was to be permanent. The original ships were followed by *Macedonian* (Downes), *Constellation* (Ridgely), and *Congress* (Henley). Of the original Pacific Squadron ships, it is the *Dolphin* which captures our attention next.

Sailing has always been an isolated occupation. A small band of men live together aboard a relatively tiny craft for months at a time and personalities sometimes clash. The expedition of Lewis and Clark along the Missouri River, over the Continental Divide, and on to the Pacific Coast in 1804 was a remarkably successful model of leadership and cooperation. Men on board ships often had no such understanding and wise leaders. So it was with the ship *Globe* in 1824. Her crew mutinied, murdered several officers, and marooned the rest of the loyal crew on an island in the Mulgraves, a part of what are now the Marshall Islands, about 2,500 miles southwest of Hawaii.

News of the incident, when received in Washington, produced outrage. On May 24, 1825, Secretary of the Navy Samuel Southard instructed the Commandant of the Pacific Squadron, Commodore Isaac Hull, to order the vessel USS *Dolphin*, under command of Captain John Percival, to sail to the Mulgraves to find any survivors of the mutiny. Percival was also ordered to proceed to the Sandwich Islands to do what he could to enforce payment of debts owed to American merchants by island rulers. It took Isaac Hull over a thousand words to write this simple order. He ended with the cheerful closing, "Wishing you a pleasant cruise, I remain your obedient servant, Isaac Hull. Sent to Lieutenant commander John Percival, commanding United States Schooner *Dolphin*."[13]

Percival had sailed two years earlier as First Lieutenant with Hull aboard USS United States. Hull's confidence in Percival was based on his seamanship rather than his diplomatic skills. Percival was a 'sailor's sailor'. He worked as hard as his crew, expected much from them, but no more than he provided, shared wine with his men, and gave no ground to anyone when it came to swearing and uttering grand oaths. His fiery temper was legend. One of his strengths was colossal pride. It was also his greatest weakness. Because of several incidents in which he was involved during his career, he was known as "Mad Jack".

Upon arriving at the Mulgraves in November of 1825, Percival found only two remaining survivors from the mutiny-stricken ship *Globe*. Cyrus Hussey and William Lay, age 20 and 18 respectively, were still alive because they had been adopted by native families.

Percival took the young men on board *Dolphin*, reprovisioned his ship, and stood for the Sandwich Islands. He arrived on the morning of January 14, 1826. It was the year after the commander of HBMS *Blonde*, Lord Byron, had ordered the first charting of Pearl Harbor. Lt. Charles R Malden's chart not published until 1841, so Percival had no knowledge of the lochs.[14]

Percival's stay in Honolulu was marred by misunderstandings, calamities, and perceived insults. The day after he anchored was a Sunday. He removed tampions, wooden plugs placed in gun muzzles for protection against fouling by the sea, from his cannon and fired the customary salute toward the fort. His salute was not answered. What Percival later observed was that missionary Hiram Bingham had set up what amounted to a religious dictatorship, declaring all forms of dancing and singing abolished, especially the hula. Otto von Kotzebue had observed that "the streets which had been full of life and animation only a year before, were now deserted. The inhabitants of every house or hut in Hanaruro were compelled to an almost endless routine of prayers".[15] Apparently this situation was in accordance with the missionaries goals. One of the sons of the original missionaries wrote, "The whole scene has no more breadth nor freedom about it than a petty New England village, but it is just as neat, trim, orderly, and silent also".[16] He went on to praise the work of his father by stating that it was but 50 years ago that the Puritans "civilized a savage nation".

Among other restrictions, no work was to be done on Sunday, and that included firing the fort's cannon to salute an arriving ship. Percival lived up to his sobriquet 'Mad Jack' and received the silence as an insult to his honor and to that of the United States. He had no way of knowing that he had arrived in the midst of a political and religious battle being fought by Bingham and his ally, regent Ka'ahumanu, on one side, and Boki, the governor of Oahu allied with local merchants on the other.

Percival never went anywhere lightly. When he invited the leaders of both sides in this dispute to meet for a festivity aboard *Dolphin*, only Boki accepted. Percival was furious. After a Long sea voyage he had ordered the schooner dressed with flags and his men were aloft in the yards as a token of his respect and honor. Percival welcomed Boki with a salute from his cannon and an announcement. How the announcement was worded is not recorded, but today it would be the honorary, "Oahu, arriving". Today, as senior officers board or leave ships, their command is announced over 1MC, the ship's loudspeaker. For example, when the Captain of the USS *Seawolf* visits another ship, the number of bells appropriate for his or her rank are rung and the announcement is made, "Seawolf Arriving". When he or she departs, the announcement is "Seawolf Departing".

Boki presented a remarkable picture, tall and splendidly dressed in the uniform of a British major general. His size, color and bearing must have been dramatic. What they spoke about is not recorded, but his comments to Percival were not impartial, given the intensity of the enmity back on shore.

The scene on Oahu looked tranquil enough. Behind the swamps of Waikiki lay a small peaceful village of about 150 thatched houses and a few buildings built of frame or stone which was called Honolulu. Around this residential area were fields of taro and fish ponds. Hiram Paulding, one of Percival's officers, wrote that when the officers went ashore, they were escorted to a large frame building called the Wooden-House, which was then occupied by an American, Captain Wilds. Paulding also wrote that he and his fellow seamen made an excursion to a valley called by the name of Pearl River. He indicated in his journal that the visit was made, but did not comment on any military value of the inlet.

The local custom at the time was to make liaisons with native girls by the simple act of placing a piece of *tapa* over her in the presence of witnesses. Each of Percival's crew, including the captain, took advantage of this custom and settled down to conduct their assigned business in the atmosphere of domestic pleasure. Of course the missionaries were trying to abolish such practices and came into immediate conflict with 'Mad Jack'. The explosive confrontation was delayed by the receipt of the news that the ship *London* (Edwards) had gone a ground on the rocks of the island of Lanai. Percival, with all his faults and personality problems, was a superb seaman. He immediately arranged to man the ship *Convoy*, because his ship *Dolphin* was undergoing repairs, and rushed to the rescue. He spent about a week off Lanai helping Captain Thomas Edwards salvage what they could and then return to Honolulu.

During Captain Percival's absence, Bingham, the missionary, had persuaded Ka'ahumanu and her associate Kalanimoku, or Billy Pitt, to enforce an order to prohibit native women from visiting the ships. Percival returned from the salvage effort on February 5, 1826 and was met by his men pleading for him to rescind the new prohibition. At a meeting on the 20th of February, which included some of the missionaries, and at which Percival was snubbed, Percival called them "a set of damned schoolmasters".[17]

On Washington's birthday, Percival called on Ka'ahumanu. The atmosphere was cool at best. The conversation that follows is reported in differing ways by different people. The consensus is:

> "Percival, 'Who governs these islands?'
> Ka'ahumanu, 'The young king' She was referring to the boy king Kauikeaouli (Kamehameha III).
> Percival, 'And who governs him?'
> Ka'ahumanu, 'I do.'
> Percival, 'And who governs you?'
> Ka'ahumanu, 'My God.' She answered, piously.
> Percival thought of her as an enthusiastic supporter of Bingham. At this point Percival ended the conversation with the explosive and accusatory words, 'You lie, you damned old bitch! Mr. Bingham controls you!'".[18]

He also warned the woman that he and his men would take severe measures if she didn't grant him the same licenses granted to Captain Lord Byron the previous year. Ka'ahumanu had learned the fear of God, instilled into her by Bingham, so Percival's threat was not as effective as it might have been.

When he was back aboard his ship, Percival opined that "the sailors would serve the missionaries right if they were to tear down their houses". He meant this as an offhand comment, but some of the sailors nearby heard the remark and took it as a license to treat the missionaries as fair game. On Sunday, February 26, 1826, his men all requested liberty. Percival granted it to one third of the crew, as was the custom. His instructions to them were to stay sober, and return to the ship promptly.

Unfortunately for everyone, the sailors fell in with several discontented seamen from merchant ships and with a few whalers who were stranded in the islands because the Hawaiians would not pay their debts to the ship masters. As they went from grog shop to grog shop, their anger intensified. They came upon Bingham and a group of his followers at a meeting and proceeded to destroy the porch they had been using. The drunken sailors smashed the windows of the house and chased the hapless Bingham down the street until he reached his own house and found refuge.

Word of the disturbance reached the *Dolphin* and Percival was overcome with embarrassment and anger. His men were instrumental in giving credence to the arguments of his new enemy. The furious captain and two midshipmen raced to the scene of the rioters and began smashing heads with clubs they had picked up along the way. Percival's rage was directed as much towards Bingham as towards the seamen, but the unfortunate tars were under his orders and were available targets upon whom to vent his anger.

Percival then went to Bingham and warned him that if the loathsome ban on fraternization were not lifted, some terrible consequences would ensue. The riot, he explained, was but one minor result. Governor Boki, without the permission of Ka'ahumanu or Bingham, rescinded the prohibition for the rest of Percival's stay in the islands. Percival reported the incident in a letter to Congressional member Hon. John Anderson, in these terms,

> "At the Sandwich Islands there was a distinction [cost] made by the chiefs between our whale ships and those of the English. To do this away, it was necessary for me to obtain .. influence over the chiefs.... by which I obtained an ascendancy sufficient to get the obnoxious regulation repealed."[19]

The captain of *London*, Thomas Edwards, whom Percival had helped when the ship grounded on Lanai's rocks, was angry at the captain rather than grateful. Percival had found an irregularity in Edward's paperwork concerning the amount of specie aboard *London* at the time of the wreck, and declared his intention of reporting it to the proper authorities. Edwards and Bingham set about preparing as many incriminating documents as they could to send back to America. 'Mad Jack' went aboard *Becket*, Edwards' new brig and confronted him. Neither was a diplomat. They had a few choice words, as preliminaries, and set to with fists, belaying pins, stanchions, an ax, and even a gun ram. Percival turned to the members of his crew who had accompanied him to *Becket* and called, "Grab the damned rascal and take that thing away from him!" Edwards fled to his cabin and Percival returned to *Dolphin* satisfied that his honor had been upheld.

Percival's assigned mission had been to rescue two marooned sailors and settle the disputes between the Hawaiian chiefs and the merchants. He did both. The whalers and merchants wrote a letter asking him to remain in Honolulu to maintain control over the zealous missionaries and the easily manipulated island chiefs. The American consul John C. Jones wrote to his superior, Secretary of State Henry Clay, that Percival had performed an essential service to American concerns in Hawaii.

However, Percival's abrasive manner had upset many people, especially the newly established dicta of the missionaries. Upon his arrival in America in 1828, a court of inquiry was convened to investigate charges brought against him, principally by Edwards, the disgruntled captain and Hiram Bingham, the missionary leader.

The court found insufficient evidence to proceed. Percival, exonerated, continued his career. He circumnavigated the globe in USS *Constitution*, retired, and lived to the age of 83.

He spent much of his retired life petitioning ("memorializing", in the vocabulary of the day) Congress for reimbursement for his expenditures during his voyage to the Sandwich Islands. One of his many pleas ended, "Wherefore your memorialist prays that he may be remunerated for the extraordinary expenses thus incurred by him in the discharge of his official duty. J. Percival."[20]

'Mad Jack' had done his duty, but he had left a legacy of confusion among the Hawaiians as well as hatred and disgust among the missionaries. When conflicting reports reached Isaac Hull, Commander of the Pacific Squadron, he determined to choose his next emissary from those with more diplomatic natures. This man was Commodore Thomas ap Catesby Jones, commander of the Peacock.

It would be difficult to find two capable, respected Naval Officers more different than Percival and Jones. One, Percival, was eager to share pleasures ashore with his men, displayed an explosive temper, and was severe in his punishment. The other, Jones, was aloof, with a regal bearing and diplomatic ability. Far more important than their differences, however, was the fact that each man could be absolutely relied upon to complete any mission on which he was sent. While Percival enforced an uneasy agreement between the merchants and missionaries, and coerced the chiefs to pay their debts to the merchants, Jones' challenge was to persuade the various feuding factions that an agreement was advantageous to everyone.

Captain Thomas ap Catesby Jones brought his ship *Peacock* into Honolulu Harbor on the afternoon of October 11, 1826. Since it was a weekday, he fired a salute and received one without incident. Unlike his predecessor he did not allow the swimming native girls aboard his ship. Nor did he demand - or accept the offer of - a grand house ashore. The Hawaiians were fearful that Jones, whose ship was larger and more menacing than *Dolphin*, would simply be a more fearsome edition of Percival. The missionaries were also apprehensive since the last crew had smashed their meeting house in a drunken spree.

Jones politely petitioned each group for an audience and wisely used this 'waiting period' to gather information. As he rode around Honolulu from meeting to meeting, he made a marvelous impression. His bearing, stature and manners bespoke the carriage and breeding of a gentleman. This impression was accurate. He was the product of an affluent family whose residence was a plantation in Virginia. His educated, intelligent manner pleased merchants. His attitude and restraint pleased the missionaries, and most of all, his quick smile and dark eyes pleased the natives. He soon acquired the title, *Ke ali'i o Ka Maka Olualu*, "The Chief with the Benevolent Eyes".[21]

Unlike Percival, Jones perceived that Ka'ahumanu, the widow of Kamehameha the Great, was the real and accepted power. He saw also, that her complete conversion to Christianity made the task of the missionaries much easier than it otherwise would have been. Therefore, when warring groups invited him to formal receptions, it was Ka'ahumanu he visited first. He won her over completely. His manners were courtly, his dress impeccable, his penetrating eyes and dazzling smile marked him for Hawaiians as an *ali'i* in his own land. Beside his naturally powerful presence, he was in fact the personal representative of President John Quincy Adams, *Ali'i Nui* of the Americans. Their continuing, increasing influence in commerce and dominance in local religion, seemed to be brought together in this one man. Ka'ahumanu saw in him the solution to most, if not all, of the current political problems.

Jones listened to the complaints of the local citizens about the 'destructive nature' of American sailors who had been left behind when their ships sailed. He investigated and found that not all of them were wastrels. Most of these men had become farmers or shopkeepers or employees of local merchants. Instead of 'rounding up the lot' as he was implored to do, he ordered his Marines to find two or three dozen of the worst trouble makers and bring them to him. Thereupon, he imprisoned them, and as quickly as he could, put them aboard whaleships and other merchantmen heading to the United States. The disappearance of this haole trash was not lost on the missionaries or merchants. The situation was mellowing, thanks to Jones' forbearance, restraint, and decisive action.

Next, Catesby Jones prepared for a grand meeting with all factions in order to settle their arguments. The meeting actually came in two parts. First, he met with the some of the members of the king's government and the *ali'i* and agreed that American merchants charged too much for many of their goods and services. Then he scolded the Hawaiians, an astonishing act in itself only possible because of his personal acceptance by the chiefs, for unwise indulgences in ships, uniforms, and other luxuries. These debts were part of the legacy of profligacy left by Liholiho years before. Captain Jones let the chiefs decide a fair amount that would retire their debts. It made perfect sense to the Hawaiians. Instead of the half million dollars demanded by the Americans, the chiefs decided that one hundred and fifty thousand dollars would be the correct amount. The merchants accepted the decision because the medium of exchange was sandalwood. They knew they could turn an enormous profit for the valuable wood in China.

Jones' other problem was the dispute between the missionaries and the local citizens, many of whom were not American. Because he had so ingratiated himself into the community, both sides in this dispute, as the Hawaiians had done previously, accepted Jones as a respected and trusted mediator.

On December 8, 1826 a critical meeting took place at the home of Governor Boki, but not in the manner anyone expected. All the elements were present for a fiery, tempestuous confrontation. What happened was truly remarkable. While the anti-missionary group complained vociferously and often against the missionaries' restriction upon native life and culture, the complaints were of a general nature. They said that they were really not interested in charging the 'longnecks', as they called the missionaries, with specific transgressions. The missionaries firmly stated that they would respond to no charges, except those presented in writing. Since the missionaries' opponents refused to place any written documents before Jones, the meeting might well have ended in failure.

Jones, however, leapt into the impasse. After a few tactful, diplomatic remarks, he declared that the meeting was a success and adjourned. Hiram Bingham, the missionary leader later declared the meeting to be a "most ... complete triumphant victory for the missionaries"[22] It was certainly a tribute to the diplomatic skill of Jones that the missionaries' opponents also felt that they had been heard and fairly treated.

Jones proposed a treaty between the Kingdom of the Sandwich Islands and the United States. In it he asked no extraordinary privileges, but only a most-favored nation status, as was enjoyed by other major nations, and the promise of strict neutrality in time of war. When the British consul, Richard Charlton, heard of the proposal, he immediately lodged a protest with the Hawaiian king. His basic objection was that the islands were a British protectorate, based on the agreement between Vancouver and Kamehameha in 1794. Ka'ahumanu, ever anxious to please Jones, was perplexed by what should be done next. The remarkable Jones again stepped into the difficult situation and pointed out that, since the British had established a consulate in the Sandwich Islands, they must have recognized the islanders' sovereignty and independence. Thus he refuted the island status as a protectorate of England and carried the argument and the day.

The treaty, the first between the United States and Hawaii, was signed on December 23, 1826 by Thomas ap Catesby Jones, King Kauikeaouli (Kamehameha III), Elizabeth Ka'ahumanu (Queen Regent}, Kalanimoku (Prime Minister), Boki (Governor of Oahu), and a number of other *ali'i*.

On January 6, 1827, Jones' crew winched the anchor to the cathead, were towed out of the harbor, and set sail for home. Unfortunately, the US Congress was not able to see with Jones' vision. They never did ratify the hard-won treaty. Catesby Jones' accomplishments, nevertheless, were monumental. He had overcome the brutal legacy of his predecessor and smoothed the way for future relations between the United States and Hawaii. The Hawaiian-American bonds Percival had forged by force and Jones had created by persuasion were on their way to becoming permanent.

Chapter 9 - Discontent and Paulet's Folly

Sereno Edwards Bishop was an author and philosopher and the first child born of missionary parents in the islands.[1] In his reminiscences of the 1830s, he wrote,

> "The Lochs or Lagoons of Pearl River were not as shoal then as now. In the Thirties the small pearl oyster was quite abundant, and common on our table. Small pearls were frequently found in them. No doubt copious inflow of fresh water favored their presence...I think the clam is still found in the Ewa Lochs."[2]

The gentry would often picnic on what is now the Pearl City Peninsula, the Waipio peninsula, and occasionally on the island of Dr. Ford. But these pleasant times for a few affluent people were not indicative of the social atmosphere of the island.

The unsettling differences between missionaries, natives, rulers, merchants, and visiting seamen continued. The missionaries were enjoying success due to their cohesion and determination. These characteristics were combined with the natives' search for some kind of spiritual anchor, having abandoned the old ways of idolatry and tabu. The *ali'i* were unable to curb the activities of heavily armed warships of other nations or the merchants who were happy to sell whiskey to sailors. They deplored the subsequent wanton conduct of the sailors. Hawaii, particularly in the heavily visited Honolulu/ Pearl River area, was not the mecca of serenity we would like to imagine.

Into this group of often malcontent people sailed Captain William Bolton Finch, USN, in command of the Sloop-of-War USS *Vincennes*. This ship was a 'plain Jane' with no figurehead or any external ornaments.[3] From Callao, Peru on July 4, 1829, she left on what would be the first Westward circumnavigation of the globe by an American warship. Captain Finch dropped anchor in Honolulu Roads on October 14, 1829. He had in his possession a letter from the Secretary of the Navy Samuel Southard addressed to "Kamehameha 3rd, King of the Sandwich Islands". It introduced Captain Finch as one who was willing to aid the good people of the island country in any way possible. It was complimentary, friendly, and cordial. Later, Finch reported his activities on behalf of the "King of the Hawaiian Islands". He seems to be the first correspondent to use that expression.[4] The term 'Sandwich Islands', or 'S.I.' was still in use in the islands at least seven years later as is illustrated by an announcement of "Vessels in Port, Saturday, August 13,1836. S.l. Sch. Pikolia (Victoria), Kanikalio"[5] As recently as 1897, the

German Minister Count Otto von Bismarck was still referring to the "King of the Sandwich Islands".6

The two familiar problems which confronted Captain Finch were the settlement of claims which had been incurred since the departure of Jones only three years earlier, and the promise by the people in charge of the administration of justice to treat American sailors fairly. On November 2, 1829 Finch succeeded in having young King Kauikeaouli (Kamehameha III), Governor Boki, regent Ka'ahumanu, and other chiefs agree to one payment of "4,700 piculs of sandalwood at seven dollars per picul, and another of 2,165 piculs of sandalwood".7 He also rounded up another group of perpetually drunken seamen and had them returned to the United States. The role of American Navy ship captains was a judicial one and they often assisted local police in dealing with errant American seamen. They were respected for fair treatment and their decisions were generally popular.

Seamen who landed in Honolulu were often just letting off steam after wretched voyages filled with back breaking work and danger from natural as well as human forces. Added to the usual rigors of being at sea was the terrible prospect of being attacked and killed by natives on foreign shores. Such a tragic event occurred on the island of Sumatra. In a small village named Qualah Battoo, the entire crew of an American ship named, ironically, *Friendship*, was massacred. Such an atrocity was not unique, but this event struck a sensitive nerve in America and Captain John Downes, USN, was dispatched in the frigate USS *Potomac* in February 1832 with orders to chastise the natives. He landed on the Indonesian island, killed 150 of the men who opposed him, and burned their village. Such harsh treatment was de rigour at that time, and effective. No further unfortunate incidents occurred there.

Downes proceeded to Honolulu and arrived off Waikiki on July 24, 1832. He was greeted by Kamehameha III, no longer a boy, who "wore a full-dress of the Windsor uniform, with gold epaulettes; a gold star on his left breast, cocked hat and sword".8 The pageantry was reciprocated by Downes in kind. His men were aloft on the yards, flags fluttered in the warm trade breeze, and two rows of Marines stood rigidly at attention as side boys. The 21 gun salute that was fired so impressed the king that he spent much of his time aboard Potomac while she was in port. Downes had a company of actors, a Corps-Dramatique, on board who, with the ship's band, put on a performance at the Theatre-Royal-Honorura.

When he was invited to the king's palace, Downes obliged and was pleased to see, prominently hanging on the wall, "a copy of the Declaration of Independence beside a portrait of former King Riho-Riho".9 A festive *luau* was organized by the king which presented an extraordinary sight to locals and seaman alike. Some merchant ships in the harbor had American

Indians from the Northwest Coast on board. They danced and whooped to the delight of all present.10

While in the Honolulu/Pearl Harbor area Downes, in the role now common for American Navy captains, settled, at least temporarily, the same old disputes among locals. After leaving Hawaii, Downes continued his journey around the world eastward, the opposite direction from his predecessor, Finch.

Life in the islands was currently peaceful, if not tranquil. Typical of the low-key activities of the local dignitaries, the British Consul Richard Charlton wrote a note to his majesty "King Tameahmeah" (Kamehameha III) and added, "will you send one of Your boys with the boys that go with the horses to prevent there being stop'd and oblige your Most Obedient Servant." A minor matter, but typical of diplomatic activity.

Soon after Downes left the Sandwich Islands, Commodore Edmund Kennedy, with another two-ship squadron, USS *Peacock* and USS *Enterprise*, continued the American Naval presence there for a short period in September of 1836 and settled more local disputes.

Yet another such 'settlement' was effected by Commodore G. C. Read, commanding a two-ship squadron consisting of his ship, the frigate USS *Columbia*, and the companion vessel, the Sloop-of-War *John Adams*. They anchored off Waikiki in October of 1839.[11] By then American ships' captains were readily accepted in the role of adjudicator and circuit judge.

After Read departed, an unwelcome group re-appeared. It was another attempt by a Frenchman to establish a Catholic presence on the islands. In late 1839, a French man of war, the sixty gun frigate *L'Artemise* appeared in Honolulu. From the first she exhibited a hostile attitude. Captain La Place refused to exchange the usual national gun salutes for the flag. He sent a battalion of one hundred and fifty men ashore with fixed bayonets. They were accompanied by a marching band and they took possession of the King's residence and the royal yacht.[12]

The king issued an edict of tolerance of all religions, but that is not what the Frenchman wanted. He demanded that the French consul have jurisdiction over any crimes committed by Frenchmen in the Islands. The Captain also ordered that a Catholic church be built in Honolulu and insisted that the flag of France was to fly over it. Furthermore, the flag must be saluted by a twenty-one gun salute from the fort.[13] The demands were arrogant and ridiculous and none, especially the last, was ever honored.

In the face of so much firepower, the king partially agreed, but he appealed to the American and British consuls. Their combined pressure on French Captain La Place defused the situation and La Place eventually sailed away, having little to show for his bellicose efforts. The king's yacht was never returned.[14]

The belligerent and forceful French had compelled the king, Kamehameha III, to grant equal rights among foreigners. He decreed that religious toleration was now the rule and he permitted the continued presence of the Roman Catholic mission.[15] Still, just a year later, Kuakini, governor of the island of Hawaii, stated that the king should give precedence to American missionaries while allowing others to practice other faiths. They had been in Hawaii first and he felt indebted to them for their first steps toward civilization. Hawaiians should allow these new missionaries to teach and preach their religion in peace out of gratitude.[16] Nothing changed after that; no declaration was forthcoming from the king, so the small group of French Catholics remained.

By 1840, advancements were made in the two areas that would revolutionize naval warfare, ordnance and tactics. One important development was the percussion cap used with flintlock muskets and the addition of lands and groves to naval ordnance. That meant powder would no longer need to be measured before every shot. On the horizon was the marvel of interchangeable parts. At sea, where no specialized parts could be manufactured, having spare parts that would fit into any appropriate weapon as a replacement would soon have a profound effect.

The next arrival of note in the Pearl Harbor area was Lieutenant Charles Wilkes, USN. He had been chosen, reluctantly, by Secretary of the Navy Mahlon Dickerson to lead an Expedition into and around the Pacific Ocean. The Navy was the appropriate agency of the government to conduct such a venture. Both the Navy and the merchant fleet needed more accurate charts because by 1835 they were sailing the oceans of the world. To illustrate how reluctant the secretary was to choose Wilkes, let us review the people who were chosen initially, late in the year 1836. The expedition was initially to be led by our old friend Thomas ap Catesby Jones, but he had a leadership conflict with Dickerson and withdrew his name in November of 1837. Three other men were selected with the following results: the first man said the ships were unfit; the second man had a dispute with Dickerson and left; the third man was Commodore Matthew Perry who declined because of other projects at the time.

The expedition was becoming a national embarrassment and an international joke. Besides the difficulty of finding an acceptable (and accepting) leader, there was endless wrangling among the scientists as to what equipment to take, what the purpose of the journey should be, and even who was 'really' a scientist.

The search for a leader continued. On January 30, 1838, a Lt. F. Gregory was selected and accepted. However, when Mrs. Gregory learned that the voyage would last three or perhaps four years, the hapless candidate soon withdrew his name. The next man chosen, Captain J. Smith, was offended by one of the proposed crew, Lt. Charles Wilkes, and left the project. Finally, in desperation, the Secretary of War Joel Poinsett, at the urging and recommendation of our old acquaintance 'Mad Jack' Percival, intervened to assume responsibility for the expedition. On April 19, 1838 he secretly appointed Wilkes, 38th on the seniority list of 40 lieutenants, to command the group of six vessels.[17]

With these six sailing ships, some ill-adapted to exploring, and approximately 300 men, Wilkes was instructed to lead this United States Exploring Expedition to the unknown areas of the world. Scientists and navigators aboard were to observe and record meteorological and hydrographic data, to explore the islands and continents, namely Antarctica, and bring back samples of natural vegetation and animals that inhabited these lands. Whether this was intended to be a naval or a scientific expedition, and no one was sure which it was, it was a daunting task. It was authorized by the government and embarked upon mainly to raise the world's opinion of the intellectual and navigational prowess of the United States.

Wilkes' flotilla, riding at high tide in Hampton Roads, just offshore Norfolk, Virginia, consisted of Sloops-of-War *Vincennes* and *Peacock*, the small schooner *Relief* the brig *Porpoise*, and two schooners, *Flying Fish* and *Seagull*. The *Relief* was interesting in that she was rigged with fore-and-aft sails bent onto her mizzen and foremast. This, of course, allowed her to sail higher into the wind than the other ships, all of which were square rigged. On Saturday August 18, 1838 the ships were ready.

With the ebb tide and a favorable wind, the time had come. Weighing orders were called through trumpets or raised on signal halyards. The deckhands leaned into the anchor windless bars and the anchors began their slow climb out of the muck at the bottom of Norfolk Harbor, spewing mud into the water on the way to the surface. Crewmen aloft, digging their toes firmly onto their footropes, removed the gaskets from the sails and let them drop and fill. On deck, sheets were drawn taut and then secured. Boatswains' pipes shrieked across the water, and the voyage was underway. Despite all the bungling and wrangling that preceded the sailing day, the sight must have been glorious. Six ships under full sail moving majestically down toward the mouth of Chesapeake Bay, past the lighthouse, and into the Atlantic. Neither observers on shore, President Van Buren among them, nor men aboard the ships realized that this would one of the last times such a sight would be seen. Regular steam service had already been established across the Atlantic. When they were far enough off shore, the sails were sheeted in to catch the wind off the port quarter, wheels turned a point or two to starboard, and a Southerly course set. As sails filled with silent power, masts groaned and leaned perceptively forward and to starboard. Port stays became taut and the ships heeled gently to starboard. The voyage of exploration was underway.

Wilkes had received these instructions, among reams of others, relating to his planned sojourn in the Sandwich Islands.

> "From the Isle of Desolation you will proceed to the Sandwich Islands, by such route as you may judge best, from the information you may receive from such sources as fall in your way. A store ship from the United States will meet you there, with a supply of provisions in the month of April 1840."[18]

The Wilkes Expedition made its way into the Pacific Ocean to explore north and south, map islands, look for new land and to describe what they encountered. Members of the expedition charted reefs, collected specimens and observed and recorded the culture of the various peoples they met.

By the time the ships of the Exploring Expedition arrived in Honolulu, several months later than April 1840 when they had been expected, much had been anticipated and written about their work. A local Honolulu weekly, *The Polynesian*, hailed the expedition's success in discovering Antarctica and hoped they would be able to clear up some points of geography around the local islands.[19] When they landed in Honolulu, Wilkes' comment was that the people they encountered were so motley he couldn't describe their dress or appearance. "There are few places where so great a diversity in dress and language exist. The streets, if so they may be called, have no regularity as to width, and are ankle deep in light dust and sand. Little pains are taken to keep them clean."[20]

What Wilkes found in Hawaii, especially in Honolulu, the city near the only viable harbor on the island of Wahoo (Oahu), was what his predecessors had found. The missionaries were attempting to recreate New England society and protect the simple people from their 'heathen' enjoyments. The sailors, drifters, and deserters, on the other hand, were doing their best to assist the native women in their 'enjoyments'. Merchants were complaining about both stiff-necked religious zealots and drunken derelicts who roamed the town. Not much had changed since Finch and Downes had left over ten years before.

Wilkes met King Kamehameha III on the 30th of September, along with the American consul, Mr. Brinsmade, Kekauluohi, the widow of Kamehameha I and prime minister of Hawaii, John Young and the king's bodyguard. Describing the king, dressed in a blue coat, white pantaloons and vest, Wilkes said that he is robust with pleasing manners and a good expression. Kekauluohi was almost six feet in height with a large frame. She was dressed in yellow silk dress with gigot and puffed sleeves and wore a tiara of beautiful yellow and scarlet feathers. Only persons of high rank could wear these rare feathers, he commented.[21]

One positive aspect of Wilkes' stay in the Honolulu/Pearl Harbor area was his accurate charting of the inlet just a few miles West of Honolulu. At the request of the King, a group of men led by Lt. John Alden, embarked in small boats and made soundings across the bar (reef) at the entrance to the estuary and up the river.[22]

This chart, dated 1840 and called The Harbor of Ewa and the Pearl River, gives extensive soundings in the entrance channel, the coral reef and at the mouth of the estuary. Charting continues inside the harbor as far as Clark Point and Bishop's Point. The surveyors did not penetrate the harbor as far as Ford Island or the peninsulas.[23]

Previous to Wilkes' chart of the Pearl River estuary, maps or charts were scarce indeed. Sometime in 1784, after Captain Clerke returned to England with the announcement of Captain Cook's death, a Mr. T. Woodman of Harrison & Co. in London carefully drafted "A New Chart of the Sandwich Islands including Owyhee where Capt. Cook was killed on Sunday the 14th of February 1 779". It shows eight major islands and identifies them as Atooi, Owyhee, Mowee, Tamoorowa, Ranii, Morotoi, Woahoo, and Oneeheow. There are a few smaller islands identified. Cook's several voyages around the islands are clearly indicated. Later that same year, R. Benard in Paris created "Carte Des Isles Sandwich". The data were apparently taken from Woodman's earlier chart as the names are spelled the same way. Benard includes an inset entitled, "Plan de la Baye de Karakakooa", where Cook landed on the big island of Hawaii and subsequently died.

Two other maps or charts preceded Wilkes' work. One is a map of Honolulu in 1810 compiled by Dorothy Barrere for the Bishop Museum in 1957. Her data were extracted largely from "Fragments of Hawaiian History", a record of trails and sites by John Papa Ii in 1810. Also there was a map drawn from a survey made by Lt. Charles Malden, an officer aboard HBMS *Blonde* in 1825.

The Wilkes Expedition left after several months in the islands. They headed toward the west coast of North America where they explored and mapped the coastline, river outlets and islands.

On Wednesday November 17, 1841, the U.S. Ship *Vincennes*, the schooner *Flying Fish*, and the Brig *Porpoise* arrived in Honolulu again, this time coming from Monterey in California.[24] Wilkes' says that the first of his ships "on the 23rd of September 1841 made the island of Oahu and by four o'clock saw the town of Honolulu."[25] This was a much shorter visit and was a prelude to their heading homeward.

Having completed his work in the Sandwich Islands, Wilkes was ready to leave Hawaii, but found it necessary to hire sailors in place of those who had left the expedition. Instead of resorting to hiring the worn-out vagabonds of all nations, he wanted to hire a number of Kanakas. The authorities agreed provided the men were returned after their services were no longer needed. Five hundred men showed up ready to take the jobs. Captains Hudson and Wilkes chose about fifty, all able-bodied, active young men in perfect health.[26]

Lieutenant Charles Wilkes, USN, was a determined and thorough explorer and a very able seaman, but he was a strict disciplinarian, too strict according to some of his men. When he and his ships returned to the United States in June and July of 1842, after four years, the nation was more interested in Westward expansion on land than in his historic sea voyage. The reception was between apathetic and hostile. Much of the scientific work was hailed as brilliant, but Wilkes faced a court martial for his treatment of his men during the voyage. The testimony of his officers and crew revealed his character. They called him tyrant, violent, overbearing, and insulting. He was convicted of seventeen counts of illegal punishment. He was so disgraced that his description of the Antarctic Coast was cast in doubt. After many months, the penalty meted out by the tribunal was "a public reprimand by the Honorable the Secretary of the Navy".[27]

His charting of Pearl Harbor, however, was accepted, and rightly so, for the shape of the coastline and his soundings of the entrance were accurate. He described the inlet as a lagoon that had been partly filled with alluvial deposits.

"At the request of the king, we made a survey of it [Pearl Harbor]: the depth of water at its mouth was found to be only fifteen feet: but after passing this coral bar, which is four hundred feet wide, the depth of water becomes ample for large ships, and the basin is sufficiently extensive to accommodate any number of vessels. If the water upon the bar should be deepened, which I doubt not can be effected, it would afford the best and most capacious harbor in the Pacific."[28]

For the next few years, mainland America turned its attention to the argument between the advocates of steam-driven engines and those who favored sails. The former group asked, "Why tack so slowly and laboriously into the wind when an engine will drive a ship straight into the eye of the wind?" The other side asked, "Why carry a multi-ton engine plus vast quantities of wood or coal when a sailing ship can sail at no propulsion cost and save all that space for cargo?" Of course they both had valid points, but were short-sighted. An obvious temporary solution was a combination of both steam and sail. Steam for light airs and upwind work; sail for downwind running. From their debut in the early 1840s through the Civil War, such combination ships would roam the seas. Several sailing captains lodged complaints which today seem facetious, that the smoke from the steam engine exhaust got their sails and uniforms dirty.

A more serious problem was the danger of fire aboard the mostly wooden ships. On the combination ships the danger was great due to the possibility of sparks from the stack blowing into the after sails, should they be rigged at the time. The Navy was prominent in the development of spark arresters, and suffered less damage from fire than many merchant ships. Another problem was the enormous side or stern wheels required to propel the vessel. These made the ships vulnerable to enemy fleets and pirates. A Swedish engineer, John Ericsson developed a screw propeller in 1844 which operated underwater and eliminated the large wheels previously needed.

American naval presence in the Pacific was significant and growing. By 1842, Thomas ap Catesby Jones was Commander of the Pacific Squadron. His report in the form of a letter to Secretary of the Navy Abel P. Upshur, dated August 31, 1842, summarized the US force in the area. Note that the only criterion used was number of guns.

"Statement showing the number and forces of the Naval Forces of the United States now employed in the Pacific Ocean.

Frigate	United States	52 Guns
Sloop	Cyane	20 do
do	Dale	16 do
do	Yorktown	16 do
Schooner	Shark	12 do
Total		116 Guns

Further Report on foreign powers afloat.

Peruvian	24 Guns
Sardinian	16 Guns
Chilian	51 Guns
French	238 Guns, 1800 tns
English	166 Guns"[29]

Commodore Jones had the authority to assign a U.S. Naval Storekeeper to a post in the islands. From his "Flagship United States in Honolulu Roads" Jones wrote,

"William Hooper, Esq.[rc],
Sir, There being no United States Navy Agent, nor Naval Store-Keeper at Honolulu, or any other post within the Hawaiian groupe, I request you to take upon yourself the duties of those officers for the time being. (Signed) Very Respectfully &c. Thos ap C. Jones, Commander in Chief of the Pacific Squadron."[30]

With a flourish of his quill pen and a few random splatters of ink, Jones' secretary added the affirmation of authenticity, "The foregoing is a True Copy. Henry La Reintrie, Secly."[31]

The United States was well represented in the Pacific, but was still outgunned by the French and British. It was at this time that Secretary Upshur asked Congress to establish a naval base along the West Coast, or in the Hawaiian Islands and to double the number of vessels now employed in the Pacific.[32] Also, in August of 1842, a Bureau of Yards and Docks was established.[33] That same month saw congressional approval of the establishment of a coaling station at Honolulu. The subject of a naval base in Hawaii was receiving serious attention. Secretary of War Daniel Webster affirmed that the United States did not intend to annex the Hawaiian Islands, but would oppose with force a similar attempt by any of the Great Powers.[34] This application of the Monroe Doctrine was to be tested sooner than Webster or anyone else expected. On February 10,1843, into the harbor of Honolulu, and the pages of Hawaiian history, sailed HBMS *Carysfort* under command of brash young British Captain Lord George Paulet.

Two months previous to Paulet's arrival, Richard Charlton, the British consul in Honolulu, a fervid anti-American, perceived that he had been ill-treated in a land transaction with American merchants. This position was later commented on by Sanford Dole in a paper in which he stated "It had been a new departure to admit that the people had any inherent right in the soil".[35] Charlton petitioned King Kauikeaouli (Kamehameha III) for redress. Both the king and his regent, Kinau, turned a deaf ear to Charlton's plea. The consul sailed for London to present his case, augmented by several other alleged grievances he had accumulated. His journey took him from Honolulu to the coast of Mexico, across the Isthmus by mule train, on a boat to New Orleans, thence by train and carriage to New York, and finally by ship to England. On this trip, the plot thickened considerably.

While in Mexico, Charlton met Captain Lord George Paulet, a young officer commanding Her Britannic Majesty's Ship *Carysfort*. Paulet was no friend of the Americans. When he heard of Charlton's mission, he set sail for Honolulu, with his superior's consent. His superior was Rear Admiral Sir Richard Thomas, commander of the British Pacific Squadron. As often happens in the flow of human events, a simple lack of communication caused a calamity. Just one week after Paulet had sailed, Thomas received instructions from the Admiralty in London that Britain had no desire to infringe on the independence of the Sandwich Islands. Paulet, however, was happily ignorant of his government's position. He was already off and running with the opportunity to further his career with a spectacular colonization triumph and, with the same stroke, unseat the Americans from their position of prominence in the islands.

Immediately upon anchoring and securing his ship in Honolulu Harbor, Paulet petitioned the king for a private audience. The king refused, but suggested that his minister, Dr. Judd, would be pleased to meet with the British Officer. Paulet, taking the suggestion as an insulting excuse, responded with a set of six demands with which the king must comply by 4 o'clock the next afternoon. "Otherwise" Paulet continued, "I shall be obliged to take coercive steps to obtain these measures for my countrymen"[36]

Into this atmosphere sailed USS *Boston* under the command of Captain Long, USN. When he was informed of the threat and impending confrontation, Long commandeered some small boats from ships in the harbor and sent them to Reynold's Wharf to rescue any American citizens who might have desired to board his ship for safety. He had no authority to defy Paulet, but he bristled at the actions Paulet threatened to take.

The arrival of *Boston* was met with rejoicing by the local American citizens, who were just as accurately called 'foreigners' as Paulet and his crew were. The extent of the American enthusiasm was expressed by the harbormaster, William Paty,

> "Hurra! Hurra! Hurra! for the Stars and Stripes! Hurra! for our gallant Navy! For our glorious Country! Oh, ye Yankees who live at home at ease, how little can you imagine the stirring thrill of joy and pride that agitates the bosom of your countryman who, roaming far away in foreign lands, and in the midst of trouble, difficulty and danger, hears the cry of Sail O! and the next moment he sees the Stars and Stripes floating over the brave hearts and powerful batteries of an American Ship of War."[37]

During this time the Navy had been experimenting with various seaboard social policies. Their goal was to achieve something between temperance and total abstinence, in the ration of grog each crewman had always expected. One of the less unsuccessful plans was to offer each man six cents per day in lieu of his tot of grog. The crew of USS *Boston* was not only morally firm, they were generous as well. In Honolulu, they presented their combined 'grog money' to the chaplain of the American Seamen's Friend Society.[38]

A little over a week later, on the 25th of February, 1843, Paulet sent armed sailors and marines ashore to the palace. He entered without an announcement or requesting permission and proceeded to lower the Hawaiian flag and raise the British Standard. In the face of overwhelming force, the king agreed to cede his kingdom to the British until his position could be restored. In a short address from the palace, the king indicated that he had "given away the life of our land"[39] Dr. Judd had been working at length to reach a compromise. His efforts were exhausting. On the evening of the cession, Mrs. Judd wrote,

> "After the cession my husband came home and threw himself down, utterly exhausted in body and mind, after the sleepless week of fasting and torture. I sat by him two hours, ransacking heart and brain for arguments of consolation."[40]

Paulet entrenched his position by assuming all jurisdiction over foreigners.[41] He ordered all Hawaiian flags destroyed and all departures from the islands were to be approved by him. The royal yacht *Hooikaika*, was taken by Paulet and rechristened *Albert*. The Ladd Company of Honolulu had previously chartered the ship for a voyage to Mexico to tend to some business activities there and in America. Paulet approved the voyage and ordered his emissary to go along as a passenger carrying the report of his actions to his superior, Admiral Thomas. The cloak-and-dagger aspect of this whole incident reached its peak when a young man was 'hired' by the Ladd Company officials as a clerk. In truth, he was recruited by Dr. Judd, the American serving as the king's minister. Publicly Judd placed a notice in a local newspaper, the Temperance Advocate and Friend, on May 10, 1843 declaring his resignation in protest of Paulet's actions.[42] Privately he arranged to send a secret emissary to England to plead the Hawaiians' case. The emissary, J.F.B. Marshall, was wisely chosen. He was, several years after this strange incident, considered by President Lincoln to become the Honolulu commissioner.[43]

But his first diplomatic mission was fraught with the stuff of action-adventures. He was appointed by Dr. Judd in the most clandestine manner. The king, who had fled to Wailuku, Maui after the cession, returned to Oahu by canoe at night, and met with Judd, Marshall, and a clerk at midnight in the royal tomb in Honolulu.[44] The king returned to Maui via canoe without Paulet ever learning of the secret mission. Marshall was armed with documents describing Paulet's intrusive actions which had the signature of the king and the seal of his Kuhina-Nui, Great Minister.

Marshall proceeded to Mexico aboard the Ladd ship on March 11, 1843, traveled through the United States to Boston and met with Secretary of State Daniel Webster at his Boston residence. Webster's public reaction to the news was, "The United States will interfere by force if the British government do not disavow the acts of Lord Paulet". Marshall reports that Webster's private comments were, "If the British government does not disavow these acts, we'll make a fuss."[45] Marshall then sailed on to England where he presented the case for the Hawaiians to proper personages in London. The English were nonplused by news of Paulet's actions. They had sent specific instructions to Admiral Thomas to support any claims of Englishmen in the islands, but no intention of such an occupation was implied nor to be inferred. Paulet, remember, had sailed before Thomas had received these instructions.

Marshall was informed by Mr. Addington, an undersecretary at the Foreign Office, that the English had not been desirous of assuming any jurisdiction over the islands or interfering with the king's sovereignty. However, to save some dignity, and until he learned what had really happened, Addington added, "but charges against the king are very serious and must be disposed of or the king must grant redress".[46]

During this short period of British occupation and dominance, Commodore Lawrence Kearney arrived from China aboard the frigate USS *Constellation*. When he saw the British flag flying over the palace he quickly ascertained the actions which had brought this deplorable situation about. He filed a formal protest with Paulet's 'minister' and returned to his ship. To further indicate his feelings, Kearney had his sailmaker fashion a "flag of the Sandwich Islands" and defiantly flew it from the truck of his mainmast and fired a salute in its honor.[47] The British were surprised because they had ordered the destruction of all such flags. Kearney also had his crew put on a festive dinner to which all the local Hawaiian royalty were invited. Tempers were rising.

At the same time Marshall, the Hawaiian king's emissary reached Mexico on his way to London, Admiral Thomas learned of the cession Paulet had gained by force of arms. He set sail from Valparaiso aboard the British frigate *Dublin* and reached Honolulu on July 28, 1843. On arrival, Thomas sent a note to the King. "Sir," he wrote, "It being my desire to obtain the honor of a Personal Interview with His Majesty, King Kamehameha." The translation flows in beautiful Hawaiian, "Aloha oe, No ko'u makemake e mahaloia mai au i ka halawai pu me ka Moi Kamehameha III."[48]

After consulting with Paulet and the Hawaiians separately, he rescinded the cession as "having completed its mission and so removed the necessity of acting any longer under the provisional cession".[49] Paulet was ordered to withdraw all his men, return to his ship and stay aboard, awaiting further orders.

Thomas' official record of the cession, or *Olelo Hooakoka* was printed in English and Hawaiian in a joyous edition of the Temperance Advocate in July of 1843.[50] The Hawaiian version contains an interesting phrase. Judd's "Her Britannic Majesty" is "Li'i Wahine Beretania" in Hawaiian. Beretania was the Hawaiian transliteration of Britannic and today is the name of an important street in Honolulu. 'Li'i Wahine' means 'female chief' or Her Majesty.

Charlton's claim, the original excuse given for the British intrusion, remained in litigation for years.[51] Paulet explained his actions by saying that he was prompted by fear of French action *a la* Tahiti, rather than by any thought of intimidation.[52]

The king, on July 31, 1843, at the old stone church called *Kawaiahao*, ordered the Union Jack lowered and the Hawaiian flag raised to its proper place over the palace. In "An Act of Grace" His Majesty King Kamehameha III made a declaration of three parts.

"We, to manifest our joy at the Restoration of our
National Flag, hereby Proclaim,
First, That none of our Subjects shall be punished... for
any act committed between the 25th of February, 1843, and
the date herein.
Second. All prisoners from Hawaii to Ni'ihau, are to be
immediately discharged.
Third, all Government business will be suspended for
ten days that all people may be free to enjoy themselves."[53]

The entire city as well as ships in the harbor joined in the celebration. So ended one of the most bizarre events in Hawaiian history.

With some apprehension lingering after the imbroglio, on August 3, 1843, Commodore Catesby Jones arrived in Honolulu on his flagship USS *United States* accompanied by USS *Cyane*. He wrote to Secretary of the Navy Abel Upshur, "My presence is needed here to look after the interests of our countrymen, now more complicated than ever. Our merchants and citizens beg me to remain until irregularities resulting from the English occupation are adjusted. When I leave it will be for Callao via the Marquesas and Society Islands. Jones, Commanding Pacific Squadron."[54]

The dust did not settle completely on this incident. Three months later, Captain A.I. Dallas, now Commander in Chief of the Pacific Squadron, in a letter to Secretary of the Navy Upshur, pointed out that the terms of the rescission, "have not as yet been fully carried out by Admiral Thomas in as much as he still keeps possession of certain papers belonging to individuals residing here". In a hawklike comment, he added, "Had I here been present I should not have permitted him [Paulet] to fire on the town".[55]

The Polynesian, a prestigious local Hawaiian newspaper edited by John Jarves, published a long letter in November criticizing and complaining of the many actions and other factors of this whole incident.[56]

As the Paulet affair faded from memory, residents of Hawaii returned to their previous activities and problems. Merchants wrangled with the government, sailors continued to plague the longnecks and missionaries vigorously renewed their efforts to save Hawaiians from their sinful enjoyment of life. It is tempting to write that the Hawaiian way of life was changing, implying a slow, natural, peaceful evolution. However, such was not the case. Hawaiian life was being thrust into a new world by a series of confusing and often heartbreaking solutions to crises. And as far as influencing these events is concerned, the native Hawaiians had little control.

Chapter 10 - The Great Mahele

Several developments important to the US Navy occurred in the US during the 1840s. In the small town of Annapolis, Maryland in 1845, George Bancroft, Secretary of the Navy, obtained the old Fort Severn to become a training school for midshipmen. He did not ask Congress to authorize this, but obtained permission via War Department General Order Number 40 issued on August 15,1845. He moved existing classes from a small Navy school in Philadelphia to the new 'Academy' at Fort Severn and appointed Commander Franklin Buchanan as the first Superintendent on October 10, 1845.[1] The new commander spoke to the students on their first day about the rules and expectations of the new institution.

> "The government, in affording you the opportunity of acquiring an education, so important to the accomplishments of a naval officer, has bestowed upon you an incalculable benefit."[2]

So it has proved over the years. The United States Naval Academy at Annapolis, on the Severn River, has produced naval officers successfully for over 150 years.

The Board of Navy Commissioners, created by Congress in 1815, had become ineffective. By 1842 action was demanded and in August Congress accepted the recommendations of a group of Naval officers and replaced the board with five bureaus: Construction & Repair, Ordnance & Hydrography, Medical, Supply and Yards & Docks.[3]

Our old acquaintance, 'Mad Jack' Percival, a little older and no doubt a little wiser, was in command of USS *Constitution* when she anchored in Honolulu Roads November 16, 1845. The *Polynesian* noted the arrival and followed the article by reprinting Oliver Wendell Holmes' "Old Ironsides".[4] This famous poem was written to arouse national enthusiasm to prevent the 45 year old ship from being sent to the breakers. It worked.

Aboard the grand old lady was a young US Marine Lieutenant named Joseph W. Curtis. He was studious and intelligent and the perfect choice for a certain mission. The United States, France, and Great Britain were never really comfortable with the situation in the Sandwich Islands. Each knew that either of the other two had the power to overthrow the monarchy any time they felt they were justified in doing so. Each frequently protested, as we have seen, the actions of one or both of the other two. At this time, and in this atmosphere of suspicion, Dr. G.P. Judd, the king's advisor or prime minister, who had aided explorer Captain Wilkes a few years before, wanted an expert opinion on the best way to defend Honolulu if the need should arise. Since he had been an American medical missionary, his greatest concern was about further assertive action the British or the French might take.

He cordially invited Curtis to his office and discussed the possibilities of defense of the islands. From these conversations came the assignment of Lt. Curtis, USMC, to study the situation and prepare a report for Judd. Permission was granted, through the proper chain-of-command and Curtis began to investigate possible defensive sites. He regarded the old fort at Honolulu, built in 1816, as worthless. He completed his study, but before he could submit it to Judd, he was ordered to return to his ship and sail for Mexico.

During the voyage, he wrote the report and on February 21, 1846, sent it to Dr. Judd via the USS *Cyane*. With great foresight, he recognized the barren, swampy land and long sloping hill, *Pu'uloa*, adjacent to Pearl River, as the best central location for a Naval installation. His vision went beyond the impenetrable reef and the distance from Honolulu, the only town of any size on the island.[5] His report stated,

> "..all the work might be going on at once, together with
> that of clearing out the reef both at Honolulu and Pearl Harbor...
> And I may call your attention to the vast importance of the
> harbor at Pearl River. The perfect security of the harbor, the
> excellence of its water, the perfect case with which it can be
> made one of the finest places in the island, all combine to make
> it a great consideration."[6]

Dr. Judd's reaction was enthusiastic. He responded to Curtis, "If we are to exist as a nation, we shall then turn our attention to the improvements you propose."[7] He assured the young Marine Lieutenant that he had made a most favorable impression upon all the officers of the government with whom he had come into contact and expressed his wish that Curtis would be able to return to Hawaii before his final trip back to the east coast. He added, "This I think, is probable, as the contest with England will eventually bring ships of war more or less to this port."[8] As sometimes happens, this prophetic report by Curtis was set aside for what were perceived to be more important matters, and remained for decades in a dusty camphor wood chest in the attic of the Iolani Palace in Honolulu. It is now among the documents preserved in the Archives of Hawaii.

Honolulu was the first popular port for whalers in Hawaii. Everything the captain needed, such as provisions and supplies, especially water, was available. What the lowly sailor wanted, women and liquor, he was also able to find. When the staunchly Christian governor of Maui died, the port town of Lahaina became popular because of the immoral inducements that were suddenly for rent or sale there. Lahaina was an open roadstead, popular in winter when humpback whales come to calve. Whale ships brought new ideas, new wealth and new products. They brought sailors willing to pay for anything Hawaiians had to sell. And they brought more diseases against which Hawaiians had no immunity.

In addition to whalers, many United States Navy ships called at the islands. They usually anchored at Honolulu, but also at Lahaina on Maui, and Lihue on Kauai. It was their first stop out of Callao, on the west coast of South America, a prime port for US Navy Pacific Squadron ships. The logs of many ships such as USS *Congress* in June of 1846 and USS *St. Mary's* in August of 1854, detail their stays at the islands.[9]

The idea of a US Naval presence in this area was popular among the leading citizens of the islands. The Honolulu weekly journal, *The Polynesian*, commented editorially in 1841 that a naval base should be established here to protect the interests of American citizens engaged in the whaling industry.[10]

In this atmosphere of increased activity on the seashore as well as the land, King Kamehameha III and his advisors in 1839 adopted a statute that amended fishing laws. It set aside the area seaward of the reefs for use by the Hawaiian people to fish. The waters within the reefs, or where there was no reef one mile from the beach, were limited to the use of the *ali'i*, the great chiefs and their tenants.[11]

Foreign pressure led Kauikeaouli, Kamehameha III, the brother of Liholiho, to begin reforming his realm into the image of a western nation. In 1839, he declared a list of the rights of his subjects. In 1840, he took over the educational system and that year a constitution was drawn up by a group of Hawaiians who had been educated by local Protestant missionaries. This document included establishment of a legislature, to which representatives were elected, a cabinet, a civil service and a basic judicial system. By 1845, Hawaii had a government created in the image of European and American nations. By this time, there were about two thousand non-Hawaiian permanent residents in the Pearl Harbor and Honolulu area. The kingdom of the Kamehamehas, fifty years old in 1845, had never been strong. All three kings had floundered their way to 19th century western-style sovereignty and nationhood, beset on all sides by those who would influence them, direct them or grasp control from them. Hawaii had weathered all of these attacks by foreigners, churches, businessmen, sailors, residents and even Hawaiians.

The greatest, most important change that occurred in Hawaii in the 1840s had little to do with foreign adventurers, traders or religious zealots. It was internal rather than external. Called The Great *Mahele*, it was the distribution and re-organization of land and re-defined the ownership of land by the King and high ranking chiefs. *Mahele* means to divide or share in Hawaiian. According to some this was a complete disaster.[12] Others describe it as a change that brought equity and order to Hawaii's troubled land situation, even though many felt they had been cheated and their rights had been disregarded.[13]

The basic unit of land in Hawaii was a traditional section called an *ahupua'a*. This was a triangle, its apex in the mountains its arms sweeping wide toward the sea and its base a line outside the reef and parallel to the land. All island resources were available in this area from food to building materials. Each ahupua'a was owned and controlled by a chief of high standing and his land was the basis of his power. Commoners could move from one ahupua'a to another without restriction, unlike feudal serfs, but lived under the jurisdiction of the chief who controlled the land where they settled. They worked and produced food for him as well as their own families, just as serfs in medieval Europe had done.

The changes were recommended by a Land Commission which had been appointed by the government in 1848. Members John Ii, J.Y. Kaneoha, John Ricord, and William Richards were all prominent businessmen or had posts in the government. The Attorney General was the fifth member of the commission.[14]

The purpose of changing the land ownership system to follow western ideas was to identify which land belonged to the king, which to the chiefs and to control and organize land deals. It also intended to stipulate which land could be sold, with an eye to the 'highest and best' use of land and to end the feudal system of land tenure. Agreement was a long time coming, however. Discussions continued for a year in the Privy Council and in the Legislative Assembly. The Land Commission, which was slated to implement this system, was originally intended to last for two years. They finished in 1858 after ten years of grueling work.

By that time, many who had dragged their feet over changing the system had begun to realize that to retain the old pattern would hamper the growing economy of Hawaii. Finally it was agreed by all that the king would retain private lands that had traditionally been controlled by the ruler. One third of the remaining lands were allotted to the Hawaiian government, one third to the chiefs and the last third to the common people and tenants.[15] In the end, commoners had only 1 % of the land.[16]

The law transferred the traditional communal ownership of land to private ownership. As with native groups in many regions who had always depended on land for subsistence, American Indians for instance, it was a radical change. For Hawaiians, land had always been held by the community that lived on it. Everyone expected to share in the fruits of that land. Changing this to private ownership would keep it from being used by anyone else. It was a hard lesson.

Under the agreement called the Great Mahele, crown lands traditionally owned or controlled by the king, were inalienable and inheritable only by the Hawaiian crown. The law now specified the amount of land the crown could lease out and limited the time of a lease to thirty years.

Kamehameha III, Hawaiians J. Pi'ikoi and M. Kekuanaoa and two hundred and forty other high ranking chiefs, haole residents John Young and G. P. Judd and others, joined to create this agreement. It was implemented between January and March of 1848 in spite of never having been put to a vote of the citizens.

The basic purpose of the *mahele* was to replace the old native system with a new one that was closer to the European idea of land ownership. This would allow progress and enable Americans and Europeans to buy land in the islands. It was touted by some as preparing Hawaiians to join the mainstream of modern nations. It certainly took away traditional approaches to living, and their ideas of land use and ownership. By this time the Hawaiian Islands were too small, with too many residents, to continue to live by the old 'feudal' system. So many foreigners had settled in the islands and so many native Hawaiians had perished from disease or alcohol, that Hawaiians were now in a minority. They no longer owned or controlled their land, they were no longer uniquely Hawaiian and never would be again.

No systematic land survey was made until 1870. Boundaries were vague and ownership still unsettled twenty years after the *mahele*. By then, western ideas of land ownership were firmly in place and the *ahupua'a* was just a memory. In 1900, non-Hawaiians would own four times more land than native Hawaiians. There were fewer and fewer 'pure' Hawaiians. From a population estimated by Captain Cook in 1779 at 300,000, the population of pure Hawaiians fell drastically to 30,000.

More changes were soon to assail Hawaii, more incursions and attempts by foreigners to secure footholds in the islands. In the next several years, sugar became the most important business in Hawaii and Pearl Harbor became the logical center for the defense of United States interests in the Pacific.

Chapter 11- Politics and Sugar

Unfortunately Hawaii had not seen its last intervention by a foreign power. Another group of Frenchmen came in 1849. The French frigate *La Poursuivante* and the corvette Gassendi, commanded by Admiral de Tromelin, anchored in Honolulu Harbor and sent ashore small boats full of armed men. They occupied the old fort there and once again the king's yacht was commandeered.[1] However, the French colony was so small and weak that the Admiral received no support from his countrymen. A show of force in protest against the French by both the British and Americans convinced Tromelin to return to his ship and leave the islands. When he left, the episode was over. The king's yacht, however, was never returned.

In the 1850s, President of the US, Franklin Pierce, sent David George to the islands to negotiate a treaty of annexation which would prevent any further incursions by foreign powers. The Hawaiians did not request it. After five years of deliberation and negotiation, the proposed agreement fell dead on the sword of one provision. That provision, suggested by a few expansionists in congress, was eventual statehood for Hawaii. It was unacceptable to congress and was rejected. This first attempt at annexation was puny at best for neither the United States nor Hawaii were ready for it.

The number of foreign attempts at intervention diminished for a few years. Hawaii was still independent and King Kamehameha III, Kauikeaouli, was still in power. However, Hawaii had still not been accepted as a sovereign nation among the family of European nations. This was a keenly desired goal of Kamehameha III, his predecessors, and his successors.

One factor that deterred many Europeans from serious thoughts of annexation was its location. This beautiful archipelago is the most remote group of islands in any ocean, far from the centers of European power. The powerful western European nations had too many other political fish to fry to be concerned over Hawaii.

It was clear to many that the Americans were overwhelming the islands. The efforts of the missionaries, the firm establishment of American businesses, along with the protection of American naval forces, were insinuating American culture into the everyday life of the Hawaiian people. This was not a new scenario. United States citizens had moved into the area west of the Mississippi River, although the land clearly belonged to Mexico or the native groups who had occupied it for centuries. The same thing was happening in Hawaii. The days of the monarchy were numbered, many predicted, though the kingdom was more resilient than most people realized. It withstood the onslaught of westerners for another forty years.

There were times when annexation seemed expedient to various kings as the only viable way to forestall revolutions, which were frequently rumored to be imminent. It would also stop avaricious foreigners from exploiting the islands. At times the situation became so bad that surrendering sovereignty to the United States seemed to be the king's only way out. His advisors and cabinet always managed to avert the crisis to maintain their independence. These respites from danger may have been due to astute political actions by Hawaiian politicians or to disagreements among their opponents. Which ever it was, it meant that the government avoided any action at all. Annexation did not become a reality in the 1850s, but it would be suggested again. And the next time, Pearl Harbor would be an essential part of the new proposals.

The Hawaiian government, especially the rulers, wanted to be on an equal footing with other nations. It was not easy to gain such recognition because the perception of Hawaii in the halls of Europe was as a race of savages playing at nationhood, guided by some British and American advisors. It wasn't easy for Hawaiian diplomats or representatives to be taken seriously because their land and their regime had so little power. Hawaii's geographic location in the Pacific Ocean was unique. To Europeans, it was perceived that while Hawaii was important to the British and Americans, their loyalties were elsewhere. Hawaiian sovereignty was young, its rulers were inexperienced and unstable. The tiny country so far away was difficult to deal with in what was deemed proper diplomatic negotiations.

The Hawaiians did make some diplomatic progress. They were able to sign a 'most-favored-nation' treaty with Norway, Sweden, Denmark, and a few German states. This success was not due to the importance of Hawaii to these European countries, but because the treaties were requested by Hawaii. The nations were only slightly involved in trade with Hawaii, but for the Hawaiian king, it was a start. Eventually this idea was expanded to England and to the United States. France refused to participate.

The political status of Hawaii was still vague. There was a king, but no military force to protect the nation. Some residents wanted Hawaii to create such an army for protection. A good number of American residents in Hawaii, even second-generation residents, wanted annexation to America. Others wanted much stronger trade agreements with America and England, corroborated by treaty. Some Hawaiian government representatives were working toward asserting their independence by traveling to European capitals to negotiate new treaties. The United States government talked of signing a treaty giving Hawaii equality in relations with them.

King Kamehameha III wrote a document placing his realm under the protection of the United States until France would recognize Hawaii's independence. France would not do so and rejected all attempts at compromise. French representatives finally withdrew from Hawaii.[2]

Treaties are only as good as men believe they are. Over the years, especially in the 19th century, treaties were frequently broken by all sides.

This fact was true all over the world, but it did not stop politicians from negotiating new treaties. They were often not legally binding, but were always politically useful.

The need for the annexation of Hawaii to the United States faded when France withdrew and other foreigners lost interest around the middle of the century. The islands were no longer under siege and Europe seemed ready to leave them alone. In order to plead its case as a modem country, Hawaii needed to have a city. Honolulu, therefore, was declared to be a city in 1850.[3]

At that time another strong voice was heard to make two points: the Hawaiian Islands are important to the United States, and they would be a danger if in foreign hands. Captain (later Admiral) Samuel F. DuPont commanded *USS Cyane* which frequently took him to the islands in the course of his duties. His military opinion was unambiguously stated in a report to Secretary of the Navy William B. Preston in 1851.

"It is impossible to estimate too highly the value and importance of the Sandwich Islands, whether from a commercial or military point of view. Should circumstances ever place them in our hands, they would prove the most important acquisition we could make in the whole Pacific Ocean, an acquisition intimately connected with our commercial and naval supremacy in those seas; be this as it may, these islands should never be permitted to pass into the possession of any European power."[4]

Rulers of fledgling nations often view constitutions as expedient documents that will corroborate power and are a vital means toward establishing their rule. For some, a constitution is not created because it is philosophically right. Soon it was clear that the Hawaiian constitution, created in 1840 under the influence of the missionaries, lacked important provisions and had to be redone. Kamehameha 111, with surprising arrogance, declared he would create a new one.

The constitution of 1852, which would not be the last such document of the 19th century, included the right of every adult male, native born or naturalized, to vote to elect representatives to the lower house of the Hawaiian legislature.[5] To many this was not an acceptable concept. Men of many nationalities other than Hawaiian lived in the islands by 1852. The idea that all of these men would be eligible to vote was, for some men in the government, far too democratic. It would hand over the kingdom's government to the poor and the ignorant.[6]

Twenty-five Americans and twenty-one Englishmen were part of the government at the time. All had guaranteed their allegiance to the king, but Hawaiians remained suspicious of their motives and loyalties. The Hawaiians did nothing and suffered the presence of the *haoles* because they could not yet operate the government without their help.

Hawaii was slowly strengthening its tenuous independence, but there was still the question of whether or not it could survive as an autonomous nation. One way or another the tiny new country had successfully withstood incursions by the French, the British and by some Americans. The word 'annexation'had been heard from several countries. Rumors appeared at this time of a secret deal by a group of Americans, financed and controlled by a shipping millionaire. His plan, according to the rumor, was to buy the islands outright for five million dollars.[7] There is no evidence the proposal ever reached the king, nor that it was ever seriously pursued.

At this time, 1853, the United States Navy, perceived by the Hawaiians to be one of the most powerful western navies, was actually in deplorable shape. The US Navy has had a saw-like curve of progress. The six splendid ships of 1797 had transformed a weak group of colonies, forced to depend on armed merchantmen for defense, into a world class naval force. Then, after the serious decline following the War of 1812, the Navy was strengthened to meet the challenge of the Algerine pirates. By 1853 many of the ships which had served the country so well were tired, obsolete, and unfit to fight effectively. The United States did not have one ship equal to the first class warships of European nations.

To correct this dangerous discrepancy, Congress, reacting in 1853 to the persuasion of Secretary of the Navy James C. Dobbin, authorized the construction of six screw propelled, steam driven frigates plus five shallow draft steam sloops-of-war.[8]

Progress was also being made on the dipJomatic front. In 1854 Commodore Matthew Perry concluded his famous Treaty of Kanagawa which opened Japan to commerce with the west. His course to Japan had been from Norfolk, Virginia, south and east around the Cape of Good Hope, past Singapore, and then into Japanese waters. When the treaty was completed, his fleet returned along the same route except for the two ships USS *Susquehanna* and USS *Mississippi* which cruised east across the Pacific and home via Cape Horn.[9] Some sources do not indicate that *Mississippi* stopped at Hawaii.[10] But her need for coal and other provisions would seem to indicate that such a stop would have been mandatory. Other sources show that the two frigates "also called on their way heme from Japan, in the latter part of October 1854, and remained a week off the port of Honolulu."[11]

That same year, a group of Americans decided that Hawaii was a likely candidate for conquest. They were even less successful than the French had been in 1849. Labeled 'filibusterers', they were a group of adventurers, soldiers of fortune and failed gold miners from California infused with expansionist dreams. Their goal was to take territory for the United States, and for their own enrichment. Raiding countries in Mexico, Central and South America, they created confusion, but none of their efforts were successful for any length of time. One of these was Sam Brannen who had spread news of the discovery of gold in California five years before.

With twenty-five men, Brannen chartered the ship, *Gamecock*, and set sail from San Francisco to invade Oahu. He planned to create his own government with himself as governor. When Hawaiian officials heard of their impending arrival, they called on Captain Gardner and the US Marines of USS *Vandalia*, which was anchored in the harbor.

When the Californians swaggered into Honolulu, they were confronted by US Marines, trained by Sgt. J. Read, and their ship was impounded. No one in the Hawaiian government would receive them and they hadn't the firepower to oppose the marines or even the weak Royal Guards. Having failed to attain their goal, the Californians left Hawaii.[12] Read and Gardner received letters of gratitude from the king and the bond between the US and Hawaii grew stronger.[13] Although this particular problem was over, foreign interference would appear again.

The same year, 1854, saw advances in the tools and weapons of war. One was the invention of metal cartridges by the firm of Smith and Wesson. These eliminated the separate and cumbersome operations of measuring and loading gunpowder, ramming the shot home, removing the ramrod, and standing clear all before a pistol, rifle, or cannon could be fired. Steam engines, metal cartridges, iron ships, and reorganization all contributed to updating the navies of the world. The U.S. Navy was changing.

Hawaii was also changing. It is difficult today to separate Honolulu from Waikiki, but the difference was easy to see in 1854. Hawaiian author George S. Kanahele quotes a Mr. George Washington Bates as describing the two areas thus: "Honolulu was a noisy, dusty money-grubbing port town of 14,000 inhabitants, including hundreds of foreign residents and visitors. Its maze of streets were mostly narrow and crooked, filthy lanes were often used as race courses for reckless riders and their horses." It was a city of "yelping dogs, rattling carts, saluting cannon, and carousing drunks. Over 600 ships a year called at its harbor discharging passion-starved sailors and whalers who rioted for sport."[14] A local newspaper added that there were those who were against all street nuisances including "yelping curs, biped nudity, horse racing and &c."[15] In contrast, Waikiki, just a few miles away, was *kua'aina*, which is a word meaning "a land of people who are simple and unpretentious. Their values were family-oriented and they toiled mainly in the Taro fields."[16]

In Honolulu, some business liaisons were being forged which were mutually beneficial, but too often the natives, in their desire to emulate wealthy, powerful foreigners, would sacrifice too much when entering into a deal, and retreat a little farther from their old ways. This trend of departure from the old systems had started before the first westerners came, but it certainly accelerated with their arrival. To the natives, the missionaries seemed so sure, so confident in their religion. Ships of foreign powers were able to sail anywhere in the world, an ability the Hawaiians had long since lost, though many shipmasters reported having excellent Kanaka sailors among their crews. *Kanaka* was the term for man in Hawaiian. It also could refer to a low order chief, just above a commoner.

Some observers may view these relentless changes as a series of debacles for the Hawaiian people. Others may recognize and accept the inevitable forces of change and describe the European and American influences as a better alternative to what might have been.

Perhaps the foregoing description of a changing, growing town was a bit harsh. There was an ever growing presence of American Naval personnel and their fiscal contribution to the community was substantial. The War Department established a quartermaster's office in Honolulu in 1849 to purchase supplies for the Presidios in San Francisco and Monterey. This increased activity certainly was a stimulant to the Hawaiian economy. Beside the amounts the sailors spent personally, the Suppo (Supply Officer) of one warship reported disbursing $245,000 while in Honolulu. An office of the Navy Department was also in the city to tend to the needs of the many U.S. Navy ships visiting the growing port. American politicians, Admirals, Generals, and other prominent people were also interested in the area. All reiterated that no other nation should ever dominate the affairs of our island neighbors.[17]

King Kamehameha III, Kauikeaouli, had been king for 29 years, during many difficult times. He died on December 15, 1854 after several years of poor health, the last son of Kamehameha the Great. He was the last Hawaiian king with a direct connection to that revered leader. His successor was to be his adopted son Alexander Liholiho. Liholiho's mother was Kinau, former Kahina Nui, and his father was Mathio Kekuanaoa. Liholiho was known as Kamehameha IV.

A great many things had happened in Hawaii between 1820 and 1854. More important, perhaps, were things that did not happen. Hawaii was not taken over by the French, who by then controlled entire groups of South Pacific islands to create their so-called 'French Polynesia'. Nor was Hawaii overwhelmed by Russians and their commercial ventures. Britain and America had each had adventures in the islands, but neither yet laid claim to them. Hawaii had not collapsed into chaos, either The missionaries were still there and active, though not as powerful as they had been in the days of Hiram Bingham. The religious pioneers were celebrating their 35th anniversary in Hawaii. Children of the original missionaries still lived in Hawaii, but did not often follow the profession of their fathers. They became prosperous and many owned healthy island businesses. Later, when these same descendants gained control of the government of Hawaii, they were often called "Missionary Boys". It was not complimentary.

Life in the islands settled down and, during the late 1850s, no more intrusions occurred. It was a period which allowed the government to turn its attention to the economy. A strong and healthy business climate was vital if Hawaii were to survive and prosper. Creating a profitable industry was essential to growth and prosperity. The product which they chose to develop was sugar.

Sugar originally grew wild in Hawaii and its agricultural development and exportation possibilities made it a good choice. At first, island refining techniques were primitive, but they improved.[18] The obvious market was America. It was the closest country, albeit 2,400 miles away, and by far the largest Pacific rim consumer. Fortuitously, Americans craved sugar, great amounts of it. Sugar was the one product that might bring the balance of trade to a level more advantageous for Hawaii. Sugar related businesses began to grow, most of them owned or controlled by residents who were not native Hawaiians.

One problem in the new industry was labor. In the first few years, half of all working Hawaiians were employed in the labor intensive sugar industry. Two problems confronted the growers. There were too few Hawaiians to supply all the labor needed and those available were not disciplined workers. Contract workers and immigrants were brought from China to work in the fields and later these were augmented by more contract labor from Japan. Oriental field laborers were eager to work many hours a day for meager pay. Later more immigrants were brought in from Japan, Portugal, and the Philippines. They alleviated the immediate shortage but their presence created problems in housing and culture clashes.

The growers paid import duty and foreign product taxes on every shipment of sugar into the United States. A suggestion from the past offered a way to eliminate those expenses. If the United States annexed Hawaii, those taxes and duties would disappear. It is easy to see why the sugar company owners supported annexation. The clout of commercial necessity was added to the other forces working for annexation.

Despite their differences, the one thing the growers agreed upon was that an American connection was critical to get sugar to market. It was as simple as that. One suggestion for doing this equitably was called a reciprocity treaty. Reciprocity meant a mutual action or interchange of privileges. The first time the word was used in connection with Hawaiian sugar was in the early 1850s. Beginning as an economic expedient, reciprocity had both enthusiastic supporters and rigid opponents. Most Americans on the mainland were against it because they thought that annexation, rather than a reciprocity treaty, would guarantee the supply of sugar. Sugar growers in southern part of the United States were especially against it because of the deleterious effect it would have on the prices they were receiving for their sugar.

The reciprocity negotiations began. The first treaty that was proposed stipulated that the United States would allow Hawaiian sugar into the country without attendant, crippling import duties. For such a privilege, Hawaiian companies would sell exclusively to the United States. It was argued that this would enable Hawaii to become prosperous and maintain its independence.

The first reciprocity treaty was submitted for consideration when Alexander Liholiho became king in 1855 as Kamehameha IV. He had strong pro-British sympathies. His anti-American sentiments, and the growing American commercial presence in Hawaii, led to serious problems.

As Kamehameha IV, Alexander Liholiho ruled for nine years. He was not against a treaty with the United States that would allow Hawaiian sugar into the US duty free. It would help to keep him and his country independent. This treaty, however, went down to defeat in 1857 when the US Congress let it drop for lack of interest.

Chapter 12 - Worth its Weight in Sugar

By 1861, the United States was involved in a violent Civil War that kept their attention on the east. There was some naval activity in the Pacific, mainly Confederate, but concentrated on the west coast of the US mainland. Neither side expressed much interest in the affairs or the location of the Hawaiian Islands. It was during the first year of this war that Congress instituted the Medal of Honor. Originally it applied only to enlisted men of the Navy. Army enlisted personnel were included a year later, and army officers two years later. It was not until 1915 that Naval officers were eligible.[1]

A special squadron of four vessels, commanded by Commodore John Rogers, departed from Hampton Roads for the Pacific via Cape Horn. The flotilla included the ships USS *Vanderbilt*, USS *Tuscarora*, USS *Powhatan* and USS *Monadnock* which were intended to increase the Pacific Squadron to a fourteen ship force.[2] This extended strength seems to have been effective in thwarting Confederate plans to interrupt shipping activities on the west coast. The Confederate ships *CSA Shenandoah* and *CSA Alabama* did harass shipping and burned much of the whaling fleet in 1865, but did not seriously interrupt the flow of goods from Asia to the east coast.

In the postwar period, the Pacific Squadron, the only prewar squadron to survive the Civil War intact, underwent a number of organizational changes. Pursuant to a Navy Department circular dated April 23, 1866, the Pacific Squadron was divided into the North Pacific and South Pacific Squadrons. General Order 105, March 13, 1869, rearranged the American fleet in the Pacific into a Pacific Station, under the command of a rear admiral, and the North and South Squadrons each under the command of a commodore. A subsequent change was made on July 8, 1872, when General Order 175 stipulated that as of October 1, 1872, the Pacific Station would be divided into the North Pacific and the South Pacific Stations, thereby abolishing the North and South Squadrons. Finally, the Pacific Station was reestablished between April and July of 1878.

At the time the first squadrons were established, the highest rank in the Navy was captain. A captain commanding a squadron was often given (or assumed) the courtesy title of commodore, but it was not until 1857 that the commanding officer of a squadron was officially given a title different from the captains subordinate to him. An act of January 16, 1857, made the commanding officer of a squadron a 'flag officer'. An act of July 16, 1862, created the ranks of commodore and rear admiral and thereafter, the commanding officer of a squadron usually held one of those ranks. The establishment of other advanced ranks followed: Vice Admiral on December 31, 1864, and Admiral on July 25, 1866.[3]

After the Civil War, the US Navy again fell into a deplorable state. The 600 ships the Navy had boasted at the end of the war were reduced through attrition, scrapping and rot, to 60 vessels. No less than sixty-five ironclad ships were discarded, dismantled, or sold. With no war to fight, the 'old guard' of senior officers clung to the sailing ships with which they were familiar. Steam driven ships had been demonstrated to be capable of speeds up to 18 knots. In spite of the fact that a sailing ship could only make good an undependable 5 to 10 knots, the faster type of ship was ignored. Furthermore, Navy ships which had engines were restricted in their use. "To burn coal was so grievous an offense in the eyes of the authorities, that for years the captain was obliged to enter in his logbook in red ink his reasons for getting up steam."[4]

In this atmosphere of frugality, a group of contrarian naval officers founded the US Naval Institute in October of 1873 as a place to exchange and discuss proposals to improve the neglected US Navy. The medium they chose was a magazine called *Proceedings*. It has continued to be a forum for the exchange of ideas from that time to today.

More steps were taken to improve the Navy's condition. In 1882, Secretary of the Navy William H. Hunt instituted a Naval Advisory Board.[5] Then in October 1884, the Naval War College was established in Newport, Rhode Island. Yet another Navy renaissance had begun. The college president, Commodore Stephen B. Luce, had to consider the incorporation of the most recent developments in naval warfare: rifled barrels, breech loading, smokeless powder, armor piercing shells and automotive torpedoes. In 1870, the Gatling Gun was developed, the first machine gun. It could fire over 300 rounds per minute and rapidly exerted its influence on military activities all over the world.

Meanwhile feelings had mellowed between American and British sailors, though a sense of rivalry still existed. One incident which had the potential to expand into something very ugly, turned out to be more of a prank than an offense. In 1865, Queen Emma, the widow of Kamehameha IV, Alexander Liholiho, went to England for a visit aboard HBMS *Clio*. While there she met and became friendly with Queen Victoria. On her return trip, she traveled to America by ship, across America by train, river boat and wagon. When she left the west coast for Hawaii, she was aboard USS *Vanderbilt*, one of the four new ships in the Pacific Squadron.

Before she had departed from Hawaii, the United States shield had mysteriously disappeared from the office of the American Minister. The Minister threatened to use US Marines to recover the shield and sternly demanded its return and the identification of the man responsible for the crime. Perhaps he expected a lowly seaman, maybe drunk, to be the thief. From the ranks of the crew, however, stepped the grand young Lord Charles Beresford, a midshipman in her Britannic Majesty's Royal Navy to admit he was the gamester. Having cleanly admitted the theft, he volunteered to replace the shield, which he did in front of an amused crowd. The situation ended so amicably that a local artist sketched a picture of Beresford replacing the shield.[6] If the Beresford family has a sense of humor, a copy of this painting hangs in the family home.

Annexing the Hawaiian Islands, suggested a number of times before by people in the United States, businessmen in Hawaii and even by Hawaiian royalty when it was threatened by other nations, was suggested again. In 1854 annexation had been discussed by the king and the American Minister. The British had opposed it and denounced the United States. The Hawaiian king, Kamehameha III did not want annexation, but too many foreigners had made threatening moves towards the islands and he needed help to protect his lands. Many members of the US government weren't keen on it, either. Still, the US Commissioner in the islands, D.L. Gregg, wrote to the king,

"The strong arm of the United States has been solicited for your protection. It has been kindly extended and held out until at length self respect must soon dictate its withdrawal."[7]

USS *Portsmouth* and USS *St. Mary's* were in the harbor along with US frigates *Susquehanna* and *Mississippi*. The latter two ships were returning to the US, carrying papers from Commodore Perry on the official mission to open of Japan. They all remained, awaiting word on the annexation negotiations. Such a large concentration of US ships was seen as intimidating by islanders and foreigners, and perhaps Gregg wanted it that way. Kamehameha III felt that the tone of the note from Gregg was offensive.

Treaty negotiations were reaching the serious stage, but the idea was beginning to wear thin, and islanders were turning away from it. Then an event occurred that halted it in its tracks. The king, Kamehameha III, died and his successor, Alexander Liholiho or Kamehameha IV, broke off the talks. Even in the United States this was greeted with a sigh of relief. It was clear that such a concept was premature. Most congressmen were of the opinion that the US president, Franklin Pierce, would not sign such a treaty, anyway.

Annexation is a singularly one sided political action that proclaims the power of the taker over the area taken. It also has a colloquial meaning; taking territory without any right to it. It was clear that Hawaiians felt threatened by it, and congressmen in the US felt it was an option to be used very sparingly. Annexation of the islands was brought up again in 1867 in the United States. In a letter to Edwin Cook, US Minister to Hawaii, dated September 12, 1867, Secretary of State William H. Seward said that Cook should oppose a reciprocity treaty because it would hinder the idea of annexation.

"A strong interest, based on the annexation of the
Sandwich Islands, will be active in opposing a ratification
of the reciprocity treaty. It will be argued that the reciprocity
treaty will tend to hinder and defeat an early annexation;
which the people of the Sandwich Islands are supposed to
be now strongly inclined to.'"

Seward instructed Cook to remain in Honolulu and continue to
investigate the possibilities of annexation instead of coming home at this
time. He also stated that Cook should be governed in all his proceedings
with proper respect and courtesy to the government and people of the
Sandwich Islands. Know for your own information, Seward went on, that
lawful, peaceful annexation with the consent of the people, is desired.

Nothing happened on the annexation issue for a while and the islands
of Hawaii were left in peace. Business continued to grow, sugar plantations
expanded and merchants ships called frequently. The American presence in
Hawaii also continued to grow. By the autumn of 1867, one survey reported
that there were 42 American flags on whaling ships and merchantmen in
Honolulu Harbor and only six from all other nations. United States Naval
Captains continued to act as arbiters in the local disputes that arose.
Government and royal dignitaries and ali'i were often seen aboard US ships,
conducting business or simply enjoying themselves.

There was duty for the Pacific Squadron to attend to on the west
coast of the Americas, on the southeast coast of Asia and on several island
groups in between. Also the purchase of Alaska was anticipated, although
the actual contract was not completed until 1867, after the Civil War was
over. One of the ships from the North Pacific Squadron USS Lakawanna,
discovered the island of Midway on August 28, 1859. It is about 2,500 miles
northwest of Hawaii. In December of 1867 Congress acted to make Midway
the first overseas possession of the United States.[9]

While the missionaries eventually lost their influence as purveyors
of right and wrong in Hawaii, by 1867 one out of every four Hawaiians
belonged to a Christian Church. There were over fifty churches, the majority
of which were overseen by ordained native ministers.

From the first, churchmen had tried in vain to maintain and teach the
value of a rigid moral atmosphere in Honolulu. It was not easy as it went
against the inbred instincts and desires of ordinary Hawaiian citizens as well
as visitors. After the first wave of rigid religious Calvinist fervor and discipline
subsided, the residents began to regard the missionaries as eccentric.

According to one writer, Charles Nordhoff, the missionaries had
attained their goal of covering the islands with fruitful fields, neat pleasant

dwellings, schools, and especially with churches by 1873. As he rode around visiting various sites in Honolulu, he was impressed with the streets, the buildings and the houses, as well as the churches, because they reminded him so much of New England. The missionaries have left an indelible mark, he remarked, and he was impressed with the respect and admiration that he saw people had for them.[10] His opinion was biased perhaps and uninformed, but no less a sincere record of what he saw. The missionaries are still viewed as destroyers of ancient Hawaiian traditions and in part the accusation is true.

Shortly thereafter, leprosy appeared in Hawaii. The majority of victims were workers on sugar plantations and natives, who called it *mai pake* or the Chinese disease.[11] No one knew how it had come to the islands, but they did know it was highly contagious, especially among workers who usually slept in communal barracks. Sailors in the Honolulu/Pearl Harbor area and in Lahaina on Maui began to restrict liaisons with local prostitutes when the disease appeared. The government removed infected sufferers from society. A leper colony was created at the Kalaupapa Peninsula on the north shore of the island of Molokai. It was the usual 19th century reaction to the disease, not just in the islands, because it was dreadfully contagious and there was no known cure.

Later, bouts of small pox and measles would descend on the populace and the port of Honolulu was closed for a time. Being assailed by 'western' diseases was just one more disaster heaped upon a slowly dying people. The fact that Europeans and Asians were immune to many of these diseases was, for the Hawaiians, a bitter pill to swallow. In fact, neither Europeans nor Americans knew how to deal with, cure or prevent most of these diseases. Isolation was the only way they knew to prevent their spread. Scientists were just beginning to understand the nature of bacteria and germs. These facts do not deter some writers from accusations that Americans brought the diseases to the islands deliberately to wipe out the Hawaiians. Actually, fear of communicable diseases transcended all social strata and economic levels. Sailors were warned about the locals and locals had reason to be apprehensive about contact with visiting sailors.

An extraordinary event occurred in Hawaii in 1870. The US Marine Corps has often gallantly fought their way ashore to raise the American flag. A strange and interesting incident became a part of US Navy and Hawaiian history when the US Marines stormed ashore in Hawaii to lower the American flag. And to make it even more perplexing, that flag was flying over the American consulate!

In August of 1870, ailing Queen Kalama, relict of Kamehameha III, was reported to have expired. The news prompted the foreign consulates to lower their flags to half-mast in respect. When the report of her death was proven to be unfounded, the consulates all quickly raised their flags again. However, a month later, she actually did succumb. *The Pacific Commercial Advertiser* reported "Her Majesty Queen Kalama, widow of Kamehameha the Good, expired at her residence in this city on Tuesday last, the 20th instant, after a long and painful illness." In early 18th century papers and letters 'instant' refers to the current month. 'Ultimo' refers to the previous month. There followed some personal information about her young life, marriage etc. and the article ended with a touchingly affectionate expression of grief for her.12

All the consulate flags were again lowered to a respectful midposition, except one. The lone hold-out was the consulate of the United States. The US Minister, Henry Peirce, was away and his consul, Thomas Adamson, an antagonistic rival, decided that he could use this opportunity to embarrass his superior. He did not move the US flag.

Anchored in Honolulu Harbor, Commander William T. Truxtun, captain of USS *Jamestown* had lowered his standard in respect and was dismayed to see that the consulate ashore had neglected to do so. He dispatched a young ensign, Andrew Dunlap, to remind Consul Adamson of his omission. Adamson's response startled the young ensign. The consul stated that, since his superior, Minister Peirce, had not officially informed him of the Queen's death, the consulate flag would remain at the top of the mast. He then added a comment; he considered Dunlap's mission "a piece of impertinence on the part of your commanding officer."13

Shocked, Dunlap returned and reported Adamson's astonishing reply to Captain Truxtun. Truxtun, a patriot who was aware of the importance of friendly relations between his country and Hawaii, was above all, a military man to the core. He immediately ordered First Lieutenant Henry Clay Cochrane, along with a sergeant and four Marine privates, to go ashore and reiterate to the consul, with force if necessary, that he should comply with international protocol.

Lt. Cochrane arranged his men at the parade rest position at the foot of the consulate stairs and called upon Adamson and assistant Jonathan Christie, to lower the flag. Again Adamson declined, stating, "I do not recognize Commander Truxtun, and he has nothing to do with me at all."14 His derogatory attitude and statements could not have been more poorly selected. Lt. Cochrane entered the consulate, literally pushing Adamson and his assistant aside on the way, lowered the flag and posted a guard. Then he returned to the ship.

When Minister Peirce returned and the story was related to him, he summarily dismissed Adamson and elevated Christie to the post. He and Truxtun arranged for a 50 man detachment, in splendid dress uniforms, to march in Kalama's funeral procession as a gesture of respect. Truxtun had acted immediately on his own authority, since speedy communication with

Washington at this time was impossible. Later his initiative was rewarded and he ended his career some years later as a commodore. Lt. Cochrane continued to exercise his assertiveness, spent forty years in the service of the United States Marine Corps, and became a Brigadier General.

Local residents were unhappy that foreign troops had landed on their shores, no matter how noble the reason. The *Commercial Advertiser* headlined their coverage on September 24, 1870 with "A High-Handed Proceeding", and began the article with these words, "On Wednesday, the habitues of Queen Street were witness to a remarkable scene"[15] Truxtun's report of the incident was recorded by William Jarrett, Secretary of the Privy Council, in a six page document.[16] So ended what was probably the only time a group of US Marines have landed with the sole purpose of lowering the American flag.

Again in 1870, a reciprocity treaty was proposed. However, this time it contained provisions the king of Hawaii, by then Lot or Kamehamcha V, could not accept. This reciprocity treaty failed because the US Senate refused to support it and because the king rejected it as well. It is possible the United States congress was holding out for annexation because there were serious doubts about the King. "He's liable to a sudden decease," wrote US minister to Hawaii, Henry Peirce, to US Secretary of State Hamilton Fish in July 1871. Kamehameha V "has frequent attacks of difficult breathing and is in danger of suffocation by congestion, caused by obesity. His weight is 300 pounds."[17]

The actual cause that killed the reciprocity proposal is unclear. Whatever the reason, the treaty was now defunct and temporarily, Hawaii was the loser in the lucrative world wide sugar market.

In 1871, Henry A. Peirce wrote to Hamilton Fish. stating that the time bad come for the US to consider annexing the Hawaiian Islands.

> "I am aware that the king has no heirs. When King Kamehameha V dies, there will be an election in the legislature to determine the next king. That will produce a crisis, and will be a good time to push annexation."[18]

These developments were followed with great interest by the US Navy because annexation would certainly mean access to Pearl Harbor. Exploration had always been sporadic in the Pearl Harbor area and Cook's charts were too old to be of use. The Navy senior staff felt that this harbor could be developed into the finest harbor in the Hawaiian Islands, but they had no confidence in the old British charts.

Many Hawaiians hated the idea of cession to anyone, however, as Kamehameha V lay dying of tuberculosis or alcohol, or both, the opposition to annexation faded. His realm was in disarray. He had ruled for only nine years with little distinction except that he had the first royal palace in Hawaii built. A modest one story house, it was called the *Hale Ali'i* or House of the Chief. Later it was formally called the Iolani Palace. This small, humble structure was not the Iolani Palace that stands on King Street today. That was built fifteen years later.

When Kamehameha V died, an election in the legislature chose William Lunalilo as king. Because he was not directly related to Kamehameha the Great, Lunalilo was never referred to by the title of Kamehameha.

Despite the lamentable post Civil War state of the US Navy, recommendations concerning the value of Pearl Harbor, from both military and civilian visitors, were increasing. Admiral Alfred T. Mahan, a respected and visionary naval historian, evaluated the situation. He believed that the annexation of Hawaii was desirable for two reasons. First, the islands could serve as a provisioning and coaling station. Second, they would be the first line of defense against attack on the mainland by any Asian power. Hawaii was receiving increased attention from the United States. So much attention, in fact, that a mission was sent to Hawaii to assess the military defensive capabilities of all the Hawaiian Islands. It's goal was kept secret to avoid arousing concern on the part of the British or French.

On June 24, 1872, the Honorable William W. Belknap, Secretary of War, called two men to his office. There he explained their mission to them and gave them confidential instructions.

> "..to ascertain the defensive capabilities of the Sandwich Islands' ports in the event of a war with a powerful maritime nation."[19]

The men he selected were well chosen. Major General John M. Schofield, a West Point graduate of 1853, a man with a gallant Civil War record and a Medal of Honor recipient, was to head the team. His associate, Lieutenant Colonel Burton S. Alexander, who had also served with distinction in the war, was an engineer. Secretary Belknap firmly informed the two officers that the meeting was to be confidential and their report kept secret because it was possible that their survey could be perceived as a prelude to acquisition. The US was not ready for such publicity. The British and the French still didn't want a US presence in the Pacific.

On December 30, 1872, the two army officers boarded USS *California*, flagship of Rear Admiral Pennock, and were entered on the manifest as vacationers. The primary mission of USS *California* and the admiral was to pick up the new king, Lunalilo, in the islands and take him to the United States for a visit. However, as the Commander in Chief of the Pacific Squadron he knew the assignment of his passengers and the significance of their study.

At a formal reception at the Iolani Palace, Admiral Pennock and the two Army men were well received by Lunalilo. Schofield suggests, but does not explicitly say, that the king approved of their study. Whether Schofield presented the purpose of his survey as commercial rather than military is not known.

At any rate, with the permission of the new king, Schofield and Alexander proceeded to survey the Pearl Harbor area, the land and the lochs, and a short distance out to sea. They also toured and inspected the other islands. In his report of May 8, 1873, Schofield indicated that there were other anchorages on these islands, but they were mostly open roadsteads and incapable of being defended by shore batteries. He added that even the harbor of Honolulu could not be defended from the shore. He concluded this point by stating,

> "With one exception there is no harbor on the Islands that can be made to satisfy all the conditions necessary for a harbor of refuge in time of war. This [exception] is the harbor of 'Ewa' or 'Pearl River' situated in the island of Oahu, about seven miles west of Honolulu."[20]

Schofield and Alexander described the coral reef at the entrance to Pearl Harbor as being dead. The importance of this observation is that if a channel were dredged, Schofield says, there would be no fear of the coral refilling the void. The Pearl River harbor has water "deep enough for the largest vessels of war, and its locks [sic], particularly around Rabbit [Ford] Island, are spacious enough for a large number of vessels to ride at anchor, in perfect security against all storms."[21]

Alexander, the engineer, was of the opinion that a channel could be cut through the coral by means of a surface blasting and noted that the debris would be carried out to sea by the natural current and would not foul the harbor. He estimated the cost to be about $250,000.

Frequently Schofield referred to the possibility of the United States either annexing the Sandwich Islands or securing some kind of cession of the Pearl River estuary and adjacent lands as part of a reciprocity agreement with the local government.[22] This was a prophetic observation indeed. He was well aware that the sugar planters and manufacturers wanted to have the high tariffs, which cut down their profits, removed. In fact, his report was printed almost in its entirety in a local Hawaiian magazine with the title "Worth its Weight in Sugar—Pearl Harbor."[23] While he was in the islands, Schofield arranged to have a thorough hydrographic survey made.[24]

Schofield concluded his report with the statement, "When war has begun, it will be too late to make this harbor available and there is no other suitable harbor in these islands."[25] His report was accepted, and considered of great importance by Washington officials. Schofield appeared before a committee of the House of Representatives in Washington in 1875 and urged them to act upon his proposals.

In Schofield's final report to Belknap, he also informed the Secretary that King Kamehameha V had died and was succeeded by King Lunalilo with "an almost unanimous vote of the people." Britain and France viewed the election of the new monarch with increasing concern because of the rise of American influence.

Shortly after King Lunalilo had received them so favorably, November 14, 1873, he placed an announcement Hawaiian Gazette that he believed his legislature would not approve a cession of Pearl River Harbor and therefore he withdrew his support of the plan. An editorial comment in that day's paper opined that a lease would be more acceptable than cession. Hawaii and America were moving, politically, towards a closer relationship. In each country there were enthusiastic proponents as well as opponents.

Lunalilo did not remain long as king. He died on February 3, 1874, having named no successor. Again the Hawaiian monarchy was subjected to a vote. In the turmoil, and due to the financial Panic of 1873 in the United States, and the subsequent depression, the work of Schofield was put on the back burner. The US Navy's meager budget was spent on projects in the eastern part of the United States and its coastline. Little, if anything, was done by the US Navy in Pearl Harbor.

Chapter 13 - An Election Surprise

The veneration of Hawaiian kings by their subjects grew in the 19th century. However, the reverence paid to the monarchy as an institution was very recent. No genuine monarchy existed before 1800. Chiefs and gods were the rulers of these islands and, while they were all powerful and invincible, they were tribal leaders not kings. The respect and fear that was always paid to the chiefs and ancient gods was transferred to the monarchy when the tribal system and the religion declined in the 19th century.

While the tenure of Lunalilo was short, 1873 to 1874, it was time enough for reciprocity to be brought up again.

Hawaiian Foreign Minister Charles Bishop was in favor of reciprocity and Henry Whitney, a member of the cabinet, presented him with a new idea for the treaty. He suggested that the Hawaiian government lease Pearl Harbor to the United States for fifty years in return for access to American sugar markets, duty free.[1] The idea had merit, the king decided, because it did not involve annexation. Such a lease would bring capital, wealth and resources to the islands at no expense to Hawaii. It was a powerful, compelling argument. The suggestion was supported by American military men who already recognized the value of the harbor. American politicians liked the idea because they were sure it would lead to cession of the whole area, maybe even all the islands.

In the midst of these discussions, there was a mutiny in the Royal Barracks in 1873.[2] The bone of contention was the strict and overbearing tactics of a Hungarian officer, Captain Josef Jajczay, who trained the household guards. Honolulu was in a state of alarm and apprehension for a week. Military discipline collapsed. An offer of clemency from the king to the mutineers was rejected. The mutineers took control and dictated to the king the conditions under which they would retire. In the end, no one was prosecuted, and the mutineers were discharged from service, as was the hated Hungarian who was the focus of all the disruption. But it was obvious that the government was vulnerable and unable to defend itself.

After the upheaval was over and the excitement died down, Hawaii turned its attention again to reciprocity and cession. In the face of obvious vulnerability of Hawaii, the king tried to decide what to do about Pearl Harbor.

Before he could make any decision, William Lunalilo died in January of 1874 after only one year on the job. He, too, left no heirs and that meant there would have to be an election in the legislature. Three candidates for the job emerged, David Kalakaua, Bernice Pauahi Bishop, and Emma, the widow of Kamehameha IV. It has been said that Kalakaua was partial to Americans. However, there is some doubt of his complete sincerity. A contemporary author referred to Kalakaua as a "special enemy of the United States" and added that he "enjoyed watching white men squirm", and often spoke against

Americans.[3] He was also considered thoroughly British in his sympathies, according to another author.[4] Such conflicting reports and his subsequent actions may not be very difficult to understand. He was fighting for his political life and may have been friendly to the United States when it was to his advantage, and antagonistic when it suited him. Emma was biased toward the British and Bernice Pauahi Bishop was partial to United States interests in Hawaii, perhaps because her husband was an American, though she didn't always agree with American actions. However, she reportedly had no desire to be a queen.[5] In fact, she turned down the throne when several prominent men came calling and asked her to accept it. She remained adamant even when the dying king asked her to be his successor. In any case, it left no one for the Americans to back in this election and so they stayed out of the political thicket. Hawaii was again plunged into a struggle between several *ali'i* who wanted to rule. While the population watched, candidates waged a vigorous campaign to obtain the throne.

Kalakaua really wanted the job. In a letter to her cousin Peter, Emma assessed Kalakaua's actions. Calling him Taffy, a nickname, she said that in spite of all his faults "we must give him credit for a great ambition". She remarked that he had worked both lawfully and unlawfully to secure "his coveted object, the Throne."[6] The focus finally turned to the new legislature, chosen by the all-male electorate, where the king was to be selected.

With no notion that she would become involved in Hawaiian elections, USS *Tuscarora*, on the 20th of January, left her dock in San Francisco and headed west on the mission of taking soundings across the Pacific to Hawaii. Her purpose was to determine the best route for a proposed submarine trans-Pacific telegraph cable. A few days into her mission, the crew was surprised to see the British gunboat HBMS *Tenedos* passing them at full steam, and with all sails pulling, toward Hawaii. *Tuscarora's* captain, Commander George E. Belknap, (no relation to the Secretary of the Navy), hastened to finish the day's work and then set sail for Honolulu, correctly recognizing the importance of his presence in that city.

After Belknap arrived at Honolulu Harbor on February 3, he learned that King Lunalilo had died. Several days later, the sloop-of-war USS *Portsmouth*, captained by Commander Joseph S. Skerrett, arrived and anchored abreast of Belknap's ship. They soon became aware of the impending election, which was the reason for the British gunboat's haste. If trouble erupted from this volatile situation, each captain felt his strength might be needed.

The natives of Honolulu were almost unanimously in favor of the Dowager Queen Emma, widow of Alexander, Liholiho (Kamehameha IV). However, her pro-British tendencies were known. American citizens living in Honolulu, most of whom were allied with the missionaries and merchants, strongly opposed Emma and supported David Kalakaua, whom they perceived as pro-American. In conference with the American Minister, H. M. Peirce, Captains Belknap and Skerrett were told that local police were not adequate to quell any disturbance that might occur if Emma did not emerge as the winner.

Such was a real possibility. Some legislators were opposed to Emma's candidacy. They enlisted the support of a wealthy, powerful local merchant, A.V. Cleghorn, who was married to Kalakaua's sister, Likelike. While the little royal steamer, *Kilauea*, circled the islands, bringing legislators to Honolulu for the election, Cleghorn and his followers were campaigning for Kalakaua. They were clever men and entertained the local legislators lavishly. One bizarre incident is said to have exerted critical influence on the election.

During the campaign, Cleghorn offered a new suit to each legislator, compliments of candidate Kalakaua. One legislator, Simon Kaai, was a staunch supporter of candidate Emma. While he was being fitted for his new suit, he dropped a sheaf of papers from his pocket, or perhaps it was removed by Cleghorn's clerk. Unfortunately for Kaai the papers contained the speech presenting Emma's case to the legislative body. When the elective meeting convened on the twelfth, the hapless Kaai spoke, but none of his carefully crafted words came to mind and he mumbled a lifeless endorsement of his candidate.

The plan among the American captains and Minister Peirce was to have an American merchantman, the bark *D.S. Murray*, stand by with a signal flag furled at her masthead, ready to unfurl if help were needed. The signal would indicate trouble and the Americans would go ashore to assist the Honolulu police. All day American sailors and Marines stood by with their weapons ready and their small boats drawn alongside the ship.

The election of the new monarch took place on February 12, 1874. A large crowd gathered outside the Hawaiian Courthouse in anticipation of the announcement of Emma's triumph. The members inside deliberated for over three hours. The crowd grew impatient and restless under the hot Hawaiian sun. When they finally heard the announcement, "Kalakaua is king," they were stunned. How could this have happened? They did not realize that many members of the legislature, who were Hawaiian or half Hawaiian, had voted for David Kalakaua.[7]

Shocked gasps gave way to silence, then to ominous muttering, then angry shouting. Finally some spark ignited them and they exploded into a full-fledged riot.

They stormed the courthouse and once inside, smashed up the furniture, broke windows, and tossed books and papers onto the floor. The captain of the *D.S. Murray* broke out his flag to inform the other American warships of the disturbance and within ten minutes 150 sailors and Marines marched ashore toward the courthouse. The bluejackets were led by ships' officers, with swords drawn. The Marines, with no commissioned officers aboard either vessel, were led by Orderly Sergeants Fredricks Mann and Theodore Hoff.

The Americans passed through the ominous, threatening crowd outside the courthouse, stationed a Gatling Gun squad on the steps and entered the building. Inside, sailors with their rifles and officers with their swords, flushed out most of the rioters. Those who elected to stand and defy the armed men were quickly dispersed by a line of US Marines with fixed bayonets moving relentlessly toward them.[8] Albert Taylor in his history of the United States Navy in Hawaii engaged in a bit of hyperbole over this incident, stating, "King Kalakaua practically owed his accession to the throne the following day to the glitter and power reflected from American bayonets."[9]

The British ship HBMS *Tenedos* had come to Honolulu to aid in the celebration of Emma's victory, but when news of the result of the election and the ensuing riot reached them, their crews hurried ashore to help the Americans mop up the remaining malcontents. Once the riot was quelled, American sailors laid their weapons aside, formed working parties and damage control groups and had the courthouse restored and ready for the formal meeting the following morning.[10]

The next day, February 13, 1874, at 11:30 am, King Kalakaua took his oath of office at the *Kinau Hale*, the chamberlain's residence.

Colonel C. P. Iaukea, chamberlain under King Kalakaua and later Queen Liliuokalani, remarked of the several foreign ships anchored in the harbor at Honolulu, "They were waiting, waiting for the apple to fall into somebody's lap."[11] The Americans did not wait idly.

The Hawaiian Minister of Foreign Affairs, following King Kalakaua's instructions, expressed the government's gratitude to the American naval personnel and their actions. He thanked,

> "..the forces which were landed from the United States ships Tuscarora and Portsmouth on the 12th instant, and which have rendered such invaluable services to his Majesty's government."[12]

Shortly after he ascended the throne, Kalakaua noted that the royal palace was filthy and poor and it humiliated him to have to live in it. He was not referring to the first 'royal palace' which had been occupied by Kamehameha I. That building had been built of thatch and native fronds. It was about 100 feet long and 60 feet wide, 40 feet high,[13] a true native building.

The building Kalakaua no longer wanted to live in had been built of native coral on treeless grounds on King Street in Honolulu and completed in 1845. Five kings had reigned from this building, but it was not called Iolani Palace, or Bird of Heaven, until 1863. By 1876, it was deemed no longer prudent to try to repair it. The legislature, sensing a new prosperity under the new reciprocity treaty, appropriated money a few years later. They felt that the Hawaiian nation needed a proper monarchical palace.

The new Iolani Palace was begun on King Street in place of the old in the late fall of 1874. An Australian architect was hired, on the assumption that he understood the Hawaiian climate better than an American would. It is built of brick and concrete block with a central tower that rises 76 feet. Its appointments and furnishings were luxurious and expensive and its builders could boast that it was right up to date as it was equipped with both a telephone and gas lights.[14]

Kalakaua accepted an invitation for a visit to the United States while the building was in progress. He was heartily in favor of the new reciprocity treaty and thought a visit on his part would bring the two countries closer together and ease the path of negotiations. The trip was a total success. He left Honolulu aboard USS *Benicia* on November 17, 1874. Under the command of Captain W. F. Hopkins, the trip was very smooth and pleasant. Kalakaua was an ingratiating man and quickly became friendly with the ships' officers and crew. He was a king - there was no question about that - but he also appealed to common people. His stature, jet-black curly hair, handsome features and courtly manner charmed all who met him. He landed at San Francisco as the first reigning monarch ever to step onto the shores of the United States. He won the hearts of the people there and proceeded by train across the continent to Washington where he met President Grant and visited congress.

He returned home aboard the North Pacific Squadron flagship, USS *Pensacola*, leaving San Francisco on February 2, 1875. The ship arrived at Honolulu after a rough passage, which he took in great spirits, on February 15. The people of Hawaii presented him with an expression of gratitude for American hospitality. The king later had it printed on white satin and sent to President Grant.

The value of his trip cannot be quantified, but it certainly produced successful results. The controversial treaty which had been discussed for so long was ratified after the usual amount of congressional wrangling. One of the strong arguments in favor of this reciprocity treaty was made by Minister Peirce, who stayed behind in Washington when Kalakaua returned to Hawaii. While addressing a Senate committee, Peirce passionately argued,

> "If reciprocity of commerce is established between the two countries, there cannot be a doubt that the effect will be to hold those islands with hooks of steel in the interests of the United States, and to result finally in their annexation."[15]

In a letter to the Secretary of the Navy a few years later, Rear Admiral T.C. Stevens, Commander in Chief of the Pacific Squadron, mentioned that during the king's absence on business, "Princess Lydia Dominis received my officers." She was Kalakaua's sister, later to become Queen Liliuokalani. Stevens expressed his concern that the Chinese in the Hawaiian Islands had grown to a population of disproportionate level. There were 15,000 Chinese and all other foreigners combined were only 8,000. He suggested the stationing of a man-of-war in Honolulu permanently.[16]

On March 18, 1875, the treaty passed the Senate by a vote of 51 to 12 and the House of Representatives by 115 to 101.'[17] The idea of ceding Pearl Harbor to the US seemed to be dead. But it wasn't.

The Reciprocity Treaty of 1876 was signed and ratified by Kalakaua, in spite of the fact that it restricted his sovereign right to lease parts of Pearl Harbor to others and to do as he pleased with the rest of it. It was palatable to both parties for the time being. It was not the last word on the subject, and it had no real affect on Pearl Harbor. Schofield's survey had been done by that time and recommendations had been communicated to the government, but no action had been taken by the Navy to remove the coral reef astride the opening. The treaty was re-negotiated in eight years and still the US did nothing.

The Reciprocity treaty went into affect on September 9, 1876. All the previous negotiations had resulted in one of the longest treaties in American history. It provided the basis for close economic and political ties between Hawaii and the US. It also opened the islands to American products and gave free entry into the US for Hawaiian rice as well as sugar. Later an extension was added and the US Navy was granted exclusive rights to use Pearl Harbor as a coaling station, repair base and anchorage. No naval personnel were stationed at Pearl Harbor, however, since it was not yet a Naval Station. The Navy did not begin sending Naval attaches to overseas stations until 1882.

An important concept had been re-introduced into the highest American political circles, i.e. annexation. It was not a part of this treaty, but the camel's nose was in the tent.

About this time, there was a general realization, both in the islands and on the mainland, that people were not visiting Hawaii just to conduct business anymore, but also to enjoy the air, the sea, the scenery and the people. The word 'tourist' was not yet used in the 1880s. A short time visitor was known as a vacationer, a traveler or a sightseer. These travelers arrived in Honolulu harbor on boats from the United States and England. There they boarded boats which took them to other islands. Trans-Pacific steamers and interisland schooners began to advertise trips to Maui and other islands, especially to the big island of Hawaii on which an active volcano rumbled. A number of guide books were published extolling the merits of all the islands.

Waikiki, with its coconut groves, incredibly beautiful beach, sparkling deep blue water and foaming green surf had for some time been the playground of the kings, the chiefs and the *ali'i*, and continued to be for a while longer. Their houses were scattered among coconut trees and tropical shrubs near the beach. Soon, they were joined by wealthy *haoles*, foreigners and resident businessmen who bought lots and built their own cottages. They found the area a calm, pleasant relief from the bustling city of Honolulu.

Hawaii soon was a favorite vacation destination of the rich and famous. A number of writers arrived to rest or write, hide in seclusion or make a name for themselves. It became popular, in a perverse way, for some intellectuals who arrived on Oahu to make disparaging remarks, base a novel or an essay on the area and then go to one of the other islands and relax.

Herman Melville, Robert Louis Stevenson, Somerset Maugham and Jack London all came, criticized the status of the Hawaiians, or grouched about the climate or commented most unfavorably on the inappropriate aspects of civilization that were now ruining the islands. Mark Twain arrived in Honolulu, loved it and wrote about what he saw. His descriptions of Hawaii and its people were sent in a series of twenty letters to the *Sacramento Record Union* and published once every month or so. For these "hilarious and vividly descriptive"[18] letters he was paid $20.00 per letter. He spent only four months in Hawaii, but in this short time Hawaii made a deep and lasting impression on him as he did on Hawaii. No travel writer or visitor had ever done so much for Hawaii, and its new, blooming tourist industry, on such a short stay.[19] It was when he returned to the US after his Hawaiian sojourn that he presented his first lecture, "Our Fellow Savages of the Sandwich Islands", and created interest in the islands as well as a new career and source of income for himself. His lecture was a smash hit.

Many other visitors were just as charmed by these lovely islands as Twain was. Isabella Bird was an Englishwoman on an around the world trip, when she stepped off the steamer *Nevada* from Australia in 1873 and into a whole new world, the antitheses of the Victorian England she knew.

"Everywhere only pleasant objects meet the eye. One can sit all day on the back verandah, watching the play of light and colour on the mountains and the deep blue green of the Nu'uanu Valley where showers, sunshine and rainbows make perpetual variety."[20]

During the years of political upheaval and uncertainty, most people in Hawaii were unaffected by it. Other than politicians, a man who lived outside Honolulu or on one of the other islands, might not even know the government was in such an uproar or that his life was on the brink of change.

Ordinary people worked, played, swam, took trips, went on tours and picnics, hiked and moved from job to job and house to house. They behaved just as they had for decades and as people still do in Hawaii today.

Kalakaua had postponed his coronation until the new Iolani Palace was finished and the statue of King Kamehameha was complete and in place. Finally in 1883, the coronation of King Kalakaua and his wife, Queen Kapiolani, was held, nine years after he became king. To enhance the coronation, a Grand Opening was held at the palace and the statue of King Kamehameha the Great, the man who had united the islands one hundred years before, was unveiled in the courtyard of the *Ali'iolani Hale*, the government Building across King Street from the palace. There was a coronation dinner and a coronation ball. Bands played, flags flew, and there were dances, food and games. Warships in the harbor saluted with their guns as did the several forts on the island. Rear Admiral George Balch reported to the Secretary of the Navy, W.E. Chandler that "USS *Lakawanna* and USS *Alaska* will attend king of the Hawaiian Islands Coronation on February 12, 1883".[21] The parades, regattas and picnics were for all the people and took place mainly on the grounds of Kalakaua's new palace. At this affair and others Kalakaua determinedly revived the hula and costumed dancers put on several performances.

Not so incidentally, the king and queen were crowned as part of this celebration with two new crowns studded with diamonds, rubies and emeralds. They cost ten thousand dollars each, a tremendous expense for that time. By this time, American coinage and paper money were the medium of exchange in Hawaii. There was an attempt around 1880 to create a Hawaiian coinage to inspire confidence in the government. A handsome silver dollar was minted that bore the likeness of King Kalakaua. It was in use for several years.[23]

The expense for this grand two week celebration was extreme and extravagant. Coming after the excess and the opulence shown in the construction of the palace, it was too much for many. While European residents criticized the government for using taxes for such extravagance, native Hawaiians defended it.[24] It may have been a celebration for the local Hawaiians, but it is difficult to see any Hawaiian culture in the affair, except for 'Dandy' Ioane and his hula dancers.[25] Everything else was based on European patterns. The entertainment was European and participants dressed in sumptuous European clothing. The beautiful crowns were of European design, and much of the finery had been ordered and made in England or France. Despite foreign influences, David Kalakaua was Hawaii's king. Ironically, for a man who loved life so much, his reign would be a troubled one.

Chapter 14 - 1887: A Bad Year for Kalakaua

David Kalakaua had been elected king by a majority of the Hawaiian legislators, but among the Hawaiian citizens there were many who would oppose government policies no matter who was king. In the midst of this unrest, amid the demands for reform, a secret group was created, called the Hawaiian League. Its purpose was to try to bring agreement or to bring down the elected government. The league included well known men like Sanford Dole, who was later president of the Republic, and wealthy businessman William Castle of Castle and Cooke, a prominent Hawaiian company. Their targets were the cabinet and the legislature not the king. The Hawaiian League was created to avoid government scandals and misadventures by taking control themselves. To that end, these men, prominent in politics, business and society in Hawaii, felt a show of force was necessary. They wanted to reform the government and limit the power of the king. Some, but not all, also wanted to keep him on the throne.

Since they wanted reform, not revolt, they drew up a list of five demands and on June 30, 1887, they went to the palace to present it to the king. Though they expected to have a reasonable conversation with him, they made sure they had several units of the Honolulu Rifles at their backs when they arrived. This show of force may have intimidated Kalakaua and it may be one reason the resulting document is called the 'Bayonet Constitution'.

One of the demands of the Hawaiian League was that Kalakaua dismiss his cabinet. Another demand was the right to name the next cabinet. They also handed the king a list of concessions he must make. Kalakaua was upset, but took the proposals under advisement. While he was considering, he called on representatives of the US, Great Britain, Portugal, Japan and France to see what they could do for him.[1] To stave off a revolt, he suggested to each in turn that he would place Hawaii under that country's protection. He probably did not say, but he did not care which one took him up on it. Everyone refused. Kalakaua gave in. Two members of the Reform Cabinet which subsequently took over the posts were Americans, the Attorney General and the Minister of the Interior. All the rest were British.[2]

One of the self-assigned goals of this new so-called Reform Cabinet was improvement of the earlier constitution. It had been created by reformers who were then in the government, but it was not to the liking of the new reformers. When they finished the new document, Kalakaua had to sign it, whether he liked it or not, or risk being removed from the throne altogether. It is no wonder Kalakaua opposed it, for it took away almost all his power. It was not deemed perfect by the reformers either, but they knew it was imperative that order and tranquility be restored in the halls of government at once.

"Article I. God hath endowed all men with certain inalienable rights, among which are life, liberty and the right of acquiring, possessing and protecting property, and of pursuing and obtaining safety and happiness."[3]

So begins the 1887 Constitution. There follow eighty-two articles spelling out the way the new government would operate. It was not an organized or very thoughtful document. Article 13 stated that the government is to be conducted for the common good and not for the profit, honor or the private interest of any one man, family or class of men. This was clearly against the idea of monarchy. It was also a slap at Kalakaua's profligate spending.

Then the constitution changed course and stated in Article 21 that the government of this kingdom is a constitutional monarchy under His Majesty Kalakaua, his heirs and successors. It names Liliuokalani, his sister, as next in line for the throne. Waffling again, the document then strips the king of the right to make any decisions without consent of the legislature. It did allow him to place the country under martial law in time of danger, to coin money and it stipulated that he could not be sued. It was obvious that the legislature and the Cabinet were to have the real power.

Though it is sometimes said that this constitution took away the right of Hawaiians to vote, the constitution did not use those terms and is much less specific than that. Every male resident of Hawaiian, European or American birth or descent over the age of twenty could vote. But there were other qualifications. A voter must read English, Hawaiian or a European language and must have resided in the islands for three years. The last requirement may have led to the idea that Hawaiians had been disenfranchised. It said that a voter must own property, a provision similar to one in the original US Constitution. Those Hawaiians who were descended from *ali'i* or chiefs owned property and could vote. The commoner, the Hawaiian laborer and those descended from early natives of the islands could not afford to own property and were, therefore, not eligible to vote.

In Article 73, the constitution declared in great detail who would not be permitted to vote. The list includes anyone who is insane or has committed any one of a number of crimes. It does not specifically include Orientals, they are mentioned nowhere in the document. But Orientals could not vote unless they could show evidence that they had been born in the islands.[4] It may have been noted in a local ordinance or spelled out in a separate law, as was the 1850 Chinese Exclusion Act in California.

The constitution was introduced to the citizens and signed reluctantly by King Kalakaua on July 6th 1887.

King Kalakaua has been called the 'Merry Monarch' and he truly did love a party. He spent more money on celebrations than all his predecessors combined. His coronation was extravagant, his other celebrations were even more lavish and expensive. He staged jubilees, birthdays and dances with great regularity. He loved the sea and had his own personal boathouse built near Honolulu Harbor. It was almost a complete house, with bed, kitchen and living rooms a refuge from his duties. And he wanted a Navy of his own.

He was frustrated by his inability to rule as an absolute monarch. Because of the restrictions on his actions, he couldn't always get what he wanted. Still, he could sometimes get others to get it for him. Early in January, 1887, Walter Gibson, Kalakaua's head of government, convinced the king to approve the purchase of an old British schooner, *Explorer*. She was a merchant ship, used at the time as a guano transport. Perhaps in light of the subsequent events, that was prophetic.

The schooner, 128 feet long with three masts, copper sheathed hull and a forty horsepower coal burning engine was purchased for $20,000. She was re-christened *Kaimiloa*, Hawaiian for explorer, and armed with two Gatling Guns and four 6-pound cannon. As soon as she was refitted, this 'navy' was to be sent south and effect a union between Hawaii and Samoa, 2600 miles away, as well as other Polynesian islands.[5] Kalakaua's intention was to establish Hawaiian primacy in the Pacific as well as his own, but his timing could not have been more unfortunate.

Foreign nations were wary and watched the operation closely, especially Germany which was actively involved in the southern Pacific Ocean. The British also took a dim view of this activity. The Foreign Office sent a note to the British Commissioner in Honolulu instructing him to request the "Hawaiian government not to interfere in the political affairs and status of Samoa".[6]

Hawaiian newspapers were merciless in their sarcasm and disdain of the project, though not on political grounds. "If this steamer gets very far from home, another vessel will be required as a tender to carry coal,"[7] The basis for this remark was the fact that *Kaimiloa* could make good only five knots while burning about five tons of coal per day. Fitting out was estimated by Gibson to be only $14,000 beyond the purchase price. The reporter opined that costs were nearer $50,000. The Gazette reporter stated that this is not the time to saddle the country with "a toy ship for which she has as much need as a cow for a diamond necklace".[8]

In May of 1887 *Kaimiloa* was ready to sail for Samoa. The United States, Great Britain and Germany were all watching the progress with attitudes which ranged from concern to amusement. Gibson attempted to assure the three world powers that, although *Kaimiloa* was armed, she would not be allowed to wage war.[9] A retired British Lieutenant, George Jackson, was selected to command the ship and the crew was made up of 67 young men, 24 of whom were from the Honolulu Reformatory School. Twenty of these 'sea nen' were in the school band. After a series of gala parties and concerts, the ship sailed from Honolulu on the morning of May 18, 1887. A ship in the harbor fired a salute, but the unfortunate crew of *Kaimiloa* could not return it as they were frantically busy trying to drop the anchor to avoid ramming the saluting ship.

Kaimiloa reached Samoa on June 15 and, as she neared the anchorage, she was requested to identify herself by a German gunboat, *Adler*. For some reason *Kaimiloa* did not respond until the gun crew of *Adler* fired a shot across her bow. An observer on shore, Robert Louis Stevenson, wrote, "The *Kaimiloa* was from the first a scene of disaster and dilapidation".[10] The ship was allowed to land, eventually, in Apia harbor.

After the obligatory diplomatic visits, the band proceeded to entertain ships and crews in the harbor with a number of concerts. With Captain Jackson often ill, the rest of the crew took to the streets of Apia and generally made nuisances of themselves. They spread their form of 'happiness' to several other islands as well when their ship visited other ports. When word of this behavior reached Gibson in Honolulu, he was furious. He immediately sent a letter to the Hawaiian Ambassador to Samoa requesting his instant resignation.

Unknown to *Kaimiloa's* captain and crew, a revolution took place back home in Hawaii shortly after they arrived in Samoa, on June 30th, 1887. The Reform Cabinet and the new constitution reduced King Kalakaua's personal power and Gibson was forced to resign. Unaware that their patron, and sponsor of their voyage, had been removed from office, the crew of the *Kaimiloa* carried on as usual.

Second in command of *Kaimiloa* was Boatswain James Hilbus. When he discovered that Captain Jackson had taken ammunition, rifles, and the ship's silver service to sell for liquor, "he sent two Marines ashore to keep an eye on Jackson".[11]

With some of the crew missing, the ship sailed from Pago Pago for home in August 23, 1887. Then things took a serious turn.

The Germans, who had viewed the Hawaiian ship with suspicion ever since its arrival, declared war on a Samoan tribe which had befriended the crew of *Kaimiloa*. Prime Minister Otto Von Bismarck in Berlin, is reported to have warned, "in case Hawaii... should try to interfere in favor of Malietoa [the Samoan Chief], the king of the Sandwich Islands would thereby enter a state of war with us."[12] The German leader added, off the record, that "King Kalakaua could be told that, unless he desisted from his insolent intrigues in Samoa, we should shoot his legs in two, despite American protection."[13]

Of course, Kalakaua had no intention of confronting the Germans, nor did he have any idea of the irritating and dangerous activities of his 'navy' in Samoa. The ship was ordered home.

Kaimiloa reached Honolulu on September 23, 1887, her mission a failure. The government took no disciplinary action against the Captain or the crew, for they did not want to make a public scene and wanted to forget the entire incident as quickly as possible. The ship was immediately decommissioned and served for a short time as a quarantine barge. The Hawaiian Navy was *pau*, ended. Its inglorious tenure had been about six months. This adventure added fuel to whispers about the incompetence of Kalakaua, clearly demonstrating his extravagant, bungling and ineptitude. Kalakaua's 'navy' was first relegated to the boneyard of discarded ships in Honolulu Harbor. In 1912, she was towed out to sea, beached on Pu'uloa Flats, just outside Pearl Harbor, and burned. Later her metal parts were retrieved and sold for junk.[14]

1887 was clearly not a good year for Kalakaua.

The same year that the constitution was signed, 1887, the Reciprocity Treaty was back in the limelight. Having been valid for only seven years, it had expired in 1883 and had been renewed without discussion every year since because no one in the Hawaiian government, the cabinet, the legislature or the king, was ready to discuss it. Their attention was elsewhere as their own leadership was in disarray. Businessmen dictated to the king and a number of factions had arisen rigidly opposed to each other.

Still, discussing a treaty that was advantageous to Hawaii had it merits and was a distraction from the infighting in the halls of Hawaiian government. To make sure that the treaty was palatable to the US, the Hawaiian government offered exclusive right to use Pearl Harbor as a coaling and repair station for US Navy vessels. This was not a new idea, of course. It had been suggested and discussed. General Schofield had surveyed the area fifteen years before and reported on its feasibility. A small US coaling station had been operating in Honolulu since 1842.

During months of discussion, the British made their views known in a note they delivered to the Secretary of State in Washington. They didn't like the idea of the US in Pearl Harbor at all and cited a Franco-English compact in 1843 in which they both agreed never to take possession of the Hawaiian Islands. Then they suggested that the United States should join them in this compact and guarantee the neutrality and accessibility of Hawaiian harbors to all ships of all nations.[15]

It was to no avail. Kalakaua signed the treaty with the US in October of 1887, though he hated the price he had to pay for it.[16] He proclaimed to his people in November of 1887,

> "His majesty grants to the United States the exclusive right to enter the harbor of Pearl River and establish a coaling and repair station for the use of vessels of the United States. And to that end, the US may improve the entrance to said harbor and do a the other things needful to the purpose aforesaid"[17]

Liliuokalani, the sister of Kalakaua and soon to be Queen, was sure that the lease of Pearl Harbor to the US was a mistake. Many legislators in the US Congress did not support the idea either, because it had no clear advantage for the US. If the treaty was rejected, they thought, all the better because that might make annexation more attractive to the Hawaiians.

One cloud remained over Pearl Harbor and that was the British interest in it. The government in London was sure that the use of the harbor granted to the United States was temporary. At least that is what they wanted to believe. The British Admiralty then informed the Foreign Office that the harbor of Honolulu would be unusable by her majesty's ships. Disclaiming, in part, their previous interest, they let it be known that the fact that the Americans would now have exclusive use of Pearl Harbor, "will not prejudicially affect British Naval interests."[18]

Most people in Britain were unconcerned over increased US interest in the Pacific Ocean, but others were sure the US was trying to control Samoa and Tonga as well as the Hawaiian Islands. The actions by King Kalakaua reinforced that notion.

Referring to the United States, one English writer noted that "They seem to interpret the Monroe Doctrine as though the Pacific Ocean were an American lake". Another was unconcerned. "Hawaii is of no interest to England"[19] he said. Many in Britain disapproved of the idea that the United States might acquire Hawaii. They said the US had no right to annex a place that was so far from her own contiguous territory.[20] This comment from a nation which boasted that it ruled an empire upon which the sun never set. There was no international law to control actions of nations and nothing short of armed conflict could prevent the US from taking any territory it wanted. No powerful European nation in the latter part of the 19th century, especially Great Britain, would allow such curbs on its sovereignty. Some of the British seemed to feel that they were the only ones with the right to take over the world.

Still, the US Congress decided that this was the time to play hard ball. For the economic concessions that would be granted to Hawaii by the treaty, the US had now decided it needed a Naval Base in Hawaii and required the exclusive use of Pearl Harbor. A Naval Base is a more complex, permanent facility than simply a coaling station or repair base. It was more than Kalakaua and the Hawaiian government were ready to allow. It is possible that the US was using this demand as a bargaining chip to gain its own ends. Diplomacy often works that way. There was no consensus in the United States concerning the value of this treaty. In fact, strong opinions had surfaced both for and against it, accompanied by ambivalent feelings on ethical and political grounds.

However, now that the Germans were expanding in the Pacific, and being belligerent about it, some members of Congress became nervous. Pearl

Harbor and its possible uses played a central role in treaty negotiations and the word cession came up often. To cede a piece of land is to give up the right to it. Americans had used the tactic before and understood the concept, but it is not clear that Hawaiians did. Ever since Kamehameha 'ceded' the island of Hawaii to the British in 1794, the word had been used casually by Hawaiian kings as an umbrella that would grant them protection. They did not seem to understand that they would give up ownership of the land, too. Fortunately for the Hawaiians, Europeans had not attempted to enforce previous cessions nor had Americans.

The Reciprocity Treaty of 1887 was a compromise between US demands and Hawaiian wishes. The king requested an amendment which stated that Hawaiian jurisdiction and sovereignty over the entire territory would remain. The Hawaiian government requested that they would not be required to cede any more land for military bases. The US insisted that the Hawaiian Government not grant to any other nation the right to use Pearl Harbor at the same time.[21]

The agreement was satisfactory to both parties and was signed by representatives from Hawaii and the United States in November of 1887. It would remain in force until 1894 when it would either be renewed or renegotiated.

In spite of the green light in the use of Pearl Harbor, the US Navy had no immediate plans for it and no available money to allot to it. Nothing was done to ready it for use. In fact, work did not begin on the task of removing the reef at the entrance until the end of the century. In 1898, war between the US and Spain would draw attention to the Pacific Ocean. Until then, all during the 1880s and 1890s, the harbor remained quiescent, used only by visitors and natives, as it had been for centuries.

Chapter 15 - Ruthless Politics

In 1888 Mr. B.F. Dillingham took a number of friends and a group of employees on an excursion to the Pearl River. He reports that the guests assembled at the dock in Honolulu Harbor at seven o'clock on a beautiful, summer morning and boarded *Ewa*, a small shallow-draft steamer. With a scream of its whistle the boat left the dock and crossed the still glassy water The excursionists lined the rail, and watching dawn touch the jagged green hills to the east, they sang *Aloha Oe*, a hauntingly beautiful song composed by Liliuokalani, sister of King Kalakaua. They were in a festive mood. Looking down they saw the churning wake as the boat plowed through the shallow green water of the harbor. Looking up, they saw the little city of Honolulu framed by the towering Ko'olau mountains. As the sun rose above the crests, their dark silhouette became a rich, verdant green. The shallow water of the Harbor gave way to the deep blue of the sea as they moved offshore. Adventure awaited them.

At ten a.m. they crossed the bar, a large reef across the opening, and entered the Pearl River. Immediately, they were in a different world. They had left the dusty, noisy town of Honolulu, crossed a short stretch of open ocean outside the surf line and now their little boat chugged into the quiet, lush greenery of the Pearl River inlet. On one side of the channel, they passed a large house which apparently belonged to someone important. On the other side of the channel were the salt works. Several houses stood in a coconut grove and a mile or so on, they saw a banana plantation. As they approached Dr. Ford's Island, low and flat, they could see it was densely covered with grass and trees.

The steamer anchored and the passengers disembarked in a small boat and were taken to the island. There they had a picnic lunch and then hiked, or explored in small groups. They spent the afternoon gathering shells and visiting the sugar mill or the coconut plantation. Guitars were broken out and they proceeded to while away the afternoon singing, dancing and playing games until time to go home around four in the afternoon.[1]

This event is obviously not significant in the history of Pearl Harbor, but it gives a picture of the area in the latter part of the 19th century. It also shows how people used it and felt about it. This was the area the US Navy would later occupy and change so radically.

People lived on the land near Pearl Harbor at that time. One woman was just a child when the family moved to a house on the peninsula between East and Middle Lochs, today called the Pearl City Peninsula. Her family was well off and quite comfortable and were moving from Waikiki where they had lived next to the Sans Souci Boarding House while Robert Louis

Stevenson was staying there. They a had Chinese cook as well as a Japanese maid, a yard man, and a carriage complete with driver and several horses.

When she and her family desired to go to Honolulu, they rode a carriage to the northern edge of Pearl River lagoon, then went by the Oahu Railway which stopped at a station called Pearl City. Not much else was there at the time. She remembers the Hawaiian name for Pearl Harbor was *Waimomi* and that Ford's Island looked like a lizard basking in the sun. Coconut trees lined the white coral roadway and their house faced the peacock blue water. She and her six siblings swam and fished every day and she remembers the day Jack London and his crew brought his beloved sailing craft *Snark* into their dock.[2] This description shows that there was life outside the realm of politics and intrigue.

The Oahu Railway was built in 1889 and extended from Honolulu to the northern reaches of Pearl Harbor and eventually all the way around to the western settlement at Pu'uloa. It took people to areas where they could fish, sail boats in the calm water, swim, and have picnics.[3] As early as the summer of 1890, the Oahu Railway and Land Company advertised trips to the Pearl River or the "Inland Sea".[4] Some of this area was unknown even to people who lived nearby and the Oahu Railway was the first public transportation that could take them to see it. Until then there had been neither trails nor roads. Sailors visiting from ships in the harbor soon discovered the Oahu Railway and were frequent passengers on the little local line that eventually ringed Pearl Harbor.

Life was not all calm water and picnics here. Alice Baily Cooper, the author of these recollections, also remembers the fear, pain and devastation caused by the plague that hit the Chinatown section of Honolulu at the turn of the century and the subsequent fire that burned out of control for days.[5]

This period was a calm before a series of storms and dire changes that were on the way for Hawaii. King Kalakaua had little power remaining and there were opposing factions in the government based on reform, race and cold hard business. At this time, a group of Hawaiians, made up of *haoles* and *hapa-haoles* (a term that was often used for half-Hawaiians), created the Liberal Patriotic Association.[6] Their object was to remove the Reform Party Cabinet and restore Kalakaua's powers, by force if necessary. In July 1889 eighty men, commanded by a *hapa-haole* royalist named Robert Wilcox, marched to the palace and took control of the grounds and other government buildings. This was done without authorization from Kalakaua and when rebels invited Kalakaua to return to the palace, he decided to keep out of it, retiring to his boat house. Government troops tumbled from their beds carrying their rifles and dressing as they ran to quell the revolt.[7] Surrounding the rebels, who by then were holed up on the palace grounds, they began firing

The two groups traded fire sporadically all day. Kalakaua sent a messenger to appeal to the American Minister for help.

Unlike the self-contained, relatively bloodless revolution of 1887, this action was deemed to threaten the interests of local American citizens. The American Minister contacted Commander Edwin T. Woodward, captain of USS *Adams*, at anchor in Honolulu Harbor who sent four boatloads of Marines under the command of Lieutenant Charles A. Doven. They landed on July 30, 1889, quickly made their presence known and watched the 'revolution' evaporate. The next day, the palace guard and a few Hawaiian troops mopped up the revolutionaries and the marines returned to their ship. They had acted in this revolt as a 'force multiplier'. Whether it could be called an armed riot or a pathetic revolution, it was harmless. However, it did indicate weakness in the government and discontent among the citizens of the city. There are reports, some confirmed, some merely rumors, that there was collusion between rebels and members of the government. The important facet of this incident is that it showed the Reform Cabinet did not have as strong a hold on the government as it thought. Kalakaua was still king, albeit with very little power. Many waited for the next shoe to drop.

A more pleasant report can be made of an event in the next year, 1890. The US Navy tug USS *Iroquois* was fitted out as a hospital ship for U.S. sailors anchored in Honolulu Harbor and in the adjacent roadstead. Her activities also took her back and forth between Honolulu Harbor and the Pearl River. Hence, she was the first U.S. Navy ship to enter Pearl Harbor.

The Reform Party continued to fall into disfavor with the voting population and, after the bitter election in 1890, was voted out of office. The new group of legislators was determined to restructure the constitution yet again. During the attendant acrimony, Kalakaua became ill. He decided to go to the west coast of America to seek modern medical assistance. The United States Navy was again ready to serve the legal government. The flagship of the US North Pacific Squadron, USS *Charleston*, was put at the disposal of the king to take him to the mainland. Before he left, the ailing king named his sister Princess Lydia Dominis (better known by the lovely, fluid name of Liliuokalani) as regent. He had tried to create a Regency Committee to help her during his 1881 trip, but was unsuccessful. This time he named her sole regent.[8]

Liliuokalani's description of Kalakaua's departure from the harbor is poignant. She wrote, "Crowds witnessed his departure.... the vessels saluted the out-going ship, a royal salute was fired, and he was gone".[9] Prophetic words indeed. Kalakaua did not return alive.

King David Kalakaua, the 'Merry Monarch', suffered a stroke while in San Francisco, California on January 20, 1890. His sister and regent, Liliuokalani, would be Queen. This lovely, immensely talented, imperious, remarkable woman was about to endure an incredible sequence of events. They would include the end of the Hawaiian monarchy.

At this time 6,000 miles away, off the east coast of the United States, the Navy was experimenting with a new concept. If a small boat were swift enough, it might be able to approach a large ship, fire a torpedo, and escape without suffering damage. Such a boat successfully passed her sea trials. First *Stiletto* and then *Cushing* were capable of speeds of 22 knots. They were able to fire the new self-propelled Howell torpedoes at a safe distance.[10] The introduction of this new technique in 1890 mandated a change in currently accepted tactics. It would be, of course, a long time before such developments reached the Pacific Station. With the impetus of the newly formed Naval War College, Congress enacted legislation on August 5, 1882 stipulating that no more money should be spent on old wooden vessels. This act also provided for the appointment of a Naval Advisory Board. That same period saw the addition of a frightening new weapon to the arsenal of the Marine Corps. The Maxim gun was able to fire over 700 rounds per minute. This was twice the rate of fire of its predecessors, the Gatling gun and the Hotchkiss gun, which were brought ashore, but not used, by the Marines during the 1890 'rebellion'.[11]

In the minds of Americans, both in the islands and on the mainland, there was growing conviction that Hawaii must become part of the US. This isolated island group was too small, too vulnerable, and much too strategically located to go its own way any longer. It was feared that one of the powerful nations would soon move to assume control of Hawaii. Many Americans, especially in the military community, were adamant in their belief that, "It had better be us!" The circumstances that eventually changed the status of Hawaii and brought it under the protection of the US through annexation were neither smooth nor easy. Nor were they entirely commendable on the part of the participants on either side.

Upon hearing of the death of her brother Kalakaua, Queen Liliuokalani was informed by the cabinet that she must take the oath of office immediately. She declined and asked why she could not wait until after her brother's funeral.[12] Her advisors, who included her husband John Dominis, assured her that her immediate compliance was necessary. Finally she gave in, and later wrote,

> "Few persons have ever been placed without a word
> of warning in so trying a situation and I doubt if there was
> any other woman in the city who could have borne with
> passive equanimity what I had to endure that day".[13]

The emotional shock upon learning of the death of her brother was burden enough, but she now had to adjust to a new situation. She was to be led around, told where to go and when, told what to do and how, and given to understand that she had no influential voice in the actions of the government. Several times she writes in her memoirs of how she had been stripped of the "indisputable prerogative of the Hawaiian monarchy".[14] Often she referred to the rights of her monarchical ancestors, even though the monarchy had only been in effect for a few decades. Nevertheless, Liliuokalani had been born and bred *ali'i* and the actions of the new cabinet must have been a rude shock to her.

The Hawaii legislature continued to hold meetings as they tried to relieve the economic depression. The Queen was astonished to discover that though she was on the throne, her authority was challenged at every turn. In 1892, during the longest legislative session in Hawaiian history, numerous schemes were suggested to raise funds.[15] The controversial nature of some of these, the lottery and the licensing of opium, caused furious debates and heated discussions. The stormiest battles, however, concerned the makeup of the cabinet and this may have been the final straw that led to the deposition of the Queen. There were four different cabinets in a few months. The Queen would appoint a man to a post, the legislature would dismiss him for lack of confidence, and the Queen would swiftly appoint another man. Little progress was being made as the legislature and the Queen jockeyed for power.

Rumors flew around the government building, then leaked out and raced through the city and environs of Honolulu. They implied breathlessly that a coup d'etat was looming and the Queen would soon be deposed, or that the Queen was about to take control and throw the legislature out, or that the United States was about to intervene. Most of these things did not happen.

Finally the Queen appointed to the cabinet a number of men who were respected members of the community. Some of them were members of the Reform Party. These men were acceptable to the legislators as well. By November of 1892, the cabinet crisis had abated.

The trouble with appointing moderates to cabinet posts is that one can never be sure they will vote as the appointor intended. Liliuokalani began to doubt her conciliatory action as these men were not royalists and would not do her bidding. Rumors of clashes spilled out of the Government house again.

She decided to dismiss the entire cabinet. When she announced her decision, they ignored it. The matter moved to the Hawaiian Supreme Court and was decided in her favor. She then appointed yet another new cabinet composed of men whom she felt she could trust. Many like Samuel Parker, owner of the huge Parker Cattle Ranch on the big island of Hawaii, were part Hawaiian or married to Hawaiians. The rest were long term residents and businessmen. None of them were connected in any way to the hated missionary faction who were often called the "Missionary Boys". Uneasy calm reigned.

Liliuokalani was a conscientious Christian, attending church regularly. Still, like many Hawaiians then and now, she blamed most of the ills that plagued the islands on the missionaries and their avaricious descendants. She was not entirely wrong for they did throw out, belittle or disparage a great deal of Hawaiian culture. Unfortunately for her, she also believed that she was the sole and absolute ruler of Hawaii under the Constitution of 1887, though a careful reading of that document would show that it was not so. She believed the cabinet and the legislature were there to do her bidding. Her interpretation of the constitution was ill informed. The leaders of the government, even though they were her friends, understood its provisions in a very different way.

Liliuokalani had the imperious attitude that queens and kings often display. She believed in the divine, God-given right of kings to govern their subjects and was convinced that the only way to rule was as an absolute monarch.[16] Her people had always had kings, in her opinion, and no one had the right to overrule her actions, which were always correct, according to her memoirs. She repeatedly said that she always acted for the good of her people. Yet, on a tour of the big island, when she and the rest of the royal party rode in a carriage of native construction, she noted without comment that it was pulled by people instead of horses.[17] She expected, and was unfazed, by the use of human power for her convenience.

An occasional sympathy toward Americans is displayed in her book. When President James Garfield was assassinated, Liliuokalani reports how her brother, King Kalakaua, ordered the local stores draped in mourning and meetings were held to express sympathy for the family and for the country's loss of its President, "which we share with the American people".[18]

Her reign lasted for five years and, like the tenure of her brother, did not go smoothly. Her own actions did not help at all. Opposition factions formed; parties fell apart, and then formed and reformed. And during this period, the sugar industry was in trouble. The shortage of labor was a problem and the government was not capable of dealing effectively with this or several other challenges. During this time there was talk of annexation again. It had come up before, often when one of the kings was afraid a foreign power was about to take over Hawaii. Then he was ready to cede the islands to the United States or request annexation to protect them.

Some men, in and out of the government, thought Liliuokalani was a dangerous woman who was undermining the progress Hawaii had made toward becoming a democratic state. She knew what Hawaii needed was restoration of the monarchy to full control and a firm hand at the wheel.[19] The difference of opinion was beyond her control and her actions were disastrous for the monarchy.

Both Kalakaua and Liliuokalani have been charged with being corrupt, inefficient, and unreliable by contemporary writers.[20] The charges may be valid, but there are extenuating circumstances. It was unrealistic to expect Hawaiian kings to know how to rule legally and ethically following European patterns only one hundred years after having been shocked out of their isolation by Captain Cook. Also the devotion of Hawaiian kings to the outward trappings of European royalty convinced sovereigns, nations, and Hawaiians themselves, that these kings knew the rules and understood the diplomatic, political and legal tricks that had been practiced by royalty in Europe for centuries. Their actions show they did not.

No one involved in events of the next few years is without blame or entirely admirable. Most participants acted in their own self-interest at best and some engaged in acts that can be called collusion, greed or even treason. Trouble awaited everyone.

Chapter 16 - Monarchy is Pau

When Liliuokalani declared her intent to create and announce a new constitution to her people, she was in trouble. Her intent was to rule as an absolute monarch and restore the "ancient rights of my people".[1] In her opinion, Hawaiian sovereigns had the right to make constitutions and had always had that right. The fact is they had done so for only sixty years. The idea that a leader could simply create and declare a constitution is not consistent with the basic purpose of this kind of document. The philosophy of constitutions was created in Europe in the 18th century. The first true, working constitution had been created for the United States only a hundred years before, at about the same time Kamehameha the Great created the kingdom of Hawaii. Absolute rulers, emperors and dictators as well as kings, do not understand the purpose or the logical concept that underlies a constitution. Americans, like those men of the missionary party, had grown up under the rules and the philosophy of the world's first written constitution. The Hawaiians had not.

The confusion and chaos in the Hawaiian government extended to the mainland and caused talk of US annexation of Hawaii to rise again. Anti-annexationists saw little need for such a drastic move because the US had already been granted the use of Pearl Harbor by the Reciprocity Treaty of 1887. Why did they need these islands? The argument that every treaty is voidable made little impression on the men who held this view. Contentious debates ensued in both houses of the US Congress over annexation of the islands, though reportedly two thirds of the senators were in favor of it.[2]

Another voice, and a very influential one, added fuel to the pro-annexation arguments. Navy Captain Alfred T. Mahan wrote two major books, published in 1890 and 1892, examining the influence of sea power on history. At the time Mahan was a lecturer at the Naval War College in Newport, Rhode Island. Later, in 1886, he became its president. He argued that a nation can only be great if it can maintain a navy powerful enough to control the seas that adjoin it. He advocated the use of the battleship as the central feature of the navy and, in a number of reports to Congress, he suggested that the United States should assume control over the Hawaiian Islands to protect them from China.[3] Because he praised the British Navy, his books took England by storm. Even the German Kaiser, Wilhelm II ordered a copy for every German ship. Because of America's expansionist atmosphere at the time, his books also did well in the United States.

He wrote many articles and books and an often recurring theme was that it would be bad for the United States if a foreign power were to gain control of these islands.[4] Mahan wrote to Theodore Roosevelt, before he became President, and urged his support for the annexation of Hawaii. Roosevelt, in a confidential reply said that he agreed with Mahan. "If I had my way, I would annex these islands tomorrow and build a Nicaraguan Canal at once."[5]

Some say the Hawaiian Islands were already an economic colony of the United States and had been since passage of the Reciprocity Treaty of 1875.[6] Many in the US resisted the idea of taking over a sovereign country with no diplomatic excuse.

At the same time this was being debated, the monarchy of Hawaii was in sore trouble and had reached its lowest level with fewer and fewer supporters. There were members of the cabinet who were convinced that Queen Liliuokalani was planning to take the government into her own hands.

In fact she was. A ceremony was planned by her supporters for January 14, 1893, with her full knowledge. At the Iolani Palace, she would introduce her new constitution to her subjects. One of its major features was that only true Hawaiians would be eligible to vote. She intended to read it to her assembled nobles first and then from a balcony at the Iolani declare it to the assembled multitude. When members of the cabinet heard of her plan, they convinced her to postpone the announcement. She appeared on the balcony anyway, but promised only that she would present them with a new constitution soon. At least that is what *haoles* in and out of the government thought she said. Her speech was given in the Hawaiian language, so members of the cabinet could not be certain of what she said or what she meant. Their apprehension became intense. They believed they had to act immediately.

On January 16, 1893, leading men in the current government, all of them pro-annexationists, formed a Committee of Safety, also known as the Committee of Public Safety. It was composed of five Hawaiians, five Americans, one Englishman and one German.[7] Its aims were to depose the Queen and convince the United States to annex Hawaii. The queen could not understand why they felt she was unfit to rule.

The monarchy was to be replaced at first by a Provisional Government which would firmly establish law and order in the beginning. The men who perpetrated this overthrow might well have failed if they had not had whole hearted support of the current United States Minister to Hawaii, John L. Stevens. He promised to supply troops to protect American interests and to recognize the new government immediately.[8]

At this point, the United States became interested in the fate of Hawaii again. Many in congress felt that annexation was the only way to settle the problem of Hawaii. They would also gain a valuable military location and protect US economic interests all in one stroke. They listened to prominent men from Hawaii, such as Lorin Thurston, explaining that in the current atmosphere good government was impossible in Hawaii.[9]

John L. Stevens, the US Minister to Hawaii, was strongly proannexation and believed that the only remedy for Hawaii's troubles was permanent association with the United States. He had come to the islands in 1889 and shortly thereafter began to work actively for annexation. The State Department supported that view for a time, but could not do so officially.[10] Stevens thought that if Hawaii did not become a part of the United States, it would be quickly taken over by the Japanese.

In response to the establishing of a Provisional Government, Liliuokalani issued a proclamation saying, without admitting that her former vow to create a new constitution was ill advised, that any changes to the constitution should be made by methods provided by the constitution. The public disclaimer was too late.

Mass meetings were scheduled on January 16th, 1893 by both royalists and annexationists. It was a potentially explosive situation and it was at this point that Stevens asked for troops from USS *Boston* to enter the city to maintain order. 162 sailors and marines arrived around five p.m. to patrol the grounds around the government buildings. Speeches were made in both gatherings, but no riots followed. The troops spent the night in Ali'iolani Hale. The Committee of Public Safety took over all the government buildings declaring that responsible government was impossible under the monarchy. They deposed the Queen, ousted her ministers and established the Provisional Government, with the stipulation that it would remain in force until a union with the United States could be arranged.

The next day Sanford Dole accepted the post of President of the Provisional Government. Dole was born in Honolulu in 1844, the son of missionaries who ran the Punahou School. He was respected by Hawaiians, including many of the natives, as well as by *haoles*. Sailors and marines surrounded the government buildings and the new attorney general declared martial law. By 5 p.m. on the 17th of January, 1893, the Provisional Government was in power as the government of Hawaii.

Liliuokalani yielded to the superior force of the United States and retired to her Washington Place home. She did not give up, however. She stated, "I am still constitutional sovereign of the Hawaiian Islands."[11] By midnight of the same day, the 17th of January, all foreign diplomats had recognized the new government. Although they were not happy that the proannexationists were in power, they applauded the stability the new government would bring. The next morning the Royal Household Guards were assembled, paid off and mustered out of service.

The Provisional Government immediately, and optimistically, chose a delegation to negotiate a treaty for annexation with the United States. These five men took their case to Washington, but the newly elected president, Grover Cleveland, refused to meet with them. The Queen sent a group of envoys, too, but they were delayed. Instead of listening to either group, Cleveland appointed James H. Blount as special commissioner to investigate and report back to him. He wanted to know the cause of the revolution that had deposed the Queen and formed the Provisional Government. He also wanted to know what Stevens' role in all this was and he wanted to know what Hawaiian citizens thought of the Provisional Government.

At the same time, because of his unauthorized actions in support of the pro-annexationists, John L. Stevens was removed as US Minister to Hawaii and the Secretary of State appointed Albert S. Willis to replace him. Stevens left the islands on May 24.

Blount arrived in Honolulu on March 29, 1893 with his wife and a secretary. The first thing he did was restore the Hawaiian flag atop the government building and then he sent American troops back to their ship. Hawaiians were overjoyed as they thought he was about to restore their Queen. He wasn't, but he probably would have if he had possessed the power. He had told no one what his instructions were and gave no indication of what he had learned in his investigation. Liliuokalani wrote of Blount later that he was fair, impartial, courageous and absolutely right in declaring that she was the rightful ruler of Hawaii.[12]

After about four months in Hawaii, Blount departed on August 9, 1893, still revealing nothing of his findings or conclusions. He could have remained as minister to Hawaii, but refused, leaving before the new minister, Willis, had arrived.

In his final summation to Secretary of State Gresham, Blount defended the Queen and advocated restoring her to the throne of Hawaii. He does not give his reasons for this, but he has been judged by several modern writers. One is particularly pungent and very precise.

"Blount slanted his report and the interviews contained in it. He allowed only testimony that built a case for restoring the queen to power. He failed to interview any of the members of the Committee of Public Safety to get their views nor did he interview any of the officers from the *Boston*. Blount made a case against Stevens, citing his desire to see Hawaii annexed and his over eager recognition of Provisional Government. Finally, he failed to mention the declining nature of the monarchy and the fact that it had existed only because the great powers in the Pacific had allowed it to exist."[13]

Queen Liliuokalani spoke of Mr. Blount in a rather different manner. She described him as, "selected by reason of his perfect impartiality... After digesting a mass of testimony on both sides, he decided that I was the constitutional ruler of the Hawaiian Islands." About his conduct she wrote, "I must speak in the terms of the highest praise. He first met the parties opposed to my government," and "afterwards took statements of the government and royalist side."[14]

Neither Cleveland nor his government knew of the realities or shortcomings of Blount's report, for no one gave any other point of view to the government. Cleveland acted on its recommendations without asking anyone else's opinion, rejecting annexation and ordering the Queen restored to the throne. Blount's one-sided report, therefore, led directly to the subsequent actions taken by the men of the Provisional Government.

In spite of Blount and his report, the idea of annexation gathered momentum, moving forward like a relentless steamroller. Many Hawaiians, however, still supported the monarchy and were avidly interested in restoring Liliuokalani to the throne. Some tried legal means, traveling to Washington at their own expense to appeal to the US government for help. Others were sure that only direct action in Hawaii would work.

Rumors arose about attacks on the government and troops were placed on alert again. Plots were hatched that would take control of the government for the Queen. There were conspiracies, counter plots and intrigue, stealthy movements at night, a cache of arms landed on the beach in the dark, a furtive group whispering about a plan, others burying rifles and ammunition in the shadows, or hiding guns in the corner of the Palace grounds. None of these plans ever bore fruit. An accidental shooting occurred amid the plotting and the would-be rebels fled into the mountains to the east. After a week of scrabbling around in the wilderness, they surrendered.

The new US Minister, Albert Willis, arrived bringing with him instructions to arrange a peaceful restoration of the Queen to the throne. It did not happen. The situation was becoming even more bizarre.

In October of 1893, W.W. Gresham, Secretary of State, sent a confidential telegram to Albert Willis. He told Willis to inform the Queen that,

"When reinstated, the President expects that she will pursue a magnanimous course by granting full amnesty to all who participated in the movement against her, including persons who are or have been connected with the Provisional Government depriving them of no right or privilege which they enjoyed before the so-called revolution. All obligations incurred by the Provisional Government in due course of the administration should be assumed."[15]

It was not unconditional support for the Queen and her notion of absolute power, nor was it a strong reprimand of the Americans who had made such a revolutionary move. It was designed to mollify all parties quietly. At a meeting with the former queen, Willis apologized on behalf of the United States. Then he asked if, when restored to the throne, she would give amnesty to these men who had deposed her. Willis, according to his report, was startled by the Queen's reaction. He reports that she said,

> "My decision would be as the law directs, that such persons should be beheaded and their property confiscated by the government."[16]

Later she denied that she used the word beheaded and added that she actually said that those guilty of treason should leave the country forever.[17] Queen Liliuokalani remembered that she said to Willis,

> "Our laws read that those who are guilty of treason should suffer the penalty of death. He (Willis) then wished to know if I would carry out that law. I said that I would be more inclined to punish them by banishment, and confiscation of their property to the government."[18]

She felt the interview was an informal unrecorded exchange of views. Later, when Willis presented her with a transcript of the meeting to sign, she opined that there might have been a secret stenographer behind a Japanese screen in the room of the original meeting with Willis. Still, she signed the transcript.

US Secretary of State Gresham wrote a letter recounting the interview with Liliuokalani. It was published in local newspapers on November 24, 1893 just as many in Hawaii had decided that the US was about to restore the Queen to the throne by force. Even Rear Admiral John Irwin, Commander of the North Pacific Squadron[19] expected to receive orders to land and oust the Provisional Government.

Willis informed the Provisional Government, in a letter to Sanford Dole, of actions proposed by the Cleveland administration, including the restoration of the Queen and amnesty for the present government. Dole replied to Willis, on December 23, refuting every point that Cleveland had made, based on Blount's report. It made Cleveland look ridiculous. The biggest stumbling block, and the most embarrassing, was that Stevens had already committed the US to protecting Hawaii. Cleveland could not very well declare war on a territory the US was already protecting. In January of 1894, he figuratively threw up his hands in disgust and turned the whole matter over to the Congress. Joseph Nawahi strongly supported Hawaiian independence in widely distributed publications written in Hawaiian.

The Provisional Government had been disavowed by the United States Government, on the grounds that they had not acted with the approval of the Hawaiian people, nor had they asked the consent or acquiescence of the citizens of Hawaii. These men, so certain that their actions were correct and admirable, so positive that the US government would be grateful for their gift, felt backed into a corner. Many still wanted annexation, but were startled and then angered when President Cleveland repudiated them.

In order to maintain control of the Hawaiian government until a more supportive US President was elected, they created a new constitution and declared Hawaii a Republic on July 4, 1894. They lowered the American flag and raised the Hawaiian standard again. Sanford Dole was elected as President of the Republic and the men of the Provisional Government were installed in the same jobs in the Republic. The governmental changes were merely semantic. Within two days of the proclamation, all foreign governments had recognized the new regime.

The Republic began without fuss or fanfare. On July 4, 1894, a ceremony was held on the steps of the building which had been the king's palace and today is again called the Iolani Palace. In 1893, it had been renamed as the Government Executive Building[20] and here Dole officially proclaimed the Republic of Hawaii. Later he sent a letter to Cleveland to announce the new entity. In reply, he received from the US official recognition of his new government. Royalists sent a delegation to Washington only to learn that the United States government would do nothing. They also carried their plea to European nations to no avail. Royalists in Hawaii tried to stir up native Hawaiians and other royalists for several months. They found little support for restoring the queen.

Then an event occurred which is startling, even in this weird scenario. The new Republican government was hesitant about taking this next step, but when Royalists exchanged gunfire with troops, and were taken in custody, they felt it was necessary.

On January 16, 1895, Liliuokalani received two men in the parlor of her home on Washington Place, Deputy Marshall Arthur Brown and Captain Robert Waipa Parker. To her utter astonishment, they had a warrant for her arrest. The charges were threefold. First, she had conspired, the warrant stated, to create a new constitution; second, she signed a lottery bill and, third, she proposed to issue licenses for the importation and sale of opium.[21] They would not let her hold the warrant nor read it. It was clear that they expected her to go with them without a fuss.[22] She did.

The men took her by carriage to the Iolani Palace and led her upstairs to a large, airy, uncarpeted room. It contained one bed, a sofa, a chair, a bureau, and a chiffonier plus several other pieces of furniture. There was a bathroom and a verandah. She was left there with the comment that this was to be her future home and if she wanted anything, she should ask the man on guard at the door.[23] Her description is calm, but she must have been humiliated and horrified that this could be done to her, the Queen of all Hawaii. She was in prison.

Chief Justice A.F. Judd, ordered all her papers confiscated from the Washington Place home the next day to be used in a trial of those who had conspired against the government.

The next logical step was abdication, but Hawaiian Attorney General A.G. Smith told Liliuokalani that she could not abdicate because the monarchy had already ended two years before when she had tried to make her own constitution. Nevertheless, on January 22, 1895, a paper was handed to her, which contained the necessary words of abdication. She was expected to sign it. It had been prepared by A.S. Hartwell, whom she identifies as the lawyer for the men in power. She had not intended to abdicate, she says, and the idea did not originate with her. Liliuokalani says she was threatened with the fact that all rebels and royalists who had taken part in the aborted revolts would be put to death if she did not sign. If she did sign, all the men who had been arrested the same time she was, would be released. Understandably she laments,

> "Think of my position, - sick, a lone woman in prison, scarcely knowing who was my friend, or who listened to my words only to betray me, without legal advice or friendly counsel, and the stream of blood ready to flow unless it was stayed by my pen."[24]

She was confined without legal counsel until February 8, 1895 when she was taken to the former throne room of the Palace and put on trial for the previously cited charges. Her position was, "I was a martyr to the cause of my people, and proud of it".[25] She denied any thought of treason or knowledge of any arms buried in the Palace garden. She rationalized her intention to create a new constitution by explaining that those kings who had ruled Hawaii before her had set the precedent. Her responses always expressed self-approval and frequent condemnation of her 'enemies'. All her statements were self-serving, but after all, she had no one to defend her.

On February 27, 1895 the trial concluded. She was declared guilty on all counts and sentenced to five years hard labor and a fine of $5,000. She returned to her cell a heartbroken woman. The full severity of the sentence, however, was never carried out. On September 6 she received a partial parole and was transferred to her home at Washington Place with "only sixteen servants".[26] The following year, on February 6, 1896, her parole was extended, but she was still confined to the island of Oahu. That October all of the restrictions were lifted, her passport was returned to her and she was free to go where she wished.

She records with warmth that Rear Admiral Irwin, Commander of the North Pacific Squadron, left his flagship USS *Philadelphia* and called upon her during her period of confinement. This was an act of kindness she said she would never forget.

As soon as she signed the abdication document, the Hawaiian monarchy, which had lasted less than one hundred years, was *pau* - officially at an end.

Liliuokalani lost the throne when she tried to declare her own constitution. By the end of the 19th century such a tactic was no longer tenable. In the eyes of most Americans, monarchs and constitutions have never operated well together. England has a successful Constitutional Monarchy without a written constitution, but it had developed over centuries long before the idea of a written constitutions even existed.

The Queen wanted to govern according to her own rules. The men who usurped her power formed a new government which they ran by their own rules. While they called it a 'democracy' it was really an oligarchy. The name they chose, the Republic, sounded familiar to Americans whose favor they required to effect passage of their highly desired annexation bill. They had to create a workable government while they waited for a new president to be elected to replace Grover Cleveland. They hoped for a man who could recognize the importance of Pearl Harbor and the islands.

The men of the Hawaiian Republic had snatched a sovereign nation from its rightful ruler. They justified it on the grounds of protection, expediency and politics. The Hawaiian people and the United States Navy were moving, as they had been for over a century, toward an as yet undefined affiliation and that union was imminent.

Chapter 17 - Confluence

American missionaries have long been castigated for their intrusion into the lives and culture of the Sandwich Islanders. American businessmen have been called ruthless in their treatment of the natives. American politicians were branded as unscrupulous in their machinations during the latter half of the 19th century. Nevertheless, it was Americans with missionary zeal, business experience, military power, and political acumen that created the American/Hawaiian merger and enabled the Hawaiians to learn to cope with the modern world into which they were rushing faster than any canoe could ever have taken them. The languid, tranquil river of Hawaiian life and the vibrant, tumultuous American lifestream were coming together. The great confluence would soon be a fact, and just as irreversible as the coming together of two mighty rivers.

In March of 1897 William McKinley entered the White House as the 25th president of the United States. Sanford Dole could not have been more pleased. The Democratic candidate who ran against McKinley, William Jennings Bryan, was a near-isolationist and an avowed foe of big business. McKinley's administration, on the other hand, was staunchly pro-business and encouraged an assertive foreign policy. In Hawaii, the Republic, which had so far had a controversial and tenuous existence, saw renewed hope for their goal of annexation. Republic President Sanford Dole and his wife went to Washington to plead the case of the Hawaiians and to show the lawmakers a typical Hawaiian leader who was responsible and concerned, wanting the protection of the United States.

Upon his return to Honolulu, Dole optimistically, but without authorization from Washington, decided to limit or prevent any more Japanese workers to be imported into Hawaii. This would bring two major countries to the possibility, if not the brink, of war.

There were already many Japanese workers in Hawaii and many people, both private citizens and government officials, thought they would soon crowd out whites as whites had done to Hawaiians.[1] By 1897, Japanese made up one fourth of the Hawaiian population, which made them the largest single ethnic group in Hawaii. More important eventually was the perception that the Japanese were interfering in the business of Hawaii and trying to influence the actions of the U.S. Government. U.S. Senator Hoar told President McKinley that the Hawaiian Islands would be taken over by Japan if the U.S. did not soon prevent it.[2] It was an interesting position to take, considering the recent actions of the founders of the Hawaiian Republic. The rise of Japanese influence in the Pacific and their development of political sophistication was astonishing when one considers that they had opened their ports to the world less than fifty years before.

The importation of Japanese to work in sugar and pineapple fields in Hawaii raised their ethnic representation to more than that of the Chinese, the previous focus of Hawaiian xenophobia. Almost immediately after McKinley was in office, Dole, without consultation, moved to prevent Japanese immigrants from entering Honolulu. Of course, the Japanese government protested firmly to Washington. President McKinley ordered Rear Admiral L.A. Beardslee, Commander of the Pacific Squadron, to transfer the cruiser USS *Philadelphia* and the sloop-of-war USS *Marion* to Hawaii. The Japanese counteracted in April by sending the powerful battle cruiser *Naniwa* to anchor abreast the American ships in Honolulu Harbor. McKinley's response was to order Beardslee to send his four remaining ships to Hawaii. Assistant Secretary of the Navy Theodore Roosevelt, a devout expansionist, was advised that there was a "very real present danger of war".[3]

McKinley and Roosevelt stood firm and ordered the battleship USS *Oregon* to stand by in case of trouble. They almost transferred the aging battleship USS *Maine* to Hawaii, but decided to leave her in the Caribbean.[4] The next year *Maine* was blown up and sunk near Havana, an act which soon precipitated the Spanish-American War.

By the autumn of 1897 the Japanese retreated, apparently seeing no need to exacerbate the situation. Having saved face by a show of force, they withdrew their ships and assigned them to other duties. The crisis calmed and possible hostilities were averted.

The diplomatic crisis, and McKinley's firm and successful handling of it, brought attention back to Hawaii. The U.S. Navy, after previous requests had been turned down by the congress, was finally given authorization to spend $100,000 to survey and to dredge a channel into Pearl Harbor.[5] To put this amount into perspective, an 1898 advertisement in a local Hawaiian newspaper offered "House and lot, 7 rooms with electric lights and modern improvements for $4,750."[6]

It was during the crisis with Japan that Captain Caspar F. Goodrich and the faculty at the Naval War College prepared the strategic Plan Orange for possible use against Japan. He recognized that such a war would be fought at sea and devised a scheme in four parts. First, the Atlantic Squadron would assemble on the East Coast and provision there. Second, they would steam around Cape Horn to San Francisco. Third, the fleet would proceed to Hawaii, and fourth, it would seek, engage and destroy the Japanese fleet. He expected the enemy fleet to be located in the Philippine Island area. A battle plan that required two or three months to get to the battle made sense in 1897. The plan was never set into motion, of course, but his work laid the basis for strategic planning for decades of naval officers to come.[7]

Every European nation in the 1890s, including the new German Empire, was following the lead of the British Empire and casting about the world for territory to acquire and rule. America was slow to join this colonial activity, having already spent much time and money conquering her own continent. Still, America had taken the time and energy to claim the island of Midway in 1867 and bought Alaska the same year. Hawaii would not be America's first overseas acquisition, if annexation occurred. America was on the way to joining the world as an imperial power.

For the time being, though, Hawaii was in limbo. Many felt that it was of strategic importance to the protection of the west coast of the United States as well as the 'isthmian canal'. There was no Panama Canal yet, but it was being planned. American war plans after 1896 always included the requirement that Pearl Harbor must be manned by the U.S. Navy in order to safeguard the coast and to act as a major Pacific base.[8]

Hawaiians felt that if the United States really wanted the islands, they would find a means. If they did not, then some other powerful country would likely move in. This became clearer after the fact. The U.S. rejected the 1893 annexation treaty when the islands were not needed and accepted the 1898 treaty when they were. The need for Hawaii was first recognized as a coaling and provisioning station, and then as an essential location for protection of the west coast of the mainland. After the outbreak of the Spanish-American War in February of 1898, Hawaii achieved a new level of importance because of Spanish possessions in the Western Pacific, especially the Philippine Islands.

At the beginning of the war, the attention of congress was naturally on the crisis in the Caribbean. Soon, the vulnerable position of Hawaii was brought to their attention. Committees on Foreign Relations in both houses drafted resolutions of annexation which passed by large margins. The war with Spain was heating up and wise men realized it would soon spread to Asia. Now, the U.S. needed Pearl Harbor.

Members of congress were surprised when Japanese diplomats protested the recent action of congress concerning the Hawaiian Islands. Annexation, the Japanese Ambassador told the Secretary of State, would endanger Japanese citizens who lived and worked in Hawaii. This reading of the situation in Hawaii was reinforced by Dole's actions banning Japanese immigration. The Japanese charged Hawaiian and American governments with prejudice against Orientals in general and against the Japanese in particular. The charge was certainly true, corroborated by the attitude of many Americans and Europeans in Hawaii and the Chinese Exclusion act of 1882. Vetoed by the president, the bill of annexation did show what was to come as well as the measure of the feelings of Americans.

Many Hawaiians were concerned with what they perceived as the 'Oriental' problem. On January 31, 1898, a Honolulu newspaper displayed a headline, "An Annexation Amendment". Senator Bacon of Georgia, who was on record as being against annexation, introduced to the Senate an amendment. He wanted any annexation treaty that was submitted to be put to a vote of the citizens of Hawaii and to make acceptance of the treaty depend on the results of that vote. The vote would exclude Japanese or Chinese voters.[9] The reporter thought the amendment would not be accepted. He was correct; it was dropped. By June, a newspaper headline proclaimed, "Annexation is Demanded" and the article reported that there was tremendous pressure being brought on U.S. Senators by the leading citizens of Hawaii and those who were in favor of the action. At the time, the paper reported, 46 members of the Senate were in favor of annexation, 22 against, and 20 declined to give an opinion.[10] The paper printed names of the men in each category.

When news of the outbreak of the Spanish-American War reached the islands, Hawaii suddenly needed the protection of the United States. The Hawaiian Islands were vulnerable and many thought they should be annexed immediately[11] because the United States needed Hawaii. A case in point was the request by L.A. Thurston, hoping put more pressure on for annexation, when he suggested that the coaling station be strengthened.[12]

Until this time, the Hawaii government had wrestled with three major options concerning their role in the war. One was to do nothing. Another was an announcement of neutrality. A third was active support of the United States.

The first choice might have been interpreted as an invitation by the Spanish to occupy the islands and include them in their Western Pacific holdings. The United States might interpret the second choice as an ungrateful response to the assistance they had provided over several decades. Should Spain decide to take the islands, there was no viable force to oppose them but the American fleet. The islands were vulnerable. The Hawaiian government could not declare itself neutral because that act would be interpreted as an unacceptable offense in the eyes of the United States and would ruin chances of annexation.[13] The Republic had been formed in the first place with the goal of annexation and they did not want to jeopardize their chances now.

Dole and his cabinet announced support for the Americans and displayed it by hosting American troops as the ships stopped in Honolulu on their way to the Philippines. This was before Dewey's victory was known, and the war practically won, but the action endeared the Hawaiian people to Americans on the mainland. Their final choice of action was a pragmatic one.

During the spring of 1898, the Hawaiian government extended every possible kind of help to the United States. They became a base for operations against Spain in the Philippines. They even offered to supply a battalion of Hawaiian volunteer soldiers for Cuba, but the idea was politely rejected by Washington. During the war, when U.S. ships arrived in Honolulu full of soldiers, they were welcomed, entertained and fed at the expense of the

Hawaiian government. Many of these soldiers returned home after the war with a better understanding of Hawaii and the *Aloha* spirit.

It has been suggested that if the Spanish-American War had not come when it did, if Dewey had not gone to the Philippines to fight, Hawaii would not have been annexed for years, if ever.[14] Although the war was advantageous for the annexationists, there are several writers who say that the war had little to do with the fact of annexation.[15]

The joint resolution of annexation finally passed the House of Representatives on June 15, 1898, the Senate on July 6, and was signed by President McKinley on July 7. At this time, the Women's Hawaiian Patriotic League collected more than 20,000 signatures on petitions against the annexation. Whether this constitutes an angry protest, as some writers imply, depends on your point of view.[16] There was no rioting or violent reaction to it. One notable provision was omitted from the proposal made by the Hawaiian delegation which had presented the document to the government. Financial provision that had been requested for the deposed Queen was not included in the final version of the treaty. On August 12 the Hawaiian Islands were officially annexed and thereby formally made a Territory of the United States. Sanford Dole was appointed the first governor.

It is interesting to note that even while these official events were taking place, businessman Walter F. Dillingham made a survey for a projected railway to be built over the Pali, the road over the Ko'olau mountains to the east shore.[17] He had confidence that the event would happen and his business would prosper.

Full instructions covering the annexation ceremony were sent in care of Admiral Miller on USS *Philadelphia*. Admiral Miller arrived on August 3, 1898, joining USS *Mohican*, which was already anchored in Honolulu Harbor standing by to participate in the ceremonies. He and US Minister Sewall, would conduct all the necessary formalities to consummate the delivery of the islands to the United States. An envoy had also come to Hawaii on *Alameda* with instructions for the payment of an indemnity of $75,000[18] to Japan to settle immigration problems. It was to be paid before formal transfer of the territory was made. Cooper, the envoy who was also helping with the annexation papers, was warned by the US State Department that Japanese Minister Hoshi, who had concluded this settlement, would stop at Hawaii on his way back to Japan." Presumably the motive was to spur the Hawaiian government to take care of the matter.

Early in the day, Friday, August 12, 1898, a large throng gathered at the Iolani Palace, called the Executive Building at the time. People crowded onto the grounds filling lawns, benches and walkways as well as the streets outside the gates. Dignitaries filled the balconies and porches. Almost everyone wanted to witness this historic event. Many native Hawaiians, however, chose to boycott it. Liliuokalani, understandably, her entourage and her relatives would not attend the ceremony. Instead they met at her home on Washington Place to commiserate over their fate. It is not known if they sang Liliuokalani's lovely song, *Aloha Oe*. In the despair and sorrow they must have felt, it would have been appropriate.[20]

Rear Admiral J.N. Miller, Commander of the Pacific Squadron, ordered Marines and sailors from the USS *Philadelphia* and USS *Mohican* a ashore to participate in annexation ceremonies. According to Lieutenant Lucien Young, "The force under arms ...consisted of four companies of bluejacket infantry and two of artillery.... The Hawaiian troops lined up on each side of our column".[21] Admiral Miller is said to have been instrumental in subduing American sailors who may have planned to celebrate in too raucous a manner in front of the Iolani Palace where the formal proceedings took place.[22]

US Minister Sewall opened the ceremonies with a speech and then read the resolution of annexation. President Dole gave a speech and formally presented the Hawaiian Islands to the United States, whereupon he immediately became Governor Dole. Then, at precisely eight minutes to noon,[23] the Hawaiian flag was slowly lowered while the band played *Hawaii Ponoi*, the Hawaiian National Anthem. This event contained an element of pathos as the life of the dying nation passed away. As the crowd grew quiet with the solemnity of the occasion, the mournful notes of Taps drifted out over the area. The Hawaiian flag was reportedly cut up into small pieces and passed out as souvenirs.[24] Ceremonies concluded with the playing of the Star Spangled Banner as a 36 foot high American flag was raised over the center tower of the Iolani Palace while smaller flags were run up on the corner towers.[25]

> "One of the most gratifying spectacles of the occasions, especially to those Americans who witnessed our flag being hauled down by Blount, was the rehoisting of the same flag on the same flag-pole over the same building, simultaneously with the lowering of the Hawaiian flag [of the republic] on the Executive Building. I was enabled to obtain this flag immediately after it was hauled down five years previously and carefully preserved it, fully believing that sooner or later there would be a call for it to go up again."

So recalled Lucien Young. He had given this flag to L. A. Thurston in May of 1898 with the request that it be used for the ceremony. McKinley approved of the proposition as did Dole. The flag that Blount had hauled down five years before, now proudly rose to its old position.[26] There were tears of joy in the eyes of many, tears of sorrow in the eyes of others. The headline in the evening paper reported cheers and tears for the flag and "Old Glory waves triumphant!"[27]

The ceremonies were fittingly concluded with a ball which took place in the old Throne Room of the palace. Both the new flag and the old were woven into the decorations and light refreshments were served throughout the evening for the dancers.[28]

American flags, shields, buttons and patriotic decorations were on sale four days later in Honolulu at the Golden Rule Bazaar on Fort Street.[29]

A Hawaiian Commission from the US Congress, Senator Collon and Congressman Hitt, arrived in Honolulu on August 17th, 1898. Their task was to tour the islands, listen to the citizens and make recommendations for legislation that would affect and improve conditions in the islands.[30] They were reportedly thrilled and enthralled with Pearl Harbor which they toured on September 1.[31] They embarked in a steam launch from USS *Philadelphia* for a thorough cruise of Pearl. They commented on "miles of natural wharfage and space and depth... here almost everything is made by nature."[32]

The annexation of Hawaii to the United States would change the political atmosphere not only of the Hawaiian Islands as a whole, but of Pearl Harbor in particular. No immediate changes occurred, of course, but eventually Waimomi, or Pu'uloa, or Pearl River, would become something entirely different, and events would take place there that would shake the world. American, Hawaiian, Japanese, Chinese, and Portuguese citizens of the Hawaiian Islands, whether they liked it or not, were now American citizens.

Two vastly different cultures had now come together; the United States, represented by many prominent businessmen and now the government of the United States, and the Hawaiian people. Now they were bound together legally and politically. At this moment the population of Hawaii consisted of Hawaiian and part-Hawaiian *kamainas*, laborers from Japan, China, and Portugal, merchants and residents from England, Germany and America and visitors from many other countries. While still *haoles*, Americans could no longer be called 'foreigners'. The entire resident population was American. The Hawaiian lands that made up Pearl Harbor were now in the hands of the United States and soon would be controlled by the U.S. Navy. Hawaii and the Navy had been joined. The Great Confluence was a fact.

Chapter 18 - The New Territory

When the dust settled and annexation was passed, there was work to do, work that would last a good two years. An organic act had to be created to set up an annexation document. Specifics had to be dealt with and decisions had to be made. The government had to be re-worked in the image of the law of the United States. This was no small task. It commenced with a report from the Hawaiian Commission. Men appointed by U.S. President William McKinley were to implement Public Resolution No. 51, entitled "Joint Resolution to provide for annexing the Hawaiian Islands to the United States" It was drawn up and approved on July 7, 1898.[1]

The most important single fact of this document was that the Republic of Hawaii ceded absolutely, without reserve, all rights of sovereignty over the islands and their dependencies, all crown lands, harbors and ports, public buildings, military equipment and public property of every kind and description that belonged to the government of the Hawaiian Islands "together with every right and appurtenance thereunto appertaining".[2] This included the five major islands, Kauai, Oahu, Molokai, Maui and Hawaii. Also included were Ni'ihau, Lanai, Necker, Laysan, Gardiner, Lisiansky, Ocean, French Frigate Shoals, Palmyra, Brooks Shoal, Pearl and Hermes Reef, Gambia Shoal and Dowsett and Moro Reef.[3] Midway Island had been independently acquired by the United States on August 28, 1867.

One minor though important point was that the commission which was mapping out the laws for Hawaii was instructed by President McKinley to include nothing looking toward statehood. Hawaii was to be more like the District of Columbia, he believed, than other territories.[4]

The Senate and House of Representatives of the United States accepted the cession, ratified and confirmed the annexation. With this, years of furious debate over the right and the necessity of annexation came to an end. Then the work began. For, in spite of a number of Americans who had worked in the Hawaiian government for years, there was much to do to create a new government. Details of the bill providing a government for Hawaii was published on the front page of the Honolulu Evening Bulletin.[5]

One of the stickiest points was the right of citizens, that is all males over the age of twenty, to vote. The American idea of universal suffrage, which still did not include women, presupposes a certain level of education and understanding of what is meant by a republican government. The population of Hawaii by 1900 was a conglomeration of many races and nationalities of people from many countries, some with decidedly non-democratic governments. The commission report broke the voting population of 110,000 into eight groups. The island government and business was dominated by the American element, the commission report says, but there were only 4,000 American citizens in the total. Combining Japanese and Chinese in the islands, there were 46,500 Orientals and 39,000 Hawaiians. That meant Americans would be in the minority. Despite the numerical disadvantage, Americans displayed zealous political ambition and skill. They succeeded in acquiring and maintaining control in several areas.

During the transition time, the government of the Republic of Hawaii continued to operate as it had for years. That is, Sanford Dole was the president and his cabinet was made up of the same men who had held the offices during the Republic. The legislature was relatively unchanged as well. Most ordinary citizens, though, were unaffected by the changes or by the effort to create a new working government. They went about their usual business, fishing, working in the sugar cane fields, selling papers or operating the downtown trolley. How did they feel about the annexation, how did they like being citizens of the United States? It is hard to tell because they weren't considered important and few reporters went to the trouble of interviewing them. It certainly made little difference in their lives unless they owned land, worked for the government or the military.

The men who were concerned with the government wanted the territorial government handled in specific ways and with great care. These so-called "representative men"[6] had been successful in their quest which began by deposing Queen Liliuokalani in 1893. Some called them arrogant and the epithet is justified. They had wanted the United States to take control of the islands and they had succeeded. The reasons were considered to be secondary.

Still, they didn't intend to allow the powerful American government to collide with, or oppose, the way they wanted the government of the islands to operate. There were restrictions they wanted included in their operating system, even if they were not commensurate with the American constitution. For instance, voting rights for all citizens were a major concern. They wanted to keep irresponsible people from being able to influence the election of men to high office. What they did was to institute restrictions similar to those the Founding Fathers of the new United States had placed on voting a hundred years earlier. At that time a man had to be responsible in order to vote, that meant he had to own property. In Hawaii, however, there was a different twist on the idea. The restriction desired by men like Sanford Dole was based on race. Dole and others believed that the Hawaiian native should not be allowed to vote just because he was of the right age. Many believed natives were not yet responsible. It was understandable from the point of view of the men who controlled the government, but it was anti-democratic. The basic fact was that if native Hawaiians were allowed to vote, they would outnumber Americans almost ten to one. It was an unendurable prospect for men like Dole who had been in control for so long. Orientals were not allowed to vote at all.

Changes in this policy would not be made by the Hawaiians, but would have to come from the mainland. To take advantage of Dole's experience and expertise, President McKinley appointed Dole to the commission to draft an organic act for the Territory of Hawaii. The first report on Hawaiian Territory was read to the senate on December 6, 1898. It included facts about Hawaii such as the location of the various islands and their climate as well as particulars such as agriculture, the fisheries and culture. It also explained the leper colony on Molokai, housing some 1,200 lepers at the time. Harbors and landing places were depicted in detail, especially the location and attributes of Pearl Harbor. The document may have been the first time that members of the U.S. Senate heard such details about the islands. It also discussed man made Hawaiian institutions such as churches, prisons, newspapers as well as the need for an oceanic telegraph cable.

The Annexation document finally got around to discussing the make up of the legislature of Hawaii, qualifications for voting and the laws of Hawaii.

> "The existing laws of Hawaii not inconsistent with the Constitution and the laws of the United States or of this act shall continue in force subject to repeal or amendment by the legislature of Hawaii or by Congress."[7]

The commission left several issues alone. They stumbled on labor and left the problem unsolved. Since the act annexing Hawaii was passed prohibiting further Chinese immigration, sugar planters had been importing Japanese labor. They needed cheap labor to make their plantations profitable and that meant contract labor. Too many Japanese were being brought to the islands but maybe that could be solved, some Commissioners thought, by using white labor. It wasn't.

The commission could not agree on the creation of a cabinet or advisory council to aid the new Territorial government. Some believed that the territorial government would be subordinate to the government of the US and would have limited authority. Others, "gentlemen of great experience and wisdom"[8], thought a cabinet was necessary. One firm statement the document did make was;

> "The underlying theory of our Government is the right of self-government, and a people must be fitted for self-government before they can be trusted with the responsibilities and duties attaching to free government."[9]

The report made by the commissioners included two additional items. One was related to the silver coinage of Hawaii which was to be accepted at par, but not reissued. The other had to do with postal savings banks in Hawaii which would be terminated. Sanford Dole included a minority report which he suggested that the governor be given more power to employ and discharge members of the government.

The government set up by the organic act and put into affect on April 30, 1900 included a two house legislature. The Senate would be made up of fifteen men and the House of Representatives would be thirty. The governor and the secretary of state were to be appointed by the President of the United States, as had been the practice with US territories for many years. All persons who were citizens of the Republic on August 12, 1898 would be citizens of the United States. Included in this organic act was a copy of the Constitution of the United States, with all the amendments up to the 15th amendment of 1870.[10] Eligible citizens could vote for legislators and would elect a delegate to the US Congress. This representative of Hawaii would have a regular seat in the US House of Representatives. He would be able to introduce bills, but would have no vote. This is still standard procedure in US territories.

The US government assumed operation of many institutions that are run by the government agencies, such as customs, the post office, immigration, and higher courts.

It was no surprise when President McKinley appointed Sanford Dole as the first governor. This completed a continuity from the Provisional Government of 1893, to the Republic of 1894 to the Territory of 1898.

All citizens of the Republic became citizens of the United States when the new government went into affect. Orientals were still unable to vote as they had not been citizens of the Republic. Property qualifications were abolished, which meant all non-oriental men over twenty could vote. Women, of course, were excluded. Hawaiians, excluded because of property requirements, suddenly became a majority of the electorate. Only five percent of Hawaii's citizens were of American or British descent and this would lead to many a battle.

There were three political parties in Hawaii at the beginning of the new century; Republican, Democrat and a new local group called the Home Rule Party. Made up of natives and part-Hawaiians, this party was under the leadership of Robert Wilcox, that old revolutionary agitator from the now-defunct Liberal Patriotic Party revolt of 1889 and 1895. Rough days were ahead.

Wilcox was constantly advised by constituents to vote only for Hawaii, and to make race the primary criterion on which to base every decision.[11] Needless to say, with so large a majority of the voters, the new party did well in the first election, gaining a clear majority in both houses. Wilcox was elected as the first representative to the US Congress.

When the first legislature met in 1901, it was a mess.

"The first territorial legislature was worse than anyone thought it could be. Even their most serious efforts were frivolous."[12]

Hawaiians had the majority but they had no real experienced leaders. Perhaps they should have retained Wilcox at home, but there is no indication that it would have done any good. They were legally bound by the organic act to conduct all legislative sessions in English, but the Hawaiian members ignored the law and insisted on carrying on all official business conversations in Hawaiian. They argued over trivialities, blocked every move by the other parties, no matter what its merit. Most writers on the subject are of one mind about the behavior of this legislature, i.e. it was a shambles and a disgrace.[13]

Buoyed by their victory in the election, they thought they were in complete control, that they could have it all back, and that they really had power. They were protected by the United States so they could act on their own terms. Some of those terms included revenge on the powerful people who had taken away their land and culture. They may have had some justification in that feeling, but it is clear that they did not know what to do or what was needed.

After two months of this impasse, not a single program had been accomplished, at a time when a great deal needed to be done. Dole was disgusted at the deadlock, especially when he had to call a special session of the legislature just to get enough money to keep the government in operation. After two years of this shilly-shallying and irresponsible behavior of the legislature, Dole resigned in frustration. He became a judge of the US District court in Hawaii. Theodore Roosevelt, then US president, appointed George R. Carter as governor. Nothing really changed when the new governor stepped in because Carter was a member of the same group of rich, white businessmen who had engineered the Republic as well as the annexation and he had been part of the government for some time.

At this point one of the more interesting figures enters the Hawaiian political scene. He was the remarkable Prince Jonah Kuhio Kalanianaole Pi'ikoi. Anyone who has spent any time in Hawaii will recognize the fact that there are three streets in Honolulu bearing three of his names, a remarkable accomplishment for anyone, in public office or not. He was the nephew of Kalakaua's wife Queen Kapiolani. Liliuokalani named him one of the heirs to her non-existent throne, along with David Kawananaka, when Princess Kaiulani died in 1899. He was, with Liliuokalani and Kawananaka, the only 'royal family' left in Hawaii.[14] He did not expect to rule as a king.

Kuhio joined the Republican Party hoping to influence them into creating jobs for Hawaiians and making things easier for the natives. Many Hawaiians followed him away from the Home Rule Party especially when he defeated Wilcox as representative to the US Congress. He wanted land for Hawaiians and, according to reports, especially wanted to restore their dignity. He was not able to achieve his goals, in spite of being elected to his seat in the congress ten times.

The one thing he supported that was successful was the creation of county governments. This was thought to be a way to dilute the power of the influential men in Honolulu. In July of 1905, five new counties were created in the islands, but it was not as simple as one county on each major island. Oahu and Hawaii were each separate counties, but Kauai county included the private island of Ni'ihau. Maui county included Lanai, Kahoolawe, and Molokai, except for the Kalawa leper colony, which is today called the Kalaupapa Peninsula, on the north shore of the island. The leper colony had no representation in the legislature and no county government except a sheriff. In 1931 it was transferred to the control of the Health Department, and was closed in the 1960s.

The counties elected seven supervisors, a commensurate number of sheriffs, clerks and other minor officers under the county act bill. Fifty years later, these counties would become a part of the new state government, but at this time they could only assess real estate and set their own tax rates for it. It was a modicum of local power, but it was a beginning. Prince Kuhio could well be proud of the accomplishment. He was not, however, sanguine about the survival of his people. In 1920, he prophesied sadly,

> "If conditions remain as they are today, it will only be a matter of a short space of time when this race of people, my people, renowned for their physique, their courage, their sense of justice, their straight forwardness and their hospitality, will be a matter of history."[15]

In 1919, Kuhio introduced the first Hawaii statehood bill into the House of Representatives and repeated the process in 1920.[16] Neither bill made it out of committee. The debate would grow and continue for thirty-five years. Kuhio and his followers failed in many of their efforts, but this fact does not diminish his foresight and motives in trying to improve conditions for Hawaiians. He was often by-passed or overlooked both in Washington and in Honolulu. It is reported that he secretly harbored the desire to be appointed Territorial Governor of Hawaii,[17] but the time for a native Hawaiian to be placed in such a position had not come yet. He died in 1922, before he could finish his work.

The US federal government began to spend money in Hawaii for internal projects such as roads, bridges and harbors, especially Honolulu harbor. In 1897, Dole had pushed through the building of a trans-island highway across the Pali, a high pass through the Ko'olau Mountains on the eastern side of Oahu. It was officially opened in 1898, a tremendous accomplishment in sheer engineering difficulty.[18] It had to be constantly improved over the years by the federal government. In 1908, the most powerful lighthouse in the world was built on Makapu'u Point. It's light was visible fifty miles away.[19] These were expenditures the Hawaiian legislature could not have afforded. For one thing, as soon as Hawaii became a part of the United States, all customs revenues went to the U.S. not the island government and they lost part of their previous income.

The transition from native society to monarchy to republican government to territory was now complete. There was only one step to go: statehood. Great changes had come in the last few years and it was clear that Hawaiians could never go back to the way it was before. Hawaii could never be the idyllic, pastoral paradise that many remembered, no matter how some wished it could. No matter who is deemed to blame or who the dupe, the reality of Hawaii will be as it is today, a part of the United States.

While the politicians struggled to create a viable, workable government, extraordinary events occurred, including an outbreak of plague, a catastrophic fire in Chinatown, controversies about labor, Orientals and more. While these substantial problems were resolved, two important changes were taking place; the acquisition of Pearl Harbor and the creation of a Naval Base.

Chapter 19 - Acquisition of Pearl Harbor

Pearl Harbor was studied and mapped over the decades with increasing accuracy beginning in 1825 when Lt. Charles Malden of HBMS Blonde made the first detailed survey. In 1894, men from USS Philadelphia surveyed the reef at the entrance to Pearl River to determine what was needed to open the channel for major ships. Important to that project were borings taken from the outer harbor to ascertain the nature of the material to be removed. This 1894 survey was augmented in 1898 by another exploration by men from the gunboat uss Bennington. Both were inexpensive studies and approved as part of the ships' operational routine. In 1897, $50,000 was requested from Congress to begin work on the channel. The request was denied.[1]

A story in a local newspaper indicates the attitude and conduct which prevailed in Honolulu when American Bark *Sea King* arrived, commanded by a Captain Wallace. He spoke Diamond Head at 4:30 in the afternoon and asked to be reported, but was told there was no communication with Honolulu. The pilot said it was too late to go to the ship that day and he would wait until the morrow. The captain entered the harbor anyway. In bringing the pilotless ship to anchor, one of the crewmen got tangled in the anchor chain and needed medical care. When the pilot finally came aboard the next morning, Captain Wallace was in a rage and "said naughty words to them". The story continues, "For all the naughty and bad things he said to the officers, the captain is going to be complained of at Police Headquarters".[2] This was a front page story in the quiet little town of Honolulu.

An often overlooked event occurred at this time which may seem somewhat anachronistic, but it was a fact. On May 6, 1896, an obscure professor named Samuel P. Langley constructed a device, propelled by a light engine, that flew, unmanned, for about two minutes and covered a distance of some 3000'. Two years later, on March 25, 1898, Assistant Secretary of the Navy Theodore Roosevelt penned a memo to the Secretary, John D. Long, with a statement which neither of them realized would have thunderous implications, "The machine has worked. It seems to me worthwhile for this government to try whether it will not work on a large enough scale to be of use in the event of war."[3]

Long approved a study committee to look into possibilities. The chairman of the committee was Commander C. H. Davis USN. Their reactions were enthusiastic and in their report, they suggested three uses for the 'launching car' . First, as a means of reconnaissance; second, as a means of communication other than land or sea, and third, as an engine of offense with the capacity of dropping, from a great height, high explosives into a camp or fortification. They concluded the report with an enthusiastic recommendation that Professor Langley's experiments continue with government support.

This event, which could have heralded the initiation of air power in the United States, was aborted by a report from the Board of Construction which had the power of approval or veto,

"The Board has the honor to report that it has considered the within subject, and is of the opinion that such an apparatus as is referred to pertains strictly to the land service and not to the Navy. The Board believes that it is not expedient at this time for the Navy Department to carry on experiments or furnish money for the purpose."[4]

With the Spanish-American War commanding the attention of the government, the 'flying apparatus' project was dropped.

Pearl Harbor would be of little military value to the United States unless several problems were overcome. The entire area surrounding the estuary was comprised of privately owned land which was largely agricultural. There were severe water problems, alleviated by wells sunk on Ford's Island and a few just east of Pearl, near Honolulu. The old coal shed built during the Civil War, with an original capacity of a thousand tons, was dilapidated to the point of uselessness. The Pearl River was still busy with commercial fishermen, and the Oahu Railway and Land Company was constructing a railway to and across the base of the Pearl City peninsula. In short, the United States had a new Territory, but one with several problems lying between the swampy area guarded by a shark goddess and a viable Naval Station.

Because of Navy determination in the post-Civil War era to confine propulsion to sail whenever possible, the coal shed at Honolulu had fallen into disuse. At the outbreak of the Spanish-American War in May of 1898, the American Consul General, William Haywood, immediately went about purchasing all the available coal in Hawaii. It would be over a month before more coal would arrive from San Francisco. He was given authorization by Congress on the 4th of May, 1898.[5] The accumulated coal needed to be stored so he requested four new sheds be built which could handle 20,000 tons.

Realizing that the Honolulu/Pearl Harbor area would be of paramount importance in resupplying Dewey's ships, which were carrying troops, livestock, and equipment, steaming between the U.S. west coast and the Philippines, the Navy sent Commander Z.L. Tanner to plan wharves at Honolulu and to survey the Pearl] River Harbor for immediate and possible future use.[6] Haywood's sheds were approved and the wharves were built at cost of $69,600.[7]

In November of 1898 various parcels of land were set aside by Presidential Proclamation for use by the Navy. Nobody objected because many of the lots were under water.[8] The plan was to use dirt from dredging operations to fill and raise the land. Captain E.D. Taussig of the gunboat USS *Bennington* suggested a small force of U.S. Marines should be garrisoned at the developing station.[9] After more coal arrived from California, Haywood sold much of his recently acquired coal to the Oahu Railway and Land Company.

By May of 1899, the U.S. government deemed that this area, quickly developing into an important military area, should have a naval officer in charge. Consul Haywood was replaced by Commander John. F. Merry. Merry acknowledged his appointment in a letter to the Chief of the Bureau of Equipment (U.S. Navy), "I have the honor to report my at arrival at Honolulu and the relief of Consul General Wm. Haywood. Very Respectfully, J.F. Merry, Commander, USN."[10] The name of his station was Naval Coal Depot, Honolulu, T.H. While there were nine designated Naval Districts established in 1898, the nearest one to Hawaii was on the west coast of the mainland. It was not until April 18, 1916, that Hawaii was included in what was called the 14th Naval District.[11]

Merry went to work immediately at a furious pace. If his accomplishments were proportional to his correspondence he must have achieved a great deal. To say that he was a prolific letter writer would be an understatement. Unfortunately, he used an early form of green carbon paper which has not withstood the ravages of time and much of his correspondence is illegible.

Starting in June of 1899 his letters were titled "U.S. Navy Coal Depot, Honolulu, T.H." In subsequent letters, mostly written to the Chief of the Bureau of Equipment, he outlined the various problems which he faced and his proposed solutions for them. His recommendations were sound and usually met with approval.

Hawaii was soon to become electrically connected with islands to the west. On May 6, 1899, the USS *Nero*, equipped for deep sea soundings, sailed from Honolulu Harbor, explored the route from Hawaii to Midway, Guam, and the island of Luzon, in the Philippine Islands. After completing over 850 soundings and sailing 4800 miles, the Navy decided on a route that was practical enough for a telegraph cable to be laid. The survey was finished by August of 1899.[12]

Merry was not without an assertive spirit for in one of his letters, he included an interesting request, "I am in need of a horse or team. If it were not that I have a bicycle and use it constantly, I don't know how I could get about in hot sun. My livery bill would be large."[13] His request apparently did nothing to diminish his stature in the eyes of his superiors, for on July 27 the Secretary of the Navy, John D Long, ordered Commander Merry to prepare a "report to the Department of your recommendations re acquiring property at Honolulu for a naval station or converting property now in US hands for that purpose".[14]

Much of the land around the Pearl River and the lochs and a short distance inland was owned and operated by the Trustees of the Bishop Estate. Bernice Pauahi Bishop had left these lands in a trust upon her death in 1884. Commander Merry's letter to these trustees on September 16, 1899, requested the price the trustees would ask if the property from "Kianapua'a Point to the East Loch" were for sale.[15] He sent similar letters to other owners of properties in the desired area. One, to a Mr. Brown elicited a terse, "No! I am absolutely opposed to the United States getting control of my land."[16] Merry wrote to the U.S. government and urged immediate action, because "if the Navy doesn't secure it [the land] I fear it will be exchanged or disposed of in some way".[17] In that report (hand written, of course) he included legal advice, extensive engineering comments, and reasons for each of his recommendations.

In that same report, he prophetically opined, "If Honolulu becomes a Naval Station, it might be desirable to erect a Naval Hospital Site - NE side of Punchbowl - 20 acres". Years later this site became the location of Tripler Hospital, a noted landmark today. And then, to reiterate his sense of urgency, "the land officer has been very busy accepting many applications coming in for exchanges". Sensing that the Navy was ready to purchase land parcels in and around Pearl Harbor, the owners were busily exchanging their properties' tax bases, which raised the values. Local media were aware of this and were definitely on the owners' side. From an editorial,

> "Occasional bits of information come from Washington that the Pearl Harbor improvement project is being attended to and that operations initiating the erection of a fortress, the deepening of the harbor and the construction of wharves are about to begin. The Secretary of the Navy has lately been seized with the apprehension that the landholders in the vicinity of the lochs are going to try to make some money out of Uncle Sam by stiffening the value of certain properties most desired by the government. This is natural and if true is commendable on the part of the fortunate real estate owners there. The U.S. Government has had nearly a quarter of a century to consider the matter, and if values have increased with the progress of the Islands it is not the fault of the property owners who have been patiently paying taxes on their algeroba forests all these years in the hope that some day the long contemplated naval station would materialize".[18]

The opportunistic land owners were soon to be shocked. Someone in the US Congress noticed that the Hawaiians enjoyed use and possession, but not title to their land. And when they learned that the use and possession were rescindable by the US, they lost any hope of excessive remuneration. Before that knowledge came to their attention, many different opinions were expressed concerning ownership of land in the Honolulu area.

Nearby in Pearl Harbor, legal maneuvering over the land was becoming more and more hostile. While the combatants were snorting and pawing the ground, Merry continued his investigation of the area.

One of the problems reported by Merry was the shortage of water in the area. The Pearl River only ran full when it rained and otherwise remained subject to incoming sea waves and tides and was brackish. He reported "A 10-inch well recently sunk on Ford's Island at depth of 480 feet produces 500,000 gallons per day".[19]

General Order #530 of November 17, 1899 reidentified the Coal Depot as a Naval Station. Merry was named commander[20], to which he replied, "I have the honor to acknowledge receipt of Department's Order #196037 directing me to assume command of the U.S. Naval Station, Honolulu, T.H."[21]

Just as the initial organization problems were being solved, suddenly all work came to an abrupt halt with the outbreak of Bubonic Plague in December of 1899.[22] Until the following February, when the threat subsided, Commander Merry took great care with the lives of his men against this new menace and placed the Naval Station under quarantine. During this time of inactivity, Merry requested $12,000 to construct a residence for the commander. Actually it could not properly be called an inactive period for Merry, because his work and correspondence continued as Commander of the new Naval Station. He served with distinction in that position until relieved by Rear Admiral W.H. Whiting on July 31, 1902.

Merry's recommendations created the patterns that shaped Pearl Harbor. His vision, sense of urgency and the persuasive manner he used in his abundant correspondence clearly showed the need for the acquisition of land in and around Pearl Harbor. He outlined which parcels of land were needed and for what reason. He constantly reminded the people in Washington, six thousand miles and two months away, of the action required to make the proposed Naval Station a reality. The political reasoning for acquiring a Naval Facility in the Pearl Harbor/Honolulu area in the first place had always been the prevention of any European power from acquiring the islands. In 1898, the United States obviated that possibility by annexing the islands. The current threat was not foreigners, but the new Americans who lived in Hawaii and owned the desired plots of land.

Partially due to Merry's urging, but also because of other problems around the world, Navy Secretary John Long created a General Board on March 3, 1900 with Admiral George Dewey, the hero of Manila Bay, presiding. This board oversaw the activities of the Pearl Harbor Board and, on April 19 Secretary Long informed Naval Affairs Committees of Congress that his department approved the board's recommendations. His report concluded,

> "Pearl Harbor can be successfully defended, rendering its anchorages safe from outside attack, and it possesses a comparatively large deep-water anchorage, capable of expansion if needed. And it should also be borne in mind that it is the only defensible harbor within the entire Hawaiian group".[23]

General Order #538 of February 2, 1900 again renamed the new station, this time to Naval Station, Hawaii. Optimistically, Merry had used the term in a letter of December 6, 1899. In June 1900, Congress appropriated $25,000 for machine tools for repair of Naval Vessels.

Almost everyone agreed, for many reasons, that Pearl Harbor was essential. But, other than Commander Merry's recommendations, with which no one disagreed, nothing was done. The Navy Department had not allocated the $100,000 authorized for dredging. When asked why, RAdm Royal B. Bradford answered that the Pearl Harbor Board believed it to be an insufficient amount.[24] Rather than use the funds available, he chose to do nothing. His point was that the land should be acquired before dredging was started.

There was a small but significant minority, however, who expressed a different opinion about Pearl. In 1901, Admiral Robley 'Fighting Bob' Evans, later to command T.R. Roosevelt's Great White Fleet, noted four deficiencies of Pearl Harbor as a Naval Base. First, the absence of high ground near the harbor made detection of approaching ships difficult. Second, the islands were not self-sustaining. Third, Hawaii had no major industrial facilities. The small Navy Yard, or 'plant', was already the largest such establishment on the islands. Finally, he stated his concern about the large percentage of residents who were Japanese.[25]

Congressional committees listened to his points but felt they were outweighed by the strategic advantages of Hawaii's location and the other advantages of Pearl Harbor. In March of 1901, Congress appropriated $150,000 for the purchase of land and for channel dredging. That same act authorized $107,000 for machine shops, including a smithery [sic] and foundry.[26]

Plans were made by an engineering company in San Francisco for a channel 30' deep, 200' wide for a distance of 3085'. This channel was to lie between two outcroppings of coral. Bids were advertised in the local news media. The contract was to be awarded on the 27th of February, 1901. One writer editorialized, "A small city will grow up on the peninsula and the pressure on the limited confines of Honolulu harbor will be considerably relieved when there are thirty feet of water on the bar"[27] The first contract was won by Clarke and Henry of Stockton, California at the rate of 44 3/4 cents per yard to remove sand only. Unfortunately, after the sand was removed, submarine coral heads remained which made navigation hazardous to all but very small watercraft. Dredging would continue for the next few years as a channel widening and deepening project. Then, a program was inaugurated to dredge the channel and harbor continuously.

One of Merry's recommendations to the Navy Department in early 1900 was to have a battalion of Marines located at the new Naval Station in Honolulu, or in Pearl Harbor if the plans for its development were carried out. That recommendation was not acted upon until almost four years later. However, in the interim, U.S. Marines were on board various U.S. ships in Honolulu Harbor, and often stood by for whatever they might be called upon to do.[28]

Merry had done a magnificent job while in command of the Naval Station. His foresight, wisdom and initiative had laid the groundwork for acquisition and further development. He remained in Hawaii but relinquished command of the Naval Station to LCdr Pond in a letter to the assistant Secretary of the Navy.

"Sir,   Nov. 13th, 1900
1. I have the honor to inform the department that in obedience to its order I have this day turned over the command of this Naval Station to Lieut. Commander Chas. F. Pond, U.S.N."[29]

LCdr Pond's assignment was as (acting) commander and was not confirmed. Merry remained officially the commander until relieved by RAdm W. H. Whiting in July of 1902.

Honolulu Naval Station received its first Civil Engineering Officer, Captain F.C. Prindle in early 1901 who acted as the Public Works Officer. He assisted Merry until he was relieved a year later by Captain U.S. White. Their engineering reports corroborated the reports Merry had been sending Washington.[30]

In the spring of 1901, the Bureau of Equipment of the U.S. Navy made offers to the land owners of Pearl Harbor, but to no avail. The prices demanded by the owners and those estimated by the Department were so far apart that negotiations came to a halt. Then Congress decided to acquire the land through condemnation. Lieutenant Commander Charles F. Pond, who had been named acting commander of the Naval Station, was ordered to commence condemnation proceedings.[31] Pond did so and reported the filing of the case in August of 1901.[32]

Federal District Judge Morris M. Estee commented that "Oahu condemnation proceedings would rank with the most difficult in the annals of American jurisprudence".[33] He was correct.

The Organic Act of April! 30, 1900, which followed the annexation of Hawaii, stipulated that title of all public lands belonging to the Republic of Hawaii at the time of annexation passed to the United States, but the use and possession remained with the new Territory. A critical clause in that act, which seriously affected the legal action of 1901, provided that "if at any time, the United States required it, the Territory would transfer the use and possession to the United States".

All the land surrounding the Pearl Harbor Lochs was owned by private individuals or corporations. Much of the land was planted with sugar, taro, cane or grazing grass for the cattle that roamed there. Many of the local homesteads boasted luxurious stands of banana trees and fields of pineapple. The waters were used by yachtsmen and others for recreational purposes. Also the waters of Pear} Harbor supplied local fishermen with good catches. Two large islands in the harbor, Ford's and Kuahua, were used for picnics, and to further complicate matters there was a cemetery in Pearl City with "a funeral almost every day".[34] The United States government made offers to each landowner, all of which were rejected. No attempt was made to contact the users of the water. The land the government sought was Kuahua Island (later made into a peninsula), on the southeast shore of East Loch (site of the present Navy Yard), and the southeast section of Ford's Island. That plan would allow U.S. ships to enter through the soon-to-be dredged channel, change course slightly to starboard and dock or anchor surrounded by U.S. government owned and operated land facilities. The land to be condemned by the U.S. government was approximately 720 acres.

On July 6, 1901 United States Attorney General P.C. Knox and District Attorney J.J. Dunne filed a petition which became known locally as the 'infamous' Case #3. During the next few years, pleas and counterclaims were filed, but none had the impact of this first case. It should be explored in some detail. The cover page states:

"In the District Court of the United States in and for the District of Hawaii, July 6th, 1901.

The United States of America, plaintiff and petitioner,

Vs:

1. The Estate of Bernice Pauahi Bishop, deceased et al, [five Trustees are named individually as defendants].
2. Oahu Railway & Land Company, a corporation; and
3. The Dowsett Company, Limited, a corporation; and
4. Honolulu Sugar Company, a corporation; and
5. Honolulu Plantation Company, a corporation; and
6. Chow Ah Fo; and
7. John Ii Estate, Limited, a corporation; and
8. William G. Irwin; and

9. Oahu Sugar Company, Limited, a corporation; and
10. Bishop and Company, a co-partnership.
    Defendants and Respondents.

The petition announces the U.S. position in 1901 legalese.

"Now comes your petitioner, the United States of
America, named herein above as plaintiff and petitioner, and
represents, avers, alleges and shows as follows, to wit:
    1. The USA has the right, under the 1887 treaty, to
condemn and hold any land in the Hawaiian Islands.
    2. The boundaries of the desired land are explicitly
described and refers to Map # 1739.
    3. The petition includes Kuahua Island.
    4. It is the USA's intent to acquire fee simple land.
    5. USA will build a Naval Station and maintain the
harbor.
    6. Refers to the congressional authorization.
    7. USA will acquire Oahu Railway land.
    8. Lists current owners and/or lessees.
    9. The owners refused USA's reasonable offer.
    10. $16,800 is the reasonable market value.
    11. U.S. will do all the work required.
    12. All legal steps have been taken by petitioner."[35]

The above document took about 40 pages of legal sized paper. It was
accompanied by an affidavit by Lieutenant Commander Charles F. Pond,
(Acting) Commandant, U.S. Naval Station, T.H. The total amount to be paid
for the land amounted to $133,640. The court found in favor of the plaintiff.
The 1st National Bank of Hawaii was named depository for the payment funds.[36]

The case dragged on with several ancillary legal actions filed and
counterfiled. The courtrooms both of Honolulu and San Francisco were filled
with continuances, appeals, writs of error and more appeals. From Honolulu,
the case of Honolulu Sugar Company was remanded to Circuit Court of
Appeals for the Ninth Oistrict in San Francisco. They sent it back to Honolulu
for a new trial which did not get underway because a settlement was reached
before the trial date. The Oahu Railway Co. deeded its land to the U.S. for
$1.00 in return for a perpetual lease to its right-of-way. Other land acquisition
proceedings followed until 1993 and will probably continue.[37]

The case was covered in local newspapers as "Uncle Sam Makes
His Plans Known. Will Establish Immense Fortifications and Naval Station".
In the article that follows that headline, the writer states, without comment,

the essential elements of the case.[38] The final hurdle had been cleared. First by annexation, then by condemnation, Pearl Harbor was about to become what some have called, the United States' Gibraltar of the Pacific.

Chapter 20 - The Marines Land

The United States Navy had obtained the right, by treaty, to use Pearl Harbor in 1876. In the treaty of 1887 those rights were redefined to include exclusive use of the harbor. However, almost no development was done because the coal station at Honolulu, small as it was, was sufficient to supply the needs of the few ships in the Pacific which were steam driven. The Spanish-American War demonstrated the need for more facilities.

The General Board had been created in 1900 by Navy Secretary John D. Long. Board members strongly influenced the passage of a bill in 1903 which provided for the construction of five battleships.[1] Also they recommended establishing a Coal Depot at Pearl Harbor with a capacity of 100,000 tons.[2]

Several US Navy senior officers had turned suspicious eyes west from Hawaii toward the Orient. Sometime near the turn of the century, Japan replaced China as the Asian menace. Radm Albert Barker, president of the Pearl Harbor Board (a local subordinate of the General Navy Board) wrote,

"Were I the Japanese Admiral with the power to act, I should get the Japanese vessels ready for service in their respective ports, so as not to attract too much attention, then issue orders to go to sea to rendezvous on a certain day at the Hawaiian Islands."

Admiral Barker then continued ominously

"I would arm the adult Japanese population to the number of 25,000, hoist the Japanese flag over the islands, attack and defeat the US vessels - for all could easily be destroyed, as they would be tied up head and stern in Honolulu Harbor. If the Japanese mean business they will endeavor to take the Islands and attack the fleet by surprise."[3]

Pearl Harbor was assuming more military significance each day. With the 'isthmian canal' through Panama under construction, commercial shippers could easily see that the route from Panama to any Asian port would pass the Hawaiian Islands. Since the port of Honolulu would no doubt prosper and increase its capacity, the United States decided to re-locate its growing military operations to the nearby Pearl Harbor, another reason attention turned to the development of the Naval Station there.

The Appropriations Act of March 3, 1901 provided that the Secretary of the Navy should "acquire land for a naval station and harbor and channel defense at Pearl Harbor, Hawaii." Further, "For maintenance of the colliers, pay, transportation, shipping, and subsistence of civilians, officers and crews, and all expenses connected with naval colliers employed in emergencies which cannot be paid from other appropriations, $350,000."[4] These plans were no secret. One reputable journal reported, "Arrangements are being made for the establishment at Pearl Harbor in the Hawaiian Islands of a naval station, roughly estimated to cost the government $5,000,000."[5]

In July of 1901, a page one article in a Honolulu newspaper carried the headline, "BILL TO MAKE HAWAII A STATE. Delegate Wilcox Declares His Views in Plain Terms." 'Plain terms' referred to the intensity with which Wilcox attacked the suggestion that Hawaii be made into a congressional district of the State of California.[6]

From the initial land acquired by the US government, the Naval Station at Pearl Harbor expanded with the acquisition of small parcels. That process continued for several decades.[7] By 1903 work had begun on grading and building on Kuahua Island and the southern tip of Waipio peninsula.[8]

This same year saw the first channel completed through the bar outside the Pearl Harbor entrance. It was only 30' deep and about 200' wide. That allowed the small gunboats USS *Petrel* and the USS *Iroquois* and other small commercial vessels to enter.[9] The channel was heralded by a local magazine as the "opening of Pearl Lochs" which pointed out that the cane grown on Ford Island will be taken by barge to the Waipio peninsula and there loaded onto ships to go to the mainland mills, rather than making the train trip to Honolulu Harbor.[10]

A small problem was encountered during the digging of this channel which was a portent of the catastrophe that would come later. Two dredges intended for use in the digging were towed to the site on barges. Warnings that the area was guarded by the shark goddess went unheeded. On the night of their arrival, an unseasonable "Kona storm arose and, before it was possible to tow the shallow draft machines into shelter, one dredge was torn loose from its moorings and sank almost in the middle of the channel"[11]. The other dredge was beached near Queen Emma's Point and was later salvaged. The Navy had indeed encountered its first instance of *pilikia* (trouble).

An inter-departmental imbroglio developed in May of 1903. The US Treasury Department stated its desire to use a portion of the Naval Reservation at Honolulu (probably Ford Island or Sand Island) for an immigration station. The Assistant Secretary of the Navy sent a terse note rejecting the proposal. He followed that action with a letter to the Naval Station Commander to "notify Commissioner Sargent and the Territorial

Government to vacate all lands occupied by them belonging to this department and take possession".[12]

Meanwhile, the business of the Navy proceeded. On October 24, 1903 the Commandant of the Naval Station, Rear Admiral S. W. Terry, ordered the Commanding Officer of the USS *Iroquois* to "proceed to sea to-night at such hour as you may deem most advantageous ... to search South and East of Oahu as far as [the island of] Hawaii, if necessary, to recover the missing boat of the French Barque *Conetable de Richmont* off French Frigate Shoals. Wishing you success in this mission to succor distressed seamen, I am ..etc."[13] The secretary was to supply name, rank and other details.

Part of the duties of any station commander is that of host to visiting dignitaries. One distinguished visitor displayed uncommon foresight. Major General Arthur MacArthur, Civil War hero and father of World War II General of the Army Douglas MacArthur, called upon the station commander, Rear Admiral S. W. Terry and Territorial Governor George R. Carter.[14] During his visit the general commented that Hawaii would be counted upon to be the focus of defense for the entire western United States. Later, in a letter to the Attorney General of the United States, MacArthur wrote of the importance of Hawaii to both commercial and military interests of the US. He said that "Hawaii's remoteness is a perfect defense against an unexpected raid."[15] Upon their departure they were honored with a 17 gun salute.[16]

With the completion of the channel through the bar at the entrance to Pearl Harbor, Secretary of the Navy William H. Moody, ordered that any foreign man-of-war or public vessel desiring to visit the harbor must first obtain permission from the Department of State.[17] Considering the depth of the new channel and the draft of major warships, this order might seem premature. However, the idea of such caution was valid.

Always when the United States desires its property protected, the first ones to be called are the United States Marines. The years 1903 to 1907 have left us with a legacy of correspondence that indicates that bureaucratic ineptitude and red tape are not new inventions.

Having decided that there should be a contingent of Marines stationed in the Honolulu/Pearl Harbor area, the Commandant of the Marine Corps sent a cablegram to RAdm Terry asking, "Where will Marines be located?"[18] Terry immediately replied, "The Navy has eight acres. Marines may use one acre."[19] After determining that the space suggested was sufficient, General Elliott cabled Terry and advised him that "Captain Albertus W. Catlin, USMC will be transferred from Philippine Islands to Territory of Hawaii to command the Marine Barracks, to be established at Navy Yard under your command."[20] General Elliott, of course, must have expected some permanent quarters would be supplied. Not only was no permanent building planned, there weren't even adequate quarters for the original group of Marines who would be posted to Hawaii. Part of the reason can be inferred from the following exchange.

RAdm Terry, on December 18, sent a cable to General Elliott. "Request permission to spend $5,000 on barracks."[21] The reply came, not from General Elliott, but from a Major Denny of the Quartermaster Corps. With no preliminary explanation, it stated, "$500 authorized."[22] Terry's reply cablegram was sent to General Elliott, not to the USMCQM. It was immediate and clear, "$5,000 is necessary. $500 totally inadequate".[23] After waiting three weeks, RAdm Terry took a different tack and wrote to the General. In this letter he mentioned, "I have received no answer for my request for necessary funds. Captain Catlin is here and I find myself somewhat embarrassed".[24] The letter had some effect, but not much. General Elliott cabled RAdm Terry, "$500 more authorized. Total = $1,000".[25] The Marine captain had already arrived, the detachment from California was due in a few days, nothing was prepared for their arrival, and the commandant of the US Marine Corps had authorized the Naval Station Commander to spend $1,000 on a building intended to house some 50 men! The word SNAFU (Situation Normal, All Fouled Up - a WWII expression) had not yet been invented, but it certainly would be appropriate to describe this situation.

The resourceful Admiral Terry sought frantically for a place to house the men who were expected momentarily. He and his staff found a solution, not a particularly good one, but under their desperate conditions, it was the best they could do. Terry wrote to Commandant Elliott and suggested, "We can use an empty coal shed temporarily for 60 to 75 days."[26] The coal shed he referred to was the one built in 1842, half a century before, rarely used, and never repaired. This was the 'housing' that awaited the Marine detachment. It was old, small, dilapidated, unfloored, and unlockable. It was a disaster in the midst of paradise.

Despite the chaotic and unprepared situation, the Marines, of course, landed. The following letter was sent to the Assistant Secretary of the Navy,

"Sir,

I have the honor to report the arrival today, on the U.S. Army Transport Sheridan, of Lieutenant William C. Harllee, U.S.M.C., and a Marine Guard of 49 men, all well.

Very Respectfully,
Silas W. Terry, Rear Admiral, U.S. Navy
cc: Commandant, U.S.M.C."[27]

Another letter went out that day from Hawaii. Captain Catlin, who was to command the Marine detachment, had not been idle. Although he was not the least bit satisfied with the proposed quarters for his men, he fully expected to rebuild the old coal shed or construct a new one. After all, he had 50 men at his disposal, and the work would be for their own benefit. All he needed was the money and permission to proceed. He wrote a long letter in which he indicated the urgency of his situation, "We expect a load of coal in two or three months and they will need the shed." He also sent a set of architectural drawings showing a building "as cheap as can be put up to properly accommodate 50 men and stores". His drawings are of a building 40' x 80', two story, with a dormitory upstairs. Downstairs were an office, storage space, a galley and a mess hall. There was also a detached latrine. Unfortunately, that building was never built. In that letter he also pointed out that "the medical officer does not consider it advisable to put the men in tents; the ground is very low and much sickness would result. If the men and stores had been put in tents upon their arrival here, the stores would have been ruined and the men drenched, as there has been a rainfall of about 19 inches in four days."[28] Welcome to Paradise!

Marines are always able to 'adapt and overcome' as shown by subsequent events. Four years after their arrival, correspondence still referred to the "temporary Marine Barracks", meaning the same old coal shed. Through the years letters indicate requests for material and permission to construct a floor, repair the roof, build an addition, etc. All during these years, of course, they turned out in formation for ceremonies in their spotless, splendid uniforms and, at other times, quelled trouble on the station in Honolulu and at Pearl Harbor.

Part of the trouble at this time was expected from the west. Japan and Russia were at war and the United States desired to maintain a strictly neutral position. G. A. Converse, Assistant Secretary of the Navy wrote to RAdm Terry and informed him that, "if a Russian or Japanese ship enters Hawaiian waters, show him the President's Proclamation of Neutrality (General Order #154, March 11, 1904) and request he leave within 24 hours."[29]

Not everyone was as deadly serious as historical accounts make them seem. An amusing exchange took place between Lieutenant Commander A. P. Niblack, who had relieved Pond as acting Commandant of the Naval Station, and Mr. B. F. Colley, Superintendent of the C. P. Cable Company, Midway Island, concerning the unexpected results of planned improvements. Niblack instructed Colley not to produce any bad weather with his new meteorological instruments. Colley responded, "You have a new doctor; if you don't look out you will all have poor health".[30]

LCdr Niblack, wrote a letter to Terry, who now headed the 14th Naval District. In the letter he reminded Terry of the Marines' quarters, "It is, of course, understood that the Marine garrison at this station is only temporarily occupying coal shed #1".[31] It must have sounded familiar to Terry. Another exchange of letters occurred on the same theme. In October of 1905, a year and a half after the Marines began to 'temporarily' occupy the old coal shed, a Major Charles L. McCawley, after inspecting the shed, recommended that the Marines move to tents.[32] Two months later, Mr. A. C. Wrenn, the acting Chief of Bureau of Equipment, wrote to the Commandant of the Naval Station and stated that "the Marines will stay in the coal shed".[33] Either he was unaware of the living conditions of the Marines' or he supposed that they did move to tents, Colonel F. L. Denny, the staff member who allowed only $500 to build the new building in 1904, wrote to the Commandant of the Corps the uninformed note, "The Marines on the Hawaiian Station will stay in tents."[34]

Lt. Harllee, the man in command of the first detachment of Marines that arrived at the Honolulu station on February 9, 1904, was still on duty there in October of the next year. He was in charge of defense of the post and decided he needed a 3" artillery piece. His requisition, approved by Captain Catlin, concerned this artillery piece. It was,

> "needed not only for drill, but for strategic considerations, since the white element of the population of these islands is numerically insignificant. Americans are not in the majority. Japanese are far in excess of all others combined. They are energetic and progressive and in the event of war with any nation the seizure of these islands by enemies of the United States resident here is not a possibility too remote to be considered".[35]

The message was forwarded to the Quartermaster's Office by Captain H. L. Roosevelt, USMC.

Some of the Marines' responsibilities took them to the other islands. Often this meant a short trip of a few miles. However, one problem they had to solve took them some 1800 miles away to Midway Island. A detachment of Marines under the command of 2nd LT. Clarence S. Owen left San Francisco on their way to Midway Island, On November 17, 1905, Second Lieutenant Jeter R. Horton, USMC, was ordered to go, with a detail} consisting of one first sergeant, three corporals, and 16 privates, to replace 2nd Lt. Epaminondas L. Bigler, USMC.[36] Their mission was to protect cable employees from Japanese marauders who visited the islands to kill seabirds. After Lt. Bigler got Horton squared away, he was ordered to report to US Naval Station, Honolulu, T.H., early the next year.[37]

Rear Admiral Henry Lyon relieved RAdm Terry on December 24, 1904 as Commander, Naval Station, Honolulu. He quickly requested additional work, such as widening and deepening and straightening the channel entering Pearl Harbor. His request reached Washington and was answered by Assistant Navy Secretary Truman H. Newberry with some interesting syntax, "Re: your request to widen Pearl Harbor entrance to accommodate battleships, because both local dredging companies are busy, and there are no funds available, not at this time."[38] The organizational relationships are somewhat cloudy as far as historical evidence is concerned. LCdr Niblack signed letters as "Captain of the Yard" as late as March 31, 1906. At the end of the next month, Lt. J. F. Carter was "Captain of the Yard" in his correspondence. Both men were commanding officers of the USS *Iroquois* during their tenure as 'Captain of the Yard' . At the same time Niblack was signing as indicated above, he also signed correspondence as (acting) Commandant, Naval Station, T.H.

In order to relieve and rotate the men serving under Captain Catlin, the Corps Commandant, Brig Gen Elliott, in May of 1906 ordered a detail consisting of Second Lieutenant M.E. Shearer, one gunnery sergeant, three corporals, and 21 privates, to board the Chesapeake & Ohio RR in Washington, proceed to San Francisco, thence to board an Army transport to sail to Honolulu, Territory of Hawaii.[39] The conditions the new men found in Honolulu were not much better than they had been two years before when the Marines first inhabited the old coal shed. Captain S. W. Very, USN, who had relieved RAdm Lyon in July of 1906, wrote a month later, in a 'sanitary report' that, "at present coal shed #2 is empty, and naturally it will be used only when its use is imperative."[40] That must have sounded dismal to men who were still waiting for their permanent quarters.

Living conditions were not improving. Major J. H. Russell, who later became the Marine Corps Commandant, relieved Major B. H. Fuller as Officer in Command of the Marine contingent in Honolulu. In a report to Major Russell, Lt. Bigler remarks respectfully,

> "I have the honor to report that the roof of coal shed #1, the building now occupied by the Marine Guard, is in a leaky and damaged condition. I had to move our stores to prevent damage."[41]

Later, Bigler got the Peerless Paint Company, Ltd., to fix the roof. In the same vein, Major Russell wrote to the Naval Station Commandant (sic), "I have the money and request permission to floor coal shed #1."[42] The resourceful major does not say where the money came from, but obviously the Marines were being treated in a shabby manner which is difficult to understand.

While their physical needs were apparently being ignored, the men on the Honolulu/Pearl Harbor station were at least acquiring intellectual stimuli. Captain Very ordered 25 volumes for the station library. His letter on the subject went straight from him to the Secretary of the Navy, Victor H. Metcalf.[43]

The ever resourceful Lt. Bigler wrote to his commander, Major Russell, "we have no land on Punchbowl. There are two US Navy plots available. The currently used US Agricultural Experimental Station is not desirable because it is 40 minutes march from the Naval Station. Enclosed are two plot plans and building plans (again) and request we retain three of the rooms now occupied in coal shed #1."[44] Apparently the optimistic Bigler thought his plan for new buildings might succeed. The reference to the Agricultural Station was in response to a suggestion that it be converted into a Marine Barracks. The sanguine request was forwarded by Major Russell to Captain Very. The Naval Station Commander's reply concerning the 'two US Navy plots available' was, "the tract on Punchbowl is to be used by the US Navy as a hospital, and the second location, Ka'akaukukui Reef is to used for an Immigration Station."[45]

The final communication in this series is an 'endorsement', a group of reports sent as a package, from the commander of the Navy Yard (station) to the Secretary of the Navy Metcalf. It is the second of nine endorsements.

"ENDORSEMENT. NAVY DEPARTMENT, 27 September 1907.

SUBJECT: Commanding Officer of Marines, Naval Station, Honolulu, T.H., requests that coal shed #1 be retained as barracks for the Marines at the Naval Station, Honolulu, T.H.

Respectfully referred to the Bureau of Equipment and to the Brigadier General, Commandant, U.S.M.C., for report and recommendations.

By Direction of the Secretary of the Navy: F.S. Curtis, Chief Clerk."[46]

Later in 1907, the Marine Guard, consisting of ten officers and 391 enlisted men were put 'under canvas' on a plot of land on the *makai* (seaward) side of Ala Moana Boulevard, which was later the site of Fort Armstrong. The camp was named Camp Very in honor of Captain Samuel W. Very, USN, Commandant of the Naval Station.

This communication concluded the evolution of the initial establishment of the United States Marines at the Naval Station, Honolulu, Territory of Hawaii. There are two ways to interpret this series. One is to regard this last letter as evidence that the officers had subjected their men to continued squalid living conditions in a building that was condemned 40 years before they were assigned to it. A more positive interpretation is that these events are evidence that the Marines, with youthful enthusiasm, dogged determination, and clever resourcefulness, had by 1907, made the infamous old coal shed into a viable, safe, healthful and respectable Marine Barracks.

Chapter 21 - Territorial Years

Hawaii was very different in 1900 from the rural, sparsely settled place it had been in 1800. The previous century had set it on a path toward taking its place in the 20th century world. A new note arrived in October of 1899 when H.R. Baldwin tried out his new motorcar, the islands' first automobile. He tested it as he drove along King Street past the palace at a whopping fourteen miles an hour.[1] The land and the people had been almost completely Americanized. Not all of the changes were good and some conditions were destined to get worse, but in spite of it all, Hawaii was still a place of beauty, gentle breezes, tropical plants and trade winds. Between the rising buildings and growing traffic of downtown Honolulu, one could still see striking, green mountains, gentle valleys and cobalt blue sea. Through the ensuing troubles, triumphs and controversies the physical reality of Hawaii never changed. Humans have altered the land, but they could not change the vast Pacific Ocean, the green and jagged Ko'olau Mountains or the soft, fragrant air that wraps the islands in a soothing cloak.

By the first decade of the new century, Honolulu was a city, with a telephone building, dozens of telephone operators, as well as a regular police force and a tourist agency. Hotels had been built for visitors, several on King Street, and the Moana' a new hotel sat in solitary splendor at Waikiki Beach. The latest model automobiles plied the streets alongside carriages and carts pulled by horses or mules. By the end of the first decade, there was an opera house, a museum and a university. The Bishop Museum, opened in 1903. Its purpose was to collect articles that would illustrate the ethnology of the Hawaiians as well as amass representatives of all the animals and plants that inhabit the islands.[2] The goal was preserve and display all things Hawaiian.

In 1907, the Territorial legislature established the College of Agriculture and Mechanical Arts. The first classes were held the next year with thirteen faculty members, five freshmen, five prep school students and a cow - it was an agricultural college after all. They occupied temporary quarters near town until they moved to the Manoa Valley, their present location above Honolulu, in 1912. Four degrees were conferred on graduates at the first commencement exercise in 1912. Called the College of Hawaii in 1911, it's name was finally changed to the University of Hawaii in 1920. It was soon open to everyone regardless of racial ancestry, gender or nationality. Its courses expanded from concentration on agriculture to become a certified university offering a full range of degrees.

There were hula dancers performing at several locations in Honolulu in 1900 and lei sellers displaying their wares whenever steamers full of tourists docked in the harbor. Visitors marveled at the sights, remarking on the "emerald hue" of the vegetation, "the beautiful valleys" and "sun gilding the mountain sides and brightening the plantations along the shore."[3] There were annual Hawaiian pageants and a big celebration marking the first time King Kamehameha landed on the beach at Waikiki in the 1790s. It featured native arts, dancing and music. Other parades included marching bands and floats that echoed the Rose Parade in Pasadena, which had begun in 1899.

There was also squalor, poor sanitation, daily hard work for the poor, and disease, especially in Chinatown. An outbreak of bubonic plague raced through this crowded section of Honolulu in December of 1899. Some areas were burned in an attempt to get rid of the disease. When the fire got out of control, it burned for several weeks and eventually destroyed all the buildings in the entire area, dispossessing thousands of oriental residents.

The first decade of the Territory of Hawaii was taken up with organizing, getting used to new systems and to being a part of a country with which citizens were familiar, but which had been an adversary in some eyes, a friend in others. It was clear that the acquisition of the Hawaiian Islands was not made for the benefit of her citizens, but was to the advantage of the United States. The islands were part of the defensive line that ran from the Aleutian Islands in Alaska to Hawaii to the Panama Canal Zone.[4] There was no canal yet, but America began its construction in 1904 and it would be opened in 1914. It would greatly reduce sailing time from the east coast of the United States to Hawaii. The new Territory and its attributes were depicted by Senator Morgan of Arkansas, an enthusiastic supporter of American Hawaii, as stronger, better and more useful to the US than Gibraltar was to Great Britain.[5]

The new territory was also, beginning in the spring of 1900, the center of massive political intrigue, rumor and in "an active state of ferment".[6] The causes of this were several. The Hawaiian masses could now vote, the very thing the commission, under the influence of Sanford Dole, had tried to prevent. The Hawaiians did not like already established American political parties. Their own Home Rule Party was whimsically dubbed the "Independent-Home-Rule-Republican-Any-Old-Thing-Party" by one local daily newspaper, the Pacific Commercial Advertiser.[7] That party was supported by the Independent, an anti-Dole newspaper.

William Howard Taft arrived in Honolulu in April of 1900 as an envoy from President McKinley to assess the situation regarding the first Territorial Governor. He commented on the opposition to Dole from the group that supported the monarchy in a letter to McKinley. The local Hawaiian party candidate, Harold M. Sewall, wanted the job very badly. Dole had his enemies but, in Taft's impartial opinion, "he is a man of high character and has a kindly disposition toward every one".[8] Sewall, Taft was sure, would focus on the native element, and he was likely to be troublesome. Sewall lacked patience, conservative judgment and the ability to avoid friction which made him a poor candidate for governor, Taft said. He continued,

> "It is the custom to decry the missionary element here, but it is that which gave us these pearls of the Pacific and which has really made them what they are. I do not think a missionary Governor would be a bad balance wheel for a probably native majority in the legislature."[9]

Sanford Dole's name was put in nomination before the Senate by President McKinley on May 4, and, as expected, he was confirmed as the territory's first governor on May 9, 1900.

Despite the ferment and change, despite the discussion about Pearl Harbor and the changes that were expected, life went on as usual for most Hawaiians. People still worked, played, hiked up Diamond Head, fished and swam in the warm tropical ocean. One example of this occurred on September 8, 1900.

> "In the closest, the most desperate and gamiest race ever held in the history of Honolulu boat clubs, the Healani senior crew captured the classic rowing event from the Myrtle Crew at Pearl Harbor. It was a magnificent race."[10]

The largest crowd in the history of this event arrived at 4 p.m. by rail, carriage and yacht with nearly every boat in these waters anchored just beyond the finish line. Here were a group of locals out to have a good time and take advantage of the attributes of their homeland.

A trip to Pearl Harbor from Honolulu was still a special excursion, often reached on the Oahu Railway. A train consisting of three cars and a small engine on narrow gauge tracks left from the city daily at 9 am. and circled Pearl Harbor. It carried sacks of rice, sugar, tobacco and passengers. Many of the latter spent the time watching the scenery or discussing politics in at least six different and distinct languages.

Excursionists disembarked at the station north of the harbor. "The peninsula and sleepy little Ewa lie under the mountains and by the water's edge disturbed only by the grinding of the sugar cane in the drowsy mill or the buzz of the wheels in the pineapple cannery."[11] Even while the lucky few lazed away the day, others toiled in the halls of commerce.

Tourists were arriving to see Hawaii in increasing numbers and among the main attractions were the active volcanoes on the big island of Hawaii. Oahu began to advertise that it had the most attractions for tourists even though it has no active volcano. The trees and the beaches so close to everything were distinct selling points, as were the mountains. Waikiki was touted as a bathing resort, three and a half miles from the city. The beach was long and broad enough to accommodate the whole of Honolulu at once. The water was as warm in January as it was in July, they emphasized. And still is, of course. Californians know little of the joys of surf bathing until they try the sandy shore of Waikiki, remarked a local writer.[12]

Other attractions on Oahu were the Iolani Palace, the statue of Kamehameha I nearby, Punchbowl and Tantalus Mountain, from which there were spectacular views of Honolulu and the sea, and the Pali, 1200 feet above sea level. From here one could see the spectacular Kaneohe Bay. These views are still visible from these locations, though now they are restricted by growth both vegetative and human.

Paradise of the Pacific, a popular local publication which covered all things Hawaiian, published a column in 1900 extolling the value and benefit of bathing, both in the family tub or shower and in the nearby and accessible sea. Good for the lungs, they remarked, and stirs up the bodily forces.[13]

Pearl Harbor, always a topic of interest to residents and visitors alike, was beginning to be a center of activity by the summer of 1901. Operations were commencing on the erection of a fort, the deepening of the harbor and the construction of wharves inside the harbor. Progress was watched with great interest and no activity was condemned in local papers.

In the first decade of the century, a number of people and groups, both in the islands and on the mainland, became interested in the make-up of this new racially mixed territory, and a great deal of counting and compiling of tables was done. A census done by the US in 1896 and published in 1906, estimated the total population of the islands at 90,000. Native Hawaiians living in the islands numbered about 30,000, 16,000 men and 14,000 women. Residents of American origin numbered 3,000 and British 2,000, a small portion of the population. There were 24,000 Japanese and 21,000 Chinese. Of the Hawaiians and part Hawaiians, 87% could read and write and the ratio among Americans and Europeans was the same. Among Orientals it was 50%. Whatever else the creators of these statistics were using them for, they do give an idea of the makeup of the islands at the turn of the century.

These people were interested in many things, as seen in *Paradise of the Pacific*. One of the new topics of interest in 1900 was communication with the mainland. The telegraph had finally reached San Francisco from the east coast in 1860, just in time for the population to hear about the beginning of the Civil War, but it went no further. The Atlantic Cable, which connected North America and Europe, was completed in 1858, but failed several weeks later. It was finally repaired and finished in 1866 from Newfoundland to Ireland. Such a cable was needed for the Pacific, but seemed too expensive and too arduous to be practical. Then in January of 1903, the Commercial

Pacific Cable Company was able to complete the connection. That very night Hawaiian Secretary Cooper spoke to President Theodore Roosevelt from the palace and received congratulations. From that time on, the transpacific cable was operational and Hawaii was in much closer communication with Washington D.C.[14]

The first telephone system in Hawaii was called "Mr. Bell's talkative wire".[15] In 1900, it was reported that the Marconi system of wireless telegraphy, connecting the five principal islands of the group, was about to be installed. The apparatus was already set up and was to be in operation by the end of August. It cost the Inter-Island Telegraph Co. $100,000 to create and operate this system. The men who owned the telegraph company were some of the most prominent businessmen in Honolulu.

One event of great interest to many islanders after the turn of the century was the Russo-Japanese War which began in February of 1904. The fighting did not come near Hawaii, but because it was in the Pacific Ocean, it was close enough to make some people a bit anxious. In 1898, a comment in a local paper showed that many people thought Japan aspired to become the British Empire of the Pacific and won't give up without a struggle.[16] The Russo-Japanese War was the first dispute between an Asian nation and a European one. It focused on who would control Korea and Manchuria in China. Japan wanted them both for she had few natural resources of her own and had to expand. To get these territories, Japan built a powerful Navy and with a Japanese Navy only three thousand miles away, Hawaii was more vulnerable to invasion than ever. Also there was deep suspicion among many who were concerned about the loyalties of the Japanese in Hawaii.

The progress of the war, descriptions of the battles and the status of the combatants were reported at length in Honolulu newspapers.[17] Many accounts were eyewitness descriptions written from battle fields and ports by reporters such as Jack London and Richard Harding Davis. Also there appeared in the press articles retelling the story of the opening of Japan in 1857, a Japanese officer's story of one of the battles and assessments of Japanese and Russian strengths and weaknesses.[18] The concern in Hawaii was personal.

"Hawaii comes first in Naval Importance Should War Occur," trumpeted a headline in July of 1905. The opinion was that of Congressman Loud of Michigan. The United States is aware that Hawaii stands between east and west, he said, should anything happen. Hawaii is in a peculiar position and Loud promised the Naval Station would soon be built in Pearl Harbor. It is only a matter of getting the money, he stated. It is always the problem. In the case of war with an eastern power, the United States must defend these islands, he concluded in a statement of the obvious.[19]

Japan won the war, which was a terrible shock for Europeans. It was the first time and oriental power had defeated a European one, even a weak one like Russia. The build-up of the Japanese navy was the significant part of this for those in Hawaii who paid attention to current events.

The threat was over, and the danger generally forgotten, when the war ended in September of 1905. Japan was awarded Port Arthur, Korea and the southern half of Sakhalin, an island off the far eastern coast of Russia. Their needs had been met, temporarily at least. The United States continued its slow, bumbling path toward creating a Naval Base at Pearl Harbor. The citizens of the islands went back to their usual pursuits.

"This creates greater joy in these Mid-Pacific isles than any event that has occurred since annexation," states an article in *Paradise of the Pacific* for May 1908. It refers to the bill that passed Congress the previous month that guaranteed the work of construction of the Naval Base at Pearl Harbor and other defenses could actually begin. The bill authorized three million dollars, half a million immediately available. The shouting in Hawaii, of course, was about the fact that this called the world's attention to Hawaii as nothing else had done. It was also, incidentally, notice that there would be jobs available in constructing the facilities. "Much material will be brought from the mainland, but salaries and wages will be paid here. Every art, profession, craft and trade will profit," the article concludes.[20]

By 1908, relations between the citizens and visiting sailors were old hat to *kamainas*, or old timers. Sailors had been visiting Honolulu from many nations for a hundred years, but now an event of singular importance was to take place.

President Theodore Roosevelt was well known for his aggressive expansionist policies, but what he did in 1908 showed a wisdom with which he is seldom credited. In the midst of very difficult relations with Japan, Roosevelt decided "no diplomatic act gained greater respect than a show of force."[21] He assigned Rear Admiral Robley 'Fighting Bob' Evans the daunting task of commanding a flotilla, in fact the majority of our fleet, sixteen battleships and their supporting craft to steam around the world. This fleet of ships is now routinely referred to as 'Mr. Roosevelt's Great White Fleet', but at the time it was simply called the Grand Fleet or the Battle Fleet. Americans were used to seeing white warships because ships in the fleet had been painted white since the advent of iron and steel ships in the 1880s.[22] Occasionally, spectators in other parts of the world commented that the ships would make great targets. Similar to the time when Lt. Charles Wilkes led his fleet of sailing ships from Hampton Roads, some sixty years before, these ships must have presented a grand sight. President Roosevelt aboard his anchored yacht *Mayflower*, beamed with satisfaction as he saw the magnificent ships pass in review. Each shining white vessel roared a 21-gun salute to their Commander in Chief as they cut through the icy waters of Chesapeake Bay on that cold December morning.

The fleet steamed south, making several stops on the east coast of South America, then around Cape Horn and up the coast to San Francisco. At each stop they replaced food, coal and engine parts, cleaned and fumigated and did the other necessary things required on such an arduous journey.

It became a popular avocation for Americans to follow the fleet's progress on their own maps at home. When it was announced that they would visit the Hawaiian Islands, committees of citizens met in Honolulu to decide on the entertainment of officers and enlisted men while they were in the islands. The earnest citizens did not know when the ships would come nor how long they would stay, but they wanted to provide something in return for the honor of the visit and to display Hawaii's warm, open and affectionate hospitality and its spirit of Aloha. "All agree that field sports are essential to the sailorman's pleasure," stated a *Paradise of the Pacific* article several weeks before the fleet arrived. One motive for planning these diversions was to keep sailors from visiting saloons.[23]

The lead ships appeared on July 16, 1908 rounding Diamond Head and anchored in the Waikiki Roadstead. The fleet was now under the command of Rear Admiral Sperry who relieved RAdm Evans in San Francisco due to the latter's illness.[24]

How successful the committee was in directing and curtailing the activities of visiting sailors is not reported, though there were no problems that received publicity. Wealthy pineapple and sugar growers entertained the officers royally. There was a picnic on the shores of Pearl Harbor, where workmen were digging holes for gun emplacements and working on other construction. Several participants remarked that it was a shame to spoil such a lovely spot.[25] Part of that construction was the beginning of the newly planned dry-dock. No one there that day knew, or could imagine that the Hawaiian shark goddess was about to become important to the Navy's activities.

In town, there were band concerts, fireworks and flags flying every day of the week long visit. Companies of sailors and marines paraded along Kalakaua Avenue in Honolulu during the days and did their best not to antagonize local citizens while they enjoyed themselves in this 'tropical paradise' during the evenings. The ships were splendidly dressed stem to stern with all flags flying and bands played for local visitors. Lights blazed from each ship's rigging every night. This event was planned so that the ships would be visible to everyone for the entire week they lay in the harbor.

An important part of the mission while in the Hawaiian Islands was to assuage the deposed Queen's feelings after her removal from power just a few years before. Unfortunately the extended hand was ignored by former Queen Liliuokalani. She and her entourage left the city a few days before the fleet arrived. Despite the snub, the visit was a satisfying success and when the American sailors hauled up their anchors and headed west, they left an impressed populace behind.

The ships and men were intended to spread awe for the power of the navy among Hawaiians and goodwill for the United States. However, the visit was only partially successful. It displayed undoubted Naval power, but fell short in eliciting affection for the United States.

The subsequent fleet tour of Japan was interesting in that the Japanese showed none of their recent animosity. They hosted the American fleet with impeccable grace and even enthusiasm. The two nations competed on sports fields and impromptu gatherings. At one picnic, the famous Admiral Togo, 61 years of age, was tossed three times up in the air by American Sailors and caught in a blanket, a young man's rollicking game of the time. One of the young officers' an ensign named William F. Halsey, would later say bitterly, "If we had known what the future held, we would not have caught him the third time."[26]

The fleet continued without any mishaps, across the Indian Ocean, through the recently opened Suez Canal, through the Straits of Gibraltar, and back to Hampton Roads, where they dropped anchor on February 22, 1909. Whatever the hostile press in America and Europe had printed about the cruise before it started, they were generally surprised and impressed by the fact that an American fleet had circled the globe, overcoming storms, collisions, desertions, epidemics and the kind of damage that the cruel sea inflicts on ships. Roosevelt's *fait* was certainly *accompli!* He gave European countries notice that America was a sea power to be reckoned with, and he quieted the saber rattling in Asia. He typically acknowledged the diplomatic triumph by smiling his wide, ebullient, engaging smile and saying, "Every particle of trouble with the Japanese government and the Japanese press stopped like magic."[27]

When they returned home, all of the ships in the entire fleet were painted gray, like the fleets of European countries. Whether or not tensions cooled with Japan after this singular event is not clear. Articles were written showing why those who predicted war were wrong. War between the U.S. and Japan would be unwise, if not impossible, both diplomatically and practically.[28]

As the first decade of the century came to a close, the people of Hawaii were treated to the sight of the first powered airplane to fly above the island. On December 31, 1910, a P-18 biplane, piloted by 'Bud' Masters, took to the air from the *Moana Lua* polo field, an area adjacent to Pu'uloa Road as it crosses the Lunalilo or H-1 Freeway today. Spectators gathered to watch the unusual sight and paid for the privilege. At the time, planes and pilots reached Hawaii by steamer. When the tour was over, planes were put on a ship for the trip back to the mainland. It would be years before airplane design would progress enough for a plane to fly non-stop over the Pacific, but it would come.

Chapter 22 -Two New Weapons

The first two decades of the twentieth century saw several important changes in the organization of the United States Navy and in the focus of its mission. The Russo-Japanese War of 1904-5, and its outcome, plunged a dagger of fear into the hearts of thousands of Americans. People in the western United States wanted more protection against possible menaces from the sea. Their oriental-directed xenophobia reached a peak in October of 1906 when the San Francisco school board segregated oriental students into separate schools in order to protect their own children from "association with pupils of the Mongolian race".[1] The San Francisco action led to anti-American demonstrations in Tokyo, and the Japanese government sternly protested to Washington. In Hawaii, where the potential enemy was 2400 miles closer and with a much higher percentage of oriental people, there was little evidence that any inter-racial problem existed. Honolulu at that time had 39,000 residents, of which 5,000 were *haoles*. The rest were of various ethnic groups other than Caucasian.

Plan Orange, which had been devised at the request of Navy Secretary George Meyer, outlined the actions necessary for the US Navy to take in case of war, specifically with Japan. The Atlantic fleet would assemble on the east coast, sail 'round Cape Horn, reassemble on the west coast, reprovision in Hawaii, and then proceed to the Philippines to engage the Japanese fleet. During the two or three month period of ship movement, the troops in the Philippines would have to defend their positions as long as possible. The plan was unpopular in the west because of the long delay in moving the fleet in an emergency, even after the Panama Canal opened. The plan was also unpopular in the east because it would leave the Atlantic exposed to German naval forces. Actually there were cruisers in both oceans, but at that time, battleships were considered the ultimate weapon.[2]

The civilians and the military in Hawaii were not too pleased with the plan either because they would ultimately be the first line of defense after the fall of the Philippines. The Hawaiian Islands at that time were hardly able to resist a concentrated invasion. Hawaiian leaders, convinced an invasion was possible, if not imminent, demanded completion of the many fortifications which the Army had started, and the stationing of a garrison. Hawaii was considered by the military to be in a "deplorably defenseless position".[3] The Hawaiian Territorial Delegate to the US Congress, Jonah Kuhio Kalanianaole, complained that the Navy had not turned over one bit of sod for its base. About all the Navy had done since the establishment of the Naval Station in Honolulu was to erect two radio towers that had the capability of sending signals for 225 miles and receiving messages from 140 miles.[4] The little amount of dredging that had been done allowed only the tiny gunboat USS

Petrel to enter Pearl Harbor.[5] San Francisco was 2400 miles away, and Washington 3000 miles more. What few defenses there were, were concentrated in the valley between the Waianae and Ko'olau mountains, expecting an invasion on the north shore of Oahu. Ironically, that is exactly the path flown 40 years later by the Japanese planes on their way to Pearl Harbor.

It was during this tense time that, on April 15, 1907, the Asiatic and Pacific Squadrons were combined to form the United States Pacific Fleet.[6]

Hawaiian Governor George R. Carter urged the Navy to move out of the Honolulu area into the land available at Pearl Harbor to reduce the congestion in the capital city.[7] Recognizing these and other forceful considerations, in the May 1908 Congressional Appropriations Act, authorization was finally granted to establish a Naval Station at Pearl Harbor. Each project involved was clearly outlined in the Act, with the expenditures allowed totaling one million dollars for a dry-dock and a million more for ancillary buildings and equipment.[8] Captain C.W. Parks was named the first District Public Works Officer.

Dredging an entrance channel	$400,000
Construction of Dry-docks	300,000
Erecting machine shops	100,000
Storehouses	100,000
Yard development	100,000
In All	$1,000,000

While the newly obtained Philippine Islands were not forgotten, Pearl Harbor was finally recognized as the primary defensive position of the United States in the Pacific Ocean.

Appropriations during the first decade of the twentieth century provided for widening, straightening and deepening the entrance to Pearl Harbor. Improvements were also provided for the Naval Station, in Honolulu.[9] Congress allowed, the next year, almost a million dollars for further development, including $185,000 for Marine Barracks and Officers' Quarters. These were the Marine Barracks that had been promised in 1904.

Bids for dredging were opened in Washington in December of 1908. The Hawaiian Dredging Company won the contract which was for the largest dredging project in the history of the Navy until that time. Because of some of the features of the entrance, it was also the most difficult.[10] Soon after the dredging contract was awarded, a proposal was made and a contract let for the building of a dry-dock which was to be 620 feet long. During negotiations, the length of the dry-dock was increased to 831 feet and then to 1,039 feet. While there had been doubts about the success of the dredging project, no such difficulties were foreseen for the dry-dock, a mistake that had serious consequences. It was established the cost would be $3,200,000.

In the early arguments proposing some sort of naval presence in Pearl Harbor much has been made of its value as a military defensive position against an Asian attacker. The arguments were quite valid, but the primary function initially was as a coaling station, and later as a shipyard. Except for one dreadful day in 1941, the fact is that no significant hostile force has ever entered Hawaii's domain. From the days of Commander Merry, Pearl Harbor has had five major functions: Fuel supply, repair, refuge, provisioning, and a defensive Naval presence.

Using the authorization of 1908, Navy Engineers began to survey the "barren acres of kiawe stubble, burnt cane and coral that were to become the Navy Yard at Pearl Harbor".[11] In 1910 construction was begun on tanks in the new tank farm slightly up the slope from the East Loch. There was never any attempt to disguise or camouflage these tanks, and, incredibly, in 1941 they were neither bombed nor damaged.

Another congressional act in 1910 authorized one and a half million dollars for dredging operations and over two and a half million dollars for the new dry-dock.[12] In April of 1910, two deep draft sailing vessels entered Pearl Harbor, the first ones to do so. Their entry showed that the channel was open, albeit on a limited basis. These ships were laden with lumber for the Navy's new dry-dock. Again, in 1911, the US Congress saw fit to continue to fund the work at Pearl Harbor. The total cost for dredging, dry-dock, hospital and power plant came to $2,262,000.[13]

An interesting sidelight especially concerning Pearl Harbor occurred in the summer of 1912. After a stormy session, the Senate authorized the building of the battleship USS *Arizona*, 31,400 tons, armed with 14" guns. Her keel was laid in 1914 and she was launched in June of 1915.[14] Twenty-six years later, her fate was sealed forever with that of Pearl Harbor.

In 1901, the Dillingham family had purchased much of the land surrounding Pearl Harbor abutting the parcels acquired by the US Government. Dillingham logically foresaw an increased demand for the adjacent land by the Navy for expansion and/or by developers to make residential areas for the growing number of people who were being employed by the construction activities and by the Navy as civilian workers. He wrote to an associate, Elmer Paxton, "The U.S. Government will have to pay a good price for what they propose to take from Pu'uloa under condemnation proceedings...The demand will be great for land there when the U.S. begins work in the harbor".[15] His plan was logical but doomed.

In October of 1910, the Army-Navy Board recommended to Secretary of the Navy, George von G. Meyer, that "no commercial or other private vessels of American registry shall be permitted to enter Pearl Harbor except by permission of the Commandant of the Naval Station".[16] Commander Merry had warned, in 1900, of the urgency of the US government acquiring the land necessary for the establishment of a Naval Station at Pearl Harbor. Even before him, a naval officer, Lt. Rittenhouse wrote to Merry advising him of Dillingham's scheme for local development.[17] After expending a great deal of time and money, Dillingham withdrew his efforts, realizing that the government, at any time, could assert its right of condemnation to obtain his land, whether it had been developed or not. As more concern arose concerning security of the harbor, Congress provided that,

> "For the proper control, protection, and defense of the naval station, harbor, and entrance channel at Pearl Harbor, Territory of Hawaii, the Secretary of the Navy is hereby authorized, empowered, and directed to adopt and prescribe suitable rules and regulations governing the navigation, movement, and anchorage of vessels of whatsoever character in the waters of Pearl Harbor, island of Oahu, Hawaiian Islands, and in the entrance channel to said harbor, and to take all necessary measures for the proper enforcement of such rules and regulations."[18]

Although the government had established court approved precedents concerning the land around Pearl Harbor and the islands therein, the matter of fishing rights was not clear. Japanese fishermen routinely fished the waters as leasees of the Campbell estate, the John Ii estate, and Dillingham's Oahu Railway & Land Company. The two precedents cited were the condemnation proceedings of 1901-3, and the permission granted by the Hawaiian monarchy to "reach from the shore line to as far out in the water as a man can wade"[19]. These areas had been producing from ten to fifteen tons of fish monthly. The matter of fishing rights simmered for almost a decade until, outraged by the actions of the Japanese, the Commandant of the Naval Station, RAdm Robert M. Doyle wrote to Navy Secretary, Josephus Daniels,

> "The [Japanese] boats fly the Japanese flag and never, by any chance display the American colors . . . It is strongly recommended that the Government acquire all fishing right in Pearl Harbor and that no fishing be permitted except under the immediate direction of the Commandant. . ."[20]

Meanwhile, progress was being made with dredging operations going on day and night to prepare for opening ceremonies for the Pearl Harbor entrance. The reason the dredging had to be finished was that the work was invisible from the surface of the water and the upcoming ceremonies were to include the passage of the first major warship across the bar.

On December 14, 1911, the cruiser USS *California*, commanded by Captain Harlow, steamed through the new channel. The local press reported, "The entry, through a tortuous, new channel, was made gracefully and without mishap of any character, the vessel breaking a ribbon of red, white and blue silk as she entered the channel".[21] The ribbon was stretched between two dredges named *California*, coincidentally, and Gaylord. The ship was accompanied by the inter-island steamers *Claudine* and *Helene* and a convoy of local commercial boats and private yachts. With the apprehensive eyes of hundreds of people along the shore, *California* carefully made her way for four and one half miles taking the green buoys to port and the red ones to starboard. These guides were stationed 600 feet apart. The ship majestically steamed slowly past the barges and dredges all decorated with bunting and banners, and received the customary three-whistle salutes from each workboat. USS *California* anchored safely in the East Loch near Kuahua island. The reason some local people were apprehensive was that in clearing the area where the ship would anchor, the *loko*, fishpond, of the resident shark goddess was torn out. On the occasion of the arrival of USS *California*, nothing untoward happened, but later, during the construction of the dry-dock, this concern would be justified.

Among the passengers were Rear Admirals Thomas, Southerland, and Cowles plus 250 other local military and civilian dignitaries, including Hawaiian Governor Frear. Navy personnel were excited because the entrance of this major warship meant that the Pearl Harbor Naval Station was now ready to accept any ship in the world, in a harbor that already had been proclaimed to be capable of holding the entire fleet. The local civilians were delighted because of the obvious economic impact that the new harbor and its entrance would have on their community.

The most interesting passengers onboard *California* were two old enemies. Sanford Dole, ex-president of the Republic of Hawaii, and Liliuokalani, the previous Queen of the Hawaiian Islands. He was on the flying bridge and she was surrounded by former subjects on the quarter deck. The fact that these two giants of Hawaiian history were reconciled, at least to the point of participating in these ceremonies, was impressive indeed. The day came to a gala end when the officers of USS *California* and the dignitaries were treated to a luau at *Pa'auau*, the Waipio peninsula estate of John F. Colburn. Again, both Dole and Liliuokalani were present.[22]

During this period, early in the twentieth century, two types of vehicles were being developed, both of which would be adapted as deadly weapons of war.

The Navy Department on September 26, 1910 assigned Captain W.I. Chambers to serve as officer in charge of their embryonic experimental aviation detachment. He arranged for Eugene Ely, a Curtiss test pilot, to land an airplane on platforms constructed on two Navy ships. Ely successfully landed onboard USS *Birmingham* on November 14, 1910, and later onboard USS *Pennsylvania* in San Francisco Bay on January 18, 1911. Based on these and subsequent successful demonstrations, the Office of Naval Aeronautics was established on July 1, 1915.23 The US Army was first to realize the potential of the airplane and had two Curtiss float planes shipped to Hawaii from San Francisco on the transport *Logan*. The planes, along with a mechanic and canvas hangers, arrived in Honolulu July 13, 1913. They were assigned to Fort Kamehameha, near Pearl Harbor.

The two new planes were quite different from each other in design. One was a 'pusher' type with the engine mounted behind the pilot, and the other had the engine in front of the plane in the manner we are used to seeing. Because the propeller 'pulled' the airplane, it was called the 'Curtiss tractor' plane.

The planes could not taxi on the water near the fort due to the outcroppings of coral. To overcome this difficulty, Army men constructed a small rail line from the fort to the deepwater channel and moved the planes on carts. After a few taxi tests, the pilot, Lt. Harold E. Geiger, flew the first military flight in the Hawaiian Islands. His subsequent comments were centered on the dangers present in the channel to Pearl Harbor, that is, the buoys, fishing vessels, stakes, to say nothing of US Navy ships now using the newly opened channel.[24]

Most of the initial flights in Hawaii were made by US Army pilots. The facilities at the old fort were unsuitable for the new flying machines, so the US War Department condemned and secured the balance of Ford Island for $170,262 on January 17, 1918.[25] The Army soon moved its operations to Ford Island and began to bulldoze a landing strip. The field was later, April 29, 1919, named Luke Field in honor of a World War I ace and winner of the Medal of Honor.

On November 14, 1917 Major Harold M. Clark was assigned to Hawaii as the army's Sixth Aero Squadron's Aviation Officer.[26] After several local flights from the newly constructed strip on Ford Island, he flew to Molokai and returned, thus completing the first inter-island flight in Hawaii. The date was March 15, 1918.[27] Only a year later, this pioneer of Hawaiian flight was killed in an airplane accident in Colon, Panama.[28] He, and the other brave and adventurous young men like him, introduced the 'machine that flies' to Hawaii.

In December of 1919 a Naval unit of nine flying officers, 40 mechanics, and four seaplanes arrived. Rear Admiral W.B. Fletcher, Commandant of the 14th Naval District, stated prophetically, "Seaplanes, brought by swift carriers within reaching distance, could rise from the lee of the nearest reefs to the Northward and Westward, or the neighboring islands, or from the sea itself, swoop down on Pearl Harbor and destroy the plant unless an adequate defense was provided".[29] This was by no means an isolated warning. The calls to alert Washington to Hawaii's vulnerability to air assault were loud and clear and frequent during the twenty years before 1941.

It's difficult to imagine a vehicle, other than ocean freighters, which has affected Hawaii's history as much as the airplane, both military and civilian. Supplies are now brought with astonishing speed by airplanes, tourists come by the millions via airplanes, and inter-island flights are a basis for local transit and commerce. But also, tragedy was brought by airplanes to Hawaii in 1941, and was returned furiously and successfully from Pearl Harbor via aircraft. The new vehicle was here to stay, both as a boon to mankind and as a terrifying weapon of war.

Another vehicle, this one designed to travel under the sea, was also developing during these years. The submarine arrived in Honolulu Harbor in August of 1914. Two submarines, the *F-1* and *F-3* were towed from San Francisco by the cruisers USS *West Virginia* and USS *South Dakota*. On August 2, 1914, near the entrance to Honolulu Harbor, they were set adrift and entered the harbor under their own power. They were joined by *F-2* and *F-4* on the 24th of August. Locally they were called queer little craft, but it was admitted that they were warships, they were in Hawaii and that meant they were protection for Hawaii. Their first base was an old pier which is Pier 5 today located at the foot of Richards street.

Then tragedy struck. Just a few months later, on March 15, 1915, during a test run, *F-4*, under the command of Lt. Alfred L. Ede, went down with all hands at the harbor entrance in over 50 fathoms of water. The tragedy was noted in Honolulu papers the next day, "Not in many years has the deep sympathy and horror of Honolulu been so stirred as yesterday when the news became current that one of the submarines was lost off the harbor".[30] The War Department decided to suspend submarine operations temporarily and returned the remaining three subs to the mainland.

The salvage of *F-4* was a dangerous and heartbreaking task. She went down in 305' of water at the entrance to Honolulu Harbor. The sub had a displacement of 400 tons and had been designed for 200' depth. The wreck was found by tracing air bubbles and an oil slick rising to the surface about two miles from the entrance. Because Navy had men on the scene so quickly after the accident, there was still hope for rescue of some of the crew. The maximum depth divers had reached until that time was around 200'. Two intrepid divers, Chief Gunner's Mates Evans and Agraz dove to that depth, but could neither see anything nor locate the sunken boat. The pressure at 300 feet is over 130 pounds per square inch. William F. Loughman dove to an even deeper depth but became entangled in his lines and hose. He could neither ascend nor descend. Another

Chief Gunner's Mate, Frank W. Crilley, volunteered to dive to his aid. After two hours and eleven minutes he brought his shipmate to the surface alive.

One method that held hope was to drag the sub up the ledge it was resting on into shallower water. No new equipment could be made in the few hours of life that might be remaining, so the yard tugs *Navajo* and *Intrepid* made repeated attempts to sling lines under the sub's hull and drag her, but they were unsuccessful. Local companies offered whatever they might have that could help. The Navy personnel on the scene enlisted the aid of a dredging barge. Lines were lowered and swept along the bottom until they trapped the sub. The heavy windless on the dredge hauled upward on the cable around the sub while both tugs towed sideways on their lines. Heavy cables parted under the strain with a snarl and then an explosive blast, and shot like whips back at the would-be rescuers. The sub did not move. It was concluded that she was completely filled with water and that no hope remained for her crew. The rescue efforts were sadly terminated.

Lieutenant Commander Julius A. Furer, who had been assigned to oversee the construction of the new Naval Station at Pearl Harbor was called to the scene to determine the best way to salvage the boat. The Navy was interested in ascertaining the cause of the debacle and, of course, everyone wanted the bodies recovered. He decided that a short series of lifts and tows was the best plan.

Since there was no appropriate equipment for him to use, Furer borrowed equipment from the dredging companies in the area, machinery from nearby sugar plantations, steel beams from a coal shed project, and improvised a device which looked as if it could do the job. So important was this project to the Navy that divers were ordered from New York and San Francisco to the salvage site. The divers, their gear, a recompression chamber, and a physician, Dr. George French left San Francisco aboard USS *Maryland* and arrived at the worksite on April 14, 1915.

The expert divers were descending to depths never before attained. They worked as quickly as was feasible and during the entire operation suffered no serious accidents. By May 25, the sunken sub had been moved up the slope to a depth of 48 feet. In the shallower, clearer water, the divers could inspect the hull for the first time. They observed severe hull damage which was a matter of concern. If the hull broke under the strain of further moving, the pieces of the wreck might slip back down into the channel and block shipping. Also, the opportunity to determine the cause of the disaster would be lost.

Furer decided that the only way to raise the hull intact would be to design some sort of buoyant force device that would pull the sub up evenly to the 25' depth needed to place it into Honolulu's dry-dock. He designed a pontoon system and left for Mare Island in California to have it produced.

There was less urgency now because the sub hull was stable in its current location and all hope of life was gone.

Sunday morning, August 29, 1915 Furer and his men placed slings under the sub hull, inflated the pontoons with compressed air, and successfully raised the *F-4* to the surface. Then they towed the battered hull with its tragic cargo to the dry-dock. The bodies were reverently removed and the engineers grimly inspected the hull, seeking the cause of the sinking. Almost immediately they saw corrosion around the rivet holes which had been caused by leaking battery acid. The twenty-one gallant men of the ill-fated *F-4* did not die in vain. The information learned from the salvaged hull led to significant redesign and improvement of US submarines.[31] On February 15, 1929, President Calvin Coolidge presented the Medal of Honor to Chief Petty Officer Frank W. Crilley for his heroic, selfless efforts during the attempted rescue operation.[32]

This salvage was remarkable. *F-4* was the first US submarine ever lost. The divers dove to unprecedented depths and, in so doing, developed new techniques that would be used for decades before SCUBA equipment was available. Commander Furer's pontoon system of raising the hull was innovative and would also be used in future operations. Newly designed submarines displayed a markedly safer record than the pre-*F-4* ships. The Navy was encouraged to proceed with submarine design and application. World War I was expanding and such vessels were needed. On October 14, 1915, The Navy General Board endorsed the recommendation that Quarry Point become the location of the Submarine Base in Pearl Harbor.

Four K class subs (*K-3, K-4, K-6, & K-7*)[33] were assigned to Hawaii in April of 1916, but when the US entered the war in Europe in 1917, they also were returned to the mainland. From 1917 until July of 1919, no submarines were stationed in the Hawaiian Islands. After the war, on June 25, 1919, the subtender USS *Beaver* and six subs (*R-5 to R-10*) swept into Pearl Harbor, their new home. What they found was as uninviting as the dismal reception for the US Marines had been fifteen years before. There was a creosoted-timber pier that had been installed the year before at Quarry Point in East Loch, Pearl Harbor. Behind that was 32 acres of wasteland. Their 'base' was a swamp covered with cactus. Coral heads protruded through the marsh from the land. With little help expected from Washington, the submariners turned-to and quickly made the place livable, if not shipshape. After two months they had living quarters, an administration building, and several shops. The 'quarters' was the old cruiser USS *Chicago* which was moored nearby.

General Order#510 on November 18, 1919 set the standard operating procedure for shore-based submarine installations The sailors developed the base with such efficiency that it was ready to be officially commissioned only three months later, on February 2, 1920. The first commanding officer was Commander Chester W. Nimitz. He received his orders to report to Hawaii on July 11, 1920 as CO of Submarine Division Fourteen, the Submarine Base, and the *Chicago*. Division Fourteen at that time consisted of a few junior commissioned officers and chief petty officers and about 200 men. Except for the small areas that had been cleared, the base was still a tangle of cactus plants and dense jungle. Nimitz, ever the opportunist, solved two problems with one decision. Any man who was on report received an area of vegetation to clear as punishment. Rather than being confined in the brig of the old *Chicago*, the disciplined men were outside doing physical work which was obviously beneficial to the entire division. The men responded with a loyalty which was to be seen in most of the man and women who ever served under Nimitz's command.[34]

In the face of the inadequacies of the site, he requested funds to complete the permanent base. However, he was informed by the Chief of Naval Operations, Admiral Robert E. Coontz, that fiscal limitations and the unknown outcome of the impending arms conference would force the Navy to limit the number of submarines stationed at Pearl Harbor to ten boats. However, he was promised $100,000 for waterfront & dockage development and $50,000 for battery charging equipment. To maximize the use of his meager funds, Commander Nimitz was able to obtain some surplus buildings that had been used in World War I in France.

Nimitz served with distinction as the first CO of the Sub Base until he was relieved in 1922 by Captain L.F. Welch. Twenty years later he returned to Pearl Harbor to direct the Central Pacific Campaigns of World War II and became the nation's first five-star Fleet Admiral. The submarines, called 'boats' in a respectful manner by their crews, became permanent residents at Pearl.

Meanwhile, other, less dramatic, events were occurring. The old Naval Station was moved from Honolulu to Hospital Point in Pearl Harbor in August 1913, and in August of the following year, the Marines finally moved from Honolulu to Pearl Harbor. Also, in the residential area of Pearl Harbor, $14,300 was spent building a house at 6 Hale Ali'i (now 1000 Hale Ali'i) designated Quarters A, for the use of the senior officer on the station. The significance of this house is that it is the first such house built in Pearl Harbor and now is classified as a category I historic property. The only other category I structure is Building 300, Quarters K, on Ford Island. The construction of Quarters A was under the supervision of Captain Ernest R. Gayler, CEC, USN. His son, Admiral Noel Gayler, lived in the house during his tenure as CINCPAC from September 1972 to August 1976.[35]

Pearl was becoming quite a livable place. The Surgeon General's report of 1916 described it thus,

"Electric illumination of quarters is now continuous. Telephone connection through the Yard exchange is now possible to all parts of Oahu. Lawns are being developed around the quarters, marine barracks, and administration buildings. The general sanitary condition has been good, mosquitoes are present the entire year in great numbers. Water supply is of good quality and natural drainage is good."[36]

To summarize the congressional allotments to Pearl Harbor a brief list of the acts and the major authorizations is in order:

DATE			CONGRESS/ SESSION	PURPOSE
03	Mar	1901	56:2	$150,000 establish NAVSTA P.H.
13	May	08	60:1	2m dry-dock construction.
03	Mar	09	60:2	2.2m to dredge channel.
24	Jun	10	61:2	1.5m dredging, $2.7m dry-dock.
04	Mar	11	61:3	545,000 dredging, $800,000 dry-dock.
22	Aug	12	62:2	1.05m dry-dock, $100,000 waterfront.
04	Mar	13	62:3	629,000 miscellaneous
30	Jun	14	63:2	Dry-dock limit $4,986,500.
29	Aug	16	64:1	700,000 Dry-dock.
04	Mar	17	64:2	936,000 Dry-dock.
01	Jul	18	65:2	41,275 Water facilities
11	Jul	19	66:1	Miscellaneous[37]

During the second decade of the twentieth century, war games were frequently held. Oahu was 'invaded' from two major locations. The north shore was a favorite target, the other being the Pearl Harbor area. The invading personnel were "evenly balanced forces of infantry, cavalry, artillery, and marines".[38] The previously described Plan Orange optimistically anticipated the opening of the Panama Canal and was updated in 1914 to shorten the time needed for the Atlantic Fleet to come to the aid of a stricken Philippines or Hawaii. Unfortunately, after the elaborate opening ceremonies and passage of a few commercial ships, the canal was closed because of landslides, malfunctions of the locks, and political wrangling.[39] The slides were still causing trouble a year later when USS *Missouri*, the canal's first battleship, transited the 'Big Ditch'. In a letter, midshipman William F. Dietrich, later a rear admiral, wrote to a friend, "On the north side, a sandy soil keeps slipping down and only a couple of weeks ago a slide blocked the Canal"[40]

The radio towers at Pearl Harbor were put into use for the first time on September 29, 1916. An engineer sent this message to the Secretary of the Navy at 2:30 am,

> "I have the honor to send you the first through message to Washington D.C. from Pearl Harbor Hawaii radio station, and report satisfactory progress in test of plant.
>   George R. Clark"[41]

The secretary responded half an hour later.

In July of 1919, a Naval Ammunition Storage facility was established on Kuahua Island. The first Inspector of Ordnance was LCdr J. C. Thom. Three hospital buildings were built during 1918-1919. These facilities added 90 beds, increasing the number available from 40 to 150. Later, in October of 1919, the first ship entered the newly dedicated drydock for maintenance .[42]

When the cruiser USS *St. Louis* steamed into Pearl Harbor in June of 1916, she became the first major ship to be stationed there. She was to be the flagship of Rear Admiral C. J. Boush, Commandant of the 14th Naval District. Her skipper was Lieutenant V. S. Houston. The ship served as the sub tender for the K-class submarines and as training ship for the Hawaiian Naval Militia .[41] Tensions were rising among military leaders in Pearl Harbor because a great war was being waged in Europe. No one knew how long it would last and, although it was thousands of miles away from Hawaii, no one was sure how far it might spread.

Chapter 23 - The Territory Matures

It may seem strange that World War I could affect Hawaii at all, so far are these islands from the centers of combat in the 'War To End All Wars' . But Hawaii was part of the United States now, no matter how distant, and many wanted to feel as if they were helping those in trouble. The war began in 1914 and news was avidly sought by locals whenever and wherever it was available to them. There was no real fighting in the Pacific during the war, nor was America yet involved until the last years, but Hawaiians were aware of the momentous struggle going on in far off Europe. Local groups created charities that knitted or made things for servicemen, others worked for War Relief or joined the Red Cross. Sugar prices rose dramatically and trade was disrupted and often spotty. For Hawaiians, forced by isolation to get most of their staples and clothing from overseas, it was uncomfortable, but bearable. The ocean passage between mainland west coast ports and Hawaii was probably the safest ocean route in the world at that time. The territorial government began a publicity push for local expansion of farms and fields that grew perishable food and people were encouraged to grow their own vegetables and grains.

The most unsettling aspect of World War I for Hawaii was the involvement of the Japanese in the western part of the Pacific Ocean. They had conquered Formosa (Taiwan), annexed Korea and coveted Manchuria in northern China. Since their victory in the Russo-Japanese war a decade before, the country had advanced rapidly into the modern industrial world. They had tacitly agreed diplomatically to support the Open Door Policy in China, ascribed to by all nations who had dealings in the Pacific, but only as far as they had to. Alfred T. Mahan called this a pious statement on the part of the Japanese, entirely hypocritical.[1] There were many who were watching Japan, aware of its designs on its neighbors. A few, knowledgeable about Hawaii, were concerned for its safety and dreaded the day Japan's attention strayed to the east.

Modern systems and appearances prevailed in Japan, much of it copied from the west, but one aspect of their ancient tradition remained: war would bring glory and prosperity. As the Great War ground on in Europe, Japan's attention remained on the various German possessions in the Pacific. This was the primary reason Japan entered the war on the Allied side, to the relief of some Hawaiians and the skepticism of others. England and France were the core of the Allies from the beginning in 1914, joined by the United States in 1917. Japan joined the war on the Allied side only a few weeks later. The war ended with an armistice in November of 1918, and in 1919, the peace treaty awarded Japan some of the territories it sought. It was not enough to satisfy the leaders of this overcrowded land. They needed new space and more resources for their people.

Hawaii's only real involvement with the 'enemy' in World War I grew out of a practice that was understood to be proper and safe for all nations. It was generally accepted that an enemy ship from one country could not attack a capital ship from another in a neutral harbor. The United States was a neutral party during the first three years of the war, so the nations who were participants in the war felt safe in entering Honolulu Harbor. Visiting ships from both England and Germany anchored in the harbor between 1914 and 1917. The first of a dozen German vessels took refuge in Honolulu as early as August 7, 1914, only five days after the war began.[2] By taking refuge here, five German merchant ships and a gunboat, which had escaped the British fleet, hoped to avoid capture. There were so many they left little room at the docks for others or for small boats or supply tenders. The roadstead became crowded with ships at anchor. It was suggested by someone that a portion of these many ships could be accommodated in Pearl Harbor which was a much larger anchorage. The idea was ignored, perhaps discouraged by the Navy.

The Japanese Battleship *Hizen* soon showed up, sensing prey it could capture. It began to cruise back and forth just beyond the three mile territorial limit to wait for the Germans to come out. The main target of their attention was the German gunboat *Geier* which had been given a time limit for remaining in the harbor for repairs. The Germans knew it, the Japanese knew it and the people of Honolulu, sensing a dramatic confrontation were drawn to the waterfront to watch as the deadline drew near. The action of the Japanese battleship was like that of a cat waiting for a mouse to leave its hole.

The United States government was in a strange position and finally issued an ultimatum: the German boat must leave the harbor by November 7, 1914 or remain interned for the entire war. The Germans chose to be interned and the Japanese war ship gave up and left to look for other targets. War was still a gentlemen's game at the time of the Great War and most combatants played by the rules established in Europe in the 19th century.

The German ships remained in the harbor until 1917 with no particular problems. Hawaiian Governor Pinkham communicated by cable with Washington, sometimes frantically, concerning Hawaii's responsibility and the eventual disposition of the vessels.[3] The US Navy cruiser USS *St. Louis* was always nearby, watching with great vigilance. It had been assigned to temporary duty patrolling the southern shore of Oahu, watching the harbor entrance in general and the German fleet in particular. As tensions rose between the US and Germany, the Honolulu harbor docks were closed at night to all traffic and more troops were brought into the city to protect government buildings.

In 1915, before America was involved in the war, the Revenue Cutter Service, which had been established in August of 1789, was combined with the Lifesaving Service to create a new agency - the Coast Guard. The government assigned one of their new cutters to patrol Hawaii, the cutter *USCG Thetis*, however, she was only in Hawaii part time. The islands shared this sparse protection with Alaska which was two thousand miles to the north.

But when the United States declared war on Germany in April of 1917, the situation of the interned German fleet changed. On the night of February 4, 1917, when *St. Louis* was riding at anchor off the harbor, the lookout sighted smoke coming from the ports and hatches of the German ship *Geier* and there was unusual activity on deck. Captain George R. Clark, Commandant of the Naval Station, was advised that the German ship was either preparing for a dash to the open sea, forbidden by international rules, or she was being scuttled. The *St. Louis* log indicates,

> "At 11:28 armed party of 34 enlisted men.. all from this
> vessel, left the ship to board the *SMS Geier* reportedly being
> destroyed by her crew."[4]

The boarding party went ashore near the *Geier* and assumed a position on the second floor of the Alakea Wharf warehouse where they could observe the ship. The Honolulu Fire Department was deployed on adjacent docks, a battery of field artillery was stationed behind a coal pile opposite the docked ship and two regiments of infantry were held in reserve near the Governor's Palace. Behind police barricades, people strained to see what would happen in "the first military activities on Oahu since Kamehameha I", as one spectator put it.

In a strange and rare move, German crewmen had crippled their own ship. They set fires, damaged machinery and threw instruments and ship's logs overboard. This had been the case in all of the ships in the harbor. They refused to allow anyone aboard the ships to put out the fires.

Finally a boarding party managed to get aboard the flaming *Geier* and demanded that the fires be extinguished or they would do so. The commander of the port then intended to confiscate the ship. The German Captain Grashof mustered his men athwartship facing aft where they remained at attention. Not a man moved. At this point a game of 'chicken' evolved.

The senior American officer stated that if the Germans would not cooperate, he would detain everyone on the ship until the flames reached the magazines and the entire ship would explode. Captain Grashof replied that he understood and that his men would remain where they stood. The situation was defused by a man with more good sense than rigid honor. One of the boarding party, the Chief Water Tender, made an unauthorized excursion below the main deck and discovered that the fires were mainly confined to the boiler. The prodigious amount of smoke came from open boiler doors and closed flues. He opened the flues, closed the boiler doors and shut off the incoming oil. Then he returned to the main deck.

The heat and flame vanished and the danger went with it. The Germans were forcibly taken off *Geier* and the other ships and the fires were extinguished. The crews were detained in Hawaii until passage to the mainland could be arranged. There they remained in prison camps until the war was over.

The enemy ships remained in the harbor for a time or were moved to repair facilities. The German gunboat *Geier* and her tender, the collier *Locksun*, were reconditioned at the Pearl Harbor Naval Shipyard. *Geier* became a United States second-class cruiser called *Carl Shurtz* as part of the Atlantic Fleet. Her collier, renamed *Gulfport*, remained at Pearl as an oil tender for the rest of her life.[5] The other ships were incorporated into the US merchant service.

The annual report of Secretary of the Navy Josephus Daniels, in December of the following year' stated,

> "It may be truly said that the war zone extends round the earth. This truth applies with special force to our naval station in far away Hawaii, known as Pearl Harbor. To that station, then under the command of Rear Admiral Clark, must be given credit for the first taking over of an enemy war vessel, the German Gunboat *Geier*."[6]

This was the only direct involvement Hawaii had in World War I. It was an exciting interlude and it has been said that it was instrumental in stimulating patriotism and a sense of adventure among young Hawaiian residents. The Hawaii National Guard was territorial and not used overseas, so many young men joined the Canadian, Australian or New Zealand Army to get to the fighting in France.[7] Almost a thousand men from Hawaii served in the war, of whom about a hundred were killed.[8] Germany had a difficult time with her naval forces in the Pacific which was not, of course, the primary concentration of action in this war. The German Empire controlled many islands and mainland areas in the Pacific and tried to defend them. The peace treaty eventually took away all German possessions, including Samoa and the Marshall Islands.

The war was a disaster for German companies doing business in Hawaii, too. Most German property, enemy property after the United States joined the war in 1917, was attached by the US Government. German companies were dissolved and new companies were established with new names. One such was Hackfield and Company which became American Factors, Ltd.[9] The old name was removed from its downtown building at Fort and Queen streets, a new one put up and the company was taken over and run by Alexander and Baldwin, Castle and Cook and the Matson Navigation Company, all major, powerful companies in Hawaii. One of their subsidiary businesses has become one of the more visible department stores in Honolulu and environs, The Liberty House. American Factors, Ltd. also bought three former German sugar plantations.

The populace had fond thoughts about Pearl Harbor in its old guise as a recreation and residential area not as a naval station. They also had their own ideas about the changes that were going to be made when the Navy began to build there.

> "What Pearl Harbor is going to be and what Pearl Harbor is today are as different as what the Panama Canal is today and what it was before the United States started to dig. Pearl Harbor is famous because of plans that have for years been identified with the immense protected arm of the sea. While the world thinks of Pearl Harbor as a mighty naval base that is to be, we of Honolulu are more immediately concerned with its natural attractions and residential pleasures."[10]

The citizens and the Navy had very different views of the area. Some locals saw it as a pleasure resort with delightful retreats for picnickers, trampers, hunters, fishermen, yachtsmen and motorboat folk. They hoped much of that would remain. At the same time, to the Navy it was the location of a massive dry-dock being constructed and was to become home to the Pacific Fleet.

Numerous residences, 'country houses' as they were dubbed by some, still dotted the peninsulas in Pearl Harbor. Some were owned by former Hawaiian high chiefs, like John F. Colburn, others by businessmen. As the Naval Station neared its completion, plans were made to establish a ferry service from the Naval Base to the Waipio peninsula where Navy personnel and workers lived.

All during this time, the sugar business prospered. However, until the Panama Canal opened, half the Hawaiian sugar crop had to be hauled all the way around Cape Horn, the southern tip of South America, to the eastern seaboard of the United States. This trade gave rise to two great steamship companies based in Hawaii; the Matson Navigation Company and the American-Hawaiian Steamship Company. Between them they ran a stream of ships on the 20,000 mile trek around the Horn. The American-Hawaiian

Company alone had twenty two steel cargo ships. Steamers had cut travel time on this route to half the time it had taken a sailing ship. Eventually, new technology reduced the time to about two months.

Still, the shipping companies were overjoyed when the Panama Canal was finished in 1914. The first cargo to pass through the canal was a load of Hawaiian sugar which was ferried through on May 18, 1914. This again cut the length of the trip in half. In 1910, Matson began carrying passengers from the west coast of the United States to Honolulu in the ship *Wilhelmina*.[11] Round the world cruise ships began to put into Honolulu beginning in 1922. It was clear that it was getting easier to reach the islands and it took less time.

When the war was over in 1918, flying had become a major enthusiasm among Americans. The Navy Department had already recognized the importance of the airplane by setting up an Office of Naval Aeronautics in July of 1915.[12] Hawaiians joined the excitement when barnstormers began touring Hawaii after the war giving demonstrations of aerial prowess and taking people up at a dollar a ride. Enthusiastic crowds greeted them everywhere they performed.

By the end of World War I, the Navy, Marines and Coast Guard had enlisted forty thousand men, two thousand planes and fifteen lighter than air craft in their air divisions.[13] In 1918, Major Harold M. Clark flew a seaplane from Honolulu to the island of Hawaii. It was the first over-water flight in Hawaii. He crash landed on the slopes of Mauna Kea, but was unhurt.[14] It was not surprising that soon both military and civilian flyers would attempt to fly to Hawaii. It was a challenge that was bound to be taken up by someone. It was clear to everyone that airplanes were here to stay. In 1924 two navy planes took an admiral on an inspection tour from Honolulu to Hilo and back, about four hundred miles. This was the longest distance yet covered in the islands in one day.

Three Navy seaplanes made an attempt to fly from the west coast to Hawaii in August of 1925. Taking off from San Pablo Bay, northeast of San Francisco, they intended to take advantage of the trade winds. One of these planes turned back, one was forced down by engine trouble only three hundred miles out and had to be towed back, the third kept going. There were Navy ships stationed every one hundred miles or so, including the aircraft carrier *Langley*. The last plane continued to fly, but ran out of fuel about two hundred miles short of Hawaii. There was a ship which was supposed to have had replacement fuel, but it was out of position when the fuel was needed.

The pilot, Cdr John Rodgers, and a four member crew, had to land on the water, unable to notify anyone of their location because they had lost their radio contact. They survived because they were on a seaplane. The crew floated and drifted in the Pacific Ocean for nine days, with only three days rations, drifting toward the north west, until they were found only fifteen miles from the coast of Kauai by one of the many searching craft, a submarine. They were towed to Nawiliwili Harbor, just south of Lihue, on the south east coast of Kauai. There the airplane was repaired and refueled in a few days. The crew flew on to Honolulu. The trip was completed, though it was not an unqualified success.

The first successful non-stop flight from the mainland to Hawaii left Oakland, California just two years later, in June of 1927, only a month after Lindbergh had made the first successful solo crossing of the Atlantic Ocean. The flight over the eastern half of the Pacific Ocean was accomplished in a Fokker Trimoter monoplane. The Army lieutenants who managed this flight landed at Wheeler field just twenty-six hours out of California. The first civilian flight, only two weeks later, ended in a crash into a clump of Kiawe trees on Molokai. The pilots were lucky. They did finish and were able to walk away from the plane which was another monoplane. They, too, had run out of gas.

It was only a month later that enthusiasm for flying produced the first transoceanic flying race. A prize of $25,000 was offered by James D. Dole, president of the Hawaiian Pineapple Company. The participants were not so lucky as their pioneering predecessors. Of eight planes that began the race, two crashed at the beginning, two turned back and two disappeared somewhere over the Pacific Ocean. Only two entrants of the 'Dole Derby' were able to finish, one of whom was a resident of Honolulu, Martin Jensen. Even then, the successful finishers landed with only four gallons of gasoline left in the tank. A massive search was undertaken' all vessels of the 14th Naval District and fifty-four vessels of the battle fleet were so engaged.[15] None of the lost flyers were found and one of the search planes went down as well.[16] Ten people died trying to complete this race. It was clear to observers that the airplane was a fascinating machine, but it was not yet ready for the huge, unforgiving expanses of the Pacific Ocean.

The first flights to connect the islands began in November of 1929. This service was established and operated by the Inter-Island Steam Navigation Company.

All of this activity in the air was a portent of the future for the people of Hawaii, for the Navy and for the United States. Hawaii had gotten even closer to the mainland and easier to reach.

A new industry blossomed in the first years of the 20th century. In 1903, the Hawaiian Promotion Committee was formed with Albert Pierce Taylor was its Secretary-Director.[17] Its goal was to encourage travel to Hawaii as a vacation destination. The volume of visitors to Hawaii understandably slowed during World War I, but when the war was over, the delights of Hawaii were publicized in all parts of the country. By 1922, when the Committee became the Hawaii Tourist Bureau, almost ten thousand visitors had come to spend time in Hawaii. All of them came by steamer, the only way across the Pacific, and the steamers were probably owned by the Matson Navigation Company.

They were not the only steamers to visit Hawaii, but Matson was a home grown company and a very successful one. It carried a major portion of the tourist traffic east and west, as well as a great deal of the goods imported and exported from Hawaii.

The fastest, most expensive ship built in the United States to that time, the 582 foot *Malolo*, was launched in 1925 by the Matson Company. She was a luxury liner, no doubt about that, with seven decks, swimming pool, ballroom, theater and accommodations for 650 passengers. *Malolo's* maiden voyage was in November of 1927 and it was an unqualified success. *Malolo* made the crossing from San Francisco to Honolulu in four and a half days, which seemed far too fast for some who relished their stay in this floating hotel. Others were thrilled at the speed with which they could cross the Pacific. In Honolulu at the end of her first crossing, *Malolo* was met by dozens of canoes, as Cook had been almost 150 years before. Canoes were manned by chiefs and *ali'i* as well as residents from every island in the Hawaiian group. All must have been aware of the importance of this event, but they probably didn't dream of the volume of tourists that would eventually visit Hawaii.

Business was slow in the winter at first and the Tourist Bureau focused on this time for its advertising. Matson continued to expand in the wake of *Malolo's* popularity. Matson built the three most famous luxury liners on the Pacific route in the late 1920s and early 1930s. They were *Matsonia*, *Mariposa* and the *Lurline*.

To accommodate tourists in Hawaii, more hotels were needed. The Moana already existed on Waikiki Beach, built in 1901. The Royal Hawaiian Hotel arose a few blocks west of the Moana on fifteen acres of land leased from the Bishop Estate. This was the same spot that was occupied by the cottage of King Kamehameha V in the 1860s.[18] Both hotels were built by the Matson Navigation Company. Begun in 1925, the Royal Hawaiian had a unique design and color. It looked like a palace and its outer stucco finish was done in a coral pink. The grand opening of the Royal Hawaiian was attended by 1200 guests, celebrities, politicians, Naval personnel from Pearl Harbor and other luminaries on February 1, 1927. Coral pink it remains today, seventy years later, and it is often called 'The Pink Palace'. It has been restored to its 1920s glory and is very distinctive among a sea of high-rise hotels.

Celebrities soon discovered the *Lurline*, the Royal Hawaiian and Hawaii. Spencer Tracy, Douglas Fairbanks; Mary Pickford, Al Jolson, Bob Hope, the Rockefellers and many more were photographed on their arrival being greeted by hula maidens with arms full of leis, swimming or surfing with Duke Kahanamoku, hiking or watching a volcano. A radio program began, funded by the Tourist Bureau, in 1935. 'Hawaii Calls' was sent to the mainland by short wave at first and was a mixture of Hawaiian music and interviews of local and tourist interest. By then, many Americans were dreaming about a vacation in Hawaii. Some were returning for a second or third trip. These repeat tourists were called "comebackers".[19]

In contrast, there were parts of Hawaii that were never seen by tourists where everyone was hard at work. The major economic activity in the islands in the early years of the century was sugar with pineapple coming up fast. About fifty thousand people worked in the sugar mills and fields, which was about one third of the population. Sugar growers purchased a refinery in California in 1905 to bring more of the profits from the businesses back to Hawaii. The C and H Refinery, California and Hawaii, in Crockett can still be seen near the Carquinez Bridge where it crosses the Sacramento River on its way to San Francisco Bay.

This industry depended on cheap labor and always had. Sugar growers had imported labor from the beginning, bringing people from Portugal, Spain and the Philippines, all of whom were deemed "capable of becoming American citizens".[20] It wasn't enough. They tried to get Americans and Hawaiians to do the work, but most were not interested so the growers imported Japanese workers. It had been Chinese workers until a law banned Chinese immigration into the United States. Many Americans at the time were convinced that Orientals could not be 'Americanized.'

No one seemed to notice at first that the children of these imported Hawaiians were born in the islands and were Americans by birth and citizens by law. They were as capable of being citizens as anyone else and the former false belief faded away. As trite as the statement seems today, Hawaii is a Pacific melting pot. It is not unusual for one person living in Hawaii today to have Chinese, German, Japanese, French, Philippine and Hawaiian ancestors. Much like the mixing of ethnic groups and nationalities in the early United States, the mix of races in Hawaii today is a matter of pride to residents and government alike. These were the people who were employed at Pearl Harbor to build the Navy Base, to construct buildings, roads and houses as well as the all important Dry-Dock.

Reference has been made to the ill-fated Pearl Harbor Dry-Dock #1. Its story covers a span of time from 1908 when activities were initiated, to 1919 when the dock was formally dedicated. The first of three disasters at Pearl Harbor occurred at this time. In the beginning, no one realized how the Americans directing the building of the dry-dock and local Hawaiians were going to affect each other. The United States Navy and an important Hawaiian shark goddess were on a collision course.

Chapter 24 - Too Much Pilikia

In Hawaiian *'Pilikia'* means 'trouble'. In 1907 US Navy engineers started the design for a dry-dock at Pearl Harbor. They concurrently inaugurated plans for dredging the harbor adjacent to the proposed dry-dock. The dredging was carefully considered because of, as we shall see, the relatively delicate nature of dredging in the area immediately next to the drydock. They foresaw no difficulty in the construction of the dry-dock itself because others had been built on the mainland with no untoward results. What happened to cause a two-year project to require twelve years is a study in engineering techniques and Hawaiian lore and their interdependence.

Occasionally seagoing ships need to be laid dry, that is, they need to have work done on the bottom of their hulls. Ships that sail the oceans of the world collect an amazing assortment of barnacles and vegetation which impede the ship's progress as she tries to sail. Often the hull is damaged underwater by collisions with rocks, coral heads, or other obstructions. These ,gardens' and cracked planks must be removed and/or repaired. Obviously this work can only be done if the ship is removed from the sea.

On remote islands, ships for centuries have been careened. That is accomplished by heaving down, or sailing near a beach, carrying the anchor up onto the shore, planting it firmly, and then winching the ship aground on the flood, or incoming, tide. If possible, a beach with coarse sand was chosen whose friction would help scrape the hull as it lay. This practice is called graving from the French word for coarse sand, *greve*. As the water recedes, her bottom is exposed which not only gave rise to many ribald jokes among sailors, but also allowed them to scrape, caulk, patch, and paint, usually with pitch or tar. This work was often frantically done to complete the job before the flood, or incoming, tide arrived a few hours later.

After the work had been completed, the anchor was removed by hand, carried to the ship's small boat, rowed out to sea for a short distance, dropped and secured on the sea floor. Then the incoming process was reversed and the ship was pulled down the beach as far as her crew could manage and when the flood tide came in, the ship was floated, righted, and rode easily at anchor ready for her next voyage. That technique lasted, in one form or another, for all the centuries that man has sailed until he was able to conceive and create a 'hole' in the beach into which a ship could sail, or be towed. Then the hole, or ditch, would be closed off from the sea, pumped out, and the ship would settle onto previously set blocks to support her weight while men worked on her hull with no sense of urgency. Tides were no longer a consideration. That type of dry-dock is called a graving dock. Later engineers were able to construct floating dry-docks which meant that the repair facility could go to the stricken ship, rather than attempting to get a damaged ship to the nearest graving dry-dock. But our concern is with the graving dry-dock designed for Pearl Harbor.

The first American dry-dock was requested in 1798 by the newly formed Navy Department. However, it was not until 1825 that the US Congress asked Secretary of the Navy Samuel L. Southard to locate an appropriate site. After Southard's recommendation was accepted in 1827, Congress appropriated $700,000 to construct the first dry-dock in the Western Hemisphere at Gosport, near Portsmouth, Virginia. An engineer, Laomi Baldwin, experienced in building European dry-docks was chosen to head the project. His assistant was a young lad named William P.S. Sanger who became the first Naval Civil Engineer and held that position for 55 years.

Baldwin, working with Shipyard Commander Commodore Lewis Warrington, overcame financial constraints, laborers ignorant of the techniques needed for the new project, geological problems, uncooperative weather, and the apathy of those who did not have the vision to imagine the advantages or even the possibility of such a device. However, on June 17, 1833, the *USS Delaware*, a 74 gun, 2600 ton Ship of the Line was towed into the new structure and secured. When the coffer dam was closed behind her and the water pumped out, a cheering crowd acclaimed Baldwin's success.' The project in Hawaii, some 75 years later, did not fare so well.

The congressional act of 13 March 1908 was an important one for the Navy. It authorized $400,000 for dredging to widen, deepen, and straighten the Pearl Harbor entrance channel and for the establishment of a shipyard. This date is considered the birthday of the Naval Shipyard. A recommendation was made by Chief Constructor of the Navy, W. L. Capps, that the activities of the yard be confined to repair and outfitting and that no ship building be done. Since there were several competent yards on the west coast of the mainland which could do the building more inexpensively, that advice was heeded and there have never been any major US Navy ships built at Pearl Harbor.

The 1908 act also allowed $2,000,000 for a graving dry-dock to be constructed at Pearl Harbor. Victor H. Metcalf, Secretary of the Navy, offered plans for a dry-dock 1140' long which would have a center division so that one half could be flooded and used for smaller ships, and the entire dock flooded for major ships. His plan would need $3,500,000. Congress refused to accept his plan and allowed only enough for a dock 620' long. The bids were received and the successful bidder was the San Francisco Bridge Company whose bid was under the $2,000,000 limit set by Congress. The company was associated with the Dillingham family. Walter Dillingham was the company's Hawaiian manager and the firm's attorney was a Dillingham in-law, Judge Walter F. Frear,[2] later to become the Territorial

Governor. The contract was let on June 17, 1909 and work commenced on September 21 of that year, then sublet to the Hawaiian Dredging Company. The official designation was Pearl Harbor Dry-dock #1. The anticipated completion date was November 22, 1912.[3] The cataclysmic disaster which subsequently occurred was the result, perhaps, of a monumental omission by the Navy at this point. Excellent plans were designed and drawn, competent local workers were hired, the finest materials were used, and the experience of other dry-docks was available. What went wrong?

At this point it is appropriate to consider where the ill-fated dry-dock was to be built. Hawaiian religion, or lore, contains many stories, legends, and tales which, as with any accepted religious dicta, are based on experience and wisdom handed down through many generations. One ignores them at one's peril. The beliefs of early Hawaiians sound as quaint to western ears as Christian beliefs must have sounded to the Hawaiians when they first heard them. An open mind will attempt to empathize with the legend of *Ka'ahupahau*, the shark goddess of *Ke awa lau o Pu'uloa*, the many harbored sea of Pearl Harbor. Mary Kawena Pukui tells the legend,

> "*Ka'akupahau* and her brother were born, not sharks, but as human beings. One day a great shark god saw them and converted them into sharks like himself. Every day they swam up a stream at *Waipahu* and there they were fed on *'awa* by relatives. *'Awa* was always the food of the gods. When they became too large to swim upstream, the offerings of food were carried to the lochs for them."[4]

Ka'ahupahau was a benign goddess. Because of remorse for a young girl who had been killed by sharks, *Ka'ahupahau* decreed that no shark should harm a human visitor if the visitor had friendly intentions. For many years children played with the sharks of *Waimomi*, or Pearl Harbor. In fact, riding on their backs was a playful sport. Pukui states that to turn them, one would apply gentle pressure just back of the shark's eye.

If a visitor had evil intentions, however, or broke a kapu, the shark goddess *Ka'ahupahau* could wreak a terrible punishment. That is evident in the case of the young girl mentioned above. The pretty young girl named *Papio* enjoyed surfing at *Keahi*, between *Pu 'uloa*, or *Waimomi*, and *Kalaeloa*, now called Barber's Point. Mary Pukui continues the story,

> "One day she met *Koihala, Ka'ahupahau's* grandmother, who was busy stringing *kou, ma'o*, and *'ilima* blossoms into leis for her beloved shark 'grandchildren'. *Papio* begged for a lei, which was, according to the standards

of that time, a very rude thing to do. Each time she begged, *Koihala* refused to give her a lei. *Papio* then went to her surfing and on her return snatched one of the leis from *Koihala* and went away with a laugh. *Koihala* was filled with anger and when she took the leis to the beach, she told *Ka'ahupahau* all about it. *Ka'ahupahau*, too, became angry with *Papio*.

"*Papio* crossed the channel, found a large rock and stretched herself on it with her long, beautiful hair trailing in the water. She did not suspect that *Ka'ahupahau* had sent a shark to destroy her. *Papio* was seized, drawn under water and killed. Then her blood was spewed on the shore not far away, staining the soil there red to this day."[5]

Ka'ahupahau's son *Ku-pipi* made his home in what is now called Southeast Loch across from the island of *Moku'ume'ume*. This place was kapu, not to be defiled. This was, unfortunately, precisely the location of the Navy's planned dry-dock. The *kia'i*, or guardian of that site would "resent the intrusion of this chief's home and disaster would surely result". Two irresistible forces seemed to be on a collision course.

As construction began, an old man, *Kupuna Kanakeawe*, warned of the dangers of building at that location. The haole engineers thought he was cute. Neither he nor his warnings were of any concern to them. However, the old man continued to visit the site, bringing fish to appease the offended shark god *Ku-pipi*, son of *Ka'ahupahau*. His intent was to protect the Hawaiian workmen on the project.[6] The dry-dock itself was only one part of the project, albeit the central structure. Construction was also started on warehouses, machine shops, quarters, power plants, saw mills, blacksmith shops, and all the necessary buildings for a first class shipyard. The location was a lovely one. On one side was the beautiful lagoon. Beyond were tens of thousands of acres of sugar cane and pineapple fields. The cane reached up to the slopes of the Ko'olau ridge.[7] It was in this tranquil, serene location that the first of three catastrophic events occurred. The other two were to take place almost half a century later.

David Kanakeawe Richards, a construction expert in Hawaii, was retained to oversee the initial excavation for the dry-dock. Starting in November of 1909, he and his men lived in a settlement created just for this project named Watertown, located on the Diamond Head side of the entrance to Pearl Harbor. A few days after the digging started, Richards was approached by an old man who asked about the work. "We're digging a hole 50 feet deep" was Richards' answer. "What are you doing here?" he asked the old man, who replied, "I have come to feed my *'aumakua*, the *Ka'ahupahau*, a shark goddess"8 The old man continued to come to the worksite and offer fish to the offended *Ka'ahupahau*. When the fish were gone, then he would drop his line to get fish for himself. There was a difference between the fish he brought for the goddess and those he caught for himself. Richards and the other workmen laughed at the old man and continued their excavation.

The project was mammoth. While a crater was being dug longer than a football field and deeper than a five story building, the rock, coral, and dirt was used to build a coffer dam across the opening to the water. The dredging was begun at the outer entrance in water from 15 to 25' deep by using a steam lumber schooner fitted with hoppers and equipped with a 14" centrifugal pump, connected to a 20" suction pipe, and driven by a 275 HP steam engine. As the depth became greater and the softer material was removed a clamshell dredge, equipped with a 4 1/2 yard, 13 ton bucket, was put into use. Then, for excavating the hardest materials a drag-scraper dredge, equipped with a 3 yard bucket, was used; the bucket was sunk at the greatest possible distance from the dredge, which was moored with anchors, and was drawn in by a cable rove through a sheave at the stem of the dredge. The dredging of the channel and the dry-dock was started on August 23rd 1909 and completed on January 30th, 1912.[9] During this time in January of 1911, the small gunboat *Petrel* steamed from Honolulu Harbor and crossed the bar through the new channel into Pearl Harbor, becoming the first warship to enter. While work continued on the dry-dock, President William H. Taft closed the harbor to all commercial shipping of foreign registry.[10]

Pilings 16 inches square and 20 feet long were driven into the bottom of the crater by huge steam-driven piledrivers. These heavy vertical pilings were placed three feet apart over the entire floor of the cavity.[11] The drawings were, of course, made by hand in 1908 on linen. The workmanship is exquisite.

All the while the work progressed, the old man begged Richards to stop digging and to move away or else they would all be severely punished. Richards, who had become friendly with the old man, explained that "it couldn't be done for haoles just don't believe in that sort of thing"[12] The digging involved blasting with dynamite and then removing the loosened dirt by use of steam shovels and rail cars. Several times water would pour in from an exposed tunnel. One such tunnel was 9' in diameter coming from Halawa Gulch. That stream had to be diverted before the work could continue. Were they being warned?

By August of 1912, Congress had been convinced of the importance of making the dry-dock large enough to service the two new battleships USS *Arkansas & USS Wyoming*, so the length was increased to 1008' raising the estimated cost to $3,486,500.[13] As the dredging progressed, ships bearing millions of board feet of lumber and other needed materials and supplies, arrived from western mainland ports. The channel was deep enough in 1911 to allow the armored cruiser USS *California*, with several dignitaries, including the improbable duo of Sanford Dole and former Queen Liliuokalani, to become the first major warship to enter Pearl Harbor.

As the pilings were pounded into the ground, the engineers noticed that the land was of uneven density. Soft dirt was embedded in coral and lava rock, each with different densities and strengths. When all the pilings were finally driven, concrete was poured between and over them. A special formula of cement and sand was used that would cure underwater. Over a thousand tons of crushed rock came in daily from the quarries to be added to the cement.[14] The general shape of the dry-dock began to emerge. The U shaped cavern, open to the lagoon, rose to over 50' from its base. It widened to a width of 200' at the coping by offsets in the side walls, called altars. These altars provided balconies for access to ship' hulls and were wide enough to lay tracks for railroad cars to remove the dredged earth and carry lumber to the bottom. The walls were much thicker at the bottom than at the top, much like a dam, since, when filled, the dock sides would have to support a head of 50' of water. All this time the old man kept warning the workmen and supplying fish to *Ka'ahupahau*, the shark goddess.

The first section was sealed off from the lagoon water by means of a cofferdam so that work could begin on the next section. On February 17, 1913, the section was pumped empty and then either a vengeful *Ka'ahupahau* or inferior, unreinforced concrete caused what Secretary of the Navy Josephus Daniels was to call, "The marine disaster of the year".[15]

David Kanakeawe Richards, the assistant supervisor of the project, noted leaks, not only from the cofferdam, but from the sides of the newly poured walls. Over 50 men were working at the bottom of the dry-dock. Richards related,

> "At the end of four days our instruments indicated that the bottom would rise. All the men were ordered to come up and also the divers on the outside. Then just as the last diver emerged, section two let go its bottom, and sections one and three caved in. The sound of section two crashing was like that of an explosion of tons of black powder. It was unbelievable that those huge timbers could be crushed to splinters in so short a time. Luckily no one was hurt. Nearly $4,000,000 and four long years of hard work were destroyed in about four minutes."[16]

He remembered the old man's warning, "Byme, bye, too much pilikia". A similar description was given by Walter Dillingham,

> "At this point, the water crushed in the lower members of the cofferdam and rushed into the vortex under great pressure. In five minutes, several million feet of timber were broken into kindling wood, pumps, hoisting engines, concrete mixers, derricks and locomotives were precipitated into the tangled mass of ruins and two years work had been destroyed in less time than it takes to relate the catastrophe".[17]

More than 1000 workers were immediately laid off. The local newspapers decried the disaster and heralded the heroism of Francis 'Drydock' Smith, Richards' boss. Smith saw the scope of the crumbling monster and rushed, at his own peril, to aid workers who had been too casual about evacuating the cavern.[18] An immediate response from Washington quoted L. M. Whitehouse, a civil engineer who had been visiting the worksite as an interested observer at the time of the disaster. He stated, "The only opinion I expressed before the collapse was that the artesian water would prevent the piling from holding in the coral...I have estimated that the pressure was seventeen pounds to the square inch".[19] Rear Admiral Charles B. T. Moore was at the site because he was to relieve RAdm W. C. Cowles and assume command of the Naval Station on March 24, 1913, just 35 days after the collapse. Parts of the US Naval Station, Hawaii, had recently been moved from its previous location in Honolulu at the corner of Richards Street and the Waterfront Esplanade.[20] The balance of administration personnel were to move to Pearl on August 4, 1913,[21] Moore faced a $4,000,000 pile of twisted rail and pipe, ten-ton chunks of concrete, locomotives on end, overturned machinery, millions of feet of lumber in splinters, all in a pile of rubble, worth less than nothing because it was dangerous and had to be removed. The local *Kamainas*, old timers, just shook their heads with no surprise at all.

For the next two years, the United States Navy and the contractors stood, each pointing respective accusatory fingers at the other. Assistant Secretary of the Navy Franklin D. Roosevelt appointed Mr. Alfred Noble, a civil engineer of international reputation and respect to investigate the debacle. Noble's initial report stated that the foundation conditions were not as had been assumed and were not suitable for the structure as designed.[22] The consensus was that hydrostatic (external water) pressure caused the eruption and destruction. It was quickly decided that the government was at fault, but it took 22 months for them to admit that and negotiate a new contract for the design and construction of a new dry-dock. Based on Noble's report, Navy Secretary Daniels said, "the enormity even of this immeasurable difficulty was not fully realized at first".[23] A comment in a letter from an interested observer 30 years later stated, "There are some Hawaiians who believe that the blitz attack at Pearl Harbor on December 7, 1941, was merely a continuation of the bad luck that was initiated when the ground was broken without appropriate appeasement of the native shark gods". The writer of the letter was Admiral Chester Nimitz.[24]

The first consideration, after cleanup, was whether or not to build on the same site. Then all the previously answered questions arose regarding size, design, cost, etc. It was not until August of 1914 that the Navy confirmed the viability of the original site, approved a new design produced under the direction of Rear Admiral H. R. Sanford, the Chief of the Bureau of Yards and Docks, and Congress appropriated $4,968,500 for its construction.[25] The bickering and the cleanup process progressed simultaneously, each taking almost three years. The original contractor, San Francisco Bridge Company, and subcontractor, Hawaiian Dredging Company were awarded the contracts and began the work of reconstruction in November of 1917. Meanwhile, two significant events occurred. A radical new design was created and the project received a blessing.

The foundation of the first dry-dock was a sheet of concrete poured underwater around the pilings with no reinforcement. When the cavern was pumped dry, the external water pressure not only broke up the concrete slab floor, but slid the pilings and the attached chunks of concrete upward, destroying everything in their path. Obviously, the new design had to prevent such an occurrence. The solution was one that had never been used before.

The excavation was cleaned out to a depth of 55' and pilings were driven into the soil, coral, and rock at the base of the 'hole'. This time crushed rock was poured between the pilings and tamped to create a uniform surface. The crushed rock bed was seven feet thick. Then, instead of pouring concrete through the water onto the base, another method was devised.

The 1020 foot length of the dry-dock was divided into 16 sections. For each section a slab was built 'in the dry'. Each slab was 60' wide, 152' long, and 16' thick. They were reinforced with 1 1/16 inch diameter steel rods placed 16 inches on centers with alternate layers 18 inches above the previous layer and laid in a direction perpendicular to it. The concrete was made with a new formula and different ingredients than the concrete in the first dock and cured in the open air. Each slab weighed over 7,500 tons. As each was completed, a pontoon was built above it and fastened to it with holddown bolts. The entire assembly was floated to a position over the designed location. Huge chains were connected from the pontoon to the slab below it, the holddown bolts were backed out and the slab was lowered into position on the crushed rock bed. After all the slabs were in position, concrete was poured over the entire area to bind them together.

The final slab and the rest of the structure was completed and placed on March 25, 1919 and pumping of the dock started on March 31. We can only imagine the apprehension of the workers, the designers, the contractors, the US Navy, and the general public. Unwatering was successfully completed on April 10, 1919. With the removal of water, the entire structure rose an almost unmeasurable 3/16 of an inch owing to the elasticity of piles and soil. Of the hundreds of people there to watch the ten day unwatering process, nobody cheered. They all remembered that it was a few days after pumping out the previous dry-dock that it exploded. This time, happily, the dry-dock performed as expected and has been in service ever since.

This new design and construction was one of two events that followed the catastrophe of Dry-dock #1. The other had to do with the concerns many felt about the lack of recognition of the shark goddess *Ka'ahupahau*.

One morning in 1917 David Kanakeawe Richards, assistant to 'Dry-dock' Smith, the construction superintendent, approached Smith and suggested some kind of offering be made in the Hawaiian manner as they do on the mainland for ship christenings. He felt it would please the men who had worked for over ten years on the project. Smith told Richards he was crazy and walked away. Later, however, Governor Frear visited the site, talked with Richards, and approved the Hawaiian blessing. Considering the explosive end of the previous dry-dock, it would seem to be a small effort to spend. Even Smith began to like the idea.

Richards went to the *Kahuna Kainani*, a priestess, who lived near Waikiki. When she was told what the men desired her to do, she inspected the site and observed that it had been built on the home of the shark goddess and her son. She asked if they had experienced much trouble. A believer would say the old lady was able to sense to *pilikia* in the area. A skeptic would say she had read the local newspaper.

As the old *kahuna* proceeded with her incantations, Smith became impatient and stalked away. *Kahuna Kainani* observed, "*Hookieki no ka kanaka, e hoopai ia no oia*", or "there is punishment for those who scorn the sacred things". She then instructed Richards to leave and return to the site between two and three the next morning and recite a prayer she had prepared for him. He did so.

Richards drove to the Navy Yard gate. He relates,

"The gate is usually guarded well, but upon my arrival, I found it wide open. There was no one in sight. I went straight to the cave, filled my hand with the sacred water and recited the prayers the old woman had taught me. When all was finished, I started home happy. This time as I approached the gate, I met all the guards that should have been there as I passed through just a short time before."[26]

On his way home he was informed that Smith was in the hospital with a broken collar bone as a result of an automobile accident. Alarmed, Richards rushed to the home of the *kahuna* to inform her of the accident. Before he had an opportunity to tell her, she exclaimed, "Oh, my God! Too bad for the old man!... It's going to be a long time before he is well again". It took Smith over nine months to return to work, and then he could only work two or three days a week. Later the old *kahuna* came back to visit Richards at the worksite and said, "No more *pilikia* to this dry-dock. The next time you start a big job, don't forget to call me".[27]

With the new design and the *kahuna's* blessing, the dry-dock has operated flawlessly for over 80 years. Along with the basic structure, they built several thousand feet of wharfage, a marine railway, oil and coal storage and fueling stations, ammunition depots, stores, machine shops, a hospital and an administration building, officers' quarters, barracks, radio wireless towers, and many other facilities. The shipyard at Pearl Harbor was ready to service the Navy's largest vessels, and a world war had come and gone during its building.

Considerable interest was attached to the formal opening of the dock on August 21, 1919, by the Secretary of the Navy Josephus Daniels. Governor Charles J. McCarthy declared a special holiday and the opening was attended by about 7,000 people. Bleachers were set up around the three land sides of the dock and a speakers' platform was erected at the land end of the structure.[28] After appropriate ceremonies, Mrs. Daniels pressed an button which opened the three large sluice gates, which admitted the water to the dock, making a particularly spectacular sight.[29]

The local newspapers devoted their Wednesday, August 20, 1919 issues almost completely to the event. They displayed pictures of the exterior from several angles, the interior of pump rooms, the generators, and lists of names of those who participated in the construction. They described the enormous American flag which was proudly unfurled by Mr. Peter F. Dubois, a veteran of the Civil War who had fought under Admiral Farragut.[30]

This ten year process brought together the US Navy and the Hawaiian culture in a way nothing else ever did. Together they weathered optimism, opposition, disaster and finally triumph. No matter how one explains the collapse of the first dry-dock or the effective second one, the operation was an unqualified success.

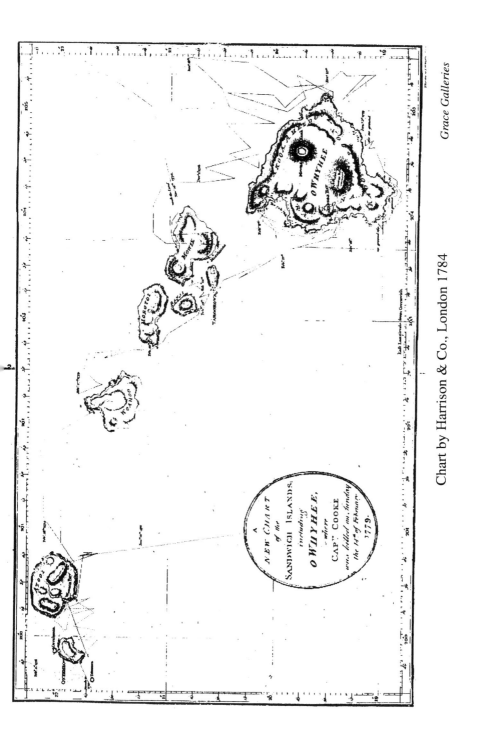

Grace Galleries

Chart by Harrison & Co., London 1784

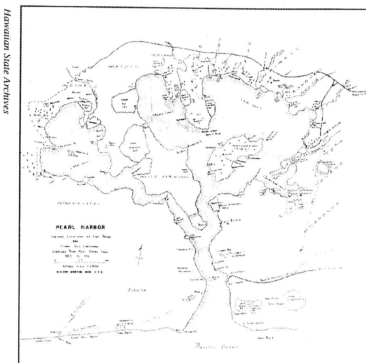

Early Maps

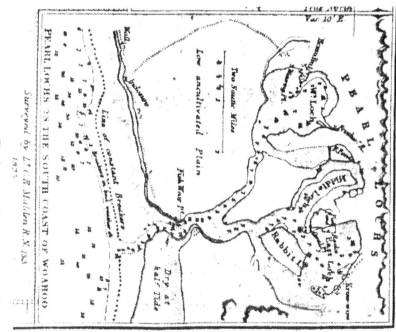

First known published chart of Pearl Harbor
Bishop Museum

Bishop Museum

Early Sandwich Island Canoe

Hawaiian State Archives

Iolani Palace, late 1800s

Her Britanic Majesty's Ship Dublin, off Honolulu, 26th July, 1843.

Sir,—It being my desire to obtain the honor of a Personal Interview with His Majesty, King Kamehameha III., for the purpose of conferring with His Majesty on the subject of the Provisional Cession of His Dominions, I have to request that you will be pleased to intimate my wishes to His Majesty in order that he may appoint the time and place where such Interview may be held.

I have the honor to be, Sir, your most obedient humble servant,

RICHARD THOMAS, Rear Admiral and Commander in Chief of H. B. M. Ships and Vessels in the Pacific.

To KEKUANAOA, Governor of Oahu.

Ko ke Lii Wahine Beritania Moku Dublini, mawaho o Honolulu, Iulai 26, 1843.

ALOHA OE,

No ko'u makemake e mahaloia mai, au i ka halawai pu me ka Moi Kamehameha III ke Lii, e kamailio pu me ia, me ka Moi, no ka Haawi ana o kona Aupuni me ka manao e hoihoia mai; nolaila, ke noi aku nei au if oe e lokomaikai mai oe ia'u a e hoopuka aku i ka Moi ko'u makemake, i hiki ia ia ke hoakaka mai i ka manawa a me ka wahi e halawai ai.

Owau no me ka mahalo kou kauwa hoolohe,

(Inoa,)

RICHARD THOMAS, Adimala Hope, a me ke ke Nui o H. B. M. mau Manuwa a me na Moku ma Moana Pakifika.

Na KEKUANAOA, ke Lii Kiaaina Oahu.

Unuhia e G. P. JUDD, Unuhiolelo a me ke Kakauolelo no ke Aupuni.

Admiral Sir Richard Thomas' request for an audience with King Kamehameha

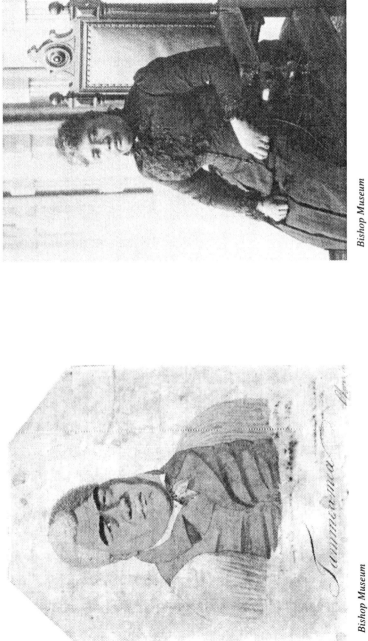

Bishop Museum

Queen Lili'uokalani, 1892

Bishop Museum

"Tammeamea" – Kamehameha, 1819
at the age of 75 insisted on being painted
in European clothing

Bishop Museum

Waikiki Beach 1920

Honolulu Advertiser

Honolulu Harbor 1880

PRNY 8-7-41 5M
Original
U. NAVAL AIR STATION, KODIAK ALASKA
NAVAL COMMUNICATIONS

Heading   RFG RC 63 F C 2 76L 071630 CBQ TARI 0 BI

From: CINCPAC   Date 7 DEC 41

To: ALL SHIPS PRESENT AT HAWAII AREA.

Info: - U R G E N T -

DEFERRED unless otherwise checked | ROUTINE .... | PRIORITY .... | AIRMAIL ....

AIRRAID ON PEARLHARBOR X THIS IS NO DRILL

U.S. Navy Department

CINPAC's announcement of attack Dec. 7, 1941

Magellan Geographix

DRAFT No. 1   December 7, 1941.

PROPOSED MESSAGE TO THE CONGRESS

Yesterday, December 7, 1941, a date which will live in *infamy*

the United States of America was *suddenly* and deliberately attacked

by naval and air forces of the Empire of Japan.

The United States was at the moment at peace with that nation and was

still in conversation with its Government and its Emperor looking

toward the maintenance of peace in the Pacific. Indeed, one hour after,

Japanese air squadrons had commenced bombing in *Oahu*

the Japanese Ambassador to the United States and his colleague delivered

to the Secretary of State a formal reply to a *recent American* message.

While This reply *stated* that diplomatic negotiations

contained no threat *or* hint of *war*

armed attack.

It will be recorded that the distance of

Hawaii from Japan makes it obvious that the attack *was* deliberately

planned many days ago. During the intervening time the Japanese Govern-

ment has deliberately sought to deceive the United States by false

statements and expressions of hope for continued peace.

Franklin D. Roosevelt Library

Original dfraft of Presidenty Roosevelt's
message to U.S. Congress Dec. 8, 1941

Franklin D. Roosevelt Library

Fleet Admiral Chester Nimitz

U.S. Navy Department

General of the army Douglas MacArthur signing
the Instrument of Japanese surrender aboard *USS Missouri*
Sept. 2, 1945

Honolulu Advertiser

Statehood – Finally!

U.S. Navy Department

USS Missouri arriving at Ford Island, June 22, 1998
USS Arizona Memorial in foreground

U.S. Navy Department, FISC
Aerial view of US Navel Base, Pearl Harbor

U.S. Navy Department
USS Carl Vinson entering Pearl – RIMPAC July 1998
USS Missouri, USS Arizona Memorial, & Adm. Clarey Bridge

Chapter 25 - Another Drawdown

After every war in our nation's history, the United States Navy has suffered a reduction, or drawdown, in size. Quantities of men, ships, equipment, and services have been maintained at existing levels or reduced. 'Do more with less', a phrase commonly heard since 1996, certainly is not a new concept.

Shortly after the first World War, Navy Secretary Josephus Daniels announced that the fleet would be divided into two sections. One section would remain in the Atlantic and the other would be assigned to the Pacific Ocean, all 64,000,000 square miles of it.[1] For the first time the major American Naval force was assigned to the Pacific Ocean.[2] While the fleet was geographically divided, it was combined, on paper for administrative purposes, in 1922, to form the United States Fleet.

Immediately concern was expressed as to the capability of west coast facilities to meet the new demands. Assuming Congress would somehow find the money to fund the required expansion, people in Hawaii received the news joyously. Some locals opined that upward of $50,000,000 would be spent at Pearl Harbor and other Hawaiian locations.[3] Such vast quantities of money, however, were not forthcoming for several years. In fact, by 1921 only $1,500,000 had been appropriated, and that was for a Naval Air Station on Ford Island. The appropriation included barracks, electric and water systems, gasoline storage tanks, hangers, officers' quarters, shops, storehouses, and a timber pier. The entire allotment, $460,675, for the balance of needs at Pearl Harbor was so inadequate that the Naval Base had to close for two weeks in 1921.[4] While major ships could moor at docks, smaller vessels had to anchor, with the danger of collision due to circular swinging with the tide and current, or moor fore and aft *mauka*, towards the mountains, of Ford Island.

In addition to military needs, which were paramount of course, Pearl Harbor required facilities for incoming fleet personnel. In 1920, sailors would arrive at Pearl hot and dirty. That was a result of shoveling coal for twenty days in 110 degrees heat of an engine room. Their fresh water allowance was 1/2 bucket per day to wash themselves and their clothes. The first job after mooring or anchoring was to coal the ship. Senior officers realized that to raise the morale of incoming sailors and to avoid embarrassing confrontations between these blackened monsters and the civilian population, shoreside quarters had to be built. Barracks were constructed by the sailors themselves and water was piped to showers.[5]

Fiscal restraints were exacerbated by an act of July 9, 1921 which stated that no person could be employed upon any public work in the Territory of Hawaii unless he is a citizen or eligible to become one. This made it difficult for Filipinos and impossible for Japanese to qualify. That in turn, meant hiring from the mainland, indemnifying the workers' passage, and paying them higher than local scale wages.[6]

Bitterness had been steadily rising among the American people against war and almost anything related to it. Some of the same arguments heard after the Revolutionary War were heard again. First, we don't need a large navy in peacetime. Second, if we continue to rearm, other nations will regard that action as provocative and will follow suit. The escalation will inevitably end in another conflict. Third, the American Navy has always been able to rise to the occasion after war starts. Fourth, if we rebuild after war starts we won't be burdened with outdated equipment; the ships and equipment will be new. The short-sightedness of these arguments have plagued Navy men for over two hundred years.

Politicians in the Harding administration and senior Navy officers were at odds over several issues. The losers in these arguments were the US Navy and the American people. As a result of their attention to these debates, the politicians were left unprepared for the scheduled arms limitation conference to be held in 1921 in Washington.

Representatives of Great Britain, the United States, Japan, France, and Italy met at the Washington conference in 1921 and 1922. On February 6, 1922, after months of wrangling over the definition of capital ships, the allowable uses of submarines, and the role of aircraft carriers, the last of several treaties was signed. Ratios were established as to the amount of tonnage of battleships each nation was allowed. Submarines and aircraft carriers were not mentioned by tonnage. For those in our Navy with vision, the vague language about carriers was a door left ajar. The partially completed battlecruisers *Saratoga* and *Lexington* were immediately redesigned and built as aircraft carriers which not only gave the United States acceptable (according to the treaty) strength in that unfamiliar area, but also allowed for the construction of two more cruisers. The two new aircraft carriers, launched in 1927 and operating from Pearl Harbor, were to play an important part in World War II only a few years later.

Woodrow Wilson was succeeded by Warren Harding in 1920. President Harding transferred the administration of Naval Petroleum Reserves to the Secretary of the Interior, Albert B. Fall.[7] This transfer was opposed by the Chief of Naval Operations Admiral Robert E. Coontz and Assistant Secretary of the Navy Theodore Roosevelt, Jr., but the transfer was made, and in the interim a fraudulent scheme was devised in Washington. Fall accepted a $100,000 bribe to lease certain oil field reserves (among them, Teapot Dome in Wyoming) to two oil companies.

Pearl Harbor was one location used to mask the fraud. Contracts were awarded to two companies for the construction of storage tanks for

1,500,000 barrels of fuel oil which they were then to fill with the oil from their oil fields in Wyoming and California. The Secretary of the Interior and the presidents of the two oil companies secretly agreed to base the pay to the companies via royalties for "the amount of oil pumped from the leases" so the incentive was to produce and store as much as possible.[8] The Navy Secretary, Edwin Denby, was neither consulted nor informed. He remained innocent, but irresponsibly unaware of the scheme.

When the illicit deal was discovered, the tanks had been built and the oil had been transferred from California to Pearl Harbor. After a number of trials, appeals, writs of certiorari and rulings from the Supreme Court, the Navy was awarded over $25,000,000 plus over nine million dollars worth of equipment which the oil companies were forced to forfeit. Secretary Fall went to prison and Secretary Denby resigned. Pearl Harbor, however, benefited handsomely from the fraud.

Despite the limitations imposed by the Washington conference, some money was allotted each year to Pearl Harbor. In 1922, six million dollars was appropriated for more straightening, widening, and deepening of the entrance channel.[9] New ships were longer and had more draft and even with the expansion of the channel, eleven ships grounded during the next seven years.[10]

The decade of the '20s saw the convening of several committees, or 'boards', usually named for the senior officer in charge. The Rodman Board in 1922 recommended Pearl Harbor and Kaneohe be expanded to be "capable of serving the entire fleet". In January of 1923 the Willard Board recommended spending $42,500,000 at Pearl with an emphasis on air power. In October of that year, the Houston Board rejected the Kaneohe proposal in favor of expansion from Pearl into the Kalihi Basin nearby and acquiring all remaining private land surrounding Pearl Harbor. This proposal had been made by Commander Merry a quarter of a century before.

Congressmen who witnessed the Navy War Games in Panama in 1923 were impressed when an airplane from the USS *Oklahoma* dropped ten unarmed bombs on the locks before a single plane got off the ground and before the anti-aircraft batteries opened fire.[11] That lesson was not lost and the Naval Air Station on Ford Island soon received $1,150,000 for hangers, a magazine, runway improvement, and supporting shops.[12] The Navy's prompt reaction to exercises and surprise orders to mobilize won favorable reviews and, despite the continued reluctance of Congress to allot money for more ships, the air arm was being steadily strengthened. Air space above Pearl Harbor was set aside for US government use only, the only exception being the Pan-American Airways company which flew the clippers into Pearl Harbor from San Francisco.

New construction reported in 1922 and 1923 included the completion of a marine railway, the 9th Division USMC barracks, and more development of the docks around Merry Point. The Marine Reservation lay *makai* (seaward) of the shipyard, then called the Industrial Plant. Dredging of the channel and anchorages continued to accommodate the increased number of ships entering the harbor. Quay walls and a pier at First Street were installed. Two concrete chimneys were constructed at the Navy Yard power plant and the Submarine Base.

Meanwhile, the world was drifting toward war as the United States became more isolationist. More limitations were put in place by conferences held at Geneva in 1927 and London in 1930. Before those conferences, however, the diminishing abilities of the US Navy was demonstrated in 1921 when Captain Thomas Hart led a flotilla of ten submarines from the east coast into the Pacific bound for The Philippines. Every one of the vessels broke down and the cruise to Manila could not get underway until every boat was repaired at Pearl harbor. These S-class subs were slow, had a limited cruising range, and suffered a frightening number of fatal accidents.[13]

Responsible men recognized the unfulfilled needs of Pearl Harbor. On May 15, 1924, Commandant Rear Admiral J.D. McDonald recommended that the planned Naval Maneuvers be scheduled with the idea of disclosing the inadequacy of the Naval Base as it had been developed to that date. He felt that the Army had taken its mission more seriously than the Navy. He cited as principal deficiencies the insufficient depth of the channel and the dangerous turns required for large ships to enter the harbor, and the lack of berthing and docking facilities.[14] The Chief of Naval Operations, Admiral R. E. Coontz agreed with McDonald's assessment and reinforced his agreement by visiting Pearl Harbor from September 9 to 23 of 1924. As a result of the visit, he approved the acquisition of a dredge for the exclusive use of the Navy, seven more buildings for Kuahua Island, storage space at the Sub Base for their enormous batteries, reinforced concrete storehouse at the Air Station, Six DT-2 planes, and several other minor improvements. He also concurred with the recommendation to acquire all the land surrounding Pearl Harbor. The Admiral returned in April of the next year with the entire U.S. Fleet for Joint Army and Navy Problem No.3, to be carried out in Hawaiian waters.[15]

On October 28 of the previous year, the submarine USS *R-1* grounded on a reef three miles west of Barber's Point. The *Seagull*, which had replaced the *Chicago* as the sub tender in early 1923, with the aid of local commercial tugs were able to pull her free and float her. Repairs were made at Pearl and she was seaworthy again in three months. There were no casualties.

On December 13, 1924, the 32 acre Aiea Naval Reservation was transferred from the War Department to the Navy Department.[16] This was part of a parcel adjacent to East Loch that had previously been designated as a military area.

During the next three years committees headed by Naval Officers Babcock in April 1925, McKay in May 1926, and Chambers in July 1926 all recommended improvements to the docking facilities. The most important recommendation accepted was a series of quay walls for capital ships on the Diamond Head (east) side of Ford Island. They were sturdy enough and spaced far enough apart to accommodate battleships. The Hanson Report in January of 1927 summarized the recommendations and the work was approved and completed. His report was an effective force in gaining the congressional act passed in 1927 for $2,805,000 to continue improvements in the harbor and almost $400,000 for the Submarine Base.

In the fall of 1923, a young Army Officer, William (Billy) Mitchell, after an inspection tour of the Pacific, warned that the Hawaiian Islands, and in particular, the great naval base at Pearl Harbor, were open to a Japanese surprise air attack. He proceeded to outline the plan that the Japanese would probably use. One of his assumptions was that Japan "knows full well that the United States will probably enter the next war with the methods and weapons of the former war".[17] Unlike the many heralds gifted with 20/20 hindsight, Mitchell's predictions were printed in the War Department Records and reside in the National Archives.

Over 3400 miles away other naval activities had been taking place which would soon affect Pearl Harbor. The Imperial Japanese Navy founded its Naval Air Service in 1912. For several years the Japanese High Command ignored this mostly experimental arm of their war machine, but by 1927 an independent naval aviation department was formed and in 1928 a formation of aircraft carriers was assigned to the Imperial Fleet. Like the Americans had done after the Washington Arms Conference of 1921-22, the Japanese converted two major ships into aircraft carriers: *Akagi* and *Kaga*. Another carrier, *Hosyo*, was added in 1928. By 1941 five more aircraft carriers were launched, *Soryu, Hiryu, Ryuzyo, Koryu,* and *Sokaku.*[18] Several of these ships were soon to head east.

It has been written that the U.S. Naval exercises of the late 1920s, in and around Pearl Harbor, provided a blueprint for the Japanese. During Naval Problem #8 in 1928 the USS *Langley* completely surprised the defensive forces at Pearl Harbor, destroying the fleet and harbor, on paper, before the defending forces left their runways or docks. Because of the limited range of airplanes of that day, the consensus was that carriers were as vulnerable as they were effective, hence they would be detected and destroyed long before they could reach Pearl.

In 1929, Naval Problem #9 planned an attack on, and defense of the Panama Canal. Admiral Reeves commanded a small carrier squadron comprised of two later-to-be-famous ships commanded by two outstanding officers. USS *Lexington*, under the command of Captain Ernest J. King, later to be Chief of Naval Operations and a Fleet Admiral, and the USS *Saratoga*, commanded by Captain Harry E. Yarnell. The air attack achieved total victory. Enough damage was theoretically done to the canal to render it useless for months. At a debriefing, Admiral Pratt, the defending Officer in Command stated, "Gentlemen, you have witnessed the most brilliantly conceived and most effectively executed naval operation in our history". Another officer, a young army captain, said that he had been walking near his quarters that morning with his adjutant who, seeing specks in the sky asked, "Frigate birds?" "Frigate birds, my eye" responded the alarmed captain, "Those are enemy aircraft and they've caught us flat-footed!". The young captain was J.B. Mitchell.[19]

Again in 1932, Yarnell, by then a Rear Admiral and one of the first flag officers with flying experience, staged a simulated air attack on Pearl Harbor. Ironically his two carriers were *Lexington* and *Saratoga*, the two carriers that escaped danger nine years later during the attack by the Japanese, which followed a plan similar to Yarnell's. Yarnell based his attack on four assumptions:

> First, a small carrier-centered task force would be more difficult to find than a larger fleet accompanied by a landing force with support ships.
>
> Second, rain squalls could cover his approach.
>
> Third, winter clouds form and cling to the Ko'olau mountains east of Pearl Harbor. Attack planes could approach undetected, break out of the cloud banks, and be over Pearl Harbor in clear skies before the defense forces would realize they were even close.
>
> Fourth, no one would expect, or be ready for, an attack early on a Sunday morning.

Yarnell's success was complete. The senior officers who were judging the 'game' concluded, however, that the entire fleet would not be in Pearl at one time and that remaining ships would find the carrier force and destroy it. Also they felt that even if all the capital ships were at anchor or docked in Pearl, their combined anti-aircraft fire would sweep the skies of enemy planes before any significant damage could be done.[20] For each dazzling demonstration of excellence and superiority of aircraft, the old-line senior officers had explanations of why things would be different in actual battle.

While the officers in command of Pearl Harbor appropriately focused on military matters, they allowed a minor problem become a monster. When the US Navy acquired Pearl Harbor at the turn of the century, fishing rights were not considered to be of importance. The *ili kupono*, small parcels, granted to the *hoa'aina*, tenants, by the king were his to fish as he saw fit. When the US included all fishing rights in the land acquisition act, a few local landowners complained via lawsuits which appraised the value of these rights at $85,000. Rather than settle for that amount, Congress argued the suits for years. During that time, the assessments and number of plaintiffs grew alarmingly. On December 9, 1930, a Commission consisting of Captain H.R. Stanford, CEC, and Commander Pollock were able to bring the matter to a mutually agreeable conclusion. By the time the cases were settled, there were over 7,000 plaintiffs and the settlement, in their favor, was $1,570,000! An expensive delay indeed.[21]

Work at Pearl continued. The war plans of 1930 called for the berthing and anchorage of 425 ships in Pearl Harbor. Surveys were made for a magazine and ammunition depot at Lualualei near West Loch.[22] Yet another contract for dredging the channel was completed. By the end of the decade, despite monetary constraints, Pearl housed a navy yard, submarine base, hospital, air station, Marine barracks, ammunition depot, railway, tank farm, supply warehouses and dozens of buildings for support activities.

The Navy had been able to obtain money for some of its projects, especially on the west coast and at Hawaii, but not nearly as much as they felt was necessary. Then Herbert Hoover became President in 1928 and proceeded to slash every Navy budget presented to him. Further drawdowns were inevitable. The great depression descended like a ghastly, dismal cloud on America and the United States Navy suddenly had, again, to 'do more with less'. The Navy was sailing into the ominous thirties.

Chapter 26 - The Ominous Thirties

Franklin Delano Roosevelt was elected President of the United States in 1932. He had always been a pro-Navy man and this attitude did not change. His assumption of office came as more than a breath of fresh air for the Navy; it was a life-saving event. Even through the harsh depths of the Great Depression Navy procurement requests were more favorably heard than before by many, but not by all. In fact Pearl Harbor was termed by some, "a billion dollar service station".[1]

Hawaii was still trying to lure tourists and conventions to the islands. The local economy was suffering. By the beginning of 1932 an estimated ten percent of the population of Honolulu was out of work.[2] No one gathered data about the unemployed outside the city. Some Public Works money came from United States government programs in 1934 such as the WPA and CCC. Many men were employed building bridges, highways, parks, and developing Pearl Harbor. The growing need for workspace at Pearl led to moving the Public Works Officer and staff to the newly built Shop 8.

In the first two years of the decade, the everlasting dredging of the entrance channel was continued, along with waterfront improvements. On Ford Island several buildings were erected for engine repair, a new runway was laid out, and the seaplane ramps were extended. A needed parcel of 3923 acres at Lualualei was acquired as was one adjacent to West Loch.[3] The munitions storage facility was moved from Kuahua Island to the new location at Lualualei on May 1, 1934. Kuahua was joined to the adjacent land by spoilage from the dredging operations and became a peninsula upon which FISC, the Fleet & Industrial Supply Center is located today.

The name 'Industrial Plant' was changed to 'Naval Shipyard', or commonly called 'The Yard'. In March of 1932 a 134 foot high Submarine escape training tower (Building 659) was finished. While no longer used for its original purpose, the tower has become a landmark which can be seen from almost anywhere in the harbor.[4]

Although every area of Pearl Harbor was expanded and improved during the 30s, Rear Admiral Orin S. Murfin, COMFOURTEEN, stated in October 1937, "The development of the base has not gone forward at a speed commensurate with its importance. It is essential that it be in all respects ready to receive and service the Fleet before [the start of] a Pacific War".[5] It was during this year that work began on the concrete moorings alongside the Southeast shore of Ford Island. Later these piers would be known as 'Battleship Row'. Also the radio towers were dismantled and moved to Hospital Point to make way for expansion of the Yard.[6]

During these years, politicians debated endlessly about the relative allowable sizes of armed forces throughout the world. All economics suffered during the first half of the decade and most were revived principally by the production of arms and ammunition. Plans were made, discarded, and replaced concerning the defense of the Pacific coast of the US mainland, but always Pearl Harbor stood as the primary focus of our defense.

With the horrors of the recent war fresh in American minds, and with the pressure on the government to reduce expenses, the people of the United States drifted toward an increasingly complacent and anti-military mindset. The old arguments of "with oceans on either side and friendly neighbors north and south, why should we need such a large Army or Navy?" reemerged. The fact that these barriers had never sufficiently protected us before did not occur to many in the civilian sector.

Relations between American civilians, Orientals and Hawaiian natives were quiet for the time being. In all the discussions about Hawaii as a melting pot and comments about how well the races got along, one group was generally ignored completely - the men of the US Army and Navy.[7] They were too transient to become a part of local society and thus were never assimilated. They were barely tolerated. Their money was welcome however, since there were so many of them and they spent so freely.

In 1931 the infamous 'Ala Moana Assault Case', often called the 'Massie Case', occurred. It was a case of rape sensationalized in the newspapers. After a long trial, a mistrial resulted. Then one of the accused, a Hawaiian boy was shot and killed. The relatives of the victim of the rape were accused, tried and found guilty. They were freed by a local judge and deported from the Territory of Hawaii.

The case was more about race and the workings of law and order in the islands than about the Navy. It did reveal the basic prejudices firmly held by honest, law-abiding citizens who lived in the islands. One result of the hysteria that followed was that sailors were kept away from Honolulu during 1932 fleet exercises which resulted in a loss to the city's businesses of about eight million dollars. Lahaina Roads was used as the fleet anchorage that year.[8] Despite such incidents, with efforts by people of good will on all sides, the US Navy and the Hawaiian people have enjoyed a mutually supportive relationship.

Japanese Premier Inukai was assassinated on May 15, 1932 and along with him the party system in Japan also died. From that time on, all Japanese governments were headed by military men who reported, of course, to the emperor. These governments ignored the terms of the Washington and London treaties and finally withdrew from them and from the League of Nations as well.[9] Amid severe secrecy, Japan laid the keels for the 64,000 ton battleships *Musashi* and *Yamoto*.[10]

US military personnel in Hawaii continued their preparations for defense against a land invasion. The Army, charged with the responsibility of protecting the Hawaiian Islands from enemy attack, saw as the two most dangerous problems, the Japanese population in the islands and food production.[11] A fire of suspicious nature caused over $100,000 damage at the Submarine Base on September 21, 1931. Later the cause was determined to be defective wiring in one of the damaged buildings, but speculations of sabotage were more widely reported than the true cause.[12]

On an afternoon on January 10, 1934, six airplanes of VP Squadron 10F, under the command of Lieutenant Commander Knefler McGinnis departed San Francisco and 24 hours later arrived and landed safely in the calm waters of Pearl Harbor, thus completing the greatest non-stop formation flight in the history of aviation.[13] Just two years later the time was cut to under eleven hours. Navy Air was maturing.

President Franklin D. Roosevelt arrived in Honolulu aboard the cruiser USS *Houston* on July 26, 1934, the first president to visit Hawaii while in office. It was his first vacation since winning the presidency in 1932. He combined it with good will visits to the territories of the US and some of its neighbors as well as some deep sea fishing with his two sons. His sojourn in Hawaii was less than successful as he was not able to buoy up the local Democratic Party. Still, he said in one letter that it had been a perfectly heavenly cruise and that Hawaii was lovely.[14]

One of the things Roosevelt did while in Honolulu was to visit the Iolani Palace. He made a speech from the King Street balcony,[15] urging that the throne room of the only Palace existing on American soil be restored and opened to the public because of its historic value.[16] He and USS *Houston* left Hawaii on July 28 and arrived in Portland Oregon on August 5, 1934.

In 1935, almost the entire US fleet that participated in war maneuvers anchored or moored inside Pearl Harbor or *Waimomi* as the papers called it. Only the two large carriers *Lexington* and *Saratoga* anchored off Honolulu, and even they could have been accommodated in Pearl by then.[17] This was a time when the fleet would announce its arrival and continuing presence by mounting lights on every mast and line of every ship and sweeping the skies with searchlights for hours each evening in a monumental display.[18] It was impossible to miss them. The Navy paid its respects to the port this way and it was an unforgettable experience. Hawaii was not the only port in which this was done. San Francisco and San Diego were also treated to this rare expression of exuberant greeting to the citizens of a port as were many other ports. After 1941, it was never done again.

In 1935, Ford Island was allocated entirely to the Navy. The Army, which had previously shared the island, moved to its new location, Hickam Field.[19] During that year, a young actress named Gloria Stuart starred in a movie *Here Comes the Navy* with James Cagney, filmed aboard the USS *Arizona*. Six years later, the ship was destroyed. Sixty-three years later the actress appeared in the picture *Titanic*.

At a dinner hosted by Governor Joseph B. Poindexter, during a visit to Hawaii on December 8, 1935, Vice-president John Nance Garner stated, "America will fight to the last man to retain possession of Hawaii".[20] Already the implication of war was mentioned at public affairs. More explicit was the opinion that, "The Japanese might get a number of airplane carriers within a few hundred miles of Honolulu then swoop over the city and drop bombs".[21]

By 1936, the Coast Guard had a base in the islands. There was a cutter, *Roger B. Taney* which had an airplane attached, two patrol boats and other small craft.[22] Boats and crews had been stationed in Honolulu Harbor for only a few years, though there had been a cutter on patrol here occasionally during World War I.

A Pan-American clipper made the first flight to Hawaii in April of 1935. The Clipper, piloted by Edward Musick, landed on the calm water of Pearl Harbor adjacent to Ford Island ahead of schedule and in perfect weather after a seventeen hour flight from Alameda, California. Hawaiian papers trumpeted a possible commuter service to follow.[23] In fact, Honolulu did become a stop on a regular passenger and mail service from San Francisco to Manila and Hong Kong via the China clipper.

One event of the late 1930s that caught the attention of the entire world was closer to Hawaii than most people realized. This was the disappearance of Amelia Earhart and her copilot Fred Noonan in July of 1937 on a flight over the Pacific. The search was coordinated by the United States Navy and involved ships of many nations. Flights to and from Hawaii were not unusual by this time, but for a woman to set off on a flight around the world, especially over that huge and unforgiving expanse of the Pacific Ocean, was daring and courageous. The whole world listened to their radios for the latest reports.

In a Lockheed Electra, Earhart landed at Ford Island on the first leg of her trip. However, on her attempted take off, the right tire blew out and she lost control of the plane. She and Noonan were not injured, but the plane was severely damaged. The flight was aborted, the plane was shipped back to the mainland aboard a freighter for repairs and the record-breaking attempt was replanned.

When the flight began again, the plan had been reworked and now Earhart and Noonan were to fly eastward around the world. One of their last stops before they tackled the Pacific Ocean was Lae, New Guinea at the end of June, 1937. That much of the trip went as planned. The plane took off from Lae on July 1 to fly 2,250 miles to Howland Island where it would be refueled. This was an island possession of the United States about 1,500 miles southeast of Hawaii. Fuel for the flight had been taken there from Hawaii on ships provided by the US Navy.

On July 2, 1937, three messages were received at Pearl Harbor from the plane, but none gave a clue as to their position. The plane was in trouble. It is not clear if the trouble was mechanical or if they were lost. Perhaps it was both. Neither the airplane nor its crew were ever heard of or seen again. The surrounding area became the major focus of the search when it was clear that her plane must have gone down.

Rear Admiral Orin Muffin, Commandant of the 14th Naval District, which included Hawaii, directed the search from Pearl Harbor. The commanding officer of the Fleet Air Base at Pearl sent a seaplane to the vicinity of Howland Island and all Naval facilities were made available to assist in the search. Also aiding in the search were the British HMS *Achilles* and a British freighter as well as elements of the Japanese navy.[24]

The American carrier USS *Lexington*, with Captain J.S. Dowell in command, led the search fleet. USS *Colorado*, a battleship which was in Hawaiian waters on a training mission, was diverted to cover the area in which the plane might have gone down. Coast Guard Cutter *Itasca* was at Howland Island and other vessels were deployed from Pearl. Admiral Murfin was ordered to coordinate all naval forces taking part in the search. Together over the next 16 days, 262,000 square miles were searched. No sign of the plane or its passengers was found or has ever been found.[25]

The search did display the strengths and weaknesses of the search systems as they then existed. It was assumed by the Navy that they would be called upon to rescue the crews and passengers of a clipper should one go down. Search patterns and protocols, therefore, were improved and they included a new organizational structure for the coordination of the Navy, the Coast Guard, and Pan-American Airways.

The United States saw Japanese expansion south as alarming. Their objective was the oil and other raw materials of Southeast Asia and Indonesia. In an effort to slow that advance, the US and Britain placed serious obstacles in the way of anyone attempting to sell oil to Japan. That was seen by the Japanese as a belligerent embargo, although that word was not used in any US announcement. With the Japanese occupation of French Indo-China, the British saw Singapore as a vulnerable target. Each side was increasingly wary of the other. The lines were being drawn. Meanwhile the US military continued to prepare for the possibility of a land invasion of Hawaii.

In order to assign construction projects to experienced civilians a consortium of three companies was formed and named the Pacific Naval Air Base Contractors. The officer in charge of the consortium was Rear Admiral Ben Moreel, Chief of the Naval Civil Engineering Corps.[26] In Pearl, or Waimomi, a contract for $15,000,000 was let for projects including fuel storage, housing, electric power and fresh water systems, increased anchorage area, and wharfage improvements. Another contract, this one for $7,000,000 was awarded on December 22, 1939 for the construction of two new graving docks adjacent to the infamous Dry-dock #1. Dry-dock #2 was 1000 feet long and capable of handling battleships. This dock was completed the first week in December, 1941 and proved invaluable in the salvage of the ships stricken during the December 7 Japanese attack. Dry-dock #3 was 500 feet long and was intended for destroyers and submarines. In 1940 other contracts were awarded for over $30,000,000 and by 1943 the amount had grown to $692,000,000.[27]

While these expanding projects were being undertaken a series of events occurred which affected the citizens of the Pearl Harbor area. On Wednesday, May 31, 1939, President Roosevelt, in an executive order, established a Defensive Sea Area which included all of Pearl Harbor and an area extending three miles to sea from the southwest corner of Pu'uloa Naval Reservation and three miles to sea from Ahua point. No craft, other than those of the US Navy or Army, could enter this area without the permission of the Secretary of the Navy whose agent in the area was Rear Admiral Orin Murfin.28 The one exception was the Pan-American Airways Clippers. The announcement came without warning and caused an enormous crowd of commercial and private fishermen at Pearl's main gate attempting to obtain permission to enter the area to fish. Also, following the fishermen came tour boat operators and pleasure craft owners. The focus of the order was to prevent sabotage. Admiral Murfin summed up the military thinking by stating, "The order gives the government a club to wield above the heads of aliens - or citizens with subversive motives - who attempt to gather information about the naval base".[29] The ban was so effective that it was not until six months after the announcement of the order that the first ship, the 57 foot sampan *Ebisu Maru* out of Honolulu, was stopped and seized for violating the ban. Captain Keli'i was fined $250 and his eight crewmen were fined $100 each. The maximum penalties allowed were fines of $5000 and 5 years in prison.[30]

In January of 1940 the civilian workers at Pearl promoted a Loyalty Oath. Over 3000 workers participated and the pledge was presented to President Roosevelt.[31] In preparation for the arrival of the US Fleet, a steel net was drawn across the entrance channel. No civilian traffic was allowed until after the fleet maneuvers were completed.[32] On Thursday, June 27, 1940, the president declared a 'national emergency' to exercise control over shipping in territorial waters. He followed that order on Friday July 5 by invoking the Export Control Act against Japan which prohibited the exportation of many strategic materials.[33]

Admiral James O. Richardson, the Commander in Chief of the United States Fleet was one of the first commanders to use the new abbreviated style of designation for commands and commanders. His title was shortened to CINCUSFLT. This usage has, with one notable exception, lasted until today. In some areas it has developed almost into an art form, e.g. Pacific Division Naval Facilities Engineering Command is, of course, PACDIVNAVFACENGCOM. The one notable exception was made in February 1941 when Admiral Husband E. Kimmel became Commander in Chief, United States Fleet. CINCUS, pronounced as 'sink us, did not seem appropriate to anyone. The fleet was renamed the Pacific Fleet and its commander was known thereafter as CINCPAC.

Admiral Richardson had more pressing difficulties than those concerning his title. He strongly objected to having the Pacific Fleet stationed permanently in Hawaii. Fleet exercises had been held in Hawaiian waters in 1920, 1925, 1928, 1932, 1933, 1936 and 1937. After the 1940 maneuvers the fleet was ordered to remain at Pearl Harbor. Richardson took his case to the CNO, Admiral Harold R. Stark, to the Secretary of the Navy Frank Knox, the Secretary of State Cordell Hull, and finally to President Roosevelt in a determined effort to have the fleet returned to San Diego. He felt that any attack on Hawaii or the Philippines would give the protected fleet plenty of time to react. Roosevelt stated that the presence of the fleet in Hawaii had already deterred the Japanese from any aggressive act. Richardson, although correct in some of his arguments, went far beyond the accepted bounds of his authority. His zeal and passion and lack of diplomacy were his doom. Roosevelt finally lost patience and ordered Richardson removed. Admiral Stark chose a young Rear Admiral, Chester Nimitz, to relieve Richardson. Nimitz declined because he felt it was inappropriate to jump over 50 senior officers to become CINCPAC, and ill will would develop. It was one of his most fortunate decisions. CNO Stark finally chose another qualified officer to replace Richardson, Rear Admiral Husband E. Kimmel.[34] Kimmel, a benevolent officer, instituted a practice of keeping almost "his entire fleet in Pearl Harbor during weekends to keep his officers and men happy".[35] While Kimmel was CINCPAC, Rear Admiral Claude C. Bloch was both COMNAVBASE and COM14ND. It was not until 1979 that these two commands were separated.

Ford Island, located in the center of Pearl Harbor, had come a long way from the conditions the US Navy found there when they arrived. *Moku'ume'ume*, as the natives called it, had been called many names. Rabbit Island, Marin's Island, Manning and Manine. Don Francisco de Paulo de Marin was its first foreign owner. He probably obtained possession as a result of a service he had rendered to King Kamehameha I, to whom he was an advisor. Marin lost control of half of it, but continued to raise sheep and goats, grow sugar and experiment with growing pineapple. He called it the Island of Little Goats.[36] He also may have been the one who brought the rabbits. Around 1818, the island was described as being two miles in circumference in the Pearl River and covered with English hares or rabbits.

The first American Naval officer to visit the island was Hiram Paulding of USS *Dolphin* (Percival) in 1826. William F. Gill obtained ownership of half the island, but this was disputed by the Hawaiian government. The island passed through a number of hands in joint deeds, leases and was sold at auction. Clear title was never recognized by the government. In 1865, the island was sold at a public auction by John O. Dominis, administrator of the estate of Kamehameha IV and husband of future Queen Liliuokalani. It was bought by James Dowsett for $1,040.

Doctor Seth Porter Ford came to Hawaii in 1851 to work as a doctor at the US Marine Hospital. He became court physician to Kamehameha IV. Ford's wife bought the island as income for their son, Seth Ford, Jr. Leases from several sugar and pineapple companies brought in a good income for him. Called Ford's Island by then, it passed through several more owners and was finally sold to the US government in 1917. It has been called Ford Island ever since.[37]

Pan-American clippers had their landing base and terminal on Ford Island, due to an agreement with the US Navy. In 1939, naval activity in Pearl Harbor had increased, due to rising tensions in the Pacific, that it was necessary for PanAm to move. A new site on the Pearl City peninsula, between East and Middle Lochs, was obtained. This was the main landing spot of the clippers until the flights ended in 1946.[38] Ferry service to the island was begun in the 1880s to facilitate the movement of sugar. The first Navy ferry to the island was in 1918. The ferries were temporarily suspended during the construction of the Admiral Clarey Bridge, completed in April of 1998.[39]

In December of 1919 the Pacific Air Detachment of the Navy was established at Pearl Harbor and the unit was moved to Ford Island in 1923. During the dredging operations in the 1930s, excess soil was added to the island to increase its size to 441 acres. Since that time, Ford Island has been an integral part of the Pearl Harbor Naval Complex.

Before Pearl Harbor became exclusively military, it was used for agriculture, fishing, and recreation. It was the yacht racing center of Hawaii in the 1930s. The first race was organized in 1915 by wealthy sloop owners who wanted to race in the relative calm of Pearl and away from the busy shipping lanes Honolulu Harbor.40 Racing off the southern coast of Oahu is too rough and windy for small sailboats. Pearl, with its ten square miles of flat, protected water, was ideal for sailing and especially for racing.

The Pearl Harbor Yacht Club was organized in 1925 and soon its clubhouse became the social center for Hawaiian yachtsmen. The clubhouse was on the Pearl City Peninsula at the edge of the water. It was frequented by the social elite of Honolulu each weekend. Parties, dances, and treasure hunts were popular and there are unconfirmed rumors that liquor was available without too much difficulty, even before the repeal of prohibition in 1933.

Pearl Harbor was also the focus of other nautical activities such as Transpacific yacht races and the local papers were quick to publicize events such as Shirley Temple being made an honorary commodore and General George Patton's arrival in the harbor on his yacht *Arcturus*. He had come to report for duty in Hawaii. The last club race was held November 23, 1941. Of course, all recreational activities were immediately terminated on December 7, and the yacht club never re-opened. By the end of the year the buildings of the yacht club became a PT Boat base.[41]

In May of 1940 a plot was discovered to blow up the oil tanks at Pearl. The Navy and FBI traced the conspiracy to a group in Mexico. Although the plot was discovered soon enough to thwart it, and the conspirators were arrested before any damage could be done, the vulnerability of the tanks was brought to official attention. Secretary of the Navy Charles Edison stated that the vital oil supplies should be stored underground.[42] He ordered a study that resulted in the Red Hill project built in 1940.

It was in 1940 that a revised edition of the Bluejackets' Manual was published. It's surprising to realize that as recently as 1940, complete instructions were given for the preparation of hammocks when piped down for inspection. The hammock was spread on deck with the mattress on it and all lines neatly flemished on top. After inspection the hammocks and mattresses were to be aired on the ship's rail, placed so that "no vacant spaces or holidays appeared". After airing, the bedding and hammocks were lashed in proper manner with seven marlin hitches. Then the clews were to be "twisted and tucked under the hitches".[43] This was the US Navy in 1941.

As the decade drew to a close, with war raging in Europe and Asia, two extraordinary events took place in Pearl Harbor. The Navy needed a floating dry-dock at Pearl. Someone remembered seeing an abandoned dry-dock in New Orleans. Investigation and studies indicated that it would be quicker and less expensive to tow the old dock to Pearl rather than to build a new one. The old dock had been built around the turn of the century and had been idling in New Orleans for the past 40 years. Its condition was checked and found satisfactory and in November 1939 plans were started to tow it across the Gulf of Mexico, through the Panama Canal, across 4700 miles of Pacific Ocean to a new home in Pearl Harbor. Such a feat was formidable indeed. Towing a ship is relatively easy because of the shape of her hull. Towing an enormous square cornered, flat bottomed piece of concrete halfway around the world required meticulous planning, outstanding seamanship, courage, and a lot of good luck. All of these elements were present. The mission was placed under the command of Commander D. R. Osborn, USN.

In the company of the tugs USS *Navajo* and USS *Capella* and a tanker, USS *Platte*, carrying fuel and supplies, the dock left New Orleans on May 15, 1940. The beast was 525 feet long, with a 126 foot beam, and a draft of 7 1/2 feet. It displaced 10,700 tons and had sidewalls of 54 feet. To anyone who has sailed, or handled a tow, those dimensions spell doom. The windage presented by the tall sidewalls was 22,500 square feet. That meant that with a slight breeze, there would be several tons of force pushing sideways to the course of the train of ships. While the captain was compensating for that force, the wind could easily change direction and/or force and slew the entire train dangerously off course. The consideration of the effect of the wind was separate from the effects of the waves and their influence on the towing tugs and the structure itself. Needless to say, constant vigilance was absolutely essential.

The train of ships reached Colon, Panama on June 11, 1940. By June 27 the monster dry-dock was disassembled and prepared to be carried through the locks of the canal, reassembled and set out to cross the Pacific. That was done successfully and on July 10, 1940, the unlikely entourage lumbered out of Balboa for the 4700 mile, 44 day trip to Hawaii.

Navajo led the procession, trailing a two inch wire hawser attached to the bow of *Capella*, which in turn trailed her hawser to the bow of the dock. The ships were spaced about 600 yards apart and made good a speed of between four and five knots over the bottom. When each tug was released to refuel, the lone remaining tug could only make 2.5 knots. During these periods the dock yawed about ten degrees on each quarter and crabbed fifteen to thirty degrees off course.

Wild events and unexpected happenings are the stuff of adventure novels. Usually the hair-raising accounts of ill-fated voyages are the result of stupidity, ignorance, lack of planning, or inexperience. None of these accompanied Captain Osborn. He and his associates planned carefully, executed impeccably, and experienced a calm, yet constantly tense and dangerous crossing. The tow boats and their exhausted, but triumphant crews arrived at the channel entrance to Pearl Harbor on August 23, 1940 and turned their monstrous, unwieldy cargo over to the harbor tugs. The tow boats had expended 356,000 gallons of fuel. Inspection revealed that along with the dock, the tugs delivered several tons of sea growth on their hulls due to the slow speed and the time at sea. Captain Osborn modestly attributed the success of the mission to good preparation and excellent crewmen, but his immaculate preparation and leadership were certainly vital factors in this most unusual voyage.[44]

The second remarkable event which occurred at the end of the decade was the start of an extraordinary engineering project. As the Navy Secretary had observed earlier, the vital, but exposed and vulnerable, petroleum supplies at Pearl Harbor should be stored underground. On the day after Christmas 1940, an army of tunneling experts from all over the country assembled at an area just toward the mountains (*mauka*) from Pearl and turned the first shovel full of earth of what was to become the largest underground facility ever built. The area was Red Hill. The project was not only enormous, but novel and daring as well. Underground tanks had always been laid in horizontal ditches. At Red Hill, the engineers, led by James Growden, designed them to be vertical. The design called for twenty tanks, each 250 feet tall and 100 feet in diameter. The successful completion of this project was an engineering marvel.

The first activity was to dig a horizontal tunnel 2000 feet into the gently sloping hill. The end of the tunnel was over 400 feet below the surface of the hill. A wide conveyor belt was built that ran the length of the tunnel and out to a newly constructed railway that extended three and a half miles to Pearl Harbor. Then twenty core holes, twelve feet in diameter, were dug 100 feet apart straight down from the surface to the tunnel. Starting at one end of the line of holes, miners were lowered until they reached the level that would be the top of the tanks. At the *mauka* end of the project this level was 175 feet below the sloping surface. At the *makai* end (toward the sea) the tank tops would be 110 feet below the surface.

When they were lowered to the 'tank top' level, the miners expanded the diameter of the shaft by blasting and picking until it reached 100 feet. Of course, the platform they worked from had to be expanded frequently for them to reach the walls. The walls were cut in such a way as to form a giant funnel so that when the rock was blasted or chipped, the loose rock fell and tumbled down the inverted funnel to the conveyor belt 200 feet below. One miner noted that most of the rock that found its way down the shaft, along the conveyor belt, onto the train, out the pier, and into Pearl Harbor, was never touched by a human hand.

Once the tank diameter had been expanded to 100 feet, the miners simply lowered the funnel shaped hole by continued blasting and digging until they reached the tunnel, which would ultimately become the bottom of that tank. Then they moved to the next small hole at the surface and repeated the process.

The tank vaults were dug twenty feet deeper than the spot where the bottom of the tanks would be so that a concrete and steel pad could be poured. Each tank sits on such a pad. Then, after the steel tank walls were assembled inside the enormous cavities, the irregular spaces between the tanks and the rock walls that surrounded them were filled with concrete which was forced into the voids under tremendous pressure. A unique method of testing for leaks was devised. It seems appropriate for this project. Each tank was slowly filled with water while crewmen with searchlights mounted in outrigger canoes paddled around the water looking for buddies, a sure sign of an unwanted orifice. The thinking was brilliantly simple. If air couldn't get in, then oil couldn't get out.

There is no way one can, in a narrative such as this, do justice to this engineering wonder, but a few statistics may indicate the magnitude of the structure. Each tank is taller than the 20 story Ala Moana building in Honolulu. Each holds more than twelve million gallons of fuel. The entire project of twenty tanks along with the ventilation machinery, railway, and piping, cost $43,000,000, the approximate cost of making one such underground tank today. Thirty-nine hundred men were involved in construction. Another, more sobering, cost was 17 fatalities, two of which were by drowning. An economy which was effected is the fact that since the tanks are up a hill from the loading dock, the fuel is gravity fed to the ships at the dock. In the case of a power outage, no interruption in fuel delivery would be experienced. To recognize the awesome performance of these men, one has only to consider that they completed the job nine months ahead of schedule - during a world war!

During the thirties as the Red Hill project was in the early planning stages, the conditions which made those years so ominous became even more so. Japan became more bellicose, the US became more firm and in 1941, the first of five frightening years of war began.

Chapter 27 - The Attack

While Japanese and American diplomats and military men were jockeying for position in the troubled Pacific, the big news at Pearl Harbor in January of 1940 was the opening of the new gate near the Submarine Base.[1] The main gate was the scene of daily congestion as the increased number of workers at the Naval Shipyard entered and left. The main entrance was later named the Nimitz Gate and the new gate became the Makalapa Gate. The new workers were engaged in a variety of projects. Kuahua Island had been slowly converted to a peninsula by using material from the endless dredging operations. With the strain on existing facilities exerted by the newly arrived Pacific Fleet, every portion of Pearl harbor needed expansion and development. By 1940, however, only eight buildings had been erected on the 120 acre site, although a 600 foot pier was built on Kuahua. It could accommodate twelve ships at any one time.

Merry Point was expanded to handle mainland cargo and to provision outbound ships to ports in the Pacific considered to be vital in case of war. The Pearl City Center Annex was built on the peninsula which separates East and Middle Lochs. Enormous storage facilities were built across Kam Highway at Manana (the Supply Center) and Waiawa Gulch (the Aviation Supply Depot). Over one million square feet of storage space was developed during 1940 and 1941. Later a salvage depot was erected at Waipio Point where parts could be cannibalized from damaged ships, and a construction center at Iroquois Point.

Additional ammunition magazines were erected at Lualualei which eventually grew to over seventy magazines during the war.[2] The increasing possibility of war hastened implementation of the plans that had been made for Pearl Harbor as well as expanding some. By June of 1940,500 men were stationed at the Submarine Base.[3] The two immediate needs were storage space for the material, and living space for the workers that were pouring into Hawaii. During 1940, over $32,000,000 was spent by the Public Works Administration on buildings and housing, with $50,000,000 more to follow.[4]

While the Navy was developing land facilities at an ever increasing rate, the fleet was increasing its activities at sea. 1940 and 1941 have been described as one continuous battle drill. One week in Pearl and two weeks at sea was the schedule. A typical dispatch was one that was received at 10:30 p.m. on a Saturday night. "Continue torpedo attacks throughout the night."[5] On November 15,1941, Sister Regina Catherine Brandt enjoyed a tour of an aircraft carrier in Pearl Harbor. She had often visited the ships for religious services, but this was simply a tour with other civilians. No security obstacles were encountered.[6]

Actors were appearing on stage who would play significant roles in the coming events. USS *Ward* was assigned to offshore patrol when she arrived at Pearl Harbor in March of 1940.[7] Admiral James O. Richardson, CINCPAC, was ordered to transfer the US fleet from San Diego to Pearl Harbor in April of 1940. He bitterly opposed the transfer and made his opinion known all the way up to President Roosevelt. The position of Roosevelt and his CNO, Admiral Harold R. Stark, was that the presence of a powerful fleet at Pearl would deter the Japanese from any excessive expansion in the Pacific. Richardson's opinion was that the Japanese showed no sign of slowing their acquisition in Asia and Southeast Asia and therefore the fleet should be in a mainland port. There they would be safe from a surprise attack and they could retaliate according to the Rainbow 5 Plan, a successor to Plan Orange on May 26, 1941.[8]

Richardson's assertion was not without support since he had successfully 'attacked and destroyed' the fleet at Pearl during exercises some years earlier. But Richardson was only an Admiral. Roosevelt was the President. Richardson was replaced. His successor was Admiral Husband E. Kimmel who assumed command on February 1, 1941.[9]

Kimmel was an experienced and valued officer, but his assignment became the most unfortunate such posting in US Naval history only ten months later. Kimmel's force was the Pacific Fleet and he became both CINCPAC and CINCUS, the latter acronym soon to be changed by Admiral King.

Vice-Admiral Shigeru Fukudome was Chief of Staff to Admiral Isoroku Yamamoto during the Japanese Fleet exercises in April and May of 1940. They confirmed their theories concerning the efficacy of attacking a surface force with aircraft, mainly torpedo planes and dive bombers. They concluded that, at that time, there were no ships capable of withstanding such an attack. Fukudome inferred that Yamamoto was thinking of the great US Fleet in Pearl Harbor.[10] Nor was the lesson of Taranto, November 12, 1940, lost on them. At that port, 24 British Swordfish torpedo planes sank the Italian fleet, including six battleships. It was the first such action in history.

Yamamoto's specific plan, called the "Hawaii Operation" was initiated in January of 1941.[11] It was a step in the realization of *Hakko Ichiu*, the idea of placing the "eight corners of the world under one roof". Such an attack was consistent with the Samurai Code of *Bushido*, or the "way of the warrior."[12]

On Sunday, March 30,1941 the United States took possession of all German ships that were in Pearl Harbor. Their crews were confined to the ships and the ships were forbidden to leave. On Tuesday May 27, President Roosevelt declared a state of unlimited national emergency. By Thursday June 12, all members of the naval reserve were called to active duty.[13] Thursday, September 11, the President gave all Navy ships the authority to attack any vessel threatening US shipping or ports. That order enabled USS

Ward to sink a Japanese submarine on the morning of December 7, 1941, the first armed conflict involving the US in World War II.

On July 8, 1941, USS *Arizona* returned to Pearl from the US west coast to participate in exercises. She, along with USS *Nevada* and USS *Oklahoma* moored alongside Ford Island on December 5, 1941.

Volumes have been written about the events and intentions leading to the attack on Pearl Harbor. Anxious to be the first to expose sensational material, some authors have speculated on the possibility of Allied leaders having prior knowledge of Japanese intentions toward Hawaii. None of the speculations has yet been verified. There were signs that anyone might have interpreted as an impending attack. No one did. A broadcaster in Honolulu opined that, "There can be no doubt that Japan would prefer to move southward. So far the restraining force has been fear of war with the United States."[14]

On Thursday, November 20, 1941, as Japan's armies moved through Indo-China and continued their war with China, Ambassador Nomura presented Japan's 'final proposal' for peace in the Pacific to Secretary Cordell Hull. Just a week later, on Thursday the 27th, CNO Admiral Stark sent a war warning to the commanders of the Pacific and Asiatic Fleets. He indicated that negotiations with Japan seemed to be near an end. If hostilities broke out, it was the US position that Japan would make the first hostile move. The enigmatic nature of the message did little to help Kimmel know for what to prepare.

Yamamoto had studied Admiral Yarnell's 'attack' in 1932 and the reasoning behind the strategy that was so successful. Attack early on a Sunday morning, use the cloud cover over the Ko'olau Mountains and the clear sky above Pearl, fly from nearby carriers, and attack with no warning. The last point is an interesting one. International law experts agreed that a declaration of war must proceed any hostile act, even if the time difference is a second. Counting on that, the Japanese planned to inform Secretary Cordell Hull in Washington of their intention to bomb Pearl Harbor and other US locations just one-half hour before the bombs fell. Of course, the bombers would be airborne at the time, but the 'formalities' would have been followed.[15]

Unfortunately for the Japanese, their message was not decoded and delivered to Hull until after the bombing started. It was a disgrace for Japan and an incredible stimulus to Americans. The word that dominated the American reaction and appeared prominently in all news reports was, "treachery".

Preparation for the attack began in peaceful Kagoshima Bay in the southern Kurile Islands. This inlet was chosen because of its similarity to Pearl Harbor. Especially important was its shallow depth of about 15 meters, or 45 feet, like that of Pearl. Special torpedoes were developed with wooden fins to maintain an operating level just a few feet below the surface. While Admiral Yamamoto would have loved to lead the attack, Vice-Admiral Chuichi Nagumo was chosen by the Japanese Naval General Staff because of his seniority. The task force was named *Kido Butai* or "strike force".[16]

The Japanese passenger liner *Taiyo Maru* entered Honolulu Harbor and docked in October of 1941. On her passage from Tokyo, the route to be used by Nagumo's Task Force had been checked by people on board. Sea conditions, weather, traffic encountered and visibility were all noted and relayed back to the attack group in Japan. While the passengers were checked carefully and thoroughly by Hawaiian authorities, the ship's company, conducting their daily routines, were not scrutinized. Later it was learned that the daily newspapers delivered to the ship contained notes and slips of paper crammed with intelligence which was taken back to Japan on the return voyage.

Operational orders were sent to the Japanese fleet by the Imperial Naval General Staff on November 5:

> "To: Commander-in-Chief Combined Fleet,
>   Isoroku Yamamoto
> Via: Chief of Naval General Staff Osami Nagano by
>   Imperial Order
> 1. The Empire has decided to schedule various
>   operational preparations for completion in the early part
>   of December in view of great fears that she will be obliged
>   to go to war with the United States, Britain, and the
>   Netherlands for her self-existence and self-defense.
> 2. The commander-in-Chief Combined fleet will make
>   necessary operational preparations.
> 3. Detailed instructions will be given by the Chief of the
>   Naval General Staff."[17]

Final preparations were made, and in utmost secrecy the task force was assembled in Tankan Bay (*Hitokappu Wan*), on the island of Etorofu just north of Hokkaido. The force was made up of six carriers, 423 airplanes, two battleships, three cruisers, eleven destroyers, three submarines, and eight tankers. It was November 22, 1941. A force of twenty submarines and five midget subs preceded the main force.

Four days later, in a thick fog, the first ships set their courses eastward. Not until the sealed, secret orders were opened did the entire group know that their destination was Pearl Harbor, Hawaii.

The Matson liner *Lurline*, on her way from Los Angeles to Honolulu, was at sea on November 30 when her radio operator, Leslie Grogan, picked up an unusual amount of radio traffic from Tokyo. The atmospheric conditions that night enabled him to read clearly the messages from Japan, all aimed at one small area in the western Pacific. His amateur, but accurate, comment was, "The Japs must be bunched up, biding time. It's safe to say something is going to happen, and mighty soon."[18]

On December 2, Admiral Yamamoto sent a message to the task force, "Climb Mt. Niitaka". It was the order to proceed with the attack on December 8, Tokyo time.[19]

December 4, 1941 in Tokyo, December 3 at Pearl, a message was intercepted by the Australian Special Intelligence Organization and by Ralph Briggs, a senior USN radioman. The message was, *Higashi no kazeame*, or "East wind rain". It indicated to all Japanese diplomats in the Pacific that diplomatic relations with the United States would soon be terminated and that all code books and documents should be burned. The Australian and Briggs both telephoned the information to Washington. It was lost among the heavy radio and telephone traffic of the day.[20] Shortly after midnight on December 6, 1941, the Christmas lights that had been blazing in and around Pearl Harbor flickered out and quiet descended on the glasslike water.[21]

At 0645 December 7, 1941, the flagship *Akagi* lowered her signal flags to half-mast. The planes on the carriers started their engines. A few minutes later the flags were raised to the truck of the mast and quickly lowered again. The first plane took off, followed by the entire first wave of 183 aircraft. Each pilot had his *hachimaki* or white scarf tied around his leather helmet. On the flight decks the crewmen cheered their comrades with hands thrown high and shouts of *Banzai!*. One hour and 230 miles later, zeroing in on Hawaiian radio stations, these young men would change the world.

About the time the attack planes were leaving the carriers, USS *Ward*, a destroyer commanded by Lt. William Outerbridge, sank a Japanese submarine just outside the entrance to Pearl Harbor. Other than having the historic distinction of being the first shot fired, the action was of little military consequence.

The first wave of Japanese planes flew southeast down the Waialua Valley, past Schofield Barracks and straight on to Pearl Harbor. Commander Mitsuo Fuchida sent the message, *Tora, tora, tora*, or *tiger, tiger, tiger*, to indicate to the carriers that the attack would be a surprise. Enjoying the advantage of complete surprise, they wreaked havoc upon the anchored ships. For the first few minutes they were aided, ironically, by the apathy of local citizens and military personnel who had been inured to the sounds of war by countless exercises and maneuvers in the area for the past few months. The bomb that fell from the first Japanese bomber was an act which began 1364 days of desperate, ruthless war.

One of the first retaliatory actions was that of Lt. Cdr. Logan Ramsey at 0758 who sent this message to CINCPAC, "Enemy air raid Pearl Harbor; This is not a drill." A few minutes later CINCPAC relayed the message to all ships in the Hawaiian area.[22] One of the first shots fired at the attacking

Japanese was that of a US Marine who, with his fellow marines, was at attention in preparation for raising the colors at 0800. One Marine noted the low flying plane and thought, as did almost everyone that fateful Sunday morning, that they were part of an exercise. However, he yelled at his sergeant, "Hey, Gunny, those are Japs!" Without a moment's hesitation, the Gunnery sergeant said, "My God, you're right" and ordered, "Music, sound 'Call to Arms!'" The newly issued M-1 Garand Rifles were pointed skyward and fired until their clips were empty. The Marine Barracks, Navy Yard Pearl, had gone to war. The brig was emptied of its twenty prisoners to make room for incoming casualties which could not be accommodated in the limited facilities at the hospital. It is notable that not one of the freed prisoners took advantage of his opportunity to flee. After performing various heroic acts, each man returned to the brig and awaited orders.[23]

Well trained men and women quickly swung into action when they had something to work with, but much needed equipment was locked in storage or destroyed. An apocryphal story is often told of a group of US Marines who went to a Ford Island supply depot to replace their exhausted ammunition clips. A supply sergeant, who had been trained and rewarded for twenty years of impeccable paper work, refused to issue any supplies without the proper forms and signatures. The marine needing the supplies is said to have rested his .45 against the supply sergeant's forehead and stated, "Here's my authorization, now issue the &*%#! ammo!." If the story isn't accurate in the details, it certainly is true in principle.

Burning planes and broken vehicles were cannibalized for parts and guns. Building 55, a three story pink art deco structure on Ford Island, had been an enlisted men's barracks. Its mess hall refrigerators were turned into temporary morgues to store bodies and parts to be identified, if possible, later.[24] The Iolani Palace, in downtown Honolulu on King Street, was emptied of its treasures and became a dormitory, Civilian Defense Headquarters and Red Cross Canteen.[25]

Firefighting equipment was strained past the breaking point. Every 'Handy-billy' (portable gasoline powered pump) in the harbor was soon in use. All the while, retaliatory efforts and rescue attempts were made almost impossible because of constant strafing by Japanese fighter planes and bombardment by Japanese bombs and torpedoes. Added to this awful scenario were the explosions of American ammunition magazines and the searing fires of the burning oil creeping across the harbor. The once dependable communication system and the chain of command which had seemed so reliable just yesterday were in shambles. Initiative became the watchword. In this chaos, countless acts of heroism went unheralded. For the 40 minutes of hell during the first wave and the equally terrorizing half hour of the second wave of bombers, survivors did what they could to save their comrades as well as people they had never seen before. Gallantry, valor, courage and bravery were commonplace. The only act of cowardice that has ever been recorded about this day was that of the people in Washington DC who refused to take any responsibility for the debacle at Pearl Harbor. They placed all of the blame squarely on Admiral Kimmel and General Short.[26]

As with any battle, once the attackers had droned away in triumph, quiet overcame the terrible scene. By 1130 that morning, Governor Poindexter had declared a state of emergency for the Territory and had ordered all civilian radio stations to cease transmitting except for emergency messages. His intent was to avoid providing any more incoming Japanese pilots or ships with clear radio beacons. Unfortunately, his precautions were about four hours too late.

Subsequent to the attack, two possible dangers consumed the minds of the defenders. The first was the certainty of a Japanese invasion. For days after the attack, the north shore of Oahu and the other islands were defended 24 hours a day against an invasion which never came. The other concern was the enormous population of Japanese in the Hawaiian Islands. Over 160,000 Japanese, forty percent of the Hawaiian population, were living in Hawaii that day. Almost 38,000 were foreign born. Americans on the mainland and in the islands had read stories for years about the 'fifth column' in Spain and then in France. It was understandable that local Japanese would be viewed with suspicion. Such an attitude was stimulated by the Japanese practice of hanging Japanese flags in their yards and creating shrines in their homes. Nevertheless, exhaustive investigations of groups and individuals after the attack revealed no evidence of cooperation between the any local Japanese-Hawaiian and Japanese military forces. An FBI agent reported to an investigating committee that, at no time prior, during or subsequent to the attack, did he see an instance of sabotage or fifth column activity by local Japanese.

There were no proven acts of sabotage or espionage by the Japanese during the war, but that doesn't mean that Pearl was free from such acts by others. The day after the attack, Bernard Julius 'Otto' Kuehn was apprehended and charged with being a Nazi spy working for the Japanese. Evidence presented by the Army and the FBI proved to a military court that Kuehn had supplied military information to Nagao Kita, the Japanese Consul General in Honolulu on December 3, 1941. Though Kuehn was sentenced to be shot, his sentence was commuted to 50 years at hard labor in Leavenworth prison.

In the immediate aftermath of such a sudden and cataclysmic attack, logic did not prevail. Emotions exploded in the Territory of Hawaii and the mainland United States. And the one word that was burned into the American psyche was "treachery". President Roosevelt, in his speech to Congress the next day asking for a declaration of war, requested that they agree that a state of war had existed since the "unprovoked and dastardly attack". He used such other phrases as "a date which will live in infamy" and "the Japanese government has deliberately sought to deceive" and "always we will remember" and "this form of treachery".[27]

During that speech, the ears and minds of every American, including those of the authors of this volume, were focused upon the radios which were delivering the president's words. Feelings of frustration, outrage, hatred and betrayal swept the country. Revenge was an obsession. Lines formed at recruiting stations long before they opened on Monday morning. From England came the British response. Winston Churchill, to the House of Commons on December 8, 1941 said. "Every circumstance of calculated and characteristic Japanese treachery was employed."[28]

The military leaders of Japan had made five mistakes, three tactical and two strategic. First, they failed to bomb the oil tanks lying unprotected on the hills above Pearl Harbor as well as four exposed submarines. Second, they did no damage to any repair facility, and third, the magazine at Lualualei Ammunition Depot was untouched. Containing thousands of explosive projectiles for the 14 and 16 inch battleship rifles and thousands of bags of powder, one hit would have damaged or sunk every ship in West Loch. Fourth, even though Admiral Yamamoto had spent a great deal of time in the United States, he and his associates underestimated the incredible resources and industrial might of a county physically untouched by war. Fifth, and by far the most important, was the inaccurate estimation of the American reaction. Never in our country's history have we been as united as we were in the days following that attack. The examples are legion on the mainland. The people living in the Territory of Hawaii were transformed by two emotions: the very real and reasonable threat of an invasion and a feeling of betrayal. One poignant comment was made by the Japanese-Hawaiian maid of Mrs. Alice Ho'ohokuokalani Hollingsworth who asked in confusion when told that the Japanese were attacking the island, "Why are they mad at us?" That morning Mrs. Hollingsworth heard a loud thump in the back yard of her home in the Nu'uanu Valley. She looked and found a five inch projectile buried in a crater in the center of her lawn. Later the shell was identified as one from a US Navy anti-aircraft gun.[29]

Xenophobic hysteria that was ripe on the mainland was not so apparent in Hawaii. Of tens of thousands of residents of foreign descent in the islands, 1400 were arrested and held temporarily at Sand Island by right of martial law. They were Japanese, Germans and Italians who had, for one reason or another, aroused the suspicions of the FBI or Army. Of these, 1000 were transferred to the mainland and the rest were released. Within 24 hours of the attack, the 40 year rule of *kama'ainas* and civilian *haoles* was replaced by military rule, General Delos Emmons as Governor.[30] Evacuation of all non-essential personnel was ordered for two reasons. First, that would leave fewer mouths to feed, as most Hawaiian food and staples must be imported, and there would be fewer people "in the way" if the Japanese invaded Hawaii.[31]

Amidst the horror and destruction of the attack, there was some good news. USS *Enterprise*, one of Japan's hoped-for targets, was en route to Pearl from Wake Island. Another would-be target was USS *Lexington*. She was at sea on her way to the island of Midway. The third US carrier, USS *Saratoga*, was in San Diego for repairs. These ships, not the battleships that had ruled the seas for half a century, formed the nucleus of the naval forces that, during the next four years, would sweep the enemy from the Pacific Ocean.

When Admiral Halsey entered the harbor the next day aboard his flagship USS *Enterprise*, his astonishment gave way to the anger of a warrior and he vowed, "Before we are through with them the Japanese language will be spoken only in hell!".[32]

It was on this day that the first indication of optimism was also expressed. Amid hundreds of gloomy, but accurate, reports of calamity, there were statements beyond the terrible truth. Captain E.M. Zacharias, of the cruiser USS *Salt Lake City*, arriving as part of Halsey's group, told his men, "There is nothing that could have consolidated public opinion and expedited our future plans of operations... as quickly as this did."[33] His immediate, accurate assessment was later copied and repeated as an original thought in almost every news medium.

Another case of dodging the bullet, literally, involves Honolulu itself. A defenseless and vulnerable cargo ship sat in the harbor at Pier 31A unloading 3,000 cases of dynamite. An errant Japanese bomb hit would have vaporized both the harbor and the city. The Japanese attack was very disciplined, but the pilots showed no initiative and missed nearly every target of opportunity presented to them. Even without these missed targets, the damage they did was mind-boggling. Twenty-one ships were sunk or damaged. One hundred and sixty two aircraft were destroyed. By far the most devastating losses were the 2,400 dead and 1,180 wounded.

During the first part of the attack, local civilians who were used to recent maneuvers, thought this was another. They gathered on hillsides for a view of the 'realistic' show. When they were disabused of that idea by KGMB and KGU, broadcasting, "This is the real McCoy", they immediately went about finding out what they could do to help.[34] The familiar 'Hawaii Calls' voice of Webley Edwards was convincing. Well trained civilian defense groups went into action. Blood donors appeared from every local and nearby area.

Civilian workers and military personnel returned to Pearl Harbor even during the attack. The roads were crowded and guards at the gates were overwhelmed trying to let qualified people in while maintaining security. Returning fisherman, ignorant of the momentous events, were fired upon and some were killed. Blackouts became mandatory. People rushed to fight the fires that raged in the center of the city, touched off by errant shells and bombs. Schools were closed on Monday December 8. Censorship of all mail and telephone calls was imposed. By the 13th, gasoline rationing was in effect.[35]

Soon camps, warehouses, military stockpiles and housing for civilian workers lined the road from Honolulu to Pearl Harbor. The harbor itself was devastated. Burning ships lay on their sides or under the water. Oil burned across the lochs. Screams of suffering men were heard, almost inaudible moans then silence from the many devastated ships. Parts of structures, weakened by the blasts, collapsed with loud bangs that startled already tense sailors and marines. More than one guard was shot by another in a tragic mistake. Despite the recent terror, expectation of an invasion, the stench of destruction from bodies, oil, smoke and fumes, rescue operations commenced immediately after the first casualty. Damage Control parties formed and saved what they could. When the salvage people arrived in the harbor, the scene that greeted them was deplorable.

To their advantage, they had undamaged repair facilities to work with, local engineering staffs available and major heavy-engineering equipment and expertise which came from the civilian sector.[36] More divers volunteered than could be outfitted. The slogan "Keep 'em fit to fight," became official. The results of these men's activities were remarkable. By the middle of February 1942, three battleships, three cruisers, one destroyer and two service vessels had been salvaged and were in service or on their way to the west coast for more permanent repairs. All returned to action within one year. Only USS *Arizona* and the target ship USS *Utah* were not raised. Books have been written, and rightly so, about the extraordinary, unorthodox and inventive efforts and achievements of these engineers and other workers under the most dangerous and difficult conditions.

Since its founding in 1921, the 'yard' had always been commanded by a naval officer, Commander of the Naval Shipyard Pearl Harbor. Now, Rear Admiral C.C. Bloch, Commandant of the 14th Naval District, decided a higher authority was required in wartime and named Rear Admiral W.R. Furlong Commandant of the Navy Yard. Captain C.S. Gillette remained in place, but as 'manager' of the yard. That title was used by Gillete and his successors until Furlong's tour ended."[37]

While hard-working engineers dealt with broken ships and overworked medical people dealt with broken bodies, the Navy and other military people had a war to fight.

Chapter 28 - War

Hawaii was at war. Beaches were strung with barbed wire and patrolled day and night by armed men. Gas masks were distributed and mass immunization was conducted against smallpox and typhoid. Preparations were made for the invasion that never came.[1] Two phrases came out of this awful day. Composer Sammy Cahn wrote words to a march composed by Don Reid. The title was Remember Pearl Harbor. It was something the nation needed. The other memorable phrase was created in the heat of battle. Chaplain Howell Forgy, aboard USS New Orleans, while passing ammunition to the gun turrets encouraged his shipmates by saying, Praise the Lord and Pass the Ammunition. Both of these phrases were made into popular and inspirational wartime songs.[2]

Such a disaster demands the replacement of those in charge. Culpability or lack of it can be investigated later. This is an inviolate military rule. On December 12, Rear Admiral William R. Furlong was designated Commandant of the Navy Yard.[3] After a brief conference in the oval office, President Roosevelt ordered Navy Secretary Frank Knox, "Tell Nimitz to get the hell out to Pearl and stay there till the war is won". Thus Chester W. Nimitz was elevated over 28 senior officers and returned to Pearl Harbor where he had established the Submarine Base some 20 years before. Nimitz had another connection with Pearl Harbor; he had been the commander of Battleship Division One, COMBATDIV ONE, with USS *Arizona* as his flagship. From December 12, when Admiral Kimmel was relieved, until the 31st, Vice Admiral William S. Pye was designated acting CINCPAC. On that same day, the 12th, Colonel H. K. Pickett, USMC became the commander of the Marine Barracks at Pearl.

December 31, 1941, on the foredeck of the submarine USS Grayling, Nimitz broke out his new four-star flag and assumed command of what was left of the United States Pacific Fleet. He converted a suite of offices in the Submarine Base to the Pacific Fleet Headquarters. One of his first acts was to retain Kimmel's staff. Nimitz was a wise man. In that act he not only re-established the morale of the crestfallen officers and won their loyalty, but he also acquired all their experience and local knowledge. And he certainly needed all the help he could acquire. Guam had fallen; Wake Island had fallen; on Christmas Day, the British had surrendered Hong Kong.

The replacements continued. A few days before Nimitz became CINCPAC, Admiral Ernest J. King was transferred from his Atlantic command and took the jobs of Chief of Naval Operations, CNO, and Commander in Chief, US Fleet, CinCUS. It was he who, agreeing with Admiral Richardson, did not like the 'sink us' sound of the acronym and changed it to COMinCH US.[4] Early in 1942 the Navy's authorized aircraft strength was increased from

15,000 to 27,500. On January 12, 1942, the enlisted strength was increased to 500,000. The Pacific military commands were reorganized by the Joint Chiefs of Staff. On Monday, March 30, 1942 the area was divided into two commands: Pacific Ocean Areas (Adm Nimitz) and Southwest Pacific Area (Gen. Douglas MacArthur). Admiral Nimitz was named Commander in Chief Pacific Ocean Areas (CINCPOA) and CINCPAC on Friday, April 3.[5]

Nimitz approved a plan submitted by his staff to carry the fighting to the Japanese elements on various islands in the Gilbert and Marshall groups. The only striking task forces he had available were TF8 (Halsey), TF11 (Brown), and TF14 (Leary). The carriers around which these forces were assembled were *Enterprise, Lexington,* and *Saratoga.* Later in January they were joined by Yorktown. They raided the Gilbert and Marshall Island Groups with limited success. The raids lasted from January until April, always keeping at least one carrier on station near Pearl. *Saratoga* suffered a torpedo hit and limped back into Pearl. The facilities there were still working at maximum capacity to repair the ships damaged in December, and the eastern Pacific was deemed fairly safe, so it was decided to send Saratoga back to San Diego for repairs.

One of Nimitz's admirals, Vice-Admiral William F. Halsey, Jr., displayed unusual vigor and initiative in these early attacks. His personality was an unexpected aid to Nimitz. Halsey spoke in salty language with earthy phrases and showed no displeasure in killing Japanese warriors. The press immediately fell in love with the feisty, skilled sailor and took much of the pressure off Nimitz, who was pleased to concentrate his attention on the monumental task he faced. America needed a hero. Some newspaperman dubbed Halsey 'Bull' and the name stayed with him through the war and for the rest of his life.

On these early raids, the loss of the Pacific Fleet's battleships which were equated by some as the 'heart' of the fleet, turned out to be not the catastrophe it seemed to be in December. The carriers were, indeed, the striking force of the future, which had suddenly arrived. The old battleships, which could make no better speed than 20 knots, couldn't keep up with the speedy carriers. During the recuperation of the battlewagons, 'hit and run' air raids were Nimitz's best weapon and he had the equipment for them. This is not to say that the day of the battleship was over. Later, during landings in several Pacific operations, and, in fact for two wars and several other operations later, battleships stood offshore and threw more ordnance into enemy territory than any other type of ship.

At Pearl Harbor, civilian life had become adjusted to wartime conditions and fear of an invasion was diminishing. The Navy was not so sanguine. It was not realized by the civilian populace at Pearl that many Japanese officers advised Yamamoto that Nagumo had been too cautious in his December attack; he could have pressed his advantage, demolished the untouched targets, and prepared the islands for an invasion. Not knowing that, the people of the islands felt more secure. Security, however, remained a high priority.

There were three degrees of 'alert' established. An ordinary alert meant that an attack was expected within one hour. A Double Alert meant that it was expected in half an hour. A triple alert indicated that some sort of attack or invasion was expected within 20 minutes.[6] In March a merchant seaman was arrested for taking pictures in Pearl Harbor. The court advised him, "You could have been taken for a spy and shot for that!".[7] They were shaken out of any complacency they might have had when a Japanese airplane attempted to bomb Pearl again. On the night of March 4, two seaplanes (the Japanese accurately call them 'floating airplanes', rather than 'flying boats'), refueled by submarines, acting on secret orders #81 and #572, flew over Pearl Harbor. The luck of these pilots was as bad as the luck of their predecessors had been good. An overcast obliterated visibility over the harbor and the Japanese dropped their entire load of bombs on an unpopulated area of Tantalus Mountain. The pilots never saw their target and the air-raid personnel never saw the planes. No damage was done.[8]

In March of 1942, the Army Air Force proposed a plan to Nimitz. It was a daring and audacious plan to bomb Tokyo. Nimitz liked the idea and asked Halsey, "Are you willing to take them out there?" to which Halsey stoutly replied, "Yes, I am". A new carrier, USS *Hornet* picked up 16 B-25s, under the command of LtCol James H. Doolittle, USA, at Alameda Naval Air Station and proceeded to the western Pacific to rendezvous with Halsey and the *Enterprise* group. The pilots had been intensively trained to take off from what appeared to be an impossibly short runway. Such large planes had never before taken off from carriers.

Halsey brought the air group (it was designed to be a one-way sortie) as close as he dared and bade them well. The April 17 (April 18 in Tokyo) mission was of no tactical consequence, but the nature of Japanese architecture multiplied each fire that the American bombs started. The Japanese people were surprised, shocked, terrified, and made to realize that war is, indeed, a two edged sword. The mission gave a remarkable boost to America's morale. President Roosevelt announced that the raiding party had come from 'Shangri La'.

In April of 1942 one of Japanese midget submarines that had penetrated and attacked Pearl Harbor was found on the bottom of the harbor and raised. It was taken to the SUBASE for investigation. It had been rammed and sunk by the destroyer USS *Monoghan*.[9]

Nimitz's chief intelligence officer, LtCdr Joseph Rochefort and his staff determined that the Japanese had withdrawn from the Indian Ocean and were going to 'soften up' the eastern end of New Guinea in preparation for invasion. Following that operation, Rochefort predicted, there would be a large operation somewhere in the mid-Pacific area. That meant, if Rochefort was correct, that a large Japanese force would soon be steaming toward the Coral Sea while a larger force would be massing for the assault on an as-yet unknown target area. The Australian intelligence unit corroborated Rochefort's estimate of the situation.

Nimitz, at Pearl Harbor, was advised on April 15 that a large group of Japanese transports (for invasion) accompanied by three carrier groups (for protection) were steaming toward the Coral Sea. With *Enterprise* occupied with the Tokyo raid, Nimitz had only *Lexington* and *Yorktown* and their supporting vessels to meet the Japanese. The matter was serious, because if the Japanese obtained a foothold in New Guinea, they could easily launch an invasion of nearby Australia. Nimitz depended on Halsey to return to Pearl for its defense and committed his remaining carriers to the Coral Sea and met the Japanese head-on. It was during this engagement, on May 8, 1942, that history's first carrier battle was fought. The main battle groups were over 150 miles apart at the closest. The offensive abilities, on both sides, were startlingly displayed. After being stung as never before, the Japanese fleet turned and ran. The Americans sunk the 12,000 ton carrier Shoho and a few smaller vessels, and the Japanese so severely damaged the 33,000 ton carrier *Lexington* that she had to be abandoned and scuttled. The other American carrier at the battle, *Yorktown*, was also badly damaged, but managed to limp back to Pearl.

The Japanese had, as at Pearl Harbor, won a tactical victory, but the strategic victory was certainly America's.[10] For the first time the Japanese advance had been stopped. It was not, to paraphrase Churchill, 'the beginning of the end', but it surely was 'the end of the beginning'.

The Coral Sea was, as Rochefort had predicted, the first of two major operations planned in May and June. Nimitz was aghast on May 27, when he saw *Yorktown* limp into Pearl Harbor listing and trailing an oil slick for miles in her wake. He had arranged to have the dry-dock blocks shaped and prepared for the damaged ship. The pathetic, valiant ship did not dock or moor or anchor; she was towed straight into the dry-dock. An engineer of several years experience, Nimitz jumped into the dry-dock before it was entirely emptied and sloshed along, inspecting and giving orders to his aides. The yard manager suggested that in three months the ship would be as good as new. Nimitz, knowing she would be needed for the upcoming assault 'somewhere in the mid-pacific', sternly told the assembled group of astonished officers, "She'll be fit to fight in three days". The Navy Yard's motto today is "We make them fit to fight".

Welding torches were already blazing. Damaged and burned equipment streamed off the ship while new parts poured aboard. The work went on 24 hours, 48 hours, 72 hours and, as the Admiral had ordered,

Yorktown steamed out of Pearl Harbor on May 30, 1942. Workmen were still on board, planes were preparing to fly to her at sea; fuel lines were barely separated when the dry-dock was flooded, she swept the harbor and stood out to sea.[11] The urgency was warranted. Admiral Halsey, exhausted by months of intense war activity, had been stricken by dermatitis and had to be replaced by Rear Admiral Raymond Spruance. Spruance was junior to Halsey and had no carrier experience, but he was respected as an intellect and strategist. Nimitz was left with a patched up carrier, *Yorktown*, another, *Saratoga*, en route from San Diego, and the *Enterprise/Hornet* force with a new commander. The Japanese fleet which was preparing to invade 'somewhere in the mid-Pacific' was augmented by the ships that had been repulsed in the Coral Sea. It was time for Nimitz to make one of those gut-wrenching decisions which are applauded if they are correct and damned if they are not. Where would the Japanese strike? There were reasons to expect the attack at New Guinea, Hawaii, Midway, or the Aleutian Islands in Alaska. Each scenario was equally plausible.

Admiral Nimitz chose to accept Rochefort's prediction that the strike would be at Midway. The intelligence officer had sent a wire intended to be intercepted that told of a water shortage on Midway. Later a Japanese radio message was discovered by Rochefort's men which mentioned a "water shortage at AF". This, when combined with a previously overheard message telling of the proposed invasion of "AF", convinced Rochefort that Midway would be the target of the Japanese invasion fleet, and June 4 would be the day of the assault. Nimitz decided to throw his entire force into a plan proposed by Spruance. Midway was to be defended. Nimitz assumed retained overall tactical command.[12] If Nimitz had been wrong, and the invasion was directed to Hawaii, Nimitz's fleet would have been out of position and cut off from any friendly port west of San Francisco. It was a decision of terrible importance and significance.

When a report was received on the morning of June 3 that unusual air activity was being observed over Dutch Harbor in the eastern Aleutians and that Pearl Harbor had been blacked out due to an 'all-out red' alert, Nimitz may have been shaken, but he displayed no trace of doubt to his staff. The Japanese attack in Alaska was a feint, the alert in Hawaii was a false alarm, and by the morning of June 4, Catalina patrol planes had sent the incomplete message "two carriers and main body ships bearing 320, course 135, speed 25, distance 180". Two carriers? Which two? Where were the others?

Nimitz was in the war room at his headquarters on Makalapa hill when the message came in. At his side was LtCdr Edwin T. Layton, Rochefort's assistant. Layton spoke fluent Japanese and was the man Nimitz wanted at his side. In fact, the report was correct, albeit incomplete. The Admiral in command of the invasion force was none other than the man who directed the attack on Pearl Harbor, Admiral Chuichi Nagumo. He expected little resistance from the land-based aircraft at Midway. Wake Island defense, although gallant and fierce, inflicted little damage on that invasion force. The Midway airplanes attacked Nagumo's lead carriers.

No one knew it at the time, but the army B-17s caused Nagumo to make a suicidal decision. Post-war reports from Japanese officers indicated that the high flying army planes did not make one hit with any of the 320 bombs they dropped. What then was their effect? Nagumo, as was demonstrated at Pearl Harbor six months earlier, was a cautious man. He received the news of land based bombers attacking his ships and decided to rearm his planes with bombs to attack Midway, rather than the torpedoes with which his planes were already armed. While the rearming was going on, his carrier decks could not retrieve his planes which were returning from Midway. The dilemma made the man even more indecisive. Air commanders were pleading for him to clear the decks so their planes could land and other officers warned that if the decks were cleared, the bombing from Midway and American carriers would continue unopposed. He finally ordered the decks to be cleared for the incoming planes. Then he delayed any offensive action until his planes were recovered, refueled and rearmed with anti-ship weapons such as armor piercing bombs and torpedoes. There is no more vulnerable situation for an aircraft carrier. His men were on deck cheering the news that their pilots had damaged an American carrier and were shouting "Banzai's when they noticed that one of them was looking aloft and screaming "Dive bombers!". When the B-17s broke off and returned to Midway, Navy planes from US carriers pressed home an attack on *Akagi*. Can anyone who has not been through it imagine the destruction caused by bombing a carrier with its deck full of airplanes, ruptured gasoline hoses spewing fuel crazily over the deck, bombs and bullets igniting and firing, and communications being destroyed? That was the fate of the *Akagi*.

Planes from the US carrier *Yorktown* had attacked the *Akagi*, Nagurno's leading carrier and flagship. When Commander Layton saw a message from Nagumo, he recognized the transmitter's 'fist', a term used to describe the technique of a Morse code sender's touch on his telegraph key. Furthermore Layton knew that the sender was stationed aboard the cruiser *Nagara*. He reasoned that Nagumo had transferred his flag to the cruiser; therefore *Akagi* must have been damaged beyond repair. Radio silence at the beginning of the battle and static during the action hampered reception at CINCPAC HQ. It also raised the already tense situation to one of frantic exasperation.

Finally messages came through indicating some American hits on carriers and support craft, but one dismal one reported that Admiral Fletcher's flagship, *Yorktown*, had suffered a fatal blow. The patched-up ship had fought valiantly, but had been torpedoed and Fletcher had to transfer his flag to the cruiser USS *Astoria*.

The battle continued throughout the afternoon of June 4. Reports indicated that four Japanese carriers had been badly damaged. *Akagi*, damaged that morning was still burning. *Hiryu, Kaga,* and *Soryu* were pouring flame and heavy black smoke into the Pacific sky. They were doomed. Search planes reported that the entire Japanese invasion fleet had turned and was steaming west.[13] Nagumo again, with Yamamoto's concurrence, showed his propensity to choose caution over audacity. The troop transports, which had followed the advance fleet, turned first and were now leading the battered and bruised 'protectors' back to Japan. But there were no Japanese carriers among them. They were at the bottom of the Pacific. The American Navy had once again, this time at a great cost, protected Hawaii from foreign intervention as it had before from the Russians, the British and the French. The battle of the Coral Sea stopped the Japanese advance. The battle of Midway struck a mortal blow against the Japanese navy. Now the United States and her allies were on the offensive.

Assessments made in the calm aftermath of the action agreed that although Japan's tonnage losses were staggering, her greatest loss was the enormous number of irreplaceable trained aviators who were shot down or flew into the sea when their fuel was exhausted. During the heat of battle, one can be jubilant at the destruction of an enemy, but in retrospect, a thoughtful person must surely recognize the valor of these young men on both sides who are forever joined in death.

The war progressed with Allied forces fighting their way from all corners of the Pacific toward Japan. At Pearl Harbor, on October 1 1942, the new Naval Supply Depot opened on Kuahua Island. Later the island became a peninsula and in 1943 the depot was renamed the Naval Supply Center and in 1993 was again renamed the Fleet & Industrial Supply Center, or FISC.[14] In September of that year, the new CINCPAC Headquarters building at 250 Makalapa Drive was completed enough for Admiral Nimitz and his staff to move in. The Admiral chose to have an enormous double-sized desk installed. It was convenient for spreading out the charts that accompanied discussions with visiting officers and, perhaps, to keep people a little more at bay from the overworked commander of thousands of men and women.

The war did not flow smoothly from Midway to the end of hostilities. There were thousands of critical decisions to be made. On August 8, the Pearl Harbor headquarters suffered the news that the Japanese had made a successful run through combined US and Australian naval forces just north of Guadalcanal in Savo Sound. The Allied losses were shocking. Sunk or damaged were the cruisers *Astoria, Canberra, Chicago, Quincy* and

Vincennes. Three destroyers and hundreds of men were also lost. The area became known as Ironbottom Sound. The Battle of Savo Island was the worst defeat the US Navy has ever suffered.[15] Admiral Fletcher, on August 24, engaged and sank the carrier *Ryujo*, but received two bomb hits which damaged *Enterprise* and killed 74 men. Fletcher was able to bring his group, including his wounded flagship, back to Pearl for repairs. Fletcher was then replaced by Admiral Halsey who had recovered from his ailment. Halsey then was appointed by Nimitz as the commander of American forces in the South Pacific, CINCSOPAC, but he had only two carriers to fight with. In mid September the carrier USS Wasp was hit by a torpedo from a submarine and was so badly damaged her captain transferred his crew and ordered her scuttled. That left Nimitz with *Hornet* as the only operational carrier in the Pacific. In a fierce battle off Guadalcanal in late September *Hornet* was hit badly and CINCPAC ordered her scuttled. It was at this time that the desperately needed *Enterprise* was repaired and sent back to sea.

Newspapers at the time correctly applauded the work by the men at the Pearl Harbor Naval Shipyard, but did not mention the loss of *Hornet*. Attrition was reducing both Pacific Fleets to shambles, but there was one difference. The Japanese were losing irreplaceable men and ships. America's shipyards and recruiting stations were accelerating their activities daily. The grim news from the sea was offset by good news from the eastern US. On August 27,1942 the first of the 45,000 ton Iowa class battleships was launched. USS *Iowa*, slid down the ways at the New York Navy Yard, with Mrs. Henry Wallace as her sponsor. After her completion and sea trials she steamed to the Pacific and contributed mightily to the American effort in that ocean.

Three interesting events occurred in December of 1942. On December 7, one year after the horrendous attack on Pearl Harbor, the submarine USS *Bowfin* was launched. She fought valiantly all through the war, sinking 179,000 tons of enemy warships and shipping and damaging 34,000 tons. She is now enshrined at Pearl Harbor as a world-class museum. On that same day, USS *New Jersey*, the second of four Iowa class battleships was launched. She slid down the ways and into history at the Philadelphia Navy Yard. America's fleet was adding muscle while Japan was watching her irreplaceable ships and men go down. Another interesting event was the reaction of Hawaiians to the attempt of some civilians to remove the military government that had been in force since the attack in 1941. On December 27, 1942, the Honolulu Chamber of Commerce wired President Roosevelt, urging him to retain the military government in Hawaii, at least until the danger passed. Most members of the civilian government had opposed the near-hysterical demands for mass internment or deportation of local Japanese, regardless of nationality.

1943 started out on a somber note for Admiral Nimitz. His close friend, Rear Admiral Robert S. English, commander of the Pacific Submarine Fleet, was killed in a crash of the Pan American Clipper in California. Also, at the end of January, he received word that the cruiser *Chicago* had been lost. The news, plus the exhaustion of dealing with daily crises for months brought on an attack of malaria which sent Nimitz to the Aiea Hospital for a few days.[16] After his return to CINCPAC headquarters, he resumed his daily routine behind that enormous desk. There was a meeting at nine o'clock during which operation reports were made. Nimitz commented carefully and helpfully on each report. Layton or Rochefort gave the intelligence briefing and discussions followed. General Emmons, the Military Governor of Hawaii often was present. At eleven o'clock the Admiral received visitors.

The visitors were usually VIPs from the states or officers with other than official business from various theaters around the Pacific. One visitor, however, was rather unusual. While home on leave, radarman McCaleb, from the destroyer *Shaw*, met Nimitz's half sister. She insisted that McCaleb say hello to the Chester and give him a note from her. When he returned to Pearl, the embarrassed McCaleb requested an audience with the Admiral through regular channels. At each level his request was inspected and questioned. At each level a surprised officer would proceed to grant the request. The meeting date was set.

As McCaleb left his ship for the meeting, he was asked by his shipmates to find out what their next assignment would be after her repairs were completed. When he was ushered into the sanctorum of Nimitz's office, he was relieved to see how delighted the Admiral was to hear from his sister and cordially he treated the nervous petty officer. Just as the short meeting broke up, Nimitz turned to radarman McCaleb and asked, "By the way, where are they going to send the *Shaw* after she completes overhaul?"[17]

One famous, or rather infamous and serious, problem that had to be solved was faulty American torpedoes. Several captains returned from sorties reporting two malfunctions. The torpedoes would explode prematurely or not at all. The most egregious example was that of one submariner who stopped a Japanese tanker dead in the water with two torpedoes. He then moved into a position on her beam and fired nine torpedoes. Every one hit, but not one exploded.

When the problem was presented to the Bureau of Ordnance, they blamed the captains of the submarines for faulty firing techniques instead of instituting a design investigation. It fell to Admiral Charles Lockwood to test the weapons and ascertain the cause of their flaws. He suspended nets and determined that they were running about ten feet lower than they should, and that there was a malfunction in the firing pin mechanism. He corrected the design and sent the results to the bureau in Washington. The failures ceased, but it was not until September of 1943 that American submariners had the proper weapons to fight their war.

In April of 1943 a stunning event took place. Admiral Yamamoto planned an inspection trip throughout the Japanese held areas of the Southwest Pacific. Layton intercepted a message that outlined the Japanese admiral's itinerary. Nimitz saw the possibility to remove an important enemy asset. He obtained permission from CNO King and Navy Secretary Knox for the assassination attempt. Nimitz informed Halsey with the words, "Good hunting and good luck". Halsey ordered a flight of P-38 fighters aloft to a spot most advantageous for the ambush. 'Test Flight' was the code phrase for Yamamoto's plane. Nimitz received the satisfying report on April 18,1943, "P-38s, led by Major John W. Mitchell, USA....shot down two bombers escorted by Zeros. One shoot believed to be test flight". April 18 was exactly one year since the Halsey/Doolittle raid on Tokyo.

The civilians in the Pearl Harbor area had suffered damage during the Japanese attack in 1941 and were refused any reimbursement by their insurance companies. Congress, recognizing their plight, passed an act which set up the War Damage Corporation. Working with local insurance companies, an agreement was made to repay each civilian who had suffered property loss. The act was made retroactive to December 7, 1941 so that the Japanese (and American) inflicted losses were covered. Since little or no damage was done after that date, the act was, in fact, an ex post facto benefit for the locals. One pleasant surprise for the adjusters was that several people whose automobiles were hit refused to enter any claim. They kept their cars as they were as souvenirs, some of them for generations.[18]

A ghastly act by the Japanese reinflamed American passions. The flyers who fell into Japanese hands during the bombing of Tokyo in April, 1942, were 'tried' and executed publicly. The scenes were gratuitously sent to newspapers around the world. Again the Japanese, in attempting to intimidate Americans, only succeeded in renewing American vigor in pressing home the war effort.[19]

As ship repair and other facilities were expanded at Pearl, construction continued at a furious pace. Five Navy housing areas were built. Area One, 90 acres, Area Two, 61 acres, and Area Three, 192 acres, contained a total of 2000 housing units for civilian workers. The complexes had schools, churches, a Fire Station, shops, and two large mess halls. Area Four was built for 2000 enlisted Navy men. Area Five was built on a 352 acre tract on Makalapa Crater. The CINCPAC building was a reinforced concrete bombproof structure, two stories high.

The beautiful Aiea Hospital was completed in November 1942. It was there that Admiral Nimitz recovered from his bout with malaria. Ford

Island was the major repair center for aircraft and 'stored' planes for use on carriers to complete their complement. The airstrip at Ewa was made into the Marine Air Corps Station and Barber's Point Naval Air Station was built using the $18,600,000 appropriated by congress in 1941.[20] In December of 1943 a new magazine was completed in Waikele Gulch. Nimitz had decreed that the incredible amount of explosives exposed to enemy bombs and accidents, had to be safely stored. The engineers response was to dig 120 tunnels, each 240 feet long. The project required nine miles of railroad track, ten miles of paved road, four bridges, and housing and messing facilities for the construction personnel.[21] 'Pearl Harbor' was fast becoming more than its humble beginnings could possibly have indicated.

Although extensive studies had been made concerning the raising of the battleship USS *Arizona*, the decision, for several reasons, including cost, value to the fleet, new battleships arriving, etc., was in favor of letting her rest in peace where she fell. Salvage operations were cancelled on May 22,1943.[22]

The composition of the workforce was diverse, but all-American figuratively and literally. Rear Admiral Furlong, Commandant of the Yard, in an article stated,

> "Half of the employees at Pearl Harbor Navy Yard are local residents. Many are descendants of Chinese and Portuguese forebears. Other local employees are Hawaiians, Filipinos, Koreans, and permanent white residents. The other half is made up of several thousand men brought from the mainland since the Japanese attack. A little over 1,000 Negroes are among these mainlanders."[23]

The Admiral chose not to mention the thousands of workers of Japanese ancestry. He did, however, mention the deplorable conditions which existed when the large contingents of US workmen started arriving in late 1940.

> "The streets were laid out in a muddy cane field. Those who lived in town disembarked from the trains in heavy downpours with water half-way to their knees. Men walked to the yard in mud and rain. Poor food was added to the annoyances of blackout, poor transportation, no entertainment, mud, rain, sleeping in quarters with strangers, and being away from the comforts of home."[24]

Welcome to paradise!

In September of 1943 a large dry-dock was completed and named in honor of Captain Robert E. Thomas (CEC) USN. Among the speakers at the dedication was Admiral Chester Nimitz.[25] He was impressed by the many snappy slogans posted around the yard, especially the one which proclaimed, "CINCPAC is proud of the record of the Pearl Harbor Navy Yard". Even the lowly yard carts were named with such inspiring titles as "Midway", "Solomons", "Coral Sea".[26] Morale was heightened by the publication of the yard paper BANNER. The first issue was printed on January 16, 1943. It came out weekly until September 9,1946. Thereafter the paper was entitled the SHIPYARD LOG. One of the articles in a later edition of the LOG told of Leaping Tuna, a caged trailer pulled by a tractor around the yard for workers' transportation. It moved at a snail's pace and never stopped. The workers simply hopped on and off at their destinations. There was also a train which stopped in front of Building 1 and ran to Iwilei. Some of the men would eat at the White Owl Café on Bethel Street in Honolulu or at the Naval Station on Ala Moana Boulevard. Although the hours worked were excessive and the pay was minimal a sense of pride pervaded the yard. Pride and Teamwork were the watchwords. Each man and woman did his or her best to complete the tasks per specifications and on, or ahead of, time.[27]

At the beginning of 1944, the exciting news at CINCPAC HQ was the launching of two more heavy battleships of the 45,000 ton Iowa class. USS *Missouri* was launched on January 29,1944 at New York Naval Shipyard, and USS *Wisconsin* joined her sisterships on the same day from Philadelphia.[28] These Iowa class battleships were examples of a serendipitous occurrence. The backbone of every fleet in the world in 1941 was thought to be the battleship. Carriers were assigned to protection and reconnaissance duty. After the attack on Pearl Harbor, which put most American battleships out of action, and after the hand wringing subsided, it was realized that for the war being fought, carriers were the weapon of choice. United States carriers were not affected by the 1941 attack, and as handled by the skilled commands of Nimitz, Halsey, Spruance and others, provided the needed striking flexibility until the battleships were repaired. Then, when the Allies took to the offense, battleships were needed to shell islands in preparation for invasions and our old ones were reconditioned and returned magnificently to service, ironically as frequent protectors of the carriers. As faster, stronger battleships were needed, the four Iowa class ships with their awesome speed and firepower, came to the fleet at the right time.

Despite their frequent differences, General Douglas MacArthur and Admiral Nimitz successfully conducted their drives across the Pacific. MacArthur, operating from Australia, moved northward toward the Philippines and Nimitz's forces drove westward, also toward the Philippines. The Japanese carrier fleet had been so mangled that they were all withdrawn to the protected Sea of Japan where they were repaired and were joined by new carriers being built nearby in Japan. Also, they had no fuel oil for their ships and planes to make extended sorties. They still did, however, have a strong surface fleet. While the Japanese were licking their wounds near home, the second disaster of the war occurred at Pearl Harbor.

Preparations were almost finished for the invasion of Saipan. On the afternoon of May 21, 1944, Pearl was crammed with ships full of men, equipment, gasoline, fuel oil, ammunition, and explosives. LSTs (Landing Ship, Tank) were moored and lashed together in near, orderly groups in West Loch. No one is certain how it started, but a small fire ignited a cache of explosives aboard LST 353. At 3:00pm an enormous explosion startled and alarmed people all over the harbor. As fire-fighting boats rushed to the group of LSTs, burning gasoline was sprayed over adjacent ships, igniting their deadly cargoes. The rescue crews displayed unbelievable courage in taking their small boats between burning ships to rescue those in the water who were still alive. At any time an adjacent ship might explode. Men on board the ships were killed instantly. People on the beach nearby were also in peril. The air in the loch was filled with parts from blown-apart engines, vehicles, weapons, and bodies. Hidden, silent fires burned below decks on some ships and at 9:30 that evening, another ship erupted 'like a Hawaiian volcano' and more fierce fires started.

In all, 127 men were killed and another 380 were injured. As soon as possible, the ships were separated and inspected for remaining dangers. The invasion fleet was rearmed, remanned, and reprovisioned and stormed onto the beaches at Saipan on schedule 23 days later. The only monument to the disaster is a table-sized plaque erected on the shore of the loch in April 1995 ,[29]

A ghost arose from three years past when, in Washington DC, the House Judiciary Committee approved legislation extending for 12 months beyond June 7, 1944, the statute of limitations for actions against civilian or military personnel responsible for the Pearl Harbor disaster December 7, 1941, and directing that court martial proceedings be instituted not later than June 7, 1945, against any involved in apparent derelictions of duty. The action was "necessary to protect rights of the military to institute proposed court martial proceedings against Maj. Gen. Walter Short and Rear Admiral Husband E. Kimmel."[30]

CINCPAC-CINCPOA staff had grown from 45 in 1942 to 250 officers in June of 1944. Most of these people were involved in cryptology efforts or working to solve the mind-boggling supply problems faced in the westward drive across the Pacific. That drive was accelerating.

Early on the evening of June 20, 1944, CINCPAC received the report that the submarine USS *Cavalla* had sunk the Japanese carrier *Shokaku*. That ship was one of only two remaining carriers that had participated in the attack on Pearl Harbor. Admirals Marc Mitscher and Ray Spruance also reported engaging and sinking enemy carriers. Apparently the Japanese fleet had taken the chance of risking the bulk of their remaining naval strength by leaving the Sea of Japan and steaming south toward the American forces. Sinking any enemy ship is significant, but with carriers, it also meant that the Japanese airplanes had no place to which they could return and land. They continued the fight, being shot and for running out of fuel, in both cases falling to the sea. Over three hundred desperately needed Japanese airplanes and pilots were lost that day. Officially the name for this action was the Battle of the Philippine Sea, but it was immediately dubbed by aviators the Marianas Turkey Shoot.[31]

President Roosevelt made an unusual journey to Hawaii late in July of 1944. He met there with Nimitz and MacArthur and finalized the strategy for the recapture of the Philippine Islands. They were not in accord when they first met, but MacArthur persuaded both the president and his some-time adversary Nimitz, that such a course was not only strategically important, but a matter of national honor. Preparations were commenced for the bombing and subsequent invasion of the Philippines. Meanwhile Nimitz's campaign northward through the Marianas was nearing completion. By the middle of August, the islands of Guam, Rota, Saipan, and Tinian were recaptured at a cost of 5,000 American lives and at the fearful cost to the Japanese of over 60,000 men. America, with the mightiest navy in history, was at Japan's front door.

On the afternoon of October 20, 1944, General MacArthur returned to Leyte as he had promised. He waded ashore and delivered a stirring speech calling for the Philippine people to "rise and strike" the dreaded enemy from their shores. One fact that American Intelligence at Pearl had not realized was that the Japanese had given up the idea of defending beaches against the murderous firepower of the new battleships. They changed their tactics and allowed American forces to land and then the Japanese would challenge them from well emplaced defensive positions.

Admiral Halsey, using the new Iowa class battleship USS *New Jersey* as his flagship, moved toward the Philippine island of Leyte in September. The Japanese committed most of their remaining naval strength in an effort to engage and defeat the American Navy near Leyte Gulf. Their strategy was to deploy three task forces. The northern force would expose itself to Halsey's reconnaissance planes. Simultaneously the central and southern forces would slip through the San Bernardino Strait and into the Pacific where the Japanese calculated that it would overwhelm the smaller remaining American group left by Halsey at Leyte Gulf. The plan almost worked.

Halsey took the bait and boomed north ready to blow the Japanese fleet out of the water. However all he encountered were planeless carriers and older ships. Admirals Kinkaid and Oldendorf were left to receive the onslaught of what was left of the Japanese fleet, still a formidable threat. From October 23 to 25, 1944, the greatest naval battle in history took place.

Over 280 ships were involved. Oddly, the atmosphere was so clear those days that communications from the ships were heard not only at Pearl Harbor, but at listening stations around the entire ocean.

Admiral Kinkaid met and engaged the enemy fleet in Surigao Strait/ Leyte Gulf. He obliterated the southern force, but needed Halsey's help to confront the Japanese central force. At Pearl, Nimitz was not his usual serene self. He finally ordered Halsey to break off and return to Leyte to support Kinkaid. The orders were mangled in transmittal and came to Halsey sounding like a rebuke. Halsey, furious, responded that he was returning to the gulf to Kinkaid's aid. As long as he lived, Admiral Halsey denied any wrong-doing in that action.

Kinkaid's defense was admirable. He and Oldendorf and Sprague, with his CVEs, 'Baby Carriers', turned back the central Japanese fleet. Among the many Japanese ships sunk during these operations was the carrier *Zuikaku*, the last of the carriers that had struck Pearl Harbor. Ironically, the USS *Ward* was also lost. She was the ship that dropped the depth bomb on the Japanese submarine outside Pearl Harbor at 0635 December 7, 1941, at the beginning of the war.

What sank the *Ward* was a land based plane. The pilot, to the amazement of American sailors, flew his deadly missile directly through all the anti-aircraft fire, into the superstructure of the ship. The men were later to learn that these suicide missions were called *Kamikaze* or Divine Wind, a term from centuries before when such a typhoon turned back the fleet of Kublai Khan and saved Japan.[32] These suicidal airplane attacks were not easily understood by people of other cultures, but were heroic to the Japanese. The American Navy had little time for philosophy; they had to deal with the new threat. They were able to withstand the severe losses inflicted and came to realize that each plane was irreplaceable. The attacks grew fewer and finally stopped. Japan's navy was "beaten, routed, and broken"[33] according to Halsey. It was indeed. They had lost 306,000 tons of warships; the Americans had lost 38,000 tons. America's naval power now ruled the entire Pacific Ocean.

The outstanding news from the Philippines contributed to the decision at Pearl Harbor and in the entire Territory of Hawaii, to terminate martial law on October 14, 1944. Although the American Navy was supreme in the Pacific, nature decided to deal a bitter blow. A typhoon overtook Halsey's task force in December of 1944 and resulted in the total loss of three ships, almost 800 men, and 186 planes. At Pearl Harbor, this incident, combined with what the press were calling 'The Battle of Bull's Run' diminished somewhat Halsey's otherwise well-deserved luster. It was a poor way to end the year.

President Roosevelt agreed with Congress that the US should have some five star senior officers to be equal in rank to those of the British. Four Generals and four admirals were chosen to be elevated to five star rank.

Admirals King, Leahy and Nimitz were selected. Halsey did not receive his fifth star until later, perhaps due to his unfortunate storm related woes. On December 19, 1944, Admiral Chester W. Nimitz was awarded his fifth star and became a Fleet Admiral, or FAdm, at a short ceremony at CINCPAC HQ at Pearl Harbor. It was the end of a successful year.

In January of 1945, Admiral Nimitz moved his headquarters to the island of Guam in order to be nearer the action and escape the increasingly crowded offices at Pearl Harbor. SeaBees, the Navy's Construction Battalions, transformed the bomb-cratered island into a viable site with roads and offices and even some landscaping. At Pearl Harbor, the HQ building had been made of reinforced concrete with thick walls. On Guam it was a wooden structure because there was no longer any threat of air attack. However, there were still Japanese soldiers on the island and Nimitz required a US Marine Guard near him at all times. Some of the Japanese were so bold as to don captured US Marine uniforms in which they actually stood in chow lines, ate GI food and then watched American movies.

It is difficult today to imagine the depth of the fury that was felt by the fighting men of 1944. A clue might be extracted from the expressions used by the Seabees who, with their bulldozers, were shoulder to shoulder with the US Marines where the fighting was most furious and dangerous. The profanity is not too surprising, but the ideas and descriptive language would be inappropriate and unacceptable today. One Seabee spoke for many when he said, "When a Marine sees a Jap he shoots the bastard's eyes out; when a Seabee spies a Jap he just spits a long, contemptuous stream of 'Copenhagen', and blinds the sonavabitch!".[34] These tough, brave men were not without a sense of humor amid the depressing, horrible environment of war. One stated, in 1944, "After we've paraded through the rubble of Tokyo on our bulldozers, we want to go back to the beach and welcome the Marines".[35]

While Japanese air and sea power no longer existed, there were still thousands of dedicated, fanatic soldiers on the islands surrounding Japan. The bloody invasions at Iwo Jima and Okinawa took a terrible toll of American lives. The author was privileged to be aboard a US Navy ship in the early 1990s when she passed Iwo Jima. The young US Marine detachment stood silently at the rail at attention in reverent respect for their comrades who had fallen there so many years ago.

Plans named Operation Olympic, the invasion of Kyushu, and Coronet, the invasion of Honshu, the main island of Japan, were drawn up weeks before Nimitz left Pearl Harbor. The time to put them into action was drawing near. FAdm King sent a letter to Nimitz, by personal courier, in which he stated that a new device was due by August 1, 1945. It was an atomic bomb whose power was equivalent to 20,000 tons of TNT. Nimitz's reaction was that August 1 was a long way off. Also Hitler had been ranting about secret weapons for a long time. Nimitz and MacArthur proceeded with invasion plans. Neither of them had any illusions about a Japanese surrender. As a token of the determination of the Japanese soldier, there is a relic in an Okinawa military museum today which is difficult to believe. It is a knife wired onto the end of a stick. It is a startling and poignant reminder of what the Japanese soldier was ready to use to oppose the largest, most powerful military force ever assembled in history.

On May 8, 1945, the formal surrender of Germany was announced at Pearl Harbor. The reaction was joyous, but it was not the wild exuberant exultation seen in England and on the east coast of the US. There was a determined enemy to defeat and still fresh in the minds of many was the unprovoked attack of four years earlier. Shortly following that good news, however, came word that Admiral Halsey had led his entire group into another typhoon. He faced another court of inquiry at which Admiral Hoover, the presiding officer, recommended that Halsey be replaced. Navy Secretary James Forrestal was on the verge of doing just that, but was dissuaded by King and Nimitz. They thought the removal of Halsey so near the end of the war would blemish his otherwise stellar career. He stayed.

After the fall of Germany, Pearl Harbor became a madhouse of visiting VIPs. The assessment of the world situation, at least in the eastern part of the mainland, was that with the Germans out and the Japanese fleet gone, we could easily enter Japan at little or no cost and tie up the one remaining loose end to the war. It was far from the truth, but didn't stop the flood of congressmen, industrial giants, and affluent Americans from coming out to 'see the war', which was still 3000 miles farther west, and to enjoy Hawaii's hospitality. Unfortunately, the strain was severe on the Navy men and women who were still working on details of Olympic and Coronet, including making estimates of the terrible losses in American lives they would both entail.

On July 25, a courier arrived at Guam from Washington via Pearl Harbor, with films of the destruction created by the new bomb at its Alamagordo, New Mexico trial. Nimitz and his staff were stunned. For the first time, he felt an invasion might not be necessary. He consulted his expert on the Japanese, Commander Layton, who assured him that there was no doubt that the Japanese soldiers, and even the civilians, would fight to their death. He reminded Nimitz of the ghastly sight of entire families leaping to their death off the cliffs at Saipan. Nimitz reluctantly continued his invasion plans.

The American Navy was patrolling the coast of Japan shelling cities at will. Waves of 500 bombers were dropping fire bombs that ignited uncontrollable fires in Japanese cities and factories. Then, the first atomic bomb was dropped on the city of Hiroshima. Pure hell descended on the people below. The loss of life was not as great as in some of the fire-storm raids, but it was so spectacular, and the unknown affects of radiation so frightening, that it caught the imagination of the world. Even then, the Japanese responded to political calls for surrender with a horrible silence. Another such bomb was dropped on Nagasaki three days later and Emperor Hirohito asked his people to surrender. He correctly saw that any further resistance in the face of such destruction would mean the end of Japan for many years, perhaps forever. He accepted unconditional surrender terms on August 14, 1945. Thus ended the most devastating war the world had ever seen. In a 1991 reminiscence, John Updike expressed the feelings of many Americans. "We carry an impression of the United States as a wounded lamb that responded like a lion."[36]

The prize for the laconic comment of the century surely must go to the man on watch on the bridge of USS *Iowa* while one of the most cataclysmic event of the century occurred. The ship was steaming west toward Tokyo Bay when a message was received. The entry in the ship's log is a masterpiece of understatement.

> "Wednesday 15 August 1945. 1230 to 1730
> Steaming as before on course 250 (T & PGC). 256
> at 24 knots. At 1236 changed speed to 18 knots. At
> 1300 COMTHIRDFLEET announced the surrender
> of the Japanese Empire and the termination of
> hostilities... At 1305 petty officer Jones was taken
> to sick bay. While he was moving a 5 gallon can of
> paint, it fell on his foot. Treated by Lt. (jg) G. L
> Marshall, (MC) USNR, and returned to duty... Made
> daily inspection of magazines and smokeless powder
> samples; conditions normal.
> JAMES R. C. CRUMLISH,
> Jr. Lt. USNR."[37]

Of course, the Lieutenant's entry was quite proper and accurate, but how could anyone suppress the desire to comment on the end of a world war, even if petty officer Jones did drop a paint bucket on his foot?

August 14, 1945 was officially designated 'V-J Day'.

From Pearl Harbor, the surrender ceremonies were planned to take place aboard USS *Missouri*. Her decks were stripped of fire-resistant wartime paint and scrubbed clean. The teak shown with a rich, beautiful glow. Admiral Spruance did not join the huge number of military dignitaries at the ceremony because he was patrolling the sky above in case a final foolish act of treachery might be launched by the Japanese. His orders from Admiral Halsey were, "Investigate and shoot down all snoopers - not vindictively, but in a friendly sort of way."[38]

Admiral Halsey proceeded to USS *Missouri* for the ceremonies. His absence from his flagship, USS *Iowa*, was duly noted in her log:

> "SUNDAY 2 SEPTEMBER 1945.0730 to 1230.
> At 0800 mustered crew on stations. No absentees.
> At 0806 broke personal flag of Admiral W.H. Halsey
> and hoisted absentee pennant, while Fleet Admiral
> C.W. Nimitz aboard USS Missouri for ceremonies
> incident to surrender of JAPAN. Made daily
> inspection of magazines and smokeless powder
> samples: conditions normal. L.A. MICHEL
> Lieutenant, USNR."[39]

The five-star flags of FAdm Nimitz and General of the Army MacArthur adorned the mast of the'Mighty Mo'. Dozens of officers and enlisted men were on deck and at every free space aloft, and chattered excitedly. They didn't notice when Commander Horace Bird announced that the senior officers were approaching. When Cdr. Bird bellowed. "All hands-attention on deck!!", the ship's company and visitors were startled into silence.

On September 18, at Pearl Harbor, a circular plaque was installed in the *Missouri's* deck at the exact spot where the surrender table had been located. Nimitz went to Yokohama and visited the old Japanese museum ship *Mikasa*, a relic of the Japanese victory over the Russian fleet in 1905. Already American sailors were talking of taking souvenirs. Nimitz immediately ordered a Marine Guard posted to prevent any vindictive vandalism and/or stripping of equipment for souvenirs. The ship, complete with all her artifacts intact, may be seen as a museum in the same place today.

For the next several months, 'demobilization' was the word on many lips. Every combat ship returning to the US was loaded with men and women from combat zones. Over 2,000,000 people were transported by military vessels. The operation was called Magic Carpet. During the first week in April 1946, the US Navy Staging and Separation Center was disestablished and its function assumed by the Naval Receiving Station, Pearl Harbor. T.H. That same week, the US Navy Barracks for Waves and several offices were closed. "The Navy had done a fine job," thought many, if indeed they thought about it at all. Now it was time to bring all the boys home. Except for senior military officers, little thought was given to how we would maintain the freedom we had so recently and so dearly protected. In 1946 the 14th ND Public Works Maintenance Division was established and in 1948 the name became 14th ND HQ Shops Division.

By mid-September, Nimitz returned his headquarters to the Makalapa location in Pearl Harbor.[40] FAdm King moved to an advisory position with the Secretary of the Navy. On November 24, Chester Nimitz became the tenth Chief of Naval Operations of the US Navy. He received the post and simultaneously turned over his CINCPAC-CINCPOA duties to Admiral Spruance aboard the submarine USS *Menhaden.* Young commander Nimitz had started the submarine base at Pearl Harbor in 1920. He became CINCPAC aboard the submarine USS *Grayling* in 1941. It was fitting that his final Pacific Change of Command would take place on the deck of a sub at Pearl.

Chapter 29 - Statehood

The US Navy emerged from the war as the most powerful fleet the world has ever seen,[1] with 90 large carriers, 23 battleships and hundreds of other ships, planes and submarines. After the war was won, it was clear that the nation could not support such a large Navy. Many believed that, since there was no nation with the naval capability to challenge the US, the Navy should be returned to pre-war peacetime levels. As to the expensive carriers, there were those who publicly said that modern aircraft have such large range, carriers are no longer needed. Others said, "Why should we need a navy at all?"[2]

While the nation wanted to return to normal levels as soon as possible, this meant serious consequences for some people. In March of 1946, the Honolulu Star Bulletin headline blared "Pearl Harbor to lay off 7,000". The drastic curtailment of civilian employees was scheduled to reduce the work force from 11,500 to 4,500 in six months.[3] It was not unexpected, of course, but still many Hawaiians would lose their jobs. The Navy also deactivated a number of bases around the islands.

Pearl Harbor was established as a U.S. Naval Base in November of 1945. This replaced the Industrial Navy Yards and created a new entity to function as a separate activity of the Navy under the command and control of the 14th Naval District.[4] It was clear that the Navy felt that its mission was important and on going. The shipyard was left intact and operational, but with cutbacks. Surplus ships and floating dry-docks were mothballed and anchored in Middle Loch. In 1946, the world's largest floating drydock, 622 feet long, was towed from Panama to Pearl Harbor. It was a self-contained unit suitable for offshore operations.[5] It symbolized the continuing role of Pearl Harbor as a repair facility.

Events both expected and unexpected marked the 1950s in Hawaii. It was apparent that the people expected to be granted statehood after the war for at least two thirds of the citizens voted for it. It did not happen immediately after the war for a number of reasons, many were difficult to understand. Also, no one expected another war, but by September of 1950, the U.S. was involved in war in Korea. The Navy and Hawaii saw the influx of a flood of people' ships and military personnel in the islands once again.

The event with the most significant impact on Hawaii was, of course, statehood. That it did not happen until the end of the decade was due to factors that were both important and trivial and generally ignored the value of the islands as a military base.

Hawaii should have become a state long before it did. The first published mention of Hawaiian statehood was in the *Northern Journal* of Lowville, New York on May 1,1849. An editorial called for immediate action by the US Congress to make it a state before the British took it from us.[6]

Hawaii was a sovereign country at the time, though it became a territory fifty years later and remained so for another fifty years. Today it is difficult to believe that our elected congressmen could have put forth such untenable and deceptive reasons for the delay that they did. Statehood is the responsibility of the Congress and certain requirements, such as population, physical and economic development, must be met before a statehood bill can pass either house. Elected representatives of the citizenry then have the awesome responsibility of accepting or rejecting the entry of a territory into the Union.

Objections to the entry of Hawaii into the union were of two kinds, physical and political. None of them were serious and many were not even valid. However, much of the opposition came from those who held deep prejudices against 'outsiders' and could not be budged, although a visit by President Harry S. Truman to Pearl Harbor on September 13, 1950 helped bring favorable attention to the islands.

The first obstacle was an old one, that Hawaii was too far away and not contiguous to the other 48 states. Some tried to use this objection against Alaska as well, whose citizens were also seeking statehood in the 1950s. Alaska had been purchased by the US in 1867 and was made a territory in 1912. This non-contiguity argument, however, was fading. Far off places were becoming more and more accessible as air travel became faster, easier and cheaper. Distance as an obstacle soon disappeared as an argument.

Two intertwined objections were anti-democratic and were also beginning to decrease in importance. These concerned the fact that there was no middle class in Hawaii to maintain the economy and that there was a very large Japanese population who could not vote under current rules and needed to be Americanized.[7] However, many of the Japanese were beginning to succeed and join the middle class, a fact that did not please many eastern congressmen.

Other obstacles were rooted in prejudice and discrimination and seldom seem to have been countered by emphasizing the value of Pearl Harbor as a Naval Base or the protection afforded by the Army, Air Force and Marines also stationed in the islands. Many senators on the east coast of the United States still thought of Hawaii as a colony, others remembered only its primitive nature when first discovered. A high profile incident of rape and murder in the 1930s, the Massie Case, had brought unwanted attention to shortcomings in the law enforcement ranks of the islands. The defendants were convicted but were prominent white Americans and were released by a local judge. This gave the impression to those in Washington, DC that law was not being administered properly in Hawaii. These were all excuses, of course, but attempts to reveal corrupt law enforcement activities were not effective even after more than twenty congressional fact finding tours to the islands.

Anti-statehood congressmen also professed to be concerned with the fact that the economy and politics in Hawaii were too strongly controlled by the Big 5.[8] These powerful companies were all owned, dominated or directed by descendants of the original missionaries of the 1820s. It is true that many major businesses, such as sugar, pineapple, transportation, communication, banking and construction were part of the Big 5 monopoly of business and had been for decades.

The fact is, a number of southern senators especially did not want Hawaii to be a part of US domestic affairs. One objected on the grounds that the state of Hawaii, with two senators, would have has much weight in any vote as two senators from New York.[9] It is hard to believe that an elected representative in a democratic government actually put forward this decidedly anti-constitutional argument. Another senator from South Carolina gave a second reason for voting against statehood. He stated that Hawaii was too oriental, too different to ever become truly American.[10] It was clear that distrust of the Japanese lasted many years after the end of World War II, even though they had long since demonstrated what good citizens they were.[11]

Communism was also used as a pretext for opposing statehood. One senator even professed to see statehood as a plot of the Soviet Union to get a seat in the Senate of the United States![12] A full scale HUAC[13] was sent to Honolulu to investigate in 1950. Although many people were investigated, primarily labor unions and the leadership of the ILWU[14], and some accused of communist activities, only seven were convicted. They were released when the committee's tactics were deemed improper by the supreme court. Some people believe that union leadership allied itself with communism only to help the union succeed. Clearly, the influence of communism in the islands was otherwise slight.[15]

Opposition to statehood also came from Hawaiians. One major, influential purveyor of opposition was the *Honolulu Advertiser* directed by its publisher Lorrin Thurston. As an important member of the 'oligarchy' that ruled Hawaii, Thurston often reminded his grandfather's readers of his role as a member of the 1898 Annexation Committee. It is clear that he wanted to maintain territorial status instead of allowing statehood because the *haole* elite could continue to control business, labor and the government in the islands.[16]

Pro-statehood advocates tried a new tactic in 1950 and, while they were not immediately successful, the effort was valuable and the result was not wasted. They called together a group of delegates to create a constitution for Hawaii to show that they were ready for statehood. They sent it to Congress, but it did not persuade recalcitrant congressmen. A revised version was used as the basis for a state constitution when statehood was granted.

Still, Hawaii had the premier US Naval Base in the Pacific and the population was far larger than the minimum required by the United States for statehood. The majority of Hawaiian citizens who were polled wanted to be a part of the United States. Against such pressure, statehood could not be opposed by specious arguments for long. Obstructionists could not stall much longer, but because they were members of important committees, they could bury statehood bills for months. They did so in spite of the report of a 1940 Senate Committee on Interior and Insular Affairs which stated, "Hawaii has met the requirements for statehood and ... is able and ready to accept the social, political and economic responsibilities of state government."[17] It took twenty years for that report to have any impact.

Hawaiians realized they put two faces on their land for the approval of the rest of the world. "Hawaii wants to be known as an enchanted land with the exotic flavor of the 'foreign', but also as a place that is as American as a hot dog in a drive-in."[18] Both aspects are essentially true.

Nevertheless, statehood did come about eventually. One major impetus that forced the hand of the opposition occurred in 1958. The bill to make Alaska a state passed congress that year. This obviated the non-contiguous objections. The prejudicial arguments and the stalling actions were also being publicized. They were so petty and discriminatory that the stubborn opposition melted away rather than capitulate.

In March 1959, President Dwight D. Eisenhower signed the bill that guaranteed statehood for Hawaii. Actual statehood was not yet official, for there were formalities to be dealt with, but when word reached Hawaii, spontaneous festivities broke out. This was followed by newspaper articles, celebratory picnics and parades. Even the local Army artillery fired a fifty gun salute to signify the fiftieth state.[19] A bonfire burned on Sand island that "served as a victory torch for statehood."[20] Processions and services of thanksgiving in churches were held and a packed rally took place in Honolulu stadium with bands playing, choruses singing and spontaneous cheering. Most Hawaiians were happy.

Officially, Hawaii became a state on August 21, 1959 with a proclamation signed by Eisenhower. By then, two senators and one representative to the House had been elected in Hawaii, plus a governor and state officials had taken their posts. The requisite installations and ceremonies were held with due solemnity. Hawaii was about to enter a new phase of history. Soon there would be an economic explosion and a radical change the face of Honolulu. The new era would strain Hawaii's resources to the limit.

Another important event occurred in the 1950s, and is now one of the major tourist attractions on Oahu, was the creation of a memorial to USS *Arizona*. It received its present form after a long process of discussion that focused first on a memorial to all the men who fought in the Pacific war. During the war, in 1944, a shrine to American service men and women had been erected in the Pearl Harbor Navy Yard. It listed the names of Americans already lost and, as the war continued, new names were added. The 20 foot high memorial stood between a giant war map and a billboard that showed war bond purchases of Pearl Harbor workers, both Navy and civilian.[21]

The Pearl Harbor Memorial Trust was also established before the war was over. It was to acquire land, and presumably raise money, for a memorial to the men who fought in the Pacific War. To be known as the Pearl Harbor Memorial, it was to be erected after the completion of hostilities.[22] Many prominent people were asked for suggestions as to the form the memorial should take and the ideas submitted were varied. Some suggested a memorial garden or a large carefully designed park with space set aside for individual memorials. Others wanted an amphitheater, civic center or public auditorium to be used for spectacles, conventions and pageants. Some wanted a simple memorial dedicated especially to the dead of Dec. 7, 1941 and others suggested a chapel in Pearl Harbor containing a mausoleum. One even suggested a visible memorial on Red Hill.[23]

In 1949 a commission was set up to raise funds for the war memorial, though the trust had been in place for several years. The next year, the focus of the memorial efforts began to center on USS *Arizona*. Admiral Radford, CINCPAC, ordered a flag to be flown on a pole erected on the aft mast of USS Arizona, which had been sunk in the Pearl Harbor attack. The superstructure of the ship was still visible above the water at Pier F-6 on Ford Island. This flag was to be raised and lowered every day.[24] These ideas and actions were soon to come together and meld into an effort to create a permanent memorial.

Several plaques were installed near the sunken ships on Ford Island in the 1950s, namely on USS *Arizona* and USS *Utah*. In 1955 the Naval Club of the United States put up a ten foot high basalt stone, with a plaque honoring the victims of the Pearl Harbor attack. It still stands on Ford Island at the edge of the water near the site of the devastation.

Five years after the end of WW II, the United States, and its prime Pacific territory were plunged into another war, this time in Korea. On Sunday June 25, 1950, Pearl Harbor received the news that the North Korean Army had attacked South Korea across the border. This war which began officially in September of 1950 and was conducted by the United Nations, brought the military to the forefront in Hawaii again. No aspect of the war took place outside the peninsula of Korea, but much of the personnel and material flowed through Hawaii. Technically it was a 'police action' waged by as many as sixteen nations of the United Nations contributing personnel and equipment to the effort. The US Navy was called upon to supply a major portion of transportation, repair and supply facilities for these forces. Naval, as well as Army strength, had been cut in half after World War II, but there were still enough ships and personnel available to send to Korea in the first month of the war. Navy and Marines from Pearl Harbor supplied a third of the operating aircraft during the conflict.[25] Military expenditures in Hawaii in 1950 alone were $265 million.[26]

Security regulations were tightened in Pearl Harbor as soon as the nature of the conflict was understood. Visits to any ship by any civilian were suspended, except for those people with valid passes. A task force was quickly organized around the carrier, USS *Philippine Sea*, which carried a complement of F9F jet fighters.[27]

"Like the mythical Phoenix bird, Pearl Harbor has risen out of its ashes of December 7 a decade ago to become once again one of the nation's major bastions."[28]

So begins a story read by many Hawaiians in a September 18, 1951 newspaper. They were assured that there were 80 ships in Pearl Harbor, including USS *Iowa*, the biggest battleship in the fleet. USS *New Jersey* was already in Korean waters and *Iowa* might join her soon, though the Navy would not confirm this. *Iowa*'s deck logs show her steaming to Pearl in 1952, presumably to continue to Korea. Later she went to Yokosuka, Japan. She was moored in Pearl Harbor in October at Berth Baker 1.[29]

It was reported at the same time that sixteen submarines were in Pearl Harbor and a similar number were prowling Korean waters. A number of cruisers and destroyers were also in Pearl, some used for training, some being repaired in the shipyard.

Pearl Harbor had particular significance as a ship repair facility, refueling and supply center during the Korean conflict. The US Navy was involved in many areas of Asia during those years including providing protection of Formosa (Taiwan) where Chinese Nationalists had settled after fleeing the Chinese Communist take over of China the year before. These operations often used the various facilities at Pearl and kept them humming.

President Harry S. Truman came to Hawaii in October of 1950 on his way to Japan to confer with General MacArthur about the strategy of the Korean War. Truman spent a day touring facilities in Pearl Harbor, to the delight of civilian and naval personnel alike. By January of 1951, shipyard workers were operating under a workload that was twice as heavy as it had been the previous year. Twice as many men were engaged in overhauling ships, making adjustments and repairing tons of ship's equipment.[30] There were 7,000 civilian employees again by that time, the first time it had approached that level since the end of World War II.

Pearl Harbor facilities were used by others, not just the US Navy. In 1952, a British ship, *SS Linaria*, was brought into the Pearl Harbor dry-dock to have repairs made to her propellers. About the same time the US President liner, *President Wilson*, had repairs made to her rudder and shaft.[31]

President-elect Eisenhower came to Pearl Harbor on the heavy cruiser USS *Helena* in 1952, returning from a tour of Korea. An honor guard, hula troupe and the Navy band were on the dock to entertain him after arrival ceremonies were completed.[32] On June 16 of the next year, the mine sweeper USS Doyle, underwent an unusual overhaul at Pearl Harbor. She was fitted out to look like the ill-fated USS *Caine* for the filming of the movie, *The Caine Mutiny*. Another Hollywood/Pearl Harbor connection occurred when USS *Hewell* was selected to be the ship featured in the movie, *Mr Roberts*.

The Korean conflict ended with a truce on July 27, 1953. After three years of bitter fighting, neither side won nor lost and the frustration of fighting such a war was glaringly apparent to all. However, the value of maintaining readiness in all fleet facilities was clear. Shortly after the truce, a newspaper report in Honolulu was headlined, "Pearl Harbor 12 years 'after'. 'Sitting Duck' for an Enemy"[33] . Reporter Jack Burby complained that the Naval Base was more vulnerable to invasion or a sneak raid than it had been twelve years before. Radar is ragged, he said, there is no anti-aircraft and no interceptor planes within 2000 miles. According to the reporter's exaggerated rhetoric, on December 7, Japanese planes had to penetrate a radar screen, fly through flak, and dodge US fighter planes. In truth no one could interpret the images seen on the mobile radar station that had been set up near Kahuku on Oahu. The flak was minimal on December 7, 1941 as few units were active and skeleton crews were on duty. And on that Sunday morning, only two American planes got off the ground, from the Haleiwa airfield, to do any damage at all.

The point of the exaggeration was obvious - it can happen again and Pearl Harbor is unprepared. No one believes Pearl Harbor will be attacked again and "it is clear that the US government is blind to its importance", the article went on. In 1953, a service magazine reported on a government listing of the most critical targets in the US needing their defenses increased. The list included Peoria, Illinois, but not Pearl Harbor.[34]

Reporter Burby stated that US defenses reside with our ships which are now based in Yokosuka, Japan and Okinawa. Hawaii is in reserve and only important if the first line of defense fails. As the Cold War grows warmer, Burby concluded, there is time to build up Hawaii's defenses, if the government understands what is happening soon enough. It's time now to put the guns back into the emplacements, to build guided-missile launchers and to cram the airfields with fighter planes not trainers, he declared.

However, he was not optimistic and he was sure that apathy reigned among the islanders. If someone were to bomb Pearl Harbor today, he stated, it would be a milk run. Burby clearly thought that it would take another such event to wake up Hawaii and the United States.

His assessment was overly dark. In the following year, it was reported in a local paper that Pearl Harbor was a modern bastion, a veritable fortress. In these times of hydrogen bombs, jet planes and atomic powered submarines, the paper noted, Pearl Harbor, the largest overseas US naval base, he wrote, is ready.[35]

Whether or not Pearl Harbor would have been ready to repel another attack in the mid-fifties is moot. It is clear that the Naval Shipyard, as it observed a half century of service in 1958, was operating at a peak and was proud of it. In observing the birthday of the facility, an open house was held on August 1 and 2. The 50,000 visitors could tour ships, a museum, a marine railway and could see a few restricted areas by bus. They could take a boat trip to the site of the sunken USS *Arizona*, though there was as yet no memorial. Operators of the shipyard and its workers were proud of the facility and happy to show it off. A banquet at the Princess Kaiulani Meeting House was attended by US Naval and Hawaiian dignitaries.

Pearl Harbor Naval Base became Pearl Harbor Naval Station on July 1, 1955, with Captain Kenton E. Price, USN, as its first commander. It was an administrative change which did not change the role of the base or its components. It merely grouped together certain operations for increased efficiency. Operating under the 14th Naval District, there were to be six major operations at Pearl from then on: Naval Station, Supply Center, Shipyard, Public Works Center, Ammunition Depot and Marine Barracks.[36]

Other articles being written in the fifties show the Navy was determined never to be caught with a large concentration of its own vessels in one place again, especially Pearl Harbor.[37] But there was also a need to keep as many ships and men on site as was necessary to protect the facility and the island. The Navy had to decide how to safeguard the fleet and protect the people of Hawaii at the same time. There were some public questions about how safe they were in Hawaii.

Pearl Harbor was still careful about security in the years after the war, but it did welcome ships from all around the world. Spanish, Canadian, French, British, Italian and Korean war vessels were all greeted with an Hawaiian Aloha. The Spanish sail training ship, the three masted square-rigger *Juan Sebastian de El Cano*, came in with all sails flying and was greeted accordingly. But this was also the time when the Cold War was heating up and when a German ship arrived, it was put under strict guard because its most recent port of call had been a Polish port on the Baltic Sea. Poland was one of the Eastern European countries that had recently come under control of the Soviet Union.

Just mauka of Pearl Harbor lies a military area which enjoys a commanding view of Honolulu and the ocean. Pearl Harbor can also be seen from this area, Halawa Heights. It was originally developed as a Navy Medical Center. On January 31, 1956, the installation was named and dedicated to General Holland M. Smith, USMC, one of the Corp' most outstanding leaders and the first commanding general of the Fleet Marine Force, Pacific (FLTMARFORPAC). Camp H. M. Smith is occupied today by

MARFORPAC and senior officers of the Pacific Naval Command. They are justifiably proud of the camp's namesake and General 'Howlin' Mad' Smith would be proud of them.[38]

In December of 1957, the first submarine to circumnavigate the globe, USS *Gudgeon*, arrived at her homeport, Pearl Harbor amid a boisterous and proud celebration. Leis were dropped on her from helicopters, fireboats sprayed both the sub and many of those gathered on the dock. Hawaiian musicians played 'Aloha Oe' and a Navy Band played 'Around The World In Eighty Days'. The ship had begun her epic journey in July and steamed over 30,000 miles. The event was historic, but to those who had been separated from their loved ones, it was a homecoming never to be forgotten.[39]

Military Personnel and dependents constituted one quarter of the total population in Hawaii in 1957.[40] The tourist business expanded by leaps and bounds after the end of WW II and again after the Korean War was over. Many servicemen had seen Hawaii during one of those wars and wanted to visit the islands with their families. The Hawaii Visitor's Bureau began this new era of promotion with a million dollar budget. The war had changed the Hawaiian economy from primary dependence on sugar and pineapple to a reliance on tourists and the military.[41] Hawaii's million dollar fishing industry had been halted and almost destroyed by the war.

The Matson liner *Lurline* was back in the passenger business by the spring of 1948 with a $19 million overhaul after her wartime service and was again operating as a luxury liner. American President Lines also resumed cruises in the Pacific that year. The *Lurline* was greeted on her first trip, as so many tourists to Honolulu had been, with a lei that was hung on her bow. Unlike those given to tourists, however, the lei for the *Lurline* was made of orange-yellow crepe paper and was 80 feet long.[42]

But most important, at least for the future of the tourist business in Hawaii, scheduled air service began in August of 1948. Jets arrived with statehood in 1959. Qantas from Australia has the distinction of landing the first jetliner at the Honolulu Airport on June 30, 1959. A champagne luncheon for 350 guests was held to commemorate the occasion, complete with an ice sculpture in the form of a kangaroo for a centerpiece.[43] Everyone realized what an important occasion this was.

By 1959 there were fifty thousand armed forces personnel on duty in Hawaii and more than $400 million was spent in the islands on military and civilian workers pay, allowances and purchases. The military was in Hawaii to stay.

The Pacific Command of the US Navy is the largest military command in the world, covering 85 million square miles. US forces, afloat or ashore in the Pacific, operate under the commander in chief of the Pacific, CINCPAC, a full admiral who is stationed at Pearl Harbor. COMUSPACFLT, commander of the US Pacific Fleet, is a full admiral and overall commander based at Camp Smith adjacent to Pearl Harbor.

The civilian area of Hawaii changed after the war as well. The population became more urban and there was a gradual decrease in the power of the 'Big 5'. Trade and wealth were being enjoyed by other companies and by Americans of oriental ancestry who had not had previous opportunities to succeed in this area.[44] Hawaii was maturing. Labor Unions became more powerful and monitored the fairness of wages and working conditions. But the biggest, most important civilian industry was soon tourism. Centered at Waikiki in the thirties, it began to spread to outlying islands in the fifties.[45]

Regard for ancient and traditional Hawaiian culture reached a low point during World War II. In the fifties, it was on the rise again, in conjunction with tourism, triggered by several events. One of these was 'Aloha Week', instituted in 1947 to draw tourists and promote Hawaiian culture at the same time.[46] It publicized traditional Hawaiian ceremonies, ancient sports, dance, song and religious festivities. Even the Navy took part in the celebration. Many events took place at a replica of a Hawaiian village constructed in Ala Moana Park.

A re-enactment of a festival given by King Kalakaua at the Iolani Palace in 1888 was part of the celebration. Much of the substance that made this commemoration possible came from newly discovered material, voice recordings of language, radio-carbon dating of archaeological discoveries and newly found and restored artifacts. This information was gathered by professionals, many of whom were from the Bishop Museum. When the original basalt ~castle' was built by Charles Bishop in 1889, the intent was to preserve and display cultural treasures of Hawaiian royalty and chiefs. Soon the museum staff began to investigate natural history and make archaeological surveys of the islands. As part of their operations, they also preserved a great deal of the extant cultural traditions of Hawaii and the South Pacific.[47]

The Polynesian Cultural Center was established by the Mormon Church on Oahu in 1963 and there has been a recent resurgence of the cultural work of the Bishop Museum. On the big island of Hawaii, an historic *heiau* site was restored and opened as a National Historic Landmark in 1961. It has the lovely Hawaiian name *Pu'uhonoa o Honaunau*. Many areas in the 'Place of Refuge' have been restored by the National Park Service. In doing so they have discovered more information about how ancient Hawaiians lived and worshipped.[48]

The rebirth of interest in Hawaiian culture was also the beginning of respectability for Hawaiian studies as an academic discipline. The recreation of a voyaging canoe, *Hokule'a*, and its voyage to Tahiti in the late 1970s, also gave it publicity. This cultural renaissance of the Hawaiian past, its music, song, dance, chants and ceremony, became an important aspect of tourism. One demonstration of this new respect was visible at the dedication of the site chosen for the new USS *Arizona* Memorial visitor center. On the program was the pastor of Kawaiahao church in Honolulu who blessed the site by sprinkling it with green Hawaiian Ti leaves. In October 1980, newspapers showed dignitaries draped with leis taking part in the ribbon cutting celebration. By the 1980s, many public ceremonies in Hawaii include lei draped dignitaries, songs, chants, dances and even prayers.

The fifties were in many ways a new beginning for Hawaii. The Navy Base was a part of the United States and Navy activities were of prime importance to US defense. Hawaii was located in the center of an area that began to attract the attention of the world, the Pacific Rim. Statehood also signaled a new phase for Hawaiians with ancient ancestry, for Orientals and those of other ethnic groups, and for those with *haole* ancestry. All were now citizens of the newest state of the United States.

Chapter 30 - Challenges

The people of the new state were euphoric, but faced some serious decisions. Many of these affected the US Navy in Pearl Harbor and other installations in the Hawaiian Islands. These challenges were those of nature, nuclear propulsion, civil changes, TV, and the seemingly endless Cold War.

All over Oahu, and especially in Honolulu, adjacent to Pearl Harbor, there was an eruption of new buildings. New offices, apartments, large condominiums, magnificent hotels, and expansion of the University of Hawaii at Manoa just a few miles from Pearl. Those few miles to anywhere on the island seemed to become shorter with the installation of arterial highways across the island and around the Diamond Head end. For a short time the facilities outgrew the need, then, like an onrushing train, traffic increased and the highways became choked each morning and evening.

Oahu has a limited amount of land and the value of every parcel of land shot upward drawing many potential buyers. People also became concerned with the effect the Navy was having on Pearl Harbor. These problems were slow in building, but were soon being brought to the attention of Hawaiian residents, citizens and visitors. Solutions were slow in coming, many of them taking years, even decades, to show any appreciable progress. Meanwhile, the Navy was undergoing considerable consolidation of its functions, especially in the Public Works Center. The public works departments of several commands, eg NAS, SUPCEN, SUBASE, MARBAR, etc., were all assigned to the Naval Public Works Center. This philosophy was reiterated later in a program called 'regionalization'. In 1967 control of PWC was shifted from 14th ND to COMNAVBASE.

Two factors brought Hawaii closer to the mainland, jet aircraft and television. Jets brought an increasing number of tourists, not only Americans from the mainland US, but newly affluent Japanese as well. Hawaii had activities which were naturals for TV. Surfing contests, the Hula Bowl, played in the new Aloha Stadium practically on the Pearl Harbor premises, and movies made in the islands all caught the interest of people around the world. The cycle of such activities drawing more tourists and vacation residents who, in turn, needed more space, continued. Unfortunately, the paradise of Hawaii also saw increases in crime, traffic, and other urban ills. In cooperation with the Navy personnel at Pearl and other USN facilities, the Hawaiian government tackled the problems head-on. Such problems are never totally solved, but the Navy and the state of Hawaii have worked together remarkably well.

Nature conspired to add to Hawaii's woes when, in February of 1960, Mount Kilauea erupted and destroyed the town of Kapoho on Hawaii, the 'Big Island'. That same year, a terrible tsunami, or tidal wave, struck the city of Hilo, also on the Big Island. Fifty-seven people died. Although these calamities did not directly affect the Navy, several Navy and Marine units sped to the scene to assist civilian agencies coping with the disasters.

In July of 1960, a most remarkable event occurred. From the submarine USS *George Washington*, the Navy's first successful undersea firing of a Polaris rocket took place. This capability enabled the US Navy to effect force while deployed in areas where land bases were not available. For such deployment, the center of the Pacific Ocean and gateway to the Indian Ocean was Pearl Harbor.

The Navy was very security conscious about these new, nuclear powered subs. During the fall of 1960 an amateur photographer, Fraser Howe, drove into Pearl trying to find the location of a surfing contest. He arrived at the main gate during rush hour and was waved through. He took some casual pictures around the base and returned to his hotel to have the pictures developed. The next thing he knew, he got an urgent call from a Navy lieutenant asking him to return to the base. Then came a knock on his door. It was the Honolulu Police. Howe called the FBI and willingly surrendered his film. No charges were made, but he was severely warned and "was still shaking" hours later.[1] There is no record of what happened to the guard who let Howe onto the base.

Ford Island had been placed on a stand-by basis in 1949. In 1962 the island was turned over to the Naval Base and the Naval Air Station was decommissioned.[2]

In the 1950s, the 'nukes', the colloquial term for nuclear powered ships, joined the Navy to stay. The first nuclear powered submarine, USS *Nautilus*, was launched on January 21,1954 and was soon followed on July 14, 1954, by the launching of the USS *Long Beach*, the first surface warship with nuclear propulsion. Then, on September 24, 1960, the nuclear powered aircraft carrier *Enterprise* joined the fleet.[3] Also, in 1954, the 14th ND HQ Shops Department (which had been the Shops Division since 1952) became the Naval Public Works Center, Pearl Harbor.

The year 1958 was a significant one for the submarine force of the US Navy. In July of that year the world's first nuclear powered submarine, SS *Nautilus*, arrived at Pearl Harbor for a two-month tour with the Pacific Fleet. Then in October, USS *Sargo*, the Pacific Fleet's first nuclear sub reported to her new homeport, Pearl Harbor. Finally, in November, USS *Grayback* arrived. She was the first submarine specifically designed to launch guided missiles.[4] She was followed the next year by USS *George Washington*, the first sub armed with Polaris missiles to enter Pearl.[5] Soon nuclear ships were making regular calls to Pearl and some were homeported there. Fear usually goes hand-in-hand with ignorance. Consequently in the sixties several demonstrations were staged, protesting the proximity of these nuclear power plants and explosive devices. In April of 1961 Rear Admiral James M. Farrin, a key figure in the Navy's Polaris program was posted as Commander of the Shipyard which gave credence to the suspicion that soon nukes would be stationed at Pearl. The Navy worried about the critical shortage of qualified seamen to man the new ships and workmen to service them. The civilians who lived nearby worried about the presence and containment of the nuclear devices.[6] The presence of ballistic missile submarines was confirmed on February 13, of the next year.[7]

The arrival of nuclear power brought some interesting activities to Pearl Harbor. Tiny Laulaunui Island was the site of a series of medical experiments on the effects of radiation on the eyesight of monkeys. A grant was obtained which entitled the experiments to be conducted for five years. Several hundred Douroucouli monkeys were brought to the island.[8]

Seven thousand miles southwest of Pearl in Southeast Asia, the communist government of North Vietnam was defying the United Nations' demand to withdraw from South Vietnam. This 'Police Action' had become a war. The situation had so deteriorated that Presidents Eisenhower and then Kennedy decided to show force in the area by deploying ships from Pearl Harbor. Admiral Harry D. Felt patrolled the Tonkin Gulf with a carrier task force and sent the carrier *Coral Sea* to the Gulf of Thailand accompanied by a Marine battalion. As more ships and supplies deployed from Pearl, 1,500 Marines landed, unopposed, and then proceeded to the border between Thailand and Laos.[9] These were the early stages of a long, ugly, divisive war. Pearl Harbor again became the arsenal and staging center for the Southeast Asia conflict. The Navy, only recently drawndown, had to increase recruiting efforts, the Shipyard hired more workers, and new warehouses were built. The perpetual dredging continued. Pearl maintained its four functions: ship repair, refueling, reprovisioning and a place of refuge.

Many local citizens were not happy with the Vietnam War nor the Navy's presence in Pearl Harbor. Protests were frequent. So frequent, and sometimes violent, that vehicles bearing a 'Peace' symbol were barred from the Naval Base. Rear Admiral Donald C. Davis Commandant of the 14th Naval District, banned the symbols because, "they might be a cause of possible violence". He referred to the abusive and obscene statements printed on barracks and other structures by visiting civilians. He allowed, however, that a bumper sticker with the word 'Peace' on it would be acceptable.[10]

At the Submarine Base in Pearl, two new ships arrived on the scene. Submarine Rescue Vessels *Coucal* and *Greenlet* stood constantly ready and prepared to rush to the rescue of any stricken sub. They were also equipped for salvage operations with deep sea divers, towing equipment, and rescue chambers.[11] As one enters Pearl Harbor from any direction, one of the first structures that catches the eye is the Submarine Escape Training Tower. Built in the early 1930s, it stands over 130 feet tall and holds 280,000 gallons of water. There are three escape locks which duplicate those on a submarine, located at depths of 18, 50, and 100 feet. Two recompression chambers are located near the tank, one at ground level and one at the top of the tower. These chambers are used in case someone has gone too deep, stayed too long, or come up too quickly. While these chambers are seldom required by the carefully observed training sailors, many amateur civilian divers have been rushed from local accidents to the life-saving chambers for resuscitation and a healthy return to the world above the sea. The safety record of the training program is remarkable; by 1962 there had been 483,000 ascents with only three fatalities.[12] The tower was used until 1982.

The 1941 attack on Pearl Harbor was an important event in the history of the United States as well as of Hawaii. To commemorate this and other such events, as early as 1949 the Territory of Hawaii had established the Pacific War Memorial Commission. Its job was to plan and raise funds for the design and erection of war memorials. By 1961, the new state of Hawaii, the US Congress and private donations had accumulated enough money to make the memorial a viable project. The USS Arizona Memorial was dedicated on Memorial Day 1962.[13] The ship itself is a war grave as well as a naval memorial.[14] Another distinction should be made, that is, while the ship's bell and the plaque are mounted on the wall of the war memorial to commemorate the ship, the memorial structure itself stands, "in honor and commemoration of the members of the Armed Forces of the United States who gave their lives to their country during the attack on Pearl Harbor, Hawaii, on December 7, 1941".[15]

Meanwhile, Pearl Harbor in general and USS *Arizona* in particular were recognized as important on a federal level. A report to the National Park Service by Regional Historian John. A. Hussey on April 16, 1962 described the history of the location, current use by the US Navy, and recommended acceptance as a historic site.[16] The harbor was designated a National Historic Landmark on June 28, 1965. At a ceremony at the USS Arizona Memorial Boat Landing, a bronze plaque was dedicated by A. Clark Stratton, Assistant Director of the Department of Interior's National Park Service.[17]

Thus began an exceedingly complicated movement toward recognition as a historic district some ten years later. The criteria for qualification are numerous and responsibility assumed by the US Navy was impressive.

The Naval Base Commander and his staff have many other responsibilities besides the memorial. Usually 'security' is thought of as awareness of enemies from outside the base, but sometimes the enemies are among the trusted employees and contractors at the naval base. Such an incident occurred in 1968 when a scheme was devised and operated by a company named East Bay Auto Supply, Inc. The officials of the company bought personal goods and billed the Naval Shipyard through the company with false invoices. Before discovery, the amount stolen was $2.7 million. The culprits were sentenced from one to seven years and fined from $25,000 to $200,000.[18] Sometimes there are devils even in paradise.

This book is about the history of the US Navy in Pearl Harbor. The reader may be interested in reading some of the colorful and technical record of a typical ship's entrance into the harbor. Following are some excerpts from the deck log of USS *Mars* as she entered Pearl Harbor in 1964:

> "Tuesday 8 September 1964
> 0955 Pilot boat alongside to port.
> 1000 Pilot Captain Taylor came aboard.
> 1001 Pilot took the con. Set special sea and anchor detail.
> 1112 Secured the special sea and anchor detail.
> Set the in-port watch.
> 1204 Moored starboard side pier Mike, Berth 1,
> US Naval Station, Pearl Harbor, Hawaii, with six standard
> mooring lines doubled and wire preventers fore and aft.
> Receiving fresh water and telephone services from the
> pier. Ship in condition of readiness six. Material condition
> Yoke set. SOPA is CINCPACFLT in Bldg 250.
>   R.A. Barnes
>   LTJG USN"[19]

USS *Mars* (AFS 1) was a supply ship. She and hundreds of other ships and thousands of men and women who served on them were still engaged in supplying the Americans who were fighting in Vietnam.

By the 1960s, the nagging problem of race relations and racial prejudice had come out into the open in the United States. Even though President Harry S. Truman had ordered racial integration of all the services in 1947, the effects of generations of racial discrimination were still seen and felt for decades. By the 1960s, Dr. Martin Luther King Jr. had defied segregation and anti-black laws, mainly in the south, and a new era had dawned. Before this, racial differences had been present, but had usually been hidden. They were seldom if ever addressed in public. The Navy, like the Army and other services, had its own racial turmoil. Since each of the services is a reflection of society at large, they all faced the same racial problems. The Navy's record of dealing with this problem was no better or worse than those of the other services or society as a whole.

The Japanese were, of course, the major recipients of racial prejudice in the Hawaiian Islands. Orientals were looked down upon and originally had been denied the vote. In World War II, some Japanese were interned for a time, but only a few were sent to mainland internment camps.[20] This was not so much racial antipathy as it was fear of subversive activities in the islands. Still, the Japanese were lesser citizens in Hawaii until they proved valuable to Hawaii's business. Racial prejudice was being overcome by pragmatic tolerance.

Many blacks in the service came to Hawaii during the war, as well as many whites from the south. With the latter came the old hatred and antipathy southern whites felt for any black person. Southern whites had actually warned locals that blacks were dangerous animals. Rumors about this race were spread around the islands, and gullibly accepted by many, because blacks had seldom been seen in Hawaii. It is hard to believe, however, that those without the experience of black people, could have been so credulous as to believe some of the outrageous stories told by southern whites.[21]

Black sailors fumed about this spread of racial hatred and blamed southerners for it. "They seem to think we Negroes have no place here of a right to the sun,'" one man complained in a letter home.[22] Some black men from the north had seldom experienced such treatment. They were raised in New York, and were no strangers to street fighting so fists often flew as whites insulted or attacked blacks. In one instance, a black man was attacked by a white. He knocked his attacker down and killed him. Cleared of all charges by a military court, the incident established the right of Blacks to self-defense.[23]

There was a attempt among southern white sailors to avoid saluting black superiors. Their commanding officers would not tolerate the insolence as this action mocked the military system. Several issued orders to their subordinates to eliminate causes of discord and present a united front. Their motive was not always social equality, but operating harmony. There was a war to win. The effort was successful, but only sporadically. Still, every member of a race or ethnic group that experienced discrimination could point with pride to individuals or units made up of members of their own groups. The majority of them had brilliant fighting records and had won medals and awards for valor and heroism.

In the Pearl Harbor Shipyard, where military and civilian workers met, housing was segregated, barbershops were segregated, but mess halls, movie theaters and other public facilities were not. All races worked side by side, with many southern Whites resenting the situation. Many Blacks felt that naval policies requiring integration of facilities were a great improvement over what they had experienced at home.[24]

Other instances of prejudice in the Navy and other services were publicized, such as the Mare Island Mutiny of 1944 in which Blacks fought back against unjust accusations and working conditions.[25] The Civil Rights movement did not arise for several decades, but it was inevitable.

In the 1970s, Admiral Elmo Zumwalt, CNO, declared, "there is no black navy, there is no white navy, there is just one navy; the United States Navy."[26] It didn't clear up all the problems, of course, and there were still very few Blacks in upper echelons of the services. Cadets enrolled in the service academies were sparsely distributed. Still, the numbers and quality of the men and women who fill those places was improving.

Lest the reader think that Blacks or Japanese are the only groups so set against, there is the vivid illustration of the Naval Academy yearbook. The US Naval Academy year book, called Lucky Bag, includes pictures of all cadets. Early in the twentieth century, it also included several unnumbered pages which were perforated for quick and easy removal. Those are the pages that included the pictures of Jewish cadets.[27]

Racial disharmony had not yet been eradicated in the services nor in society. Other types of dissension also pervade the services, such as religious discrimination, sexual harassment, etc. Some of these were just beginning to become important issues in the 1960s. Such problems still plague the Navy and all of the other services. Complete solutions have not yet been found, but they are coming.

Chapter 31 - Changes

In the 1960s and 1970s, there was an increasing awareness of a topic that affected everyone in the country. Our environment began to be closely studied by scientists who were becoming aware of its importance and investigating what human beings were doing to it. An early publication brought this idea to the attention of Americans. *The Sea Around Us*,[1] detailed the interconnectedness of sea, atmosphere, weather and human beings. The same author also sounded the alarm in a book called *Silent Spring* concerning environmental pollution.[2] Most people were just learning what the environment was, how it concerned them and how we were violating our planet. Courses in the Environment and Ecology, the study of organisms in relation to each other and their surroundings, were instituted at Universities during these years. Students began to specialize in such fields as environmental engineering, marine biology and ecological geology.

By 1970, there was an Environmental Protection Agency to monitor pollution. No state, group or service was exempt from the scrutiny of scientists and government agencies looking into its practices. Hawaii was no exception. Nor were Pearl Harbor or the Navy. One result was the construction of a fully EPA certified laboratory for analysis of drinking water in both microbiology and chemistry.

As oil and sewage spills were reported in the media, and those responsible prosecuted or sued, it was clear that pollution was the operative word and it had to be removed or prevented. For centuries, it was common practice for humans to dump or bury their waste and let them run into any convenient body of water. With the growing world population and more widespread use of land, this became unacceptable. The problem had to be attacked in each local area and there was very little cooperation or sharing of methods, much less of results. In some areas of the world, for instance, fishermen complained about the decrease in their daily catch, but would not admit that their time honored practices and over fishing had caused the decline.

One of the worst polluters was oil. By 1970, Pearl Harbor had acquired a strange looking little boat operated by the Shipyard and known as *Juicy Lucy II*. Starting life as a landing craft (LCM) in World War II, she was converted into a floating vacuum cleaner in 1970. Other attempts had been made to use barges for this job, but they proved to be ineffective. Barges were unwieldy and hard to maneuver between boats. *Juicy Lucy II* had twin engines which made her more maneuverable, and the craft could operate at low speeds. When there was an oil spill, the crew took the strange little craft to the site, anchored her next to the spill and then the crew used a long float line, which the Navy called a snake, to surround the floating oil. With an oil skimmer raft, they forced the floating oil into a sump on the craft with a suction line into a storage tank that held 6,000 gallons. When they returned to the dock, they emptied the sludge into portable tanks which took it to an oil recovery plant in the Naval Supply Center.

When there was no huge oil slick for it to operate on, *Juicy Lucy II* tooled around the harbor picking up debris, from 20 to 30 cubic yards of it on an average day.[3]

Oil was not the only thing that polluted Pearl Harbor. The Federal Water Pollution Control Administration issued a report on September 17, 1970, stating that the City and County of Honolulu, not the US Navy, were the major polluters of Pearl Harbor. There was no mention of radio-active waste in this report, but it showed that sediments and debris were smothering the oysters, which were infected with salmonella bacteria. The state was losing a half-million dollar business because of contamination.

According to the report,

> "If Pearl Harbor was officially open to the public, activities such as fishing, swimming and collecting shellfish would be hazardous to public health because of the high degree of bacterial contamination."[4]

The state ordered the city to stop dumping refuse into the harbor in April of 1 970, and the city complied. However, the waste was then diverted to a Pearl City treatment plant whose effluent was still deposited in Pearl Harbor. Two agencies, the city and the Hawaiian Electric Company, applied for permits to build plants to treat their waste and dump it into Pearl. Enforcement of the rules and changing the old ways have long been serious problems in Hawaii.[5] In a related story, the state was trying to find out the source of the high nutrient pollution in the streams that run into Pearl. Later some of the sources of pollution were identified and corrected. However, as recently as 1996, a Chevron oil pipeline ruptured and spilled thousands of gallons of fuel oil into the harbor. The pipeline was feeding the Waiau power plant. The US Navy was not involved in any way, but the spill and the cleanup efforts did force the closing of the USS Arizona Memorial for several days.[6]

The city and industry were not the only ones obstructing the effort to clean up the harbor. The Navy was not so forthcoming about its activities concerning nuclear effluent as they had been about the way they cleaned up oil. The State Health Department had repeatedly asked the Pearl Harbor Naval Shipyard to give them information that concerned their dumping of radioactive waste into the harbor. The Navy refused on the grounds that the information was secret. They were startled when the information was released to the press in Washington by US Representative from Hawaii, Patsy Mink.

Twenty four hours later, after clearing the release through the Pentagon, a Public Affairs Officer in Pearl released a statement which said,

> "The Navy's continuing surveys and
> studies on this matter conclude that there is
> no health hazard as a result of radiological
> discharges into Pearl Harbor." [7]

They also reported that the procedures used by the Navy to control discharges from nuclear-powered ships and their support facilities were effective and do protect the health and safety of the general public. No proof or methods were made public. The Navy still considered this information classified and no governmental official could be found who had access to specific information on the subject. The Navy and local governments at the time had no program of exchanging information on waste management, whether it was nuclear, sewage or oil.[8]

In 1971, a large fuel oil spill in Pearl Harbor became page one news in the Honolulu newspapers. A nuclear submarine, USS *Dragon*, accidentally backed into fleet oiler, USS *Ponchatoula*, and 16,000 gallons of fuel oil were spilled into the repair basin of the shipyard. The Navy reassured the public that they had it under control and there was no danger of the oil drifting out of the shipyard, according to RAdm Thomas B. Hayward, commander of the 14th Naval District. Most important to many, there was no damage done to USS *Dragon's* nuclear power plant or to the sub's nuclear propulsion system. Water cannons pushed the oil into an isolated corner of the basin and prevailing winds kept it there. The slick was about 60 by 100 yards in size, gradually diminishing as the Pearl Harbor Fire Department poured emulsifier on it. *Juicy Lucy 11* got into the act and helped to clean the oil and debris off the water.[9]

It was an isolated incident, but pointed up the fact that the public had become very interested in pollution, its results and especially the consequences of using nuclear power in Navy ships. That these ships shared this harbor with industry and the public was making all of them more cognizant of the uses of its waters.

In the summer of 1972, it was reported that Pearl Harbor's millions of oysters were nearly all dead. The few that survived were all right, according to the head of the Fish and Game Division, Michio Tukata, and he saw no other dead fish floating in the harbor. The deaths had occurred within a month and were not solved easily because they had no sick specimens to study, only dead ones. The Health department felt it was necessary to notify the public of the puzzling kill and that the cleanup would take some time.

Meanwhile, the Fish and Game biologist remarked that it would stink while they tried to remove the rotting oysters. Later there was a report that the deaths could have been caused by bug sprays. It was a time when DDT was beginning to be suspected in the deaths of many creatures. The incident itself was not of overwhelming importance, except to oyster fishermen, but it shows that environmental subjects were becoming important and that the sheltered waters of Pearl Harbor were not immune to damage. Fish share the harbor with oysters, clams, crabs and mussels and, of course, the ships of the US Navy. Waterfowl have reemerged and can be found in the restricted wetland areas in Pearl Harbor.[10]

By 1972, the Navy was engaged in trying to stop heavy metals from polluting the water. The Shipyard was accused of allowing toxic solutions to enter the harbor, such as chromic acid, caustic soda, sulfuric acid, silver cyanide and copper from naval shipyard shops. What was made public in January of 1972, was that many of these substances were in the storm drains, perhaps dumped there by the Navy or by civilians. A list of them was made public. District civil engineer, Captain Lewis Timberlake, admitted that they were letting the stuff go into the harbor, but that it was something everyone did at the time. A cleanup program had been instituted in 1968. The Navy had built a $7 million sanitary waste treatment plant, though they were still trying to figure out what kind of trucks could safely carry the stuff to the plant.[11]

The decade of the 1970s was a critical time for a new approach to the environment and of changing practices to reflect this new knowledge. The Navy in Pearl Harbor was not singled out for its polluting practices. The same thing was happening to every Navy and Army base, every manufacturing plant and every industrial company in the country. The attention does show how concerned the citizens, the government and the Navy were with the health of Pearl Harbor. It is now known that USS *Arizona* still leaks oil into the harbor every day, but it is deemed to be no threat to the harbor.

A few years later the AFL-CIO was asking the Navy to conduct routine physical examinations for all employees at Pearl Harbor who were currently working on nuclear submarines or had done so in the past. The president of the union, Brian Ho, estimated that 3500 people had worked on the subs since they arrived in 1962. He was concerned about the safety of workers and the efficiency of controls that had been instituted. He wanted the Navy to identify the problem publicly, if there were a problem. The Navy said their radiation controls worked, but they could not prove it.[12] The union President requested, or demanded, as the newspapers reported, an investigation. It may have been merely a ploy on his part, but it showed growing concern about toxic materials as well as ignorance of what they might do to humans. Presumably the Navy placated the union.

A few months later, there was another report that those who work at Pearl Harbor had gone through a monitoring test aimed at exposing hazards they might face from asbestos.[13] Clearly the Navy was trying to comply with fast changing scientific knowledge.

Meanwhile, the Navy was still responsible for the Pacific Fleet and its operations. Fleet exercises had been resumed after World War II and only involved United States' ships until 1971. At this time Admiral Elmo R. Zumwalt, Jr., CNO, arranged to have other Pacific rim countries participate. The event was called RimPac and was an annual event from 1971 to 1974, after which it was held every second year. RIMPAC 1998 saw naval forces from Australia, Canada, Chile, Japan, the Republic of Korea and the USA combine in naval exercises off the coast of Hawaii from July 6 to August 6. Over 50 ships, 200 aircraft, and 25,000 men and women were involved. Vice Admiral Herbert A. Browne, USN was commanding officer. After the exercise debriefing, it was 'liberty for all hands' in Pearl Harbor and environs. It is estimated that the sailors, marines and airmen boosted the Hawaiian economy by $25,000,000.[14]

In 1964, Pearl Harbor had been designated as a National Historic Landmark and was included in the National Register of Historic Places. Along with this designation was an attempt to clarify the name of the place. It is noted that Waimomi was used as a name by Hawaiians, also *Ke-awa-ku-o-ka-momi* and *Pu'uloa*, the old name. In the end the first survey reported that Pearl Harbor and Naval Base were in common usage as legal names.

The problem of being a historic place for the Navy was that it had to continue to operate in supporting Navy presence in the Pacific. This National Landmark had to continue to function as an active Navy Base and that role had to take precedence over maintaining physical facilities with no alterations as in many historic landmarks. Modifications had to be made with great care and noted with detailed documentation. The Navy and Department of the Interior had to follow the Historic Preservation Plan of 1978 and make sure that preservation efforts focused on structures with greatest historic significance without endangering the Navy's primary role as a defensive base. A revision of the plan is due in 1999.

Between September 16 and November 5 of 1977, a survey was made of every building and structure and every facility was listed in one of five categories. The first group covered those buildings that were of prominent historical importance and played a major role in the operation of the base. In Category 2 were structures that functioned as an important part of the base. Third were those of minor importance, the fourth category included those buildings that lacked importance and last were those built after 1953 which were not evaluated.[15] The survey covered all nine of the command facilities that were part of the Pearl Harbor Complex: the Naval Shipyard, Naval Station, Ford Island, Marine Barracks, Submarine Base, Naval Supply Center, Public Works Center, the Naval Magazine at Lualualei and the Navy Publication and Printing Office. The goal was to protect the historic character of the Pearl Harbor area through preservation and documentation.[16]

The key word here is documentation. Changes could be made to the buildings and sites, but careful documentation of changes must be kept. The major unique feature of Pearl Harbor as an historic landmark is its ongoing involvement as a working environment and the careful recording of those changes.[17]

The 1978 survey found 29 buildings of historical importance which fit into category number 1, genuine historic buildings. Building number 1, for instance, was built in 1913 and is now in use as an administration building. The process of change is clear in the history of this building. The original structure has had two wings and top floor added and seven annexes have been built. Keeping these records while the structures are still in use, along with repairs that must be made, is an important program at the base.[18]

Another aspect of preservation concerns historic Hawaiian fishponds. The State of Hawaii nominated *Oki-oki-lepe* fish pond, on the shores of Pearl Harbor, to the National Register on March 14, 1973 and it was accepted in April 10. Two other fishpond-swamp areas, on Waiawa, Pearl City Peninsula, and Honolulu, were brought up to standards to enable them to qualify for National Wildlife Refuge status. This latter was to mitigate the adverse effects on wildlife caused by the construction of the 'reef runway' off shore of Honolulu International Airport,[19] which is adjacent to and just east of Pearl Harbor. Another fishpond, *Pa'aiou*, was nominated but denied. A third on Laulaunui has yet to be nominated.

It was in the 1970s that there was a resurgence of interest in ancient Hawaiian culture. It had been coming for some time, but it was spurred on by the building of a large double canoe by the Polynesian Voyaging Society using old style methods and materials. The publicity gained by the several voyages of *Hokule'a* to Tahiti and back using old methods of navigation, helped to spread these ideas to other Hawaiians. Its impact was scholarly as well as cultural.

Problems other than environmental also plague the Navy. Captain Charles O. Swanson was named to command the shipyard at Pearl Harbor in July of 1972. He presided over 5,000 workers as well as its complex and expensive repair facilities. He was a popular and respected commander who solved several nagging problems in the shipyard. Because some of this work involved nuclear submarines, he was not only under the control of the Navy, but also the AEC, the Atomic Energy Commission.

In May of 1973, ten months after he arrived, he was fired, apparently by the Navy on orders from Admiral Hyman Rickover,[20] who was the head of the naval reactors division at the AEC in addition to his job as head of nuclear operations for the Navy. Some people have pointed to the conflict these jobs could represent, but none was powerful enough to oust Rickover. Union officials and several civilian employees at the Pearl Harbor Naval

Shipyard quickly asked for a congressional investigation into the incident. They claimed that Swanson was removed by Rickover only because Swanson would not follow his orders to fire certain people.

In the 1970s, Rickover was known as 'father of the nuclear submarine' and had by that time successfully gotten the Navy to change its rules so that he could remain on active duty at the age of 72. He had become the most powerful person in the nuclear Navy. The men who rushed to support Swanson pointed out that workers resented the surveillance Rickover ordered of them and that he was known in the Navy as power-hungry.[21] Rickover didn't go to Pearl at this time, but he had a staff at each naval installation which had wide authority to investigate outside military channels and report directly to Rickover. Even though Swanson raised the morale of the shipyard and was honest and careful in his dealings with the union, all of that was unimportant when he would not follow Rickover's orders.

As soon as he heard of the firing of Swanson, Hawaii Senator Daniel Inouye asked for an investigation and Representative Patsy Mink took steps to get a congressional hearing scheduled at once. CNO Elmo Zumwalt also ordered an investigation at the shipyard. Many of those concerned said Swanson's removal was not only premature, and unjustified, but it was just another overbearing tactic of Admiral Rickover.[22] Shipyard employees weren't even a part of Rickover's chain of command. The sole reason for the firing, according to everyone who was interviewed, was the fact that Swanson would not fire some people when the admiral told him to. Swanson saw no reason to fire these workers just because the admiral wanted to get rid of them. All agreed that Swanson's removal was not in the best interest of the shipyard, the workers, or the Navy.

The problem was that if they did not do as Rickover wanted, the Naval Shipyard might not get its nuclear repair license renewed. One day after the shipyard learned that it had passed inspection for the license, the employees and officers learned that Swanson was to be reinstated as their commanding officer.

When the Navy announced that Swanson was to be retained, in October of 1973, it was an amazing turnaround, according to a local Honolulu newspaper.[23] Swanson's retention was the only known case where Rickover's authority was challenged. The reinstatement was temporary, however, and Swanson left the shipyard a few months later. He was said to be going to Pacific Fleet Headquarters and later it was reported that he had to leave the Navy. Chief of Naval Operations, Admiral Elmo Zumwalt in his memoirs wrote,

"The system, alas, does not forgive anyone who takes it on as vigorously as Charles Swanson did. If he had not fallen afoul of Rickover, his ability would almost certainly have won him flag rank, and his Naval career might well have been a brilliant one. The navy also lost much when Charles Swanson was compelled to leave it. It lost his ability. Beyond that, it lost his integrity, a quality in shorter supply and of more worth."[24]

The shipyard continued to operate with a new commander, Captain Henry A. Hoffman, who had been a project officer in the development of the Trident submarine system.

As this fracas was being resolved in the Navy yard, the war in Vietnam was just winding down. Altogether 225 ships from Pearl Harbor had been committed to operations in the South China Sea and were now homeward bound. The Vietnam cease fire was signed and implemented on January 27, 1973. The Cold War, however, was not over and the Navy began to try to define its role in a world with no shooting war, but with a strange non-shooting one. The Pacific Fleet increased operations with friendly and allied navies to ensure freedom of the seas. Its responsibilities expanded to include the Indian Ocean.

Americans were aware of the Soviet Union and its army, its missiles and its antagonism to the United States. They were often not aware of Russia's goal of becoming master of the sea. The Soviet nuclear submarine fleet, largest in the world, cruised everywhere, even in the Pacific.[25] By 1970, the Russians boasted that they not only had the largest Navy in the world but the largest Merchant Marine fleet. And the Soviets had vowed to cover the world with communism, which President Truman had vowed to stop. Hence, the US was committed to stopping communism wherever it reared its ugly head. An author in the early 1970s wrote,

> "In some ways, we are an innocent, trusting, unsophisticated nation, wide-eyed and ready to believe the best of anybody. Hence we first went to Vietnam thinking that we were merely supporting the liberty of South Vietnam against the encroachment of North Vietnam."[26]

By 1973, the US and its citizens had been disabused of this notion. Riots and controversy split the nation as we struggled to get out of the mire. The Navy had fulfilled its job of moving military forces by sea, largely from Pearl Harbor, as well as the modern missions of Naval bombardment and Naval air support. When the war was, over, not won, just over, it was clear that the Navy had to continue its role of protecting the US against enemies, even if we were in a 'Cold War', and keep up with the numerous technical advances necessary to operate new, and more complex equipment. While general naval strength was reduced after the war, naval strategists began to re-evaluate the role and necessary strength of each unit of the Navy.[27]

The Navy that came home from Vietnam was filled with racial unrest, drug use and desertion, much like the society on the US mainland. It was a time of deep frustration for the Navy, and indeed for all services. Enlistments and re-enlistments dropped and warships often had to operate with 80% of their usual crew. The role of the Navy in the Pacific, based in Pearl Harbor, was debated and discussed in a study that was to assess requirements for the next twenty years. All of this was based on defense of the US against Soviet attack and the possible opening of a Pacific front to hit them in places other than those of their own choosing. Naval forces in the Western Pacific were reduced and each ship had to spend longer at sea because of budget constraints.[28]

The Submarine Base in Pearl Harbor, which had been undamaged by the bombing on December 7, 1941, was modernized and made ready for the nuclear fleet. Submarines based in Pearl Harbor had sunk 1750 Japanese merchant ships and twenty major warships in World War II and proved their effectiveness. By 1970, the SUBASE operated in 160 buildings to support a fleet of 56 nuclear and conventional submarines, four rescue ships and three submarine tenders. Almost 800 Naval personnel and 255 civilians were at work keeping the subs in trim.[29]

In 1975, the US Congress voted to include in the yearly budget, $7 million for a new Pacific Fleet Command Center at Pearl Harbor to replace the one shared with Pacific Fleet Headquarters in a World War II bomb shelter.[30] The Navy had not been entirely swept into the push to downsize the services.

The shipyard was modernized in order to keep it capable of properly maintaining and overhauling all major ships of the fleet. Technology was creating changes in ships as well as in maintenance techniques and operating equipment needed constant updating. This included the updating of docks, navigation, turning basins, dredging and anchorages.[31]

Environmental concerns grew during the 1980s in Hawaii as they did on the mainland. Early in the decade local physicists and medical doctors were in disagreement about how to describe accurately the radioactive waste materials found in Pearl Harbor. Cobalt 60 was estimated at three ten-trillionths of each gram of sediment below the submarine docks. Professor Kirk Smith of the University of Hawaii, opined that the levels found were 100 times below the margin of safety. The Navy announced, understandably, that no public health hazard exists in Pearl Harbor.[32]

Not everyone applauded the prospect of a ship bearing nuclear arms, or the presence in the islands of nuclear powered submarines.[33] Those who opposed the stationing of nuclear powered and armed ships in Pearl Harbor went to great lengths to indicate their opposition. Three anti-nuclear activists were put on probation for one year by a federal judge for trespassing at Pearl's West Loch in April of 1982. The judge stated that the anti-trespassing law was aimed at saboteurs. The three activists climbed over the fence in full view of the military security personnel and expected to be seen and detained.[34]

Workmen, who suspected they had been exposed to dangers of radiation, asbestos or arsenic, called upon the Navy to clean the harbor and cease from contaminating it. In most instances, investigation showed no danger to the workers. In 1983 some workers who were cleaning barnacles off pier pilings after a radiation spill in shipyard waters filed a work grievance against the Navy. After investigation of the ambient sea growth, such low traces of radiation were found that might be expected naturally even without the spill. The conclusion was that no safety procedures had been violated and the workers were in no danger.[35]

On another occasion, however, workers were exposed to unacceptably high levels of arsenic. Although men who were removing the anti-fouling paint from the hulls of ships by sandblasting were properly protected, two men who were nearby were not, and hence breathed the sand and arsenic-laden dust. The Navy had already cancelled a contract with the supplier of the arsenic contaminated sand because of similar problems at Puget Sound in the state of Washington, but still had a two-year supply on hand. The dangerous sand was removed, new, clean sand was acquired, and the workers showed no further sign of illness.[36]

In 1986 a large electrical transformer located near the Naval Shipyard cafeteria exploded, spraying PCB over an area of 50 by 300 yards. Captain R.E. Traister wrote a letter which was distributed to all shipyard workers the next day in which he reassured them that they were in no danger of ill effects. He also set up a medical maintenance program which monitored the health of the workers. No serious medical problems were found. The cafeteria was closed and a portion of the roof was replaced. PCB, polychlorinated biphenyl, had been used as a fire retardant until it was banned in 1979. Again, the Navy was in the midst of a phase-out program when the accident occurred.[37] While the Navy's environmental record was not spotless in the 1980s, it did indicate that the incidents were few, not serious, and were responded to quickly and thoughtfully.

A startling idea surfaced in the newspapers on a February morning in 1975. Commander A.J. Stewart, writing in the US Naval Institute Proceedings, had studied the five midget submarines that had been involved in the assault on Pearl Harbor on December 7, 1941. His news, speculation to be sure, was that he thought one or both of the missing crew members of submarine called 'Midget D' could be alive and living in Hawaii today. They could have gotten out of the sub, swum across the Keehi Lagoon, where the sub was found, and melted into the local population.[38] The idea was greeted with skepticism by many who feel that the crews could not have survived the attacks on the five subs by destroyers outside Pearl Harbor on Dec. 7 and 8. The story is fascinating, but it also points out how much interest there still was in any material that pertained to that vivid day in 1941 that changed Hawaii and the Navy.

Another curious story concerns the experimental program that was taking place on the island of Laulaunui in Pearl Harbor's West Loch. The experiments, conducted under the aegis of the Zaret Foundation of New York, had sought to find out how primates were affected by microwaves and radar The experiments were abruptly canceled by the Navy in 1971 after the records of the foundation were examined and it was determined that no useful information had been gathered. Two of the monkeys had died, which precipitated the audit. Originally the monkey's had been amassed to create a monkey breeding colony in 1964 and the Navy had granted a permit for the use of the island for five years. When the permit was canceled, after reports of secret experiments, the foundation moved out, but the monkeys remained. Several Navy men and former employees fed the monkeys until a solution was found. By 1972, there were 130 macaques, 7 gibbons, one tree shrew and two langurs which were contributing to the pollution of Pearl Harbor.[39] In the end, The Navy, with the consent of Lt. Wayne Berry, administrative officer of the Navy Environmental Preventative Medical Unit who had been taking care of them, gave most of the monkeys to the University of Hawaii and the rest to the Honolulu Zoo.[40] Even today almost any incident that pertains to Pearl Harbor deserves ink in the local newspapers.

Chapter 32 - Memorials

The inauguration of President Ronald Reagan in 1980 was a magnificently military affair. The parade through Washington was dazzling and the finale, a rendition of *The Battle Hymn of the Republic*, sung by the Mormon Tabernacle Choir, was thrilling. President Reagan proceeded to carry out his election campaign vows by asserting American determination at meetings with Soviet leaders. His goal for the US Navy was a 600 ship fleet by the end of 1989. He was faced, however, with a depleted fleet, which had been severely reduced by the Carter administration.

Not only did the Navy's construction budget increase, Navy Secretary John Lehman and CNO Admiral Thomas B. Hayward successfully started the recommissioning process for four World War II battleships, the *Iowa* class.[1] They were taken from their 'standby' condition and each was fitted out with 16 Harpoon, 32 Tomahawk missiles and received complete updating of their electronics guidance and communication systems. They also were armed with four of the newly developed Phalanx close-in weapon system (CIWS).[2] Partially because of its terrifying rate of firepower (3000 rounds per minute}, and partially because of the CIWS acronym, this weapon soon became known among the men who used it as a 'Sea Whiz'. Seamen often have slogans embroidered on the back of their coveralls. One Gunner's Mate, assigned to a Sea Whiz mount, bore the slogan, "If it flies, it dies!".

Of these four mammoth ships, the one which had the closest relationship with Pearl Harbor was, and is, USS *Missouri (BB63)*. She had already served in four major wars and made countless port visits and displayed America's Naval might to the world. Her size, speed and new weaponry were impressive to expert and layman alike. During the hottest part of the Cold War with the Soviet Union, everyone knew that there were 'certain death' missiles, located several places around the world, but few people ever saw one. These weapons assumed the role of some fatal, mysterious disease, which 'might' affect us someday. It was not so with carriers and battleships. Every port visit stated in obvious, certain terms, that President Reagan and his successor, President George Bush, had the wherewithal to enforce any American policy or protect any American property or personnel, which might be in danger.

A vast number of groups in Hawaii, both military and civilian, put forth a significant effort in 1984 to convince the Navy to homeport USS *Missouri* at Pearl Harbor. Part of the effort was based on the pride of having such a magnificent ship and her escort vessels at Pearl. Another part was pragmatic, recognizing that it would mean more work for the shipyard, and the expectation of $50 million to $60 million dollars being pumped into the local economy.[3] There was also the historical significance of the 'Mighty Mo'. It was on her deck that the Japanese signed the unconditional surrender documents in 1945 to end World War II. To lobby the Navy and other federal officials, a group was formed entitled Home Port Hawaii. A decision was expected by the end of 1984.[4]

Admiral James D. Watkins, CNO, stated that Pearl was, "militarily the best spot" for the huge ship, but added that housing, schools and other living conditions would also be factored into the decision. He also noted that her presence at Pearl would act as a deterrent to the increased Soviet submarine activities in the area.[5]

The decision did not come by the end of the year. But in June of 1985, it was announced that San Francisco would be *Missouri's* homeport, while Pearl Harbor would receive a guided missile cruiser and three destroyers. US Senator from Hawaii, Spark Matsunaga, spoke of the advantages of having the four warships at Pearl. Governor George Ariyoshi and Honolulu Mayor Frank Fasi concurred. Roy Yee, project manager of the community-government Homeport Task Force, said the decision is, "still a victory for Hawaii"[6] Mr. Yee would be heard from again, concerning the *Missouri*, a few years later, when he spearheaded a successful effort to have the old battleship 'retired' at Pearl Harbor.

A stipulation of awarding the ship to San Francisco was that the city make arrangements at Yerba Buena Island or Hunter's Point in San Francisco Bay for mooring. Long after the decision was made and irreversible, according to many interested parties, the news came that the US Congress had cut the funding for construction. The ship had been in Long Beach, California for four years, and was slated by the Navy to move to Bremerton, Washington, or Pearl Harbor. Senator Dan Inouye and Rear Admiral Stephen Chadwick, COMNAVBASE-PH, said that Hawaii could expect to receive the ship, her escort vessels, 1200 Navy people with their families, and the attendant prestige. The homes for these new residents would be on Ford Island, which would be connected to the shore by a "causeway".[7]

A bridge from the northeast tip of Ford Island to the Halawa Landing had been in the works for several years. The Navy released plans for the bridge on September 13, 1984. It was designed to have three lanes for vehicular traffic and a pedestrian walkway. Initial plans estimated the cost at $32,000,000. Ford Island was, at that time, the headquarters of the US Third Fleet.[8] Considering the $3,000,000 annual cost of operating ferries, the bridge was expected to reach an economic break-even point in 10 to 12 years. Senator Daniel Inouye announced in October that the US Congress had approved $12.5 million for construction of the "causeway".[9]

By 1989, little progress had been made, but during that year the US Senate passed and sent to President George Bush a measure to make 108 acres of federal land, the Manana Area on Waimano Home Road in Pearl City, available to the state in exchange for building the Ford Island bridge.[10]

The swap was supported by Rear Admiral Robert T. Reimann, COMNAVBASE, and signed by the president. The transaction was completed in 1993 under the aegis of Rear Admiral W.A. Retz, COMNAVBASE.

The sunken ship USS *Arizona* had initially been recognized by a temporary wooden platform erected over her midship area in 1950. In 1956 the Navy requested that a committee be formed to raise funds to create a proper memorial for this first major casualty of the war. The Pacific War Memorial Committee created a plan and Congress passed a bill for its construction. House Bill 5809 was signed by President Eisenhower in March of 1958. The Navy was to construct and maintain the memorial." The original plan was to build the memorial with donations and augment that money with government funding. Money was forthcoming, over half a million dollars, from many sources. The most celebrated donors were Elvis Presley, an entertainer, and Ralph Edwards, emcee of a TV program, 'This is Your Life'. A 1961 Presley concert brought in about 9% of the amount needed, a special TV program by Edwards raised 19%. The majority of contributions came from individuals, the Hawaiian legislature, prominent citizens and fund raisers. In the end Congress also authorized $150,000, about 29%, for construction. House Bill 44 was signed by President Kennedy in September of 1961. The oft-repeated rumor that Presley raised the funds by himself or spearheaded the drive is inaccurate and misleading, but continues to circulate.

The design of the memorial was dictated by the position of the *Arizona* and a unique requirement requested by the Navy. They wanted the memorial placed over the ship in the form of a bridge, but not touching it. It also must accommodate 200 people at once and contain the names of all the men who died with the ship.

The first design called for an underwater viewing chamber. This was summarily rejected by the Navy. The second design, by Architect Alfred Preis, was accepted and built by Walker-Moody Construction. It was dedicated on May 30, 1962. It was a prime tourist attraction from the beginning, the most visited spot on Oahu. Boats operated by the Navy ferried people to the memorial and commercial tour boats from Honolulu Harbor and Kewalo Basin cruised around it. The latter could not, and still cannot, land on the memorial itself.

The 1970s saw repeated discussions about memorials at Pearl Harbor. A proposal was made to mark the 30th anniversary of the attack by building a museum and theater at the Ford Is] and Ferry Terminal. Hawaiian Congressman Spark Matsunaga first introduced legislation in the House of Representatives in Washington D.C. for this. After gathering sponsors, he presented the idea to many of the survivors of the Pearl Harbor attack and family members.

In 1972, Warren Sessler, a private citizen announced that he was also seeking support for the idea of constructing a World War II museum at Pearl. He envisioned a 'living museum' with a low profile and plenty of greenery. In

August he publicized the idea of a private non-profit museum that would incorporate a number of the artifacts he had been collecting for years.[12] Later it was reported that he intended to join his concept with those of both Senator Inouye and Rep. Matsunaga both World War II veterans. All wanted a better facility at Pearl to explain the background of the USS Arizona Memorial.

The trouble was that while the simple white USS Arizona Memorial was a "beautiful thing to behold", according to Spark Matsunaga, the dock from which the boats took visitors out to see it was just a dock. For six years efforts had been made to get enough money to build a visitor center, theater and dock on a 10 acre parcel of land near Ford Island in Pearl Harbor. The Navy and the Department of the Interior, of which the National Park Service is one agency, could not agree on who should operate and maintain the facilities. The Navy felt that such a responsibility was not consistent with its primary function nor should a $2.5 million visitor center be built with Navy funds. The Department of the Interior refused to endorse the project because there were so many other projects awaiting federal funding at the time.

It was time to do something. As the number of visitors to the memorial grew, the rudimentary facilities became crowded and the mainland landing spot for the boats was clearly inadequate. Both government agencies were trying to avoid building this center with their own funds. Sessler declared that it would be built even if he had to support it and even it he could not get Pearl Harbor land to build it on.[13] In 1973, the number of visitors per year exceeded one million.

In 1978, an agreement was finally reached, the form of the visitor center was decided and funding would be shared between the Navy and Congress. The Navy transferred the responsibility for building and operating the center to the National Park Service and agreed to continue to supply boats and operators to take visitors to the memorial. Contracts were let and building was begun.

Groundbreaking ceremonies took place on October 19, 1978.[14] The new USS Arizona Memorial Visitor Center was complete and ribbon cutting and dedication of the new facility was held on October 10, 1980. It was the end of a long road, the culmination of the dreams and efforts of many who wanted a tasteful, beautiful facility for visitors that would complement the USS Arizona Memorial. It was a job superbly well done. The Park Service shows a film describing the events of December 7, 1941 and maintains a museum and bookstore on the site. But it is the USS *Arizona* herself that draws the majority of visitors. The gleaming white memorial that straddles the ship is dignified and offers a solemn location from which to view the ship below. One may contemplate the significance of the memorial by noting the names of the men entombed in her hull that cover the interior walls. It is a moving experience.

The visitor's center across the water on Oahu's shoreline is an oasis of tranquility amid the bustling activities of Pearl Harbor. It is accurately educational - neither minimizing nor sensationalizing the events that took place there. The area is peaceful and beautifully laid out with a garden atmosphere. The people who created it and those who maintain it have performed a service for the untold millions of people who visit this place from every corner of the world. It is a visual demonstration of the human cost of war and emphasizes the hope that such a tragedy may never be repeated. The number of visitors per year has steadily grown until in 1998 there were over one and a half million people who visited the site.

Few people are aware that the harbor contains other memorials as well. USS *Utah*, the ship moored on the west side of Ford Island on December 7, was also sunk. Originally a battleship (BB31), she was converted to an AG (Auxiliary Gunnery & Target) in 1931. She was recognized with a temporary memorial in 1971.[15] A permanent pier, flagpole and plaque were dedicated on May 30, 1972. The only previous recognition was a plaque welded to her deck in 1950.[16] Because of restrictions on civilians entering the Pearl Harbor Naval Base and the publicity that the USS *Arizona* receives, the USS *Utah* is less well known. A gallant ship for decades preceding the 1941 attack, she lies in solitary silence, seen by few. Both *Arizona* and *Utah* were mentioned in the Historic Preservation Plan of 1978, but it was not until May 5, 1989 that the two rusting giants were designated as National Historic Landmarks.

Another heroic ship which was disabled on December 7, 1941, was USS *Nevada*. She got underway and was steaming toward the harbor entrance when the officer at the con realized that, if sunk, the battleship would block the entrance for weeks, perhaps months. Harbor Control made the wrenching decision to ground the ship before she reached the entrance. This, and other gallant acts aboard the ship, were recognized on Wednesday December 7, 1983, when a plaque was dedicated at Hospital Point, across from Waipio Point, the spot where she was finally sunk. The 16 inch by five foot long plaque carries the names of the fifty sailors and seven marines who died aboard the ship that day. These numbers include two Medal of Honor winners and fifteen Navy Cross Recipients.[17]

Many unheralded aspects of the Pacific portion of World War II were carried on by US Submarines. One of them, USS *Bowfin*, was launched on December 7, 1942 and was therefore called the 'Pearl Harbor Avenger'. She fought bravely through two wars and was stricken from the Navy List of Ships on December 1, 1971. In 1972, Admiral Clarey and RAdm Lacy approached the Secretary of the Navy to acquire her as a Pearl Harbor Memorial. This started what became the Bowfin's last war, the environmental and fiscal fight to become a museum.

When it was over, *Bowfin* was towed from Seattle to Hawaii, arriving at Pearl in August. No site could be found at first. The Navy League was involved for a time and then a non-profit group was set up to take possession of the sub. She was restored and was finally moved to her present site, near the USS Arizona Memorial Visitor Center and opened to the public on April 1, 1981.

Bowfin was the only memorial at Pearl Harbor which the public can see and tour inside, until the USS *Missouri* opened to the public. It is an amazing experience for anyone who has never been inside a submarine. An instructive tape that comes with the tour explains each compartment and how many worked there and what they did when the ship was underway. By November of 1985, she had been toured by one million visitors. On January 11, 1986, she was declared a National Historic Landmark.

In July of 1988, the small submarine museum was transferred to the visitors' facility at Bowfin Park.[18] The new submarine museum and park is adjacent to the USS Arizona Memorial Visitors' Center and connected by a crosswalk. Both centers are beautifully landscaped. Three quite different experiences await one who visits the major Pearl Harbor memorials. The USS Arizona Memorial offers a solemn area to look down upon the sunken ship and recognition of the men who died there. USS *Missouri* is a gigantic ship upon which visitors are able to tour the weather decks and see some of the restored areas inboard. Aboard (inside) USS *Bowfin* people are able to see the workings of a WWII submarine.

A recent and unusual memorial at Pearl Harbor was dedicated on December 8, 1987. It was on that day, 46 years before, that 32 sailors who had been trapped below when the battleship USS *Oklahoma* rolled over and sank, were rescued by a team of 19 shipyard workers. The surviving sailors were among those who commemorated the rescue and honored the workmen by dedicating a plaque at the Naval Shipyard. The ceremony was attended by Lt. Gov. Ben Cayetano. Rear Admiral R. E. Traister, the shipyard commander, read a statement from President Ronald Reagan, praising the bravery and tenacity of the workmen.[19]

Few people know that Japanese nationals also gave money to help build a memorial at Pearl Harbor. It has 12 acrylic pedestals bearing the names of the ships sunk on December 7, 1941.[20] They surround a fountain with a flagpole near Building 150. The memorial was donated by the Honolulu Navy League and dedicated in 1992. There is another, rather strange, memorial in Pearl. When the superstructure was cut away from USS *Arizona* to allow the construction of the memorial, the removed metal was piled in an overgrown field near West Loch. Although several pieces have been donated to groups around the country, much of it remains in an undisclosed place. Some want the pieces to be sent to various museum, but that effort is still pending.[21]

Events other than environmental problems and memorial dedications were taking place at Pearl Harbor during the 1980s. A new Marine Barracks, Smedley Hall, was opened at Pearl. Colonel M.J. Dube, COMMARBAR stated in his dedication remarks that as a young single officer he had never had such luxurious bachelor's quarters. The $2.5 million structure housed 160 Marines in 54 two and three man rooms. Most of the Marines were sentries. The barracks is named for Marine Corporal Larry E. Smedley, a Marine who lost his life while earning a Medal of Honor in Vietnam.[28]

Near the end of the decade, a treasure was received by the USS Arizona Memorial Museum Association. The work of Tai Sing Loo, a photographer, was presented to the association in the fall of 1984, though the photographs did not reach Pearl until 1989. Tai was undoubtedly the best known photographer in Hawaii. He recorded events from the first decade of the century until his death in 1971. He took thousands of pictures which were sent to the National Archives after his death. In the mid-1980s his pictures plus those of several US Navy photographers were deaccessioned and sent to the National Park Service in San Francisco for storage, copying and cataloging. Photographic archivist Chase Weaver poured through the treasure and found that many were nitrate negatives and some were even on glass.[23] The 25,000 images show the formative years of Pearl Harbor as no other such record does.

Some of the events of the 1980s were not so monumental, such as the establishment of the first fast food restaurant at Pearl. When Burger King opened on October 12, 1982, at Pearl's Navy Exchange, it was the first national chain fast food restaurant on any US military base.[24]

At the time, the Naval Supply Center was still smarting from an embarrassing clerical error involving a discrepancy of several hundred thousand dollars. Their computers showed $800,000 worth of equipment that could not be located, and they had $300,000 worth of material in warehouses which the computer apparently didn't know about. Under the direction of Captain John Irons, COMNAVSUPCEN, an extensive inventory was conducted in the hope that the discrepancies would be resolved.[25] While such embarrassing errors and problems are trumpeted by the press, various commands at the Navy Base were quietly handling millions of dollars worth of contracts successfully and without mishap. In 1986 alone, $73,000,000 worth of contracts for repair and rehabilitation of ships were completed. In 1987 the number was $115,000,000; in 1988 the total amounted to $131,500,000. 1989 saw $162,000,000 in contracts completed.[26] The Naval Public Works Center, PWC, remained under the command of COMNAVBASE, but technical control was exercised by the Pacific Division, Naval Facilities Engineering Command, PACDIVNAVFACENGCOM. PWC command headquarters building is located on a 71 acre tract above Makalapa Gate, across from the Navy Commissary, off Radford Drive.

An interesting and thoughtful agreement was reached by Retz, WA Rear Admiral, COMNAVBASE, and the local governments to set aside a parcel of land for the construction of a public park on the Pearl Harbor shoreline at the end of East Loch. Debates that lasted for decades over naval security, the harbor environment, and public access to naval housing areas were settled and local residents may now take advantage of the opportunity to share this lovely area. The new facility is named Aiea Bay Park and offers a beautiful view of Pearl Harbor and the major memorials there. The first phase was dedicated on 13 October 1998 by Sutton, WG Rear Admiral, COMNAVBASE, and other officials.

Far away from Pearl the Soviet Empire was crumbling. The United States Navy was active in Pearl Harbor and both the Navy and Hawaii were benefiting.

Chapter 33 – A New Century

Pearl Harbor is changing. Its original inhabitants would not recognize much of the harbor today. What were once islands are now peninsulas. What were once marshes or constructed fish ponds are now covered with houses or industrial sections of the Navy Base. But for all those years, Ford Island, in the center of the harbor, remained an island. It too has changed, of course. The 450 acre flat island was once covered with Algeroba trees, rabbits, natives enjoying life, cultivated corn, fishermen, sugar fields and workers, tourists and boating enthusiasts. Later it became an airfield dotted with hangers, a control tower, cement runways and seaplane ramps, buildings and even a hospital. On its flanks interrupted cement piers were built where all manner of Navy ships were moored from battleships to tugboats. Houses were built and occupied in several areas.

Through it all, Ford Island was accessible only by plane or boat. In 1962 it was decommissioned as a Navy Air Field and was designated as a National Historic Landmark in 1964. In 1995, construction began on a bridge that would end its isolation. The Navy had long wanted the connection to the mainland in order to improve access to the island for 120 residents who live on it and for 3,000 workers who toil there.[1] They have had to rely on a ferry service for years and when a major overhaul of the island was planned, the ferries were seen as no longer adequate for the job.

The Navy had to request a permit from the US Army Corps of Engineers to build this mile long bridge and had to get public comments and approval to bring in 51,000 cubic yards of quarried rock for the approach to the bridge and another 30,000 yards of material for embankment fill. They also had to make arrangements for the land. The city paid $109 million for Navy land at Manana and Pearl City and the deal had to be authorized by the government with special legislation.[2] The plan was to build a cement pile-supported bridge 40 feet wide, about 650 feet of it on pontoons with the capability of opening for the passage of Navy vessels as large as aircraft carriers. The roadway would be able to carry two way traffic, and would include a bicycle path and pedestrian access.

Environmental concerns were addressed in the plans as well. Two acres of woody marsh shrubs were removed and were replanted in Honouliuli Wildlife Refuge on Ewa side of the harbor. Stress on local plants and animals was addressed as well. The Navy's studies concluded that the two major species of flora and fauna in the area, sea cucumbers and algae, are reasonably adaptable to "high stress environments and capable of withstanding constant high suspended sediment".[3]

Pontoons are used to build bridges where there are shallow depths, calm water or soft soil conditions. This was an ideal form for Pearl Harbor. Several other considerations were that it not be obtrusive in the harbor and that it should not obscure the nearby Arizona Memorial which is visible from many adjacent areas.[4] The center section of the bridge is a 930 foot long pontoon designed to retract under the bridge. It is pulled by two winches directed from a control house on the south side approach to the bridge.[5] This provides a 650 foot wide opening for ships. This design of the bridge was chosen from suggestions that included a steel swinging-gate bridge, a hinged concrete bridge, a fixed causeway, a tunnel, an elevated bridge, a vertical lift bridge and a bascule bridge. The pontoon was the least costly. It will be used only three or four times a year since most ships can operate in Pearl Harbor without the necessity of circumnavigating Ford Island. The bridge will only be opened to sea traffic when the harbor is especially crowded, as in training sessions or when there are many visiting ships. It will also be necessary when visiting aircraft carriers must leave the harbor during Kona wind conditions.[6] These are especially strong winds from the south that replace the usual trade winds a number of times a year.

The object of this outlay of $80 million was to make Ford Island more useful. At a time when many bases were being closed, Hawaii's strategic location made its continued use and renovation of primary importance. The Navy also built 300 new housing units as soon as the bridge was done and will add 900 more in the future. The population of the island could run as high as 6,000.

This was no hastily conceived idea as planning for such a bridge had been in the works for three decades.[7] It was reactivated when the campaign began to home port USS Missouri in Pearl in the 1980s. The ferry system in place at the time would not have been able to handle the traffic. Even though the decision was made to homeport the Missouri in Long Beach, the bridge plan survived.

Contracts were awarded to Dillingham-Mason, a joint operation of two Seattle based construction companies, and construction on the bridge began on October 1, 1995. It was to begin at the Oahu shoreline just north of the Halawa gate entrance and reach the island at its northeast corner 4700 feet later. Ground was broken on January 10, 1996 with the bulk of the first effort taking place on the mainland at Halawa where the approach was built. Kamehameha Highway was also widened to make way for increased traffic when the bridge was done.[8] Targeted completion date for the bridge was May of 1998.

This bridge "is the key that unlocks $400 million worth of land and an additional $750 million worth of development on it", [9] remarked the commander of Naval Facilities Engineering Command, RAdm Thomas A Dames.

Admiral Archie Clemins, CINCPACFLT, announced on April 12, 1997 that the bridge linking Ford Island with the mainland would be named in honor of ADM Bernard Clarey, a submariner who had been active in the local community after service in World War II and Korea. He was also a former Pacific fleet commander and became Vice CNO in 1973.[10] A dedication ceremony took place in April of 1998 on what is now called the Clarey Bridge. It was called by Clarey's son, Stephen, "a link between the Hawaiian community and the Navy, both of which my father loved and served throughout his lifetime".[11] That day Mrs. Jean

Clarey unveiled a plaque in honor of her late husband who died in 1996. It stands at the beginning of the bridge.[12]

On the eve of the day the bridge opened, more than sixty residents got together for a "Farewell to Ford Island" toast. The bridge as they saw it was an end to the island's special charm and unique tranquility.[13] One woman even called it Ford Island's second day of infamy. A resident of the island, she relished the idea that the only access to the island was by ferry restricted to military personnel, their families and friends. Residents got used to the fact that the ferry had limited seating, subject to a hierarchy dictated by the usual military pecking order. The two vessels that maintained the ferry schedule 22 hours a day also carried all the supplies and repair crews needed on the island. The 12 minute trip allowed socializing and a way to plan your day, said a resident. Both ferries, the *Wa'a Hele Honoa* and the *Moko Holo Hele*, will now be sealed and stored in West Loch.[14] No one knows if they may someday be re-activated.

Other residents call the new bridge a "godsend" after years of trying to make ferry connections. "The bridge will change the community," a mother of a small child who also has a full time job said, "but it's worth it."[15]

The bridge not only replaced a quaint and inefficient ferry system, it opened the island for additional Navy facilities and housing. Driving across the bridge is not yet available to all. It is open only to residents and drivers with Department of Defense stickers on their cars. Drivers also need a special Ford Island sticker to maintain the security of the island.[16] Security of the entire base remains in a top priority position. On August 21, the day after Afghanistan and Sudan were hit with several missiles, all Naval Bases increased their security awareness to "Threat Condition Alpha".[17] Doors that had been left open were not only closed, but locked. Gate guards inspected each incoming car and the credentials of the occupants more carefully, and in some cases, barriers were erected to prevent unwanted traffic.

Crossing the bridge is a new and solemn experience because it affords one an inspiring and remarkably different view of the Arizona Memorial. When USS *Missouri* came in, the view was expanded. The huge gray battleship sat bow on to the Memorial, towering over, but not dwarfing the simple, white elegance of this world famous testament to USS *Arizona*.

Another project was suggested that would link Iroquois Point, on the western shore south of the island, to the Naval Station with access to the H-1 Freeway. A ferry currently runs this route to enable those who live in Pu'uloa, Ewa Beach and Kapole'i easier, quicker access to the base and to Honolulu. Children even take this ferry to school. A few years ago, it was suggested that a tunnel would make life easier for the residents of this area on the west side of Pearl Harbor which is growing rapidly. It is a tantalizing vision unsupported by the Navy because of the enormous cost, problems of security as well as operating concerns.

A number of prominent people who live in Ewa Beach love the idea and work for it. They recognize the two major barriers to a tunnel, the cost and the

Navy's reluctance to have anything go over or under the mouth of the Pearl Harbor. It would cost an estimated 2 Billion for six lane tunnel.[18] Among the opponents of the tunnel was a local editorial writer who labeled the idea "insane". He described the rural aspect of the area west of Pearl and castigated the ridiculous idea of boosting growth and traffic by building another traffic artery that will soon be clogged.[19] That doesn't mean it won't be built eventually, but it will not be soon.

Closely allied with the new Clarey Bridge, and definitely affected by its opening, are plans to renovate and improve Ford Island. Despite its premier place in the estuary that is Pearl Harbor, the island has been relatively isolated from most of the activities at the Naval Base. Access to the island was limited to regular ferry service and a 'Gray Boat' fleet of Navy launches that shuttled between Naval facilities. Only a few people actually lived on the island and the work force there was also small. Three events occurred in the 1990s that led to great changes on the island.

First, the Navy made an agreement with the City and County of Honolulu to exchange land holdings and construct a bridge with the funds acquired. Second, the Navy cancelled the lease on the Ford Island airfield that had long been held by the state of Hawaii. The state agreed to take over the airfield at Barber's Point when the Navy closed that base in 1999. Third, the Navy selected Hawaii as the final resting place for the decommissioned battleship on which the surrender at the end of World War II was signed. USS *Missouri* arrived at Pearl in the spring of 1998.

The Concept Plan for the future of Ford Island was drawn up by a committee that consisted of flag officers from all commands at Pearl Harbor as well as representatives from other groups with interests in the island. Convening in July of 1996, this group discussed the needs of the Navy, opportunities and constraints of development, land use and traffic circulation plans. They created the guiding principles to be used in planning, continued to stress the need for a long term perspective as well as the phase out of incompatible uses. What they created was a plan for an ideal, but realistically achievable island community.[20]

The Master Plan for the island is called "Ford Island - A Navy Place". It creates a working and living area unsurpassed in any Navy installation when complete. The community will include all the amenities necessary for an island environment, but it is important to note that the island will also be integrated into the overall operation of Pearl Harbor.[21] Island land will be divided into three main sectors. The north side of the island, north of the current airfield, will be devoted to family housing and support facilities. The south side will include operational uses as well as bachelor housing. The center will be maintained as landscaped open space with recreational facilities.

The southern coast of the island will contain "Navy Square", a proposed historic and cultural complex adjacent to the island's two most famous residents, *USS Arizona* and *USS Missouri*. This area will include museums and displays designed to create understanding and appreciation of the commanding role the Navy fulfills in the Pacific, past, present and future.

This square was envisioned by the planning committee as a waterfront promenade including a large fountain with a map of the Pacific Rim and related interactive displays. Buildings flanking the square will include historic airplanes on elevators, similar to those found on aircraft carriers, as well as portions of ships, planes and submarines to provide a glimpse of life in the Navy.[22] These museums will be integrated with displays on USS *Missouri* explaining her role in World War II and the role of battleships in general.

Some historic features on the island, such as the control tower, a hanger and the runway, will be preserved. Although such remodeling may change these structures to make them accessible to the public, an attempt will be made to maintain them as close to the original as possible. To this end, a plaque in the courtyard of the hospital where an unexploded bomb fell on December 7, 1941 may have to be moved in the remodeling process. It will not be destroyed. Bullet holes still visible on the concrete runway and inscriptions on a concrete building may not survive. An informal tribute to those who died that infamous day will also not survive. According to the stories of those who live and work on the island, every few days a fresh lei is draped on a pipe where many died on December 7. The donor is anonymous and no one sees new leis being placed. When we visited, the flowers were fresh. No one knows who is responsible for this and it may be a myth, but it is a good story.

It will be a challenge to integrate significant features of the island with the new development.[23] The tower will be restored and fitted with a new elevator and observation platform providing a dramatic 360 degree view from which the entire area can be seen. The historic runway will be preserved as recreational open space and the runway numbers will be retained by planting contrasting grasses. The restored hanger may be retained for recreation or may be claimed for operational use. It could include commercial uses as well in one and two story facilities. The interior could also sustain pedestrian walkways and malls.

The projected cost of this project, as of 2001, was $540 million. The primary role of the Navy is to provide innovative leadership for the plan, like a redevelopment agency that must rely on the private sector to respond to needs and opportunities. A number of opportunities will be presented for public and private participation in the redevelopment of Ford Island. Concessions for services, such as tour boats, marinas, recreation, conference centers, housing and other commercial facilities will be made available.[24] Details will be decided by the participants and the Navy.

Publication of this plan led Navy Times to dub it "Planned paradise, Navy-Style".[25] The mission of the Navy, according to the Navy Times, is to turn 385 acres of old buildings, hangers and an airfield into a viable section of the Naval Base while retaining the sanctity of the Arizona Memorial and creating a fitting home for USS *Missouri*. One of the navy's goals is to change the hodge-podge nature of the current base. "We're trying to reduce problems created during the buildup of Pearl Harbor during World War II when our primary function was to put ships into the fight", said Capt. John Shrewsbury, Chief of Staff for the Naval Base.[26]

Shrewsbury estimates that it will take 12 years to implement this plan and to develop housing for 700 Navy families and 1,000 single sailors and officers. The plan has been praised by the Navy hierarchy and has the blessing of Hawaiians, thanks to Senator Daniel Inouye who made many of the preliminary arrangements with state and federal governments. Implementing this plan constitutes a significant challenge for the Navy and Hawaii that will last into the next decade.

Both the Navy and the Hawaiian people have become aware in recent years of the importance of the environment, defined as the conditions or influences under which any person lives or develops. We all live in two types of environment, physical and social. The physical environment includes water, food, plants, animals and air purity while the social environment is continuing cooperation and mutual understanding between communities, such as the US Navy and its civilian neighbors.

The living environment of Pearl Harbor has changed radically from the time of its formation. When the first Polynesians came to Hawaii, they brought pigs, dogs, fowl, trees, shrubs and edible roots with them to their new home.[27] These were the first in a long line of non-indigenous species that were brought to Hawaii and changed its natural environment. Besides planting new species, these settlers built fish ponds, changed the course of streams, rivers and shorelines. Of course they wisely used the fruits of local plants, animals and birds when they were needed or desired. No one believed that the islands should or could be left as they had been found for it is not in the nature of human beings of any group or origin to refrain from the use of the land just to keep it pristine and in its original form.

By the time Cook found the islands, they had been changed in another way, accidentally. Organisms had been brought to the bays and inlets on the hulls of the earliest canoes to find this land.[28] More accidental introductions of species came with European ships and small boats on hulls and in ballast water, many of which were deposited into Pearl Harbor after the channel was widened.

Intentional introduction of species came in the 1860s with the attempts to culture pearls, and to augment naturally occurring pearl beds. Around that time, scientists became concerned with the number of species that were becoming extinct and studies began on the current status of the waters and the land around Pearl as well as other areas of the islands.

Pearl Harbor was described by Europeans as early as 1820, so there is some historical basis for knowledge of the species that lived in its waters, especially the oysters which interested Europeans. The opening of the harbor by dredging in 1911 brought other species into the inlet.

Recently a study of the biodiversity of marine communities in Pearl was done by the staff of biologists from the Bishop Museum. They concluded that introduced species are few in number and also determined that there is no indication that they are monopolizing or taking over the waters.[29] This is not to say that Pearl Harbor waters are as they were in the beginning, but species that live there today are coexisting without any one strain being dominant or forcing others out.

Environmental conditions in today's Pearl Harbor are being studied with great concern by the Navy as well and play a major part in shipboard routine and the planning and execution of all operations at sea. Former CNO Frank Kelso stated recently,

> "Protection of the natural environment is mission imperative... Environmental protections and mission performance are inextricably linked."[30]

In 1996 Congress enacted a law at the request of the Navy that made the Navy a co-regulator with the EPA concerning some vessel discharges. To comply with this, the Navy and the EPA are developing pollution standards that will apply to naval vessels. These will supercede state and local requirements in the future. It is not the first such work the Navy has done. In the past few years, they have addressed environmental planning, encouraged public involvement, studied endangered species, especially marine mammals and taken care with coastal management.

Some of these areas especially concern the Navy when it uses sonar or other systems that project underwater noise from ships. Such noise can be a form of mammal harassment, according to the Marine Mammal Protection Act. The interpretation is still without a solution.[31] The end result will not be seen until well into the next century, but the Navy has been alerted to take note of these areas, to address local issues and coordinate with the concerns of the public.

In another area directly affecting the Navy, there have been oil and sewage spills in the harbor. One recent episode that did not originate with the Navy actually closed access to the Arizona Memorial for three days. This was a 25,000 gallon oil spill when an 8 inch pipeline, owned and operated by the Chevron Oil Company, broke and oil leaked onto the Pearl City Peninsula and into the waters of Pearl Harbor. The Navy immediately restricted traffic in the harbor to prevent ships from entering or interfering with the cleanup. This fuel oil is persistent and the public was warned not to fish or take crabs from the water until it was announced that it was safe to do so. The state health department reported that there was no immediate effect on people or wildlife in the area,[32] but the effect on sea life will be subject to long term study. The Chevron Company paid for the cleanup. This was but one of many such episodes, some private and some commercial, some solely the Navy's responsibility. Despite strenuous efforts to prevent such occurrences, it will not be the last.

Many fish thrive in Pearl Harbor. The area is home to many types of fish; such as *aholehole* (flagtail), *awa* (milkfish), *awa'aua* (ladyfish), *kaku* (barracuda), *o'opu* (gobies), and *papio* (jacks), as well as baitfish and anchovies. Fishing boats with special permits enter regularly to catch these fish. Oysters disappeared from the harbor a century ago, but recently clams and mussels, as wells as the oysters, have returned as a result of the improved health and cleanliness of the waters of Pearl Harbor.[33]

Today the water is clear in areas that were once turbid, the coral is returning and biologists have noted thriving oyster beds. The latter include two species which occurred naturally in these waters and one that was introduced in the 1930s. Harbor water continues to improve and the likelihood is that these returning species will do well.

Another area of the environment concerns cultural as well as physical environment. A joint operation was begun in 1994 to study Hawaiian fishponds that once existed in the harbor. The land, now owned by the Department of Defense, contains at least 26 ancient Hawaiian fishponds that have been identified. Anthropologists say the buried ponds may contain material that can be dated as well as information on environmental changes that have taken place. The State Historic Preservation Office hopes that the information that results from this study will make the ponds eligible for inclusion on the National Register of Historic Places. [34]

Cleaning up pollution is a constant and unending task. A hunt for sources of a new contamination threatening the fish was begun in August of 1998. Signs were posted to warn fishermen not to eat what they catch. Clyde Yokota, environmental program manager at Pearl Harbor, said that a two year Navy investigation of sediments and marine life showed elevated levels of some chemicals, such as PCBs, herbicides and pesticides. The problem is that Pearl Harbor, because of its formation and location, is a natural sink and is a depository for such contamination.[35]

A draft report in the spring of 1999 identified the areas that need to be cleaned up and if the parties responsible for the contamination can be identified, they will be required to pay for it.

One thing is clear, the Navy is aware of the problem. It has created committees and program managers to be responsible for the environmental health of the harbor. The various naval facilities have reduced the number of spills from Navy ships, and are working on programs to minimize the generation of hazardous waste.[36]

Environmental issues are not the only concern that are part of the Naval responsibility in Pearl Harbor. Some activities, for example, concern the weather. All Naval personnel, in cooperation with civilian authorities, take part each spring in a hurricane awareness exercise. It begins with a preset scenario, a simulation which sets up parameters for possible wind, tornado and flood damage that would directly affect Navy shore activities in Pearl. Personnel must be briefed on the requirements of the exercise and be ready to respond to simulated conditions that are designed to test and teach established procedures. The object is to be ready to protect ships and shore facilities as well as nearby homes and families from the effects of this destructive type of tropical storm.[37]

The human environment is also important to the existence of Pearl Harbor as well as the smooth operation of the Navy in the community in which it resides. In 1998, the Navy held hearings on a plan to conduct Navy missile testing at the Pacific Missile Range Facility at Barking Sands on the island of Kauai. An environmental impact statement declared that the tests will be held well offshore. The impact on the surrounding environment will be in the form of additional launch sites, installation of sensors and other equipment. Many of the missiles will be launched from aircraft or ocean platforms. Still the proposed decision drew fire, though not from locals. It was from the California congressional delegation which wanted those tests held at Point Mugu on the California coast. This is a part of the social mode in which the navy must operate into the next decade. A final decision has not been made as yet. More hearings will be held. For Hawaii, the range is an important part of the economy, environmentally safe and is vital to national security. That is the opinion of the Navy League.[38] Hawaii's second most important industry, after tourism, is the defense industry and it is a major source of local revenue. The military accounts for $4.7 billion of Hawaii's state economy, or fifteen percent of the gross state product.[39] The League is thankful that the military is in the islands to preserve freedom. The Navy spends a great deal of its budget in Hawaii and is also a good neighbor to the citizens of Hawaii. That's cooperation.

At the opening of the Admiral Clarey Bridge, Senator Daniel Inouye stated that Hawaii's strong ties with the military played an important role in the development and completion of the new bridge.[40]

Another more personal aspect was recently given publicity with an article that began, "It's been said that the toughest job in the Navy is that of a Navy spouse."[41] The Navy set aside a day in April as Spouse Appreciation Day. The Navy *ohana,* or family, recognizes and supports the spouses of its sailors and the tough job they face.

A more far-reaching event occurred in September 1998 when Interior Secretary Bruce Babbitt and other officials signed an agreement with the Hawaiian government concerning federal land. The signing ceremony took place in Honolulu at the governor's mansion at Washington Place. It was the first land transfer under the Hawaiian Home Lands Recovery Act, passed by Congress in 1995. The Department of Hawaiian Home Lands gained control of 586 acres at Barber's Point, when it was closed by the Navy in July of 1999, as well as other parcels all over Oahu. In exchange the government continued to use Hawaiian homestead land on Oahu at Lualualei and at Waimanalo. The land at Barber's Point, formerly a Naval Air Station, will be used for housing, training centers, parks and commercial enterprises, mostly for native Hawaiians.[42]

On a more personal note pertaining to integration with local society, a Senior Chief Quartermaster was once elected president of the Makaha community council, a group which is committed to cultural and economic growth in Leeward City on Oahu. This US Navy Chief, who was stationed at Pearl, instructed training on ships heading for deployment.[43] He operated in both the Navy and the community and had one foot on board and one foot ashore, as it were.

Environment also includes physical surroundings. In 1998, renovations were made to the headquarters building at the Makalapa section of the Navy Base. CINCPAC resides in this building which was built before World War II and includes underground protected bunkers for the safety of the officers. Renovations were made to all decks, new fire escapes installed, and an elevator.[44] It is in this building that Admiral Chester Nimitz had his wartime HQ. His former office now houses a small museum full of Nimitz artifacts and pictures including his oversized desk.

"We in Pearl Harbor sometime take for granted our paradise in the Pacific", began an article by RAdm William G. Sutton, then Commander of the Naval Base. Writing in Hawaii Navy News, his article was entitled "A typical week in the Navy's best homeport." He remarked that on a typical day the Navy supports ships, subs, aircraft as well as sailors and families. He is also proud that Hawaii boasts one of the best retention programs in the Navy, that is, more sailors re-enlist in the Navy in Hawaii than any other port.

On a typical day, various individuals from the Pearl Harbor complex are also at work in the community, he says. They serve as role models for local students, as volunteer scout leaders and Sea Cadet instructors. The Navy is making a difference in family housing areas, serving as members of community associations and just being good neighbors.

A part of that role is playing host to ships and personnel from the navies of other countries. Three Chinese navy warships arrived in Pearl Harbor in March of 1997. They were greeted by 300 members of the local Chinese community and Navy dignitaries. The ships, here on a four day tour, were the first regular ships of the Chinese Navy to visit Pearl. In 1989, a training ship, *Zheng* was the first ship of the Chinese Navy to visit a US port since the Chinese revolution of 1949.[45] The Chinese Navy is the second largest in the Pacific region, next to the United States, but is not a blue-water navy. Their primary task is to control coastal in Chinese waters. China is the largest Communist nation in the world so it came as no surprise when the only decks that were accessible to visitors were topside decks.[46]

The Naval Base at Pearl also welcomed the Japanese Training Squadron to Hawaii in March of 1998. Consisting of two ships, 570 crew, 160 officers, it was on a six month training cruise. Pearl was the first of 13 scheduled stops. Most of the officers are recent graduates of the Maritime Officers Candidate school in Japan. Attending the welcoming ceremonies were the Commander in Chief of the Pacific Fleet, Adm. Archie Clemins, Commander of the Navy Base, RAdm. William G. Sutton, the consul general of Japan, the commander of the training squadron, RAdm Kouichi Furusho and representatives of the United Japanese Society of Hawaii. Hosting this type of visit is part of the US Navy's social and political responsibility.

The saga of USS *Missouri*, (BB 63) her fifty years at sea and her final destination and use, has all the elements of a melodrama including an incredible journey to her final port. Launched in January of 1944, near the end of World War II, she was the last of four Iowa class battleships. In fact she was the last battleship built or that ever will be built. The firepower and ultimate value of the battleship was superseded in World War II by the aircraft carrier and later by various types of long range missiles which can deliver destructive loads farther than the 27 miles a battleship can lob a 16 inch shell.

However, weighing in at 58,000 tons, 887 feet long, powered by four 53,000 horsepower steam turbines, the range and capability of her guns were awesome when she was built. By Christmas of 1944, 'Mighty Mo' as she was affectionately called, steamed into Pearl Harbor ready to do her part to bring World War II to an end. She took the war to the enemy in Guam, the Marianas, Philippines, Iwo Jima, Okinawa and Tokyo itself.

When she entered Tokyo Bay in August of 1945, having traveled carefully through mine fields to get there, her captain and crew were not sure what to expect. Everyone was at his battle station.[47] The Japanese had surrendered on August 15, after two atomic bombs were dropped, and the formal surrender was to be signed September 2, 1945 on the deck of USS *Missouri*.

Thus, though her service in World War II was brief, her place in history was assured. She went on to see service in the Korean War, the Gulf War and took part in a show of force promoting a global naval presence when she circumnavigated the world in 1986. She was a participant in Navy RimPac exercises for the last time in Hawaii in April 1990. She was decommissioned in 1955 for the first time, recommissioned in 1986 and decommissioned again in 1991. On December 7, 1991, she took part in the 50th anniversary ceremonies in Pearl Harbor that commemorated the attack that began the war. Twice she was retired to Bremerton, Washington and spent many years there in mothballs, though there was a time in the 1970s and 1980s when visitors could walk her decks and see the bronze plaque embedded in her deck that marks the spot where the Japanese and Allied Forces signed the surrender document which officially marked the end of World War II. Still floating after six decades of service, she is history personified.

The idea for bringing the ship to Hawaii began in 1984 when the Navy League lobbied the government to homeport USS *Missouri* in Pearl Harbor. In anticipation of the move set for 1988, the Navy built a massive pier at Ford Island, Foxtrot 5. The move did not happen, due to budget constraints and the end of the Cold War, but the idea did not die. An association was formed to bring the ship to Hawaii as a museum and memorial. The consensus was that if she were maintained well, such a move would serve to show the Navy in a good light and bring work and tourists to Hawaii.[48] A host of people worked to make this event happen, but US Senator Daniel Inouye was instrumental in making it a success. A veteran of World War II himself, and injured in Germany, Inouye toiled in the Territorial Legislature before Hawaii became a state and was elected to the US Senate in 1960. He has been the senior Senator from Hawaii for almost 40 years, famous and highly regarded in Hawaii for his support of the Navy. He believed that bringing this particular ship to Hawaii as a memorial and museum would be of benefit to Hawaii as well as the memory of the sacrifices and heroic acts of World War II.[49]

"The Navy found the historic symmetry of two battleships resting in peace in Pearl Harbor too enticing to refuse - the USS Arizona, the symbol of the start of World War II and the USS Missouri, where the formal Japanese surrender took place."[50]

On May 4, 1998, the ship was signed over to the USS Missouri Memorial Association in Honolulu by Navy Secretary, John Dalton.[51] This was a donation contract which was accepted by the association and followed a long dispute with other groups and organizations which wanted her kept in Bremerton.[52] Their argument was that on the mainland, every American would be able to visit the historic ship, an argument that ignored visitors from other countries and the remoteness of the Washington site in relation to the rest of the states. These groups could not match the ambitious and extensive plans of the USS Missouri Association in raising funds, refurbishing the ship, and creating and building explanatory displays. They planned to do little more than maintain the ship as she was.

When this controversy over the fate of the *Missouri* was settled, and plans were made to tow her to Honolulu, several other problems arose. One concerned the necessity of the Memorial Association to agree to get rid of any PCBs that might remain on the 50 year old ship.[53] This was simple and did not constitute tons of material, but the formality had to be addressed. The agreement was made between the Association and the EPA which had to approve of the plan of removal. The approval was forthcoming.

Another problem had taken a back seat to this until the time drew near for her trip to Hawaii. Sitting in Bremerton waters, USS *Missouri* had collected years of alien underwater growth that could be detrimental to a closed harbor like Pearl. Environmental engineers studied the ship and the water, consulted with marine biologists and came up with a solution. The ship was towed to Astoria, Oregon where she sat for a week in fresh water at the mouth of the Columbia River, the closest fresh water estuary large enough to handle her. The theory was that this would kill marine organisms that had accumulated on the hull, especially those that need seawater to live. It was an inexpensive way to clean the ship.[54]

Her stay there turned out to be a publicity boon, a boost for the tourist economy of Astoria, because she drew 125,000 visitors and for the Missouri Association which received donations of over $35,000.[55] Under the footsteps of so many tourists, however, a number of the wooden plugs that are characteristic of a teak deck worked out and were turned into instant souvenirs.[56]

The towing contract was awarded to the tug *Sea Victory* and the battleship *Missouri* was towed out of the river at Astoria on June 3, 1998 at the end of a 40 foot chain that weighed four tons. People watched from every vantage point available. This was the beginning of a 2,300 mile journey across the largest, wildest ocean in the world.

Attention did not falter over the next two weeks. A website was established for those in the country, in the world, who wished to follow the progress of this momentous journey. Posted on the site were tracking logs, detailed maps, position reports, distance run in 24 hours, the condition of the sea and even what the crew was having for dinner. Honolulu newspapers also published details and progress of the ship every day. It was followed by thousands. The day of the arrival, the front pages of both local papers featured large pictures, special sections, diagrams and accounts of service on the *Missouri* by veterans living in Hawaii. Smaller publications and magazines carried the story as well.

On June 21, 1998, the shoreline of southern Oahu, Waikiki and Pearl Harbor were lined with spectators waiting for their first glimpse of the Mighty Mo. The support in Hawaii for this move was phenomenal and spectators waited for hours to see this historic occasion. The arrival of the ship was shown live on the computer website, a rare event.

> "Like a silent gray ghost of battleships past, USS *Missouri* slid around Diamond Head, slipped by Waikiki Beach and was gently guided and delicately docked to a Pearl Harbor Pier."[57]

This was how one Navy writer described the entrance of the long anticipated ship into Pearl. She was docked only a thousand feet from the Arizona Memorial, a little more than a boat length of the *Missouri*. The ship was at the same pier, ironically, that had been built in anticipation of her being homeported in Pearl, a hope that never took place. Now she is there for good. To secure her to the pier, 37 line handlers stood ready aboard the ship and 40 more were on the dock ready to make fast the mooring lines. All were active duty sailors and all were volunteers. It was a measure of the awe and esteem with which the *Missouri* and her presence in Hawaii is regarded.

Once the *Missouri* was in harbor, there were a number of ceremonies to celebrate her arrival and her importance. The most impressive of these was the commemoration of the signing of the surrender at the end of World War II on her decks. This took place on the 53rd anniversary of that day, September 2, 1998. Those in attendance ranged from men who had served aboard BB 63, veterans of World War II, especially those who had been aboard in Tokyo Bay on September 2, 1945, admirals, other officers, battleship sailors and their families and leading Hawaiian politicians.

World War II veterans saw the ceremony from the deck of the ship and those who had been there the day of the surrender were invited to sit or stand where they had been that day. Some shared their memories of that momentous day with the gathered crowd and some included other memories of service on the Mo. Speeches were also presented by invited VIPs, including Admirals Preuher and Clemins, Governor Cayetano, Senator Inouye and Honolulu Mayor Harris. A Navy band played, as well as a volunteer 'retired' *Missouri* band, and there was a flyover of F-15s and a cutting of the a leaf lei that proclaimed that the *Missouri* was here to stay. It was a moving ceremony, well organized, well performed and well attended.

When it was over, it was time to think of what *Missouri* is going to become. Turning a warship built for battle into a museum with interactive exhibits is no small task and planners have been discussing it for years. The current plan is to open a number of her decks for visitors plus the engine room, mess decks, bridge and CEC (Combat Engagement Center).[58] Included will be a number of historical displays, with reader boards, information on the ship herself as well as her weapons, and a special display at the spot on the starboard side of O1 deck where the surrender was signed. This is now marked with a commemorative plaque in its original location. There will be a theater, models, videos, graphic panels and other exhibits. One of the latter will include a history of American battleships from the USS *Constitution* to the last group built, the Iowa Class battleships.[59] Much of this work has been completed and more is planned.

The object of these displays is to show life at sea, and the work of the Navy and will include displays on navigation, fire control, weaponry, oceanography, radar, sonar and so on. Visitors will be able to climb up to the 05 level lookout for a fantastic view of Pearl Harbor, *mauka* to the Ko'olau and Waianae Mountains and *makai* to the shimmering blue sea. The restored decks of the ship will also be used on occasion for traditional naval ceremonies. There may eventually be a live action simulation of a battle presented in the CEC at the heart of the ship.

Many, but not all, of these exhibits or displays were ready at the grand opening in January of 1999 when visitors were first admitted to the ship. Some will take years to complete and refurbishing parts of the ship will take time as well. Access to USS *Missouri* is by bus from an area near the USS Bowfin Submarine Memorial. It takes tourists across the Clarey Bridge to the entrance near the bow of the ship. The buses feature 1940s music and news. Later the floating museum may be moved down the channel, to Pier Foxtrot 2 and Foxtrot 3, close to the spot where USS *California* was moored on December 7, 1941. This is about twice as far from the Arizona Memorial as the ship was at Pier Foxtrot 5. This purpose would be to minimize the visual impact of the huge gray ship on the pristine white solitude and serenity of the memorial over the sunken USS *Arizona*.[60] Many say she should remain with her WWII colleague.

In all likelihood, some of these plans for the museum and the renovation of the ship will change over the next few years, as will the current estimate of several million dollars for its completion. The ship has been opened in phases as displays are completed. When USS *Missouri* is integrated into the Navy's Ford

Island Plan, the plan is to have ferries or shuttle boats take visitors to Navy Square, a landscaped plaza, from where they will be able to visit the ship, the island and see the Navy in its working environment. To reach the Arizona Memorial, shuttle boats will continue to take visitors from the Visitors' Center as they do now.

The US Navy, like any enormous organization, must apply the Principles of Management to its operations. From their origins at the start of the 19th century, Navy leaders were cognizant of Planning, Organization, Actuating, and Control. Of course, the means of applying these principles vary with changing conditions, but they must have done well to have lasted as a viable entity and become the greatest defensive force in the world today.

Besides the daily minor adjustments and applications of management techniques, occasionally a major change is required. In August of 1991, the headquarters of the 3rd Fleet, commanded by Vice Admiral James Dorsey, Jr., moved from Ford Island, Pearl Harbor, to San Diego. His flagship was USS *Coronado*. In response to the unsettled situation following the collapse of the Soviet Union, our Navy transferred anti-submarine Destroyer Squadron 31 to Pearl Harbor.[61] Soviet naval presence, especially submarines, had increased in the Pacific in the late 1980s and early 90s, and no one in the United States was sure of the mission of these dangerous vehicles, nor even who controlled them.

An interesting evolution took place at Pearl in August 1991 when the aircraft carrier USS *Independence* relieved USS *Midway*. The former was headed to Yokosuka, Japan and the latter was headed to San Diego and decommissioning. Men, equipment, information and provisions were exchanged between the two carriers.[62] The scene was to be repeated in 1998 when USS *Kitty Hawk* relieved the Indy.

The joint exercises, with participants from several Pacific Rim countries continued. RimPac in 1996 suffered a disaster when a Japanese ship mistakenly shot down an American A6 jet which was towing a target. The men ejected successfully and the Japanese apologized, but it emphasized the remarkable safety record that the RimPac participants have achieved in 28 years of naval exercises.[63] The 1998 RimPac exercises involved 50 ships, including USS *Carl Vinson*, the world's largest aircraft carrier, 200 aircraft, and 25,000 men and women from six nations. All were under the command of Vice Admiral Herb Browne.[64]

In August, following the end of RimPac98, the first ship that bears the name *Pearl Harbor*, entered Pearl for a brief port visit. She is an LSD (Dock Landing Ship), commissioned on May 30 of 1998, and under the command of Commander James J. Bird, USN.[65]

While all of the previously described operational evolutions were taking place, the Navy was undergoing extensive organizational changes. During the Cold War, the Navy decentralized its operations. That is, each sub-division of a unit had an officer who was a specialist for that unit. For instance, a Naval Base such as Pearl Harbor, would have a security division for each command of the base. The reasoning was that each security officer would be most familiar with the problems of his area of responsibility. Decentralization is an effective method of allocating accountability, however it is somewhat extravagant and involves a great deal of command redundancy. With the budget constraints under which the Navy is currently operating, centralization seemed to be a logical move to make. Instead of having seven security (or food service, or public affairs, etc.) officers in command of seven separate security units, the security duties of the entire base are now combined under the command of one officer. The same philosophy also prevails in all the other command areas. The term used when the idea was initiated in early 1998 was "regionalization" or "regional maintenance". The purpose is to optimize the assets of the many infrastructures that existed in 1997 and before.

Part of the consolidation was the merger of the Naval Submarine Base Repair Department and the Shore Intermediate Maintenance Activity to become the Naval Intermediate Maintenance Facility (IMF) in May of 1995. Later, IMF and the Shipyard merged on April 30, 1998 under the command of Captain Jeffrey Conners.[66] The new unit is the largest industrial complex in Hawaii with an annual business volume of more than $300 million. This includes a direct economic contribution to the state of more than $260 million in civilian payroll and more than $18 million in local purchases of supplies and services. The Yard is a multi-million dollar facility, with 175 buildings on 155 acres. It contains four dry-docks and 12,000 feet of berthing and pier space.[67] Another merger which took place in the 1990s was the Naval Station and the Submarine Base. That consolidation was effected on October 1, 1997, with Captain George Covington assuming command of the combined facility.

Regionalization, which is still in the formative stages, allows the Navy to reduce costs at the shore establishments and use those savings for fleet readiness.[68] It is a redistribution of the limited amount of dollars available which will bring the Navy the "best value for organization and the best value for service".[69] The officer responsible for coordinating the installation of the plan was Commander Ava-Marie Howard.[70] Occasionally a newspaper writer wonders why the sailors don't repair the ships. There are two reasons. One is pragmatic and the other is the law. Sailors have among them many fine, skilled workmen, but when they are called away to sea, they obviously cannot continue a job started ashore, so a permanent workforce is necessary. The second reason is that in 1939, the US Congress passed a law that prohibits repair, construction or manufacturing work being done on board US Navy ships by Navy personnel. The only exceptions are those necessary to allow the ship to reach a United States Naval Station.[71]

In keeping with searching for ways to optimize their meager budget, the Navy has introduced some innovative programs. For instance, the Yard is exploring the possibility of expanding its internal taskload to accept such work as applying camouflage paint to Marine Corps vehicles, removing asbestos from DoD buildings all over Oahu, and welding FISC pipelines in underground tunnels within Red

Hill.[72] In one of their more unusual contractual agreements, in January of 1996 the Shipyard leased dry-dock #4 to CINCPACFLT for five years. This had the effect of reducing the Yard's maintenance costs and brought in more work.[73] These, and other programs, are part of the Shipyard's Strategic Plan. The plan defined eight issues and proposed 64 actions to address them.[74]

As with any large organization, the Navy suffers from unusual problems. One of the recent unneeded obstacles to daily operations is the introduction of a computer virus into one of the Navy's computer programs. It can affect any of the Navy's systems and they have experts who are constantly on watch for symptoms of a virus. In the Shipyard's 2000 computers alone, they suffer one virus per week.[75] Usually they are not fatal to a program, but they are always a pest and a frustration to people who are intent on maximizing their productivity. The other commands of Navy Region, Hawaii, are not immune from this problem, of course, but each is taking preventative measures to protect the security of the base and minimize the unproductive effect these viruses have.

One tragic incident occurred when, on 9 February 2001 at 1:50 pm HST, the USS Greeneville (SSN 772) collided with a Japanese fishing vessel, the Ehime Maru, in which several lives were lost.[76] That accident was an extraordinarily rare exception to the US Navy's outstanding record of safe operations in Hawaiian waters and elsewhere around the world.

On 11 September 2001, a treacherous attack on New York and the Pentagon was perpetrated by terrorists. The naval personnel of Pearl Harbor grieve for lost loved ones, friends, shipmates and acquaintances. The Naval Region Hawaii entered a state of heightened security and awareness immediately. The United States entered a war.

On a more positive note, the first ship to be named for our 50th state, the Virginia class *USS Hawaii* (SSN 776), was so designated at a ceremony which took place on 8 April 2001.[77] On 29 May 2001 the movie *PEARL HARBOR* was released amid a lavish celebration aboard *USS John C. Stennis* (CVN 74) in Pearl Harbor, a most appropriate site.

As was already mentioned, the fate of the US Navy seems to be to suffer downsizing and budget constraints after each war. The end of the Cold War was no different. In 1998, the number of US armed services active duty members dropped below 1.4 million for the first time since 1940. The Navy was authorized to have just over 370,000 total personnel in September of 1999. Early retirements and separations did not allow the Navy to meet that goal. Congress has not yet decided how to solve this dilemma. Meanwhile officers and enlisted personnel of the Navy complete their assignments, protect the nation, stand ready for any emergency - all with inadequate funds and aging ships.[78] A recent congressional defeat of a proposed increase in the defense budget "puts our country at risk. We have done to our own military what no foreign power has been able to do." said Representative Floyd Spence, House National Security Committee Chairman.[79]

As this is being written, the United States Pacific Fleet consists of about 227,000 people, 190 ships, and 1430 aircraft.[80] An illuminating summary of today's Navy, printed in the Navy Times, was entitled, "This is NOT Your Father's Navy". Their studies indicated that today's force is, "older, more married, more educated, more Southern, more female, and more diverse.[81]

In the strategic white papers, *From the Sea* in 1992, *Forward...From the Sea* in 1994, and *Vision, Presence, Power* in 1998, the Navy defined the strategic concept intended to carry the Naval Service beyond the Cold War and into the 21st century. The emphasis shifted from being cognizant of a global threat to one of being prepared to project power and influence in response to regional challenges. Such was the vision of Admiral Jeremy M. Boorda, CNO. His successor, Admiral Jay L. Johnson, used a nautical analogy when he stated that the Navy will be guided by four stars in its course into the future: Operational Primacy, Leadership, Teamwork and Pride.[82]

The man with the awesome title (and responsibility) of CINCUSPACOM, Admiral Joseph Preuher, (later to become the US Ambassador to China) stated that "Pearl Harbor remains a cornerstone to our readiness and capabilities in the Pacific. U.S. economic and social interests in Asia and the Pacific will last and depend upon the stability of our forward-based forces. These forces, in turn, depend upon the support and guidance they receive from Pearl Harbor and other Hawaiian military facilities."[83]

These men of vision are constantly working to provide a quality life environment for their sailors while staying prepared to defend the United States and her interests anywhere in the world. They are tasked to maintain the highest standards of material and personnel readiness in the face of decreasing appropriations from congress. They must deal with a sometimes hostile and often ignorant press while keeping their focus on those tasks they have defined. No doubt the new century will see such devices as CVX aircraft carrier battle groups, LPD 17 San Antonio Class amphibious assault ships, and other innovations unknown to today's Navy. Whatever the tools they are given to work with, these fine young people are standing in harm's way for us. As for those stationed in Pearl Harbor, they are almost at the point of the spear. They are working well with the local citizens and the Hawaiian People are supportive of their neighbors, the US Navy. The young men and women are secure in a fine profession and Hawaii is secure because of their presence.

What better, safer way to end a history?

PANINA

Of course a history never ends, but writers come to the end of their time. We are interested in Hawaiian history and the United States Navy. Our surprise was great when we discovered that we could find no written history of these two important sections of our society. Of course there are brilliantly written documentations of each group, but none of both and their mutual relationship. Our purpose is to fill that gap.

But don't think for a moment that our effort was altruistically inspired. We did it for ourselves and for anyone with intellectual curiosity about the US Navy in Pearl Harbor. Our research took us to the National Archives in College Park, Maryland, Washington DC, and San Bruno, California. We spent much time at the United States Naval Academy in Annapolis, at the Universities of California and Hawaii, at the Bishop Museum in Honolulu, the Hawaiian State Library, and, of course, at the Naval Complex at Pearl.

It was exciting to travel and land with the original Hawaiians, to watch Kamehameha the Great develop from a boy to a fierce warrior and wise ruler, and to note with apprehension the arrival of the first European and American sailors. It was heartbreaking to see our friends, the naive Hawaiians, being mistreated and often cheated by shrewd businessmen from foreign lands. We tolerated 'Mad Jack' Percival and admired Thomas ap Catesby Jones. We felt the anguish of the Hawaiians at the time of annexation, but could understand the reasons for it. We slogged it out with the first US Marines to be bivouacked in the mud and marsh of Honolulu, and shared their pride when they bravely and professionally maintained order during several disturbances. We grew disturbed at the enormous influx of Oriental workers, but were repulsed at the way they were treated.

When Pearl Harbor was bombed that Sunday morning, we were as frightened and confused and angry as anyone, but we pitched in and did our share 'for the war effort'. The joy of statehood was ours to celebrate along with our friends and watching the Navy develop Pearl Harbor as the premier defensive location in the Pacific filled us with pride. When we noted the resurgence of Hawaiian pride in their culture, we also felt proud.

The islands are no longer quite as languid as they once were. But they are not as warlike either. The Hawaiians are not as vulnerable to invasions or disease as they once were, but many are concerned about losing important elements of their culture. Although one can stand in a few places in the concrete canyons of downtown Honolulu and see neither mountain nor sea, their presence is always felt. The warm trade winds still waft softly over the islands and on a still, calm morning one can stand on the deck of a ship and marvel at the glassy water of Pearl Harbor. Mauka the majestic Ko'olau mountains rise defying the encroaching homes trying to climb the heights.

Occasionally a small boat crosses the harbor leaving a wake a thousand feet astern. Surrounded by Hawaiians working and Navy personnel busying themselves at their tasks, one can not easily separate them nor comprehend what these lovely islands would be like if history had not happened as it did.

We hope you have enjoyed our tour and sensed our love of the Hawaiian People and our pride in the United States Navy. Mahalo Nui.

The ship is secure. Shift colors.

Appendix I
Rulers of Hawaii

TITLE	NAME	YEARS	TENURE
Kamehameha I	Kamehameha	1795- 1819	24 years
Kamehameha II	Liholiho	1819-1824	5
Kamehameha III	Kauokeaouli[1]	1825-1854	29
Kamehameha IV	Alexander Liholiho	1855- 1863	8
Kamehameha V	Lot Kapuaiwa[2]	1863- 1872	9
	Lunalilo, William	1873- 1874	1
	Kalakaua, David	1874- 1891	17
Liliuokalani[3]	Dominis, Lydia	1891 - 1893	3
			96 years

1 Brother of II.
2 Brother of IV.
3 Sister of King David Kalakaua

Appendix II
Governors

GOVERNMENT	GOVERNOR	TENURE
Provisional	Dole, Sanford	1893 - 1894
Republic	Dole, Sanford	1894- 1900
Territory	Dole, Sanford	1900 - 1903
	Carter, George R	1903 - 1907
	Frear, Walter F	1907 - 1913
	Pinkham, Lucius E	1913 - 1918
	McCarthy, Charles J	1918 - 1921
	Farrington, Wallace R	1921 - 1929
	Judd, Lawrence M	1929 - 1934
	Poindexter, Joseph B	1934 - 1942
	Stainback, Ingram M	1942 - 1951
	Long, Oren E	1951 - 1953
	King, Samuel W	1953 - 1957
	Quinn, William F	1957 - 1959
State	Quinn,William F	1959 - 1962
	Burns, John A	1962 - 1974
	Ariyoshi, George R	1974 - 1986
	Waihee III, John D	1986 - 1994
	Cayetano, Benjamin J	1994 -

Appendix III
Secretaries of the Navy
Office established 18 June 1798

SECRETARY
Dates are listed in the form da/mo/yr

TENURE

Secretary	Tenure
Benjamin Stoddert	18/06/1798 - 31/03/1801
Robert Smith	27/07/01 - 07/03/09
Paul Hamilton	15/05/09 - 31/12/12
William Jones	19/01/13 - 01/12/14
B W Crowninshield	16/01/15 - 30/09/18
Smith Thompson	01/01/19 - 31/08/23
Samuel Southard	16/09/23 - 03/03/29
John Branch	09/03/29 - 12/05/31
Levi Woodbury	23/05/31 - 30/06/34
Mahlon Dickerson	01/07/34 - 30/06/38
James Paulding	01/07/38 - 03/03/41
George Badger	06/03/41 - 11/09/41
Abel Upshur	11/10/41 - 23/07/43
David Henshaw	24/07/43 - 18/02/44
Thomas Gilmer	19/02/44 - 28/02/44
John Mason	26/03/44 - 10/03/45
George Bancroft	11/03/45 - 09/09/46
John Mason	10/09/46 - 07/03/49
William Preston	08/03/49 - 22/07/50
William Graham	02/08/50 - 25/07/52
John Kennedy	26/07/52 - 07/03/53
James Dobbin	08/03/53 - 06/03/57
Isaac Toucey	07/03/57 - 06/03/61
Gideon Welles	07/03/61 - 03/03/69
Adolph Boric	09/03/69 - 25/06/69
George Robeson	26/06/69 - 12/03/77
Richard Thompson	13/03/77 - 20/12/80
Nathan Goff	07/01/81 - 06/03/81
William Hunt	07/03/81 - 16/04/82
William Chandler	16/04/82 - 06/03/85
William Whitney	07/03/85 - 05/03/89
Benjamin Tracy	06/03/89 - 06/03/93

SECRETARY	TENURE
Dates are listed in the form da/mo/yr	
Hilary Herbert	07/03/93 - 05/03/97
John Long	06/03/97 - 30/04/1902
William Moody	01/05/02 - 30/06/04
Charles Bonaparte	01/07/05 - 16/12/06
Victor Metcalf	17/12/06 - 30/11/08
Truman Newberry	01/12/08 - 05/03/09
George von Meyer	06/03/09 - 04/03/13
Josephus Daniels	05/03/13 - 05/03/21
Edwin Denby	06/03/21 - 10/03/24
Curtis Wilbur	19/03/24 - 04/03/29
Charles Adams	05/03/29 - 04/03/33
Claude Swanson	04/03/33 - 07/07/39
Charles Edison	02/01/40 - 24/06/40
Frank Knox	11/07/40 - 28/04/44
James Forrestal	19/05/44 - 17/09/47
John Sullivan	18/09/47 - 24/05/49
Francis Matthews	25/05/49 - 31/07/51
Dan Kimball	31/07/51 - 20/01/53
Robert Anderson	04/02/53 - 03/05/54
Charles Thomas	03/05/54 - 01/04/57
Thomas Gates	01/04/57 - 08/06/59
William Franke	08/06/59 - 19/01/61
John Connally	25/01/61 - 20/12/61
Fred Korth	04/01/62 - 01/11/63
Paul Fay (acting)	02/11/63 - 28/11/63
Paul Nitze	29/11/63 - 30/06/67
Charles Baird (acting)	01/07/67 - 31/08/67
Paul Ignatius	01/09/67 - 24/01/69
John Chafee	31/01/69 - 04/05/72
John Warner	04/05/72 - 08/04/74
J William Middendorf	08/04/74 - 20/01/77
W Graham Claytor	14/02/77 - 24/08/79
Edward Hidalgo	24/10/79 - 20/01/81
John Lehman	05/02/81 - 10/04/87
James Webb	01/05/87 - 23/02/88

SECRETARY   **TENURE**
Dates are listed in the form da/mo/yr

William Ball	28/03/88 - 15/05/89
Henry Garrett	15/05/89 - 26/06/92
Daniel Howard (acting)	26/06/92 - 07/07/92
Sean O'Keefe	02/10/92 - 20/01/93
Adm Frank Kelso(acting)	02/01/93 - 21/07/93
John Dalton	22/07/93 - 16/11/98
Richard Danzig	16/11/98 – 24/07/00
Gordon England	24/07/00

Appendix IV
Chief of Naval Operations
Office established 11 May 1915

CNO   **TENURE**
Dates are listed in the form da/mo/yr.

William Benson*	11/05/1915 - 25/09/19
Robert Coontz	01/11/19 - 21/07/23
Edward Eberle	21/07/23 - 14/11/27
Charles Hughes	14/11/27 - 17/09/30
William Pratt	17/09/30 - 30/06/33
William Standley	01/07/33 - 01/01/37
William Leahy	02/01/37 - 01/08/39
Harold Stark	01/08/39 - 02/03/42
Ernest King**	26/03/42 - 15/12/45
Chester Nimitz**	15/12/45 - 15/12/47
Louis Denfeld	15/23/47 - 02/11/49
Forrest Sherman	02/11/49 - 22/07/51
William Fechteler	16/08/51 - 17/08/53
Robert Carney	17/08/53 - 17/08/55
Arliegh Burke	17/08/55 - 01/08/61
George Anderson	01/08 61 - 01/08/63
David McDonald	01/08/63 - 01/08/67
Thomas Moorer	01/08/67 - 01/07/70
Elmo Zumwalt	01/07/70 - 29/06/74
James Holloway	29/06/74 - 01/07/78
Thomas Hayward	01/07/78 - 30/06/82
James Watkins	30/06/82 - 30/06/86
Carlisle Trost	01/07/86 - 29/06/90
Frank Kelso	29/06/90 - 23/04/94
Jeremy Boorda	23/04/94 - 16/05/96
Jay Johnson	26/05/96 - 15/07/00
Vern Clark	15/07/00

*All CNOs were (4 star) Admirals except King and Nimitz.
** King and Nimitz were Fleet Admirals (5 stars).

Appendix V
Pacific Squadron Commanders
1821-1886

Dates are listed in the forrn da/mo/yr.

UNIT	COMMANDER	TENURE

PACIFIC SQUADRON

	Ridgely, Charles G	31/03/1821
	Hull, Isaac	07/09/24 -29/09/29
	Thompson, Charles C B	07/10/29 -
	Ballard, Henry E	04/03/39
	Turner, Daniel	14/04/41
	Dallas, A J	29/05/40 -30/12/41[1]
	Jones, Thomas ap Catesby	30/12/41 -18/05/44
	Armstrong, James	08/06/44 -15/10/44
	Sloat, John D	16/10/44 -23/10/46
	Stockton, RobertF	26/06/46 -03/05/47
	Biddle, James	09/04/47 -03/11/47
	Jones, Thomas ap Catesby	11/04/47 -05/10/50
	McCauley, C S	24/01/50 -23/01/53
	Dulaney, Bladen	19/11/52 -22/04/55
	Mervine, William	04/09/54 -16/11/57
	Long, John S	24/09/57 -16/08/59
	Montgomery, J B	12/05/59 -31/12/61
	Bell, Charles H	14/12/61 -24/10/64
	Pearson, George F	24/10/64 -19/06/66

NORTH PACIFIC SQUADRON

	Thatcher, Henry K	26/05/66 -26/12/68
	Craven, T T	06/08/68 -25/06/69

UNIT	COMMANDER	TENURE

PACIFIC STATION - NORTH SQUADRON

	Turner, Thomas	26/06/69 -09/09/70
	Winslow, John A	05/07/70 -10/10/72

NORTH PACIFIC STATION

	Taylor, William R[2]	10/07/69 -13/08/72
	Pennock, A M	23/09/72 -30/12/74
	Almy, John J	02/01/75 -30/04/78

PACIFIC STATION

	Rodgers, C R P	09/07/78 -31/12/80
	Stevens, T H	01/01/80 -28/12/81
	Balch, George B	01/01/82 -22/12/83
	Hughes, A H	01/04/84 -12/20/84
	Upshur, J N Q	02/01/85 -28/12/85
	McCaulley, J W	01/06/86 -11/11/86

[1]   Some dates overlap due to the lack of cornmunications in the 19th century.

[2]   Letters are stored at NARA dated as shown with each man identifying himself as Commander/Pacific Station.

Appendix VI
Commander, Naval Station Pearl Harbor
1899-1915

The Naval Complex that we call "Pearl Harbor" today has had an interesting history of command definitions and titles. Before each list of commanders, a short explanation is given.

Commander John F. Merry, USN, relieved William Haywood as US consul in Honolulu on 28 May 1899. Merry's title was Commander, Coal Depot, Honolulu, Territory of Hawaii. On 17 November 1899, General Order #530 identified the Coal Depot as a Naval Station, Cdr Merry commanding. The succession of commanders is listed. All dates are listed in the form da/mo/yr. Final dates of command are listed.

Merry, J F*	31/07/1902
Whiting, W H	23/02/03
Rodman, H*	14/08/03
Niblack, A P*	21/08/03
Terry, S W	24/12/04
Lyon, H	24/06/06
Very, S W*	24/04/08
Rees, C P	13/12/10
Cowles, W C	24/03/13
Moore, C T B	17/07/15
Boush, C J	17/05/16

* All were Rear Admirals except Commander Merry and Captain Very. Niblack and Rodman were Lieutenant Commanders.

On 28 April 1916 the 14th Naval District was established. The orders were received on 17 May with Rear Admiral C. J. Boush assuming command. The commander's scope of responsibility included the newly dedicated Naval Station at Pearl Harbor.

Appendix VII
Commandants, 14th Naval District

COMMANDANT   RELIEVED   COMMANDANT   RELIEVED

Until World War II the District Commandant billet was held concurrently with the command of the Navy Yard.[1]
Rear Admiral Boush assumed command 17 May 1916.
Dates are listed in the form da/mo/yr.
Final dates of commands are listed.

Commandant	Relieved	Commandant	Relieved
Boush, C J	14/08/16	Olsen, C E	17/07/57
Clark, G R*	13/06/18	Dietrich, N K	23/06/58
Doyle, R M	15/05/19	Solomons, E A	23/03/61
Fletcher, W B	06/07/20	Campbell, R L	29/12/61
Shoemaker, W R	28/06/21	Duerfeldt, C H	13/03/62
Simpson, E	07/06/23	Buchanan, C A	28/05/64
McDonald, J D	25/10/27	Ferguson, G T*	23/06/64
Marvell, G R	04/08/30	Persons, H S	31/05/67
Stirling, Y	10/06/33	Sutherland, W	20/06/67
Yarnell, H E	10/05/36	Lynch, R B	19/01/68
Murfin, O S	11/04/40	Schelling, R*	12/03/68
Bloch, C C	02/04/42	Bakutis, F E	30/06/69
Bagley, D W	17/02/43	Davis, D C	13/08/70
Ghormley, R L*	25/10/44	Dobie, E W	25/11/70
Furlong, W R	28/11/44	Hayward, T D	06/12/71
Bagley, D W	25/07/45	Morgan, H S	02/06/72
Taffinder, S*	18/04/46	Payne, P E*	02/08/72
Hanson, E M	07/06/46	Butts, J L	30/07/73
Hall, J L*	24/05/48	Paddock, R A	17/05/75
Murray, S S	25/08/48	McNamara, T W	03/06/75
McMorris, C H	07/06/52	Wentworth, R S	31/07/79
Murray, S S	18/02/54		

* All officers were rear admirals except:
Vice Admiral: Shoemaker, Ghormley, Bagley, Taffinder, Hall.
Captain: Clark, Ferguson, Schelling, Payne.

On 1 July 1957 the Naval Base Pearl Harbor was placed under the command of the Commandant of the 14th Naval District.2 See Appendix VIII for subsequent commanders.

[1] *Fifty Years of Naval District Development*, History Division, Office of the CNO, 1954
[2] *Command Narrative,* Aug 1959.

Appendix VIII
Commander Naval Base Pearl Harbor, T.H.
1945-1950

General Order No. 223 of 14 September 1945 abolished the organization of Industrial Navy Yards and created in their place U.S. Naval Bases, each to be commanded by a "Commandant". In November 1946, G.O. No. 250 superseded G.O. 223, changing the title of the officer in command of each Naval Base to "Commander".[1]

Dates are given in the form da/mo/yr.

Commander	Tenure	
Rear Admiral E W Hanson	30/11/45	20/01/48
Captain F M O'Leary	20/01/48	08/04/48
Rear Admiral S S Murray	08/04/48	29/09/49
Captain C H Murphy	29/09/49	10/02/50
Rear Admiral R H Cruzen	10/02/50	31/05/50

From 31 May 1950 to 1 July 1957, the Commandant of the 14th Naval District acted as Commander, Naval Base, Pearl Harbor, T.H.[2]

[1] Command Narrative, Aug 1959. Ibid.
[2] Ibid.

Appendix IX
Commanders, Naval Station Pearl Harbor
1955-Present

On I July 1955 the U.S. Naval Station, Pearl Harbor, T.H.,
was (re)established, tasked to perform the operational functions of the
port.[1]
All officers are captains unless noted*.
Captain Price assumed command 07/01/55.
Dates are listed in the form da/mo/yr.
Final dates of commands are listed.

COMMANDER	RELIEVED
Price, K E	01/08/55
Groff, R H	30/06/57
Collier, J	01/07/58
Emerson, A T*	25/10/58
Davis, J H	08/06/60
Hogan, T W	15/06/61
Mackenzie, C J	16/06/64
Stark, H B	13/06/66
Weatherwax, J	10/06/68
Stuart, R M	28/07/70
Oliver, J	30/06/72
Hanson, T	03/07/73
Lanchantin, G*	21/09/73
Benson, F W	05/09/75
Conrad, P	15/06/78
Shapero, A C	07/08/80
Jensen, R	16/09/82
Clarity, M	21/09/84
Ferguson, M	04/09/86
Tucker, R	17/03/89
Blair, D	04/05/90
Porter, J	24/04/92
Taylor, J	03/12/93

COMMANDER	RELIEVED
Long, P	14/04/94
Kennedy, K	25/07/97
Covington, G	18/09/98
Sanford, H	23/06/00
Hughes, R	

* Emerson and Lanchantin were commanders.

Captain Covington assumed command of the Naval Station on 25 July, 1997, when it was combined with the Submarine Base.[2] SUBASE was disestablished at that time.[3]

---

[1] Command Narrative, Aug 1959.
[2] Change of Command booklet, Jul 25 1997.
[3] PAO NAVBASE Pearl Harbor 26 Oct 1998.

Appendix X
Commanders, Naval Base Pearl Harbor
1980-Present

In 1979 the 14th Naval District was disestablished.
The commanding officer of the base became titled Commander,
Naval Base Pearl Harbor, Hawaii.

COMMANDER   **RELIEVED**

All officers are rear admirals.
Rear Admiral Briggs assumed command 31/07/1979.
Dates are listed in the form da/mo/yr.
Final dates of commands are listed.

Briggs, E S	22/08/80
Anderson, S J	12/08/83
Rorie, C J	26/10/84
Boyle, H F	15/08/86
Reimann, R T	24/06/88
Chadwick, S K	20/06/90
Earner, W A	10/07/92
Retz, W A	09/09/94
Holder, G W	15/11/96
Sutton, W G	22/01/99
Townes, J W	09/02/00

• In 1999 the command name changed to Navy Region Hawaii.

Conway, R T

Appendix XI
Commander, Shipyard/IMF Pearl Harbor

COMMANDER	RELIEVED	COMMANDER	RELIEVED

All officers were captains unless noted*.
Commanding officers were titled "Manager" until 5 September 1945, after which they held the title "Commander".
Captain Yates assumed command 08/04/1921.
Dates are listed in the form da/mo/yr. Final dates of command are listed.

Manager

COMMANDER	RELIEVED	COMMANDER	RELIEVED
Yates, I I	25/01/24	Holtzworth, E***	24/04/61
Hamner, E C**	12/05/26	Farrin, J***	27/05/63
Duncan, P C	30/03/29	Wright, E***	29/12/66
Gay, J B	30/04/29	Sherwin, S	09/02/67
McDowell, C S	31/03/30	Fee, J***	19/12/67
Buchanan, P*	30/06/30	Barnhart, R	30/01/70
Stuart, HA	14/07/32	Wilson, K	18/05/72
Buchanan, P**	29/08/32	Wilson, K***	01/07/72
Evans, J S	23/02/35	Swanson, C	30/10/74
Hird, H B**	21/04/39	Hoffman, H	15/03/76
Gillette, C S	24/05/42	Hoffman, H***	30/07/76
Paine, R W	19/10/44	McArthur, J	31/07/80
Kell, C***	05/09/45	Marnane, T	03/05/85
		Camacho, R****	10/01/86
Commander		Traister, R***	27/05/88
Kell, C***	25/06/46	Coyle, M	09/06/89
Dreller, L***	28/07/48	Kell, R	25/06/93
Cowdrey, R T***	25/10/50	Gehrman, F	26/05/95
Lillard, J S	27/11/50	Haberlandt, F	30/04/98
Dow, W R***	23/03/54	Conners, J D	10/06/01
Pyne, S N***	21/07/56	Edwards, J	
Leahy, W***	12/06/58		

* Buchanan was a lieutenant commander on his first tour.
** Commanders.
*** Rear admirals.
**** Camacho was a commodore.
Rear Admiral W R Furlong assumed a special command "Commandant of the USNSYPH from 12 December 1941 to 1 December 1945.[1]

---

[1] Command History USNSYPH

Appendix XII
Commander, Naval Supply Center Pearl Harbor

SUPPLY OFFICERS IN COMMAND NAVAL SUPPLY DEPOT

All officers are captains unless noted*.
Captain Shaffer assumed command 12 April 1943.
Dates are listed in the form da/mo/yr.
Final dates of commands are listed.

COMMANDER	RELIEVED	COMMANDER	RELIEVED
Shaffer, H M	30/04/43	Killeen, J P	05/05/44
Gaffney, J J*	01/08/43	Norton, H J	31/08/45
Eddiegorde, E	08/04/44	Dekay, C G	01/01/46

SUPPLY OFFICERS IN COMMAND NAVAL SUPPLY CENTER

Dekay, C G	25/01/46	Fox, W V*	10/03/49
Mayo, A H*	26/03/46	Thomas, G L	26/04/49
Skillman, J H	28/01/47	Wood, J E*	27/11/49
Jecklin, J J	23/02/47		

COMMANDING OFFICERS NAVAL SUPPLY CENTER

Wood, J E*	13/11/51	Farley, W B	30/07/70
Kretz, C H	26/12/51	Condon, T P	24/08/70
Bauernschmidt*	14/01/54	Dunn, G G	31/07/72
Herlihy, J L*	24/02/56	Chapman, E C	27/09/73
Fahlbusch, H**	19 06/56	Kocher, E M	09/04/75
Parks, J D*	27/07/58	Kocher, E M*	11/06/75
Becknell, T*	21/07/61	Dickey, W H	06/07/77
Atkinson, W L	07/08/61	Schanz, T L	13/06/79
Bourgois, A*	01/10/63	Caverly, M K	30/07/81
Stokes, M G	27/01/64	Irons, J H	05/08/83
Sherwood, S*	14/06/65	Kittock, K E	28/06/85
Guelff, P H	14/07/65	Erickson, R C	19/06/87
Bloxom, E	29/06/67	McClure, J M	21/08/90
Johannesen, W	17/07/67	Sullivan, M P	26/06/92
Scheela, J J	20/08/69	Schmitt, N J	01/03/93

* Rear admirals.
** Fahlbusch's rank was commander

COMMANDER	RELIEVED	COMMANDER	RELIEVED

COMMANDERS, FLEET & INDUSTRIAL SUPPLY CENTER

Schmitt, N J	22/07/94
Wagner, J Q	09/08/96
Nanney, R G	26/06/98
Caldwell, G	11/08/00
Knaggs, C O	

Appendix XIII
Commander, Submarine Base Pearl Harbor

COMMANDER	RELIEVED	COMMANDER	RELIEVED

All officers were captains unless noted*.
Commander Nimitz assumed command 15/06/1920.
Final dates of command are listed.

COMMANDER	RELIEVED	COMMANDER	RELIEVED
Nimitz, C W*	1922	Gibson, R	1964
Welch, L F	25	Duncan, M	66
Martin, F C*	28	Purinton, D	66
Bronson, A	29	Grossetta, W	69
Wortman, W K	32	Poteet, A	69
Osterhaus, H W	34	Lewis, J	70
Koch, R A	36	Ingraham, T*	71
Culp, R S	38	From, J	72
Scanland, F W	40	Ruch, M	72
Carter, W R	41	Tomb, P	75
Daubin, F A	42	Richard, J	77
English, R H	42	Reifler, G	77
Brown, J H	43	Kelley, F	78
Edmunds, C D	43	Reifler, G	78
Aldrich, C E	44	Mathis, H	80
Swineburne, E R	46	Smith, W	80
Olsen, E	48	Kennington, W	82
Follmer, L D	48	Stubbs, G	84
Christensen, W N	50	Wright, L	86
Andrews, C H	52	Marshall, J	88
William, J W	52	Fast, R	90
Weiss, D F	54	Coughlin, F	92
Garrison, M E	56	McHugh, M	94
Hendersen, C M	58	Hofwolt, G	95
Parham, W B	60	Gustin, B	96
Bunting, D	60	Covington, G	98
Latham, R	64		

* Officers Nimitz, Martin, and Ingraham were commanders.

Captain Covington assumed command of the combined Naval Station and Submarine Base on 07/25/97 at which time the SUBASE was disestablished.

Appendix XIV
Commander, Marine Barracks Pearl Harbor

Dates are listed in the form da/mo/yr.
First Lieutenant Harllee assumed command 09/02/1904.
Final command dates are listed.

COMMANDER	RELIEVED	COMMANDER	RELIEVED
1stLt Harllee, W	09/02/04	Col Brooks, C	10/11/43
Cap Catlin, A	11/07/04	Col Webb, J	16/04/45
Maj Fuller, B*	22/08/06	Col Holdahl, T	24/10/45
Maj Russell, J*	04/01/08	Col Jeschke, R	22/09/47
Maj Long, C	13/11/10	Col Wulbern, F	12/12/47
Maj Neville, W	27/04/13	Col Monsoon, G	20/05/48
Col Myers, J	02/04/14	Col Rudd, R	08/06/48
Col Cutts, R	30/06/15	LCol Hays, G	02/08/48
Cap Clinton, T	06/09/16	Col Puller, L	15/07/50
1Lt Zane, R	01/10/16	Col Victory, R	17/06/52
Cap Clinton, T	13/02/18	Col Burton, C	22/06/54
LCol Beaumont	13/01/20	Col McHaney, J	10/08/56
Col Myers, J	05/08/21	Col Reinberg, L	20/07/58
Col Thorpe, G	16/06/23	Col Nelson, W	21/08/59
LCol Hoadley, W	13/06/23	LCol Ferguson	04/12/59
Col Bradman, F	13/07/25	Col Reeve, D	30/06/63
Col Hall, N	30/07/27	Col McMillan, J	30/06/65
Col Huey, J	10/09/29	Col Leineweber	28/07/67
Col Taylor, C	14/06/32	Col McLeod, S	11/07/68
Col Hall, D	18/10/33	Col Fry, W	03/08/71
Col Evans, F	23/01/37	Col Thomas, A	30/06/75
Col Henly, J	23/06/37	LCol Lee, V	24/08/75
Col Drum, A	22/06/39	Col Haggerty, J	11/08/76
LCol Bourke, T	25/07/39	LCol Lee, V	03/11/76
Col Denig, R	20/06/40	Col Lippold, O	26/20/79
Col Jackson, G	27/08/40	Col Koethe, F	03/06/82
Col Pickett, H	12/12/41	Col Dube, M	20/06/85
Col Jackson, G	20/06/42	Col Tilley, W	25/08/88
Col Gale, T	30/10/42	Col Bartels, W	12107/90
LCol Cuttle, K	12/01/43	Col French, J	28/07/92
		Col North, W	29/07/94

* Majors Fuller and Russell later became Commandants of the United States Marine Corps.

On 31 July 1994, the Marine Barracks command was disestablished and the marines on duty were posted to other stations.

Appendix XV
Public Work Center

All officers are Captains unless noted.

Officers in Charge	Tenure	
Shaid, Henry C.	July 1954	May 1956
Byrnes, William J. *	May 1956	Aug 1956
Plumlee, Charles H	Aug 1956	Jan 1957

Commanding Officers		
Plumlee, Charles H.	Jan 1957	Jun 1959
Curren, Howard F.	Jun 1959	Jul 1961
Frorath, John W.	Jul 1961	Aug 1964
Burke, John L.	Aug 1964	Mar 1967
Locke, Harry A. *	Mar 1967	May 1967
Rogers, William R.	May 1967	Jul 1968
Hiegel, James A.	Jul 1968	Jun 1970
Ashley, Donn L.	Jun 1970	Jul 1974
Wynne, William E.	Jul 1974	Jun 1976
Haynes, Howard H	Jun 1976	Jun 1978
Newcomb, Frank M.	Jun 1978	Aug 1979
McNeill, James E.	Aug 1979	Jul 1982
Kau, Julian M.F.	Jul 1982	Sep 1984
Emsley, Thomas H.	Sep 1984	Oct 1986
Gallen, Robert M.	Oct 1986	Jul 1989
Nash, David J.	Jul 1989	Jul 1991
Rispoli, James A.	Jul 1991	Jul 1994
Dew, Fred W.	Jul 1994	Apr 1996
Delker, James L.	Apr 1996	Jul 1998
Loose, Michael K.	Jul 1998	Apr 2000
Mustain, Jenifer K	Apr 2000	

*Officers Byrnes and Locke were Commanders, USN.

Appendix XVI
Naval Base Pearl Harbor

Commands

COMNAVBASE*
  Chief of Staff
    Staff
  Civilian Personnel Office**
  FISC
  Meteorology/Ocean Center
  Naval Air Station, Barber's Point[1]
  Naval Dental Clinic
  Naval Legal Service
    Civil Matters
    Trial Service Office, Prosecution
  Naval Magazine, Lualualei
  Naval Medical Clinic
  Naval Shipyard[2]
  Naval Support Force, Antarctica
    Christchurch, New Zealand
  Navy Exchange**
  Pacific Missile Range, Barking Sands
    Kauai
  Public Works Center
SUBASE[3]

* Rear Admiral.
** Managed by civilians. All other units are commanded by USN Captains.

Two units report to Washington DC.
  Naval Security Group Activity
  Naval Computer & Telecom Station
  Area Master Station

---

[1] Closed July 1999.
[2] Combined with Intermediate Maintenance Facility, April 1998.
[3] Combined with NAVSTA October 1997.

Abbreviations

(Sources are in bibliography by last name of author.
Abbreviations below are periodicals or organizations.)

AF	Advocate and Friend
AH	American Heritage
AHR	American Historical Review
AS	American Scientist
ANC	Army and Navy Chronicle
ASCE	American Society of Civil Engineers
EB	Evening Bulletin
FISC	Fleet Industrial and Supply Center
FR	Friend
HA	Honolulu Advertiser
HAA	Hawaiian Almanac and Annual
HC	Hawaiian Chronology
HG	Hawaiian Gazette
HHS	Hawaiian Historical Society
HHR	Hawaiian Historical Review
HIG	Hawaiian Island Gazette
HJH	Hawaiian Journal of History
HNN	Hawaii Navy News
HON	Honolulu Magazine
HS	Hawaiian Star
HSB	Honolulu Star Bulletin
HVCB	Hawaii Visitors' ~ Convention Bureau
HW	Harper's Weekly
IT	Invention and Technology
JPS	Journal of the Polynesian Society
LOC	Library of Congress
LOG	Magazine of PHN ship yard
MPM	Mid Pacific Magazine

NARA	National Archives and Records Administration
NIP	Naval Institute Press
NCE	Navy Civil Engineer
NPS	National Park Service
NT	Navy Times
PAT	Pacific Submarine Command, Patrol
PACDIV	Pacific Division Naval Facilities Engineering Command
PCA	Pacific Commercial Advertiser
PHR	Pacific Historical Review
PH	Paradise Holiday
POP	Paradise of the Pacific
PHNSY	Pearl Harbor Naval Ship Yard
PHSL	Pearl Harbor Shipyard Log
POLY	Polynesian
PPM	Pan Pacific Magazine
SB	Star Bulletin
SIG	Sandwich Islands Gazette
SIM	Sandwich Islands Monthly
SCI	Science Magazine
TA	Temperance Advocate
TH	Territory of Hawaii
USDI	United States Department of the Interior
USNA	United States Naval Academy
USNHC	United States Naval Historical Center
USNIP	United States Naval Institute *Proceedings*
USNWR	US News and World Report
WDC	Washington, District of Columbia

Notes:

Chapter 1

1   Kyselka, p. 12.
2   Carr, p. 59.
3   Kyselka, p. 117f.
4   HHS, 1909, p. 29.
5   Foster, p. 61.
6   O'Hawaii, TV Documentary, writ. Tom Coffman, Dir Robert Bates, Hawaii Public TV, 1995.
7   Kame'eleihiwa, p. 19.
8   Barrere, Summary, p. 1.
9   Foster p, 51.
10   Barrere, Summary, p. 15.
11   MacDonald et al, p. 424-6.
12   SB, Dec 7 1987, p. A2.
13   POP, Holiday Issue 1941, p. 108.
14   Fornander, vol II, p. 48.
15   Sterling & Summers, p. 49.
16   Taylor, Leighton, p. 19.
17   Sterling & Summers, p. 41.
18   Broughton, p. 72.
19   Sterling & Summers, p. 51-2.
20   HHS, 1943, p. 56.
21   Sterling & Summers, p. 44-46.
22   Ibid, p. 46.
23   POP, May 1936, p. 10.

Chapter 2

1   POP, June 1892, p. 2.
2   HHS Paper #1, Jan 28 1892, p. 4.
3   POP, Feb 1937, p. 9.
4   Ledyard, Plate XXI: p. 155.
5   Price, p. 252, Cook's Journal for Sunday Dec 30 1778.
6   Delano, p. 396.
7   Foster, p. 68
8   Foster p. 72.
9   Ledyard, p. 155.
10   HHS, 1922, p. 13.
11   Sterling & Summers, p. 57.
]2   Ibid, p. 51.
13   Pukui, p. 88.
14   HHS, 1913, p. 27.
15   HHS, 1927, p. 9.
16   Dye vol 1, p. 63.
17   Ibid, p. 64.
18   Dye v. 1, p. 69.

19   Wisniewski, Rise and Fall, p. 16.
20   HHS, 1913, p. 27.
21   Delano, p. 392.
22   Vancouver, vol III, p. 10.
23   HHS, 1940, p. 37.
24   POP, Jun 1915, p. 6.
25   e.g. Daws p. 38; Wisniewski, Rise & Fall, p. 18.
26   HHS, 1913 p. 21.
27   Vancouver, p. 29.
28   Ibid, p. 31.
29   HJH, vol XX, 1986, p. 5.
30   Smith, Bradford, p. 12.
31   HJH vol XX, 1986, p. 11.
32   Vancouver, p. 56.
33   POP, Jun 1939, p. 17.
34   Scott, p. 798.
35   Foster p. 75.
36   HHS, 1927, p. 12.
37   USNIP, Nov 1945, p. 1336,
38   Foster, p. 80.
39   USNIP, Nov 1945, p. 1337.
40   Ibid, p. 1339.
41   Campbell, p. 127.
42   Delano, p. 388.

Chapter 3

1   USNHC: http://www.history.navy.mil/
2   Hearn, p. 239.
3   NCE, Summer 1976, p. 8.
4   Hearn, p. 5, 7.
5   Hearn, p. 242.
6   Miller, p. 33.
7   Miller, p. 42.
8   POP, Feb 1937, p. 9.
9   Allen, p 50,51.
10   Jefferson to Monroe, Aug 11 1786.
11   Jones to Francois-Louis Teissedre de Fleury, Dec 1787,
      Smithsonian Institution, Washington, D.C.
12   Navy Register, p. 14, NARA, WDC.
13   FR, Oct 1937, n.p.
14   Portlock, p. 72-74.
15   POP, Oct 1926, p. 17.
16   Scofield, p. 309.
17   Ibid.
18   Ibid.
19   Ibid, p. 310.
20   Delano, P. 400.

Chapter 4

1   George Washington, "Fifth Annual Address to Congress,"
Dec 3, 1793, The Writings of George Washington from original
manuscript sources, 1745-1799 John Fitzpatrick Ed, 39 vol
(Washington: Government Printing Office, 1931-1944) 33:166.

2   NCE, Summer 1976, p. 9.

3   Archibald, p. 28.

4   USNHC, http://www.history.navy.miV

5   USNHC, http://www.history.navy.mil/USS Constitution/

6   Miller, p. 102, from an 1812 Broadsheet.

7   NARA, M625, RG 45, 1973.

8   Barratt, p. 4.

9   Pierce, p. 38.

10   Ibid.

11   Ibid, p. 37.

12   Ibid, p. 39.

Chapter 5

1   Emmons, p 65.

2   USNIP, Oct 1956, p. 1136.

3   Ibid.

4   Porter to Hamilton, NARA San Bruno CA.

5   USNIP, Oct 1956, p. 1138.

6   Ibid, p. 1137.

7   Gruppe, p. 112.

8   Porter, p. 15.

9   Porter, p. 23.

10   USNIP, Porter, p. xix.

11   Ibid, p. xx.

12   Porter, p. 266.

13   Ibid, p. 268.

14   The Register of Shipping for 1813. London Society of Merchants,
Shipowners and Underwriters.

15   Porter, p 515.

16   Ibid, p 517.

17   Report of Gamble, Aug 30 1815, Niles Weekly Register, p. 293.

18   Porter, p 523,4.

19   Ibid, p. 524.

20   Ibid, p. 525.

21   ANC, Sept. 22 1836.

Chapter 6

1   Daws, p. 54.

2   HHS, Oct 1927, p. 13.

3   Langdon, p. 72f.

4   HHS, Oct 1927, p. 11.

5   Gast, p. 180.
6   POP, Mar 1938, p. 20.
7   Wisniewski, Rise and Fall, p. 24.
8   Daws, p. 55.
9   Foster, p. 76.
10   HHS, 1916, p. 37 - 8
11   Foster, p. 76.
12   SCI, Jul 1976, p. 299.
13   HHS, 1923, p. 54. - 61.
14   HHS, 1923, p. 57.
15   Judd, Anthology, p. 23.

Chapter 7

1   Russ, Revolution, p. 93.
2   Kraus, p. 12.
3   Smith, Bradford, p. 171.
4   Bingham, p. 170.
5   Ibid, p. 123.
6   Ibid, p. 124.
7   MPM, Feb 1912, p. 168.
8   Macrae, p. 18.
9   Bingham, p. 153.
10   Ibid, p. 155.
11   Daws, p. 66.
12   Ibid, p. 105.
13   Ibid, p. 56.
14   Macrae, p. 20.
15   Daws, p. 74.
16   Daws, p. 75.
17   Macrae, p. 29.
18   USNIP, May 1930, p. 404.
19   Macrae, p. 18.
20   Macrae, p. 37. Incidentally, none are identified as Methodists.
21   John Arrowsmith, London Nov 7, 1843, Archives of Hawaii.
22   Morrell, p. 64.
23   Daws, p. 77.
24   Macrae, p. 43.
25   Macrae, p. 19, fn 19.
26   Macrae, p. 20.
27   Log of Cyane, Log of Vincennes, Archives, USNA Annapolis.
28   HHS, 1907, p. 11.

Chapter 8

1   David Floyd, NARA Microfilm archives, p ii.
2   HHS, Dec 1900, p. 16.
3   Pierce, p. 44.
4   Ibid, p. 39

5   Kotzebue, p. 215.
6   Daws, p. 51-53.
7   PHR, 1933, p. 85.
8   Ibid, p. 89.
9   Ibid, p. 90.
10   Knox, p. 150.
11   Aaron Mitchell et al to President Monroe, Nantucket, Dec 1824
     House Report # 92, US Cong 28:2, p. 9-10. HHS 1930, p. 18, 19.
12   Knox, p. 150.
13   US Congress, 21:2. Aug 14, 1825. American State Papers.
14   Chart # 437m Archives of Hawaii.
15   AH, Apr 1971, p. 33.
16   Judd, p. 68.
17   USNIP, Jun 1943, p. 860.
18   AH, Apr 1971, p. 30-37, 85-87.
19   Percival to Anderson, Jan 17 1833. American State Papers,
     US Cong 21:2.
20   American State Papers, Documents, US Cong 21 :2, Jan 11 1833.
21   Bailey, Paul, p. 163.
22   HHS, 193O, p. 21, p. 303.

Chapter 9

1   HHS, 1913, p. 32.
2   HA, Mar 4 1926.
3   USS Vincennes official information booklet, p. 8.
4   POP, Feb 1937, p. 29.
5   SIG, Aug 13 1836.
6   HHS, 1964, p. 17.
7   HHS, 1928, p. 21.
8   USNIP, Aug 1927, p. 912.
9   POP, Feb 1937, p. 29.
10   Ibid, p. 30.
11   USNIP, Jun 1943, p. 862.
12   Young, p. 230.
13   USNIP, Aug 1927, p. 913.
14   Ibid, p. 914.
15   PHR, 1933, p. 97.
16   Morrell, p. 71.
17   Stanton, p. 61.
18   J.K. Paulding to Wilkes, Aug 11 1838.
19   POLY, Oct 3 1840, p. 1.
20   Wilkes, p. 471.
21   Ibid, p. 475.
22   Wilkes, p. 218.
23   Atlas of Charts Vol II, U.S. Exploring Expedition. Philadelphia,
     C Sherman and son Printers, 1858. Chart # 66.
24   POLY, Nov 20 1841, p. 95.
25   Wilkes, p. 471.

26   Wilkes, p. 473-4.
27   Stanton, p. 288.
28   Wilkes, vol iv, p. 79.
29   Jones to Upshur, Aug 31 1842, NARA.
30   Jones to Hooper, Aug 6 1840, NARA.
31   Ibid.
32   Love, v, 1 p. 177.
33   NCE, Summer 1976, p. 6.
34   Love, v. 1, p. 182.
35   HHS, Paper #3, Dec 5 1892.
36   Kuykendall, vol I, p. 214.
37   USNIP, Aug 1927, p. 915.
38   Langley, p. 34,5.
39   TA, Feb 28 1843.
40   Judd, IV, p. 117.
41   HHS Paper #7, 1895.
42   TA(Extra) Jul 31 1843.
43   POP, Nov 1937, p. 8.
44   HW, vol LXVII, Sept. 1883, p. 511-520.
45   Ibid, p. 516.
46   Ibid, p. 517.
47   POP, Nov 1936, p. 56.
48   Thomas to Kamehameha III, Hawaiian Archives.
49   Judd, Anthology, p. 65.
50   Hawaiian Archives.
51   Hobbs, p. 38.
52   HHS, 1957, p. 18.
53   Documents, "An Act of Grace", Hawaiian Archives.
54   Jones to Upshur, Aug 7 1843 and Aug 19 1843, NARA San Bruno.
55   Dallas to Upshur, Oct 1 1843.
56   POLY, Nov 15 1843, p. 1.

Chapter 10

1   Love, p. 193.
2   The Record, NARA, Mar 1998, p. 24.
3   Langley, p. 28.
4   POLY, Nov 22 1845, p. 114.
5   USNIP, Aug 1927, p. 916.
6   Van Brackle, p. 6.
7   USNIP, Aug 1927, p. 917.
8   USNIP, Aug 1927, p. 917.
9   Archives, Nimitz Library, USNA.
10   Solomons vol I, p. 3-5.
11   Van Brackle, p. 4.
12   Kame'eleikiwa, p. 8.
13   Judd, Anthology, p. 142.
14   Hobbs, p. 39.
15   Chinen, p. 16.
16   Foster, p. 78.

Chapter 11

1   USNIP, Aug 1927, p. 917.
2   Wisniewski, Rise and Fall, p. 48.
3   Ibid, p. 52.
4   HA, Jul 8, 1956.
5   Daws, p. 107.
6   Cabinet Council Minutes, Kingdom of Hawaii, Mar 3, 1864
    Archives of Hawaii.
7   Daws, p. 147.
8   Langley, p. 32, 33.
9   Spence, p 204.
10 Dictionary of American Naval Fighting Ships, vol IV, 1969, p. 387-8.
11 HHS, 1895, p. 9.
12 Ibid, p. 4.
13 POP, Nov 1937, p. 51.
14 Kanahele, p. 119.
15 POLY, Nov 9, 1844.
16 Kanahele, p. 119.
17 USNIP, Aug 1927, p. 918.
18 Daws, p. 174

Chapter 12

1   PAT, Feb 4, 1939, p. 3.
2   Navy Dept., Civil War, vol III, p. 105.
3   US Navy Reg 1782 - 1882, p 14, NARA Mcrflm Publn, Dale Floyd.
4   Miller, p. 193.
5   Navy Register, Statutes, vol 22, p 291, Aug 5, 1882.
6   USNIP, Aug 1927, p. xxxv.
7   HHS, 1895, p. 12.
8   Microfilm roll T 987 Seward to Cook NARA San Bruno.
9   Love, p. 325.
10 Judd, Anthology p. 68.
11 Daws, p. 209.
12 PCA, Sept. 24, 1870, p. 1.
13 USNIP, Jan 1971, p. 63.
14 Ibid, p. 64.
15 PCA, Sept. 24, 1870, p. 1.
16 USNIP Apr 1929, p. 314, Hawaii Archives.
17 Peirce to Fish, Feb 28 1871, T-987 NARA San Bruno.
18 Ibid.
19 AHR, Apr 1925, p. 561.
20 Schofield to Belknap May 8, 1873, NARA I, WDC.
21 AHR Apr 1925, p. 563.
22 Ibid, p. 564.
23 Ibid.
24 Map # 448, USNIP May 1930, p. 405.
25 Van Brackle, p. 8.
26 Schofield to Belknap Report p. 1, May 8, 1873, NARA I WDC.
27 HG Nov 14, 1873, p. 1.

Chapter 13

1   Tate, p. 83.
2   PHR Nov 1962, p. 349-358.
3   Daws, p. 196.
4   Kuykendall, vol II, p. 5.
5   Ibid.
6   Ibid, p. 4.
7   Daws, p. 201.
8   HHS, 1912, p. 14.
9   USNIP, Aug 1927, p. 920.
10   USNIP, Dec 1938, p. 1764.
11   USNIP, Aug 1927, p. 920.
12   USNIP, Dec 1938, p. 1764.
13   HA, Oct 13, 1946, p. 2.
14   HHR, Apr 1963, p. 43.
15   Wisniewski, Rise & Fall, p. 68.
16   Stevens to Hunt May 15, 1881, NARA San Bruno.
17   PHR, June 1945, p. 157.
18   Dye, p. 98.
19   Ibid, p. 103.
20   Bird, p. 33.
21   Balch to Chandler, Nov 15 1882, NARA San Bruno.
22   HON Nov. 1987, p. 249.
23   Wisniewski, Rise & Fall, p. 78.
24   Ibid, p. 77-8.
25   Photos, Hawaii State Archives.

Chapter 14

1   Wisniewski, Rise & Fall, p. 84.
2   Ibid, p 84.
3   HAA, p. 33.
4   Daws, p. 252.
5   HHS, 1964, p. 9.
6   USNIP Apr 1940, p. 518.
7   HG, Jan 25 1887.
8   Ibid, Feb 18 1887.
9   HHS, 1964, p. 7.
10   USNIP, Apr 1940, p. 518.
11   HHS, 1964, p. 17.
12   US Cong 50:1, House Ex Doc. 238 p. 60.
13   HHS, 1964, p. 17.
14   Ibid, p. 18.
15   USNIP, May 1930, p. 406.
16   HON. Nov 1987, p. 287,
17   Van Brackle, p. 11.
18   PHR, Nov 1962, p. 335.
19   Ibid, p. 337.
20   Ibid, p. 338.
21   Stevens, p. 180.

Chapter 15

1   POP, Dec 1888, p. 4.
2   POP, June 1948, p 11 f.
3   Pop, Dec 1889, p. 1.
4   Pop, July 1890, p. 2.
5   POP, Jun 1948, p. 12.
6   Wisniewski, Rise & Fall, p. 87.
7   Liliuokalani, p. 200.
8   Ibid, p. 207.
9   Ibid.
10   Miller, p. 225.
11   US Navy in Cuba & Hawaii, Stackpole, n.p. 1898.
12   Liliuokalani, p. 210.
13   Ibid, p. 210.
14   Ibid, p. 21.
15   Wisniewski, Rise and Fall, p. 94.
16   Ibid, p. 91.
17   Liliuokalani, p. 17.
18   Ibid, p. 85.
19   Ibid, p. 263.
20   Russ, Revolution, p 349.

Chapter 16

1   Liliuokalani, p 237.
2   Osborne, p 3.
3   Mahan, Interest, p. 47.
4   Pratt, p 16.
5   HHR, Oct 1964, p. 175.
6   Pratt, p 34.
7   Daws, p. 272.
8   Ibid, p 236-8.
9   Daws, p. 267.
10   Pratt, p 49.
11   Wisniewski, Rise & Fall, p. 98.
12   Liliuokalani, p. 235.
13   Wisniewski, Rise & Fall, p. 99.
14   Liliuokalani, p. 235-236.
15   State Dept., Documents # 4, NARA San Bruno.
16   Wisniewski, Rise & Fall, p. 100.
17   Liliuokalani, p. 246.
18   Ibid, p. 246.
19   Wisniewski, Rise & Fa]], p. 100.
20   Nawahi, Joseph Kahooluhi, np
21   HHR, April, 1963, p. 45.
22   Liliuokalani, p 237-241.
23   Ibid, p 267.
24   Ibid, p 268.
25   Ibid, p 274.
26   Ibid, p 279.

26 Ibid, p 296.

Chapter 17
1   Morgan, p 130.
2   Wisniewski, Rise & Fall, p 107.
3   Love, p. 386; Mahan p. 505.
4   Love, p 386,7.
5   Hitch, p. 123.
6   EB, Dec 23, 1898, p. 7.
7   Love, p. 386,7.
8   Morgan, p. 1.
9   EB, Jan 31 1898, p. 1.
10   Ibid, Jun 4 1898.
11   Osborne, p. 135.
12   AHR, Apr 1931, p. 555.
13   Ibid, p. 552.
14   Ibid, p. 556.
15   Ibid, p. 560.
16   Foster, p. 82.
17   HS, Aug 11 1898, p. 1.
18   POP, Mar 1938, p. 5.
19   Day to Cooper, Telegram July 8 1898, Roll T987 NARA San
Bruno.
20   Wisniewski, Rise &: Fall, p. 109.
21   Young, p. 301.
22   Solomons vol I, p. 5.
23   HS, Aug 17 1898, p. 1.
24   Liliuokalani video, Hawaiian History.
25   Cohen, Images, p. 291.
26   Young, p. 303.
27   EB, Aug 12 1898, p. 1.
28   Ibid.
29   EB, Aug 16 1898, p. 4.
30   Ibid, Aug 17 1898, p. 1.
31   Ibid, Sept. 2 1898, p. 1.
32   Ibid.

Chapter 18
1   USCong 55:3 Senate Document # 16.
2   Ibid, p. 1.
3   Organic Act, p. 1, Hawaiian Archives.
4   EB, Sept. 1, 1898, p. 1.
5   Ibid, Dec 23 1898, p. 1.
6   Wisniewski, Territorial Years, p. 5.
7   USCong 55:3 Doc. 16, p. 16.
8   Ibid, p. 17.
9   Ibid, p. 18.
10   Organic Act, Hawaiian Archives.
11   Wisniewski, Territorial Years, p. 11.
12   Daws, p. 294-5.

13   Wisniewski, Territorial Years, p. 12.
14   Daws, p. 295.
15   Ibid, p. 296.
16   Ibid, p. 333.
17   Wisniewski, Territorial Years, p. 12.
18   Dye, p. 163.
19   Wisniewski, Territorial Years, p. 15.

Chapter 19

1   Coletta, p. 433.
2   EB, Jul 1 1901.
3   Turnbull, p. 1.
4   Ibid, p. 2.
5   USCong 65:3 Senate Docs #418 p. 126.
6   Snowbarger, p. 116.
7   Van Brackle, p. 21.
8   Ibid, p. 20.
9   POP, Holiday Issue 1936, R 56.
10   Merry to Chief of Bureau of Equipment, 28 May 1899,
      NARA San Bruno.
11   Fifty Years of Naval District Development, History
      Division, Office of the CNO, 1954.
12   Van Brackle, p 21.
13   Merry to Chief of Bureau of Equipment, July 11 1899.
14   Long to Merry July 27, 1899.
15   Merry to Bishop Estate Trustees, Sept. 11 1899.
16   Brown to Merry, Aug 15 1899.
17   Merry to Bureau of Equipment, Sept. 18 1899.
18   POP, Jun 1901, p. 16.
19   Merry to Bureau of Equipment, Sept. 19 1899.
20   Allen (acting SECNAV) to Merry, Nov 17 1899.
21   Merry to Navy Department, Dec 6 1899.
22   Solomons vol II, p. 6.
23   Coletta, p. 433.
24   Ibid.
25   Evans, p. 22 - 24.
26   US Cong 56:2 Acts, Mar 3 1901, p. 170.
27   POP, Feb 1901, p. 9.
28   POP, Holiday Issue 1936, p. 56.
29   Merry to Asst. SECNAV, Nov 13 1900, NARA San Bruno #294,
      RG 181.
30   NCE, Summer 1976, p. 19.
31   Asst. SECNAV to Pond, Jun 21 1901, NARA San Bruno.
32   Pond to Darling, Aug 3 1901.
33   Coletta, p. 434.
34   POP, Jun 1901, p. 16.
35   US Cong 56:2, Mar 3 1901.
36   Pond to Merry, Feb 18 1901.
37   Records and Abstracts, PACDIV Pearl Harbor.
38   EB, Jul 8 1901, p. 1.

Chapter 20

1	USNIP, May 1955, p. 615.
2	Braisted, p. 135.
3	Coletta, p. 435
4	USCong 56:2, p. 165.
5	Army & Navy Register, Jan. 11, 1902.
6	EB, Jul. 12, 1901, p. 1.
7	District Land Register 14ND-DPWO-11011/5 (6-61), PACDIV.
8	Van Brackle, p. 26.
9	Rpt/Bureau of Equipment 1903 p. 339, PACDIV.
10	POP, Jan. 1903, p. 7.
11	USNIP, May 1930, p. 407.
12	Darling to Treasury, Jun. 2, 1903, NARA San Bruno.
13	Terry to CO Iriquois, Oct. 24, 1903, NARA.
14	USNAVSTA Log, Nov. 27, 1903, NARA.
15	MacArthur to USAG, Feb. 2, 1904, AGO 453450, RG 94, NARA.
16	USNAVSTA Log, Nov. 28, 1903.
17	General Order #158, Apr. 28, 1904.
18	Elliott to Terry, Oct. 19, 1903, NARA.
19	Terry to Elliott, Oct. 19, 1903.
20	Elliott to Terry, Nov. 24, 1903.
21	Terry to Elliott, Dec. 18, 1903.
22	Denny to Terry, Jan. 2, 1904.
23	Terry to Elliott, Jan. 3, 1904.
24	Terry to Elliott, Jan. 25, 1904.
25	Elliott to Terry, Feb. 6, 1904.
26	Terry to Elliott, Feb. 6, 1904.
27	Terry to Asst. SECNAV, Feb. 9, 1904.
28	Catlin to Elliott, Feb. 9, 1904.
29	Converse to Terry, Nov. 16, 1904.
30	Niblack to Colley, Jul. 11, 1904.
31	Niblack to Terry, Apr. 14, 1905.
32	McCawley to COMUSMC, Sept. 22, 1905.
33	Wrenn to Niblack, Nov. 9, 1905.
34	Denny to COMUSMC, Nov. 20 1905.
35	Harllee to COMUSMC, Oct. 30, 1905.
36	Elliot to Horton, Nov. 17, 1905.
37	Elliott to Bigler, Jan. 8, 1906, NARA.
38	Newberry to Lyon, Feb. 26, 1906.
39	Elliott to Shearer, May. 14, 1906.
40	Very Rpt, Aug. 10, 1906.
41	Bigler Rpt to Russell, Nov. 15, 1906.
42	Russell to Very, Dec. 7, 1906.
43	Very to Metcalf, Apr. 6, 1907.
44	Bigler to Russell, Aug. 13, 1907.
45	Very to Russell, Aug. 14, 1907.
46	Endorsement, RG 181, Entry 410, Sept. 27, 1907, NARA

Chapter 21

1   HHR, Apr 1963 p. 47.
2   Blackman, p. 177.
3   POP, July 1898, p. 101.
4   Dulles, p. 134.
5   Ibid p. 24.
6   HHS 1955, p. 14.
7   Ibid.
8   Taft to McKinley, Apr 27 1900, McKinley papers, LOC.
9   Ibid, p. 15.
10   HS, Sept. 10 1900, p. 3.
11   POP, Aug. 1897, p. 119.
12   POP, Jul 1900, p. 8.
13   Ibid.
14   HHR, Apr 1963, p. 47.
15   POP,Aug 1900, p. 1.
16   EB, Aug. 16 1898, p. 1.
17   e.g. EB, Jul 1 1905.
18   Ibid.
19   EB, Jul 14 1905.
20   POP, May 1908, p. 1.
21   Baer, p. 45.
22   Hart, p. viii.
23   POP, May 1908, p. 1.
24   Patrol, Oct 21, 1939, Run 42.
25   Hart, p. 181.
26   Howarth, p. 287.
27   Baer, p. 46, fn. 53.
28   Early Sunset Magazine 1908, p. 77.

Chapter 22

1   US Cong 59:2, Sen Doc #147.
2   Love, p. 437-8.
3   Linn, p. 85.
4   Hitch, p. 123.
5   MPM, May 1917, p. 424.
6   Navy Dept. History, p. 1.
7   Coletta, p. 436.
8   USCong 60:1, May 13 1908.
9   Ibid, Jun 7 1900, Mar 3 1901, Jun 29 1906, Mar 2 1907.
10   USNIP, May 1930 p. 408.
11   Pearl Harbor Naval Shipyard booklet, 1990.
12   US Cong 61:2, Jun 24 1910.
13   US Cong 61:3, Mar. 4, 1911.
14   US Cong 62:2, Aug 22 1912.
15   Dillingham to Paxton, Apr. 27, 1900, Dillingham Papers, Hawaiian Archives.

16   Dewey to Meyer, Oct. 28, 1910, Letters to SECNAV 1885- 1926, RG45 M89, NARA.
17   Rittenhouse to Merry, Dec. 28, 1887, NARA RG 45.
18   USCong 62:2, Aug. 22, 1912.
19   Snowbarger, p. 128.
20   Doyle to Daniels, Apr. 30, 1919, RG 45 M89 NARA.
21   POP, Jan. 1, 1912,R27.
22   POP, Jan. 1, 1912, p. 27-29.
23   Swanborough & Bowers, p. 2.
24   Domance, p. 23, 24.
25   District Land Register, Document #012, PACDIV.
26   Horvat, p. 33.
27   Ibid, p. 52.
28   POP, May 1919, p. 11.
29   Solomons vol 11, p. 7.
30   HSB, Mar. 16, 1915.
31   Patrol, Dec. 1997/Jan. 1998, p. 13.
32   Bartholomew, p. 10-12.
33   Solomons vol II, p. 7.
34   Potter, Nimitz, p. 132-135.
35   Dodge, p. 1-3.
36   Ibid, p. 6.
37   Oden, p. 327f
38   POP, Oct. 1912 p. 1.
39   Baer, p. 52.
40   USNIP, Jun. 1961 p. 158.
41   Van Brackle, p. 48.
42   Ibid, p. 55.
43   POP, Jul. 1916, p.24.

Chapter 23

1   Seager, p. 489.
2   HHR, Apr. 1963, p. 47.
3   Ibid.
4   Log of USS St. Louis, 1128, Feb. 4, 1917, USNA.
5   USNIP, Apr. 1935, p. 496-7.
6   Daniels Rpt, Dec. 1, 1918; Jones p. 216.
7   Wisniewski,TerritorialYears, p. 19.
8   Day, p. 261.
9   Kuykendall, Hawaii, p. 271.
10   POP, Jan. 1912, p. 27.
11   Day, p. 262.
12   Swanborough and Bowers, p. 2.
13   Ibid.
14   PPM, Jan./Mar., 1937, p. 19.
15   Van Brackle, p. 81.
16   Ibid, p. 264.
17   MPM, May 1917, p 417

18   Kuykendall, Hawaii, p. 195.
19   POP, Apr. 1938, p. 16.
20   Day, p. 233.

Chapter 24
1   USNIP, Jul. 1970 p. 60 - 67.
2   Braisted, p. 41.
3   Command History PH Naval Shipyard, July 1959.
4   HHS, 1943 p. 56.
5   Ibid, p. 57.
6   SB, Feb. 5, 1983, p. A6.
7   POP, Dec. 1, 1912, p. 71.
8   USNIP, May 1944, p. 538.
9   ASCE, Transactions Paper #1354, 1915.
10   Coletta, p. 439.
11   US Navy Plan Files, PACDIV, Sept. 18, 1910.
12   USNIP, May 1944 p. 538.
13   USNSY, And So It Was p. 7.
14   MPM, Jun. 1911, p. 608.
15   SECNAV Rpt 1913, p. 16, NARA.
16   USNIP, May 1944, p. 539.
17   Coletta, p. 441.
18   SB, Feb. 18, 1913, p. A1.
19   SB, Feb. 19, 1913, p. A1.
20   POP, Mar. 1913, p. 7.
21   USNSY Command History, Jul. 1959, R 6.
22   USNIP, May 1930, p. 409.
23   USNSY, Command History, p. 3.
24   USNIP, May 1944, p. 537.
25   Ibid, Sept. 1914, p. 1505.
26   Ibid, May 1944, p. 544.
27   Ibid, p. 545.
28   POP, Sept. 1924 p. 16-17.
29   Navy Department, Activities, p. 251-2.
30   SB, Aug. 21, 1919 P. 2.

Chapter 25
1   USCong 60: I May 27, 1919, House Naval Affairs Committee.
2   NHC Website, http:www.history.navy.mil/.
3   SB, Jul. 10, 1919 p. A1.
4   Solomons vol II, p. 5.
5   Ibid, p. 7.
6   Snowbarger, p. 210.
7   Executive Order #3474, May 31, 1921.
8   Snowbarger, p. 196-199.
9   Coletta, p. 448.
10   Snowbarger, p. 195

11   Morison, p. Iii.
12   Snowbarger, p. 204.
13   Coletta, p. 563.
14   Van Brackle, p. 71.
15   Ibid, p. 76.
16   Executive Order #2566, Mar. 28, 1917.
17   SB, Dec. 6, 1962 p. A1.
18   USNIP, Jun. 1942 p. 885-6.
19   USNIP, Feb. 1950 p. 163-169.
20   Humble, p. 24-25.
21   Somolons vol II, p. 15.
22   Van Brackle p. 88.

Chapter 26

1   Colleta, p. 450.
2   Wisniewski, Territorial Years, p. 411.
3   District Land Register, PACDIV.
4   Submarine Base Brochure.
5   Van Brackle, p. 92.
6   PHNSY Command History, p. 11.
7   Daws, p. 312.
8   Solomons vol II, p. 17.
9   USNIP, April 1955, p. 415.
10   Morison vol III, p. 31.
11   Coletta, p. 450.
12   SB, Sept. 22 1931, p. A1.
13   PPM, Jan. 1937, p. 21.
14   Roosevelt, p. 411.
15   HA, Oct. 13, 1946, R 2.
16   HHR, Apr. 1963, p. 48.
17   Solomons vol II, p. 19.
18   Scott, p. 835.
19   Morison vol III, p. 32.
20   POP, Jan. 1936 p. 31.
21   Ibid, p. 18.
22   POP, Holiday Issue 1937, p. 74.
23   HA, April 17, 1935, p. 1.
24   POP, Aug. 1937, p. 7.
25   Earhart Search, File A1937, A4-3, Boxes 92,93, NARA San Bruno.
26   Solomons vol III, p. 2.
27   Navy Dept., Building, p. 122-124.
28   SB, May 31, 1939, p. A1.
29   Ibid, Jun. 2, 1939, p. 3.
30   Ibid, Dec. 2, 1939, p. A1.
31   Ibid, Jan. 13, 1940, p. A1.
32   HA, Feb. 11, 1940, p. Al.
33   Navy Dept., Chronology WWII, p. 5.
34   Morison vol III, p. 38.
35   Ibid, p 39

36   POP, Sept. 1937, p. 25.
37   Ibid, p. 31.
38   Cohen, Orient, p. 90.
39   Dodge, Ford Island History Summary, PACDIV n.p.
40   SB, Dec. 7, 1983, p. A1.
41   Ibid, p. 3.
42   SB, May 3, 1940, p. A1.
43   US Navy, Bluejackets' Manual, 10th Ed., p. 16-17.
44   USNIP, Sept. 1941, p. 1241-1254.

Chapter 27

1   SB, Jan. 13, 1940, p. Al.
2   Coletta, p. 455-6.
3   Patrol, Aug./Sept. 1997.
4   USNSY, And So It Was, p. 37.
5   Solomons vol III, p. 4.
6   Sr. Regina Catherine Brandt, personal communication.
7   USNIP, Dec. 1973, p. 850.
8   Morrison vol III, p. 128
9   US Navy Dept., Chronology WWII, p. 7.
10   USNIP, Dec. 1955, p. 1317.
11   Feis, p. 1941.
12   McComas, p. 1, 10.
13   US Navy Dept., Chronology WWII, p. 8.
14   Ewing, W. Oct. 16, 1941.
15   USNIP, Dec. 1955, p. 1322
16   McComas, p. 45.
17   Imperial Naval General Staff, Order No. 1, US Navy Dept.
18   Matson, p. 85.
19   USNIP, Dec. 1955, p. 1326.
20   McComas, p. 33, 44.
21   IIA, Dec. 8, 1981, p. B1.
22   NARA Website http://www.nara.gov/exhall/originals/fdr.html.
23   USNA, Shipmate, Dec. 1973, p. 16-20.
24   http://www.navytimes.com/world p. 1 .
25   HHR, Apr. 1963, p. 49.
26   USNWR, Feb. 4, 1955, p. 130.
27   Roosevelt to Joint Session of Congress, Dec. 8, 1941.
28   Weintraub, p. 645.
29   Mrs. Alice H. Hollingsworth, personal account Nov. 1996.
30   Jones, p. 299.
31   Brown, p. 50.
32   Potter, Bull Halsey, p. 13.
33   Weintraub, p. 631-2.
34   Brown, p. 32.
35   Kuykendall & Day, p. 257.
36   Bartholomew, p. 58.
37   PHNSY, Command History p. 12.

Chapter 28

1   Kuykendall & Day, p. 259.
2   Cohen, p. 254.
3   SB, Dec. 31, 1941, p. B1.
4   Potter, Nimitz, p. 9.
5   Navy Dept., Chronology, p. 16,22.
6   Sr. Regina Catherine Brandt, Personal Communication.
7   HA, Mar. 8, 1942, p. AI.
8   USNIP, May 1953, p. 478, 484; both local newspapers Mar. 5, 1942.
9   SUBASE History, p. 3.
10 Potter, Nimitz, p. 63-77.
11 SB, Jun. 7, 1992 p. A 21.
12 Potter, Nimitz, p. 89.
13 Ibid, p. 91-105.
14 SB, Oct. 2, 1982, p. B4; FISC Command History.
15 Potter, Nimitz, p. 181.
16 Ibid, p. 219.
17 Ibid, p. 224.
18 Ewing, Good Evening, p. 66, Broadcast Feb. 11, 1943.
19 Ibid, p. 8, Broadcast April 22, 1943.
20 Snowbarger, p. 259.
21 Navy Dept., Building, p. 130-147.
22 Ibid, p. 130.
23 POP, Dec. 1943, p. 4.
24 Ibid.
25 HA, Sept. 18, 1943, p. A1.
26 Ibid, Jan. 20, 1943, p. 2.
27 Joe DeMattos, LOG, Dec. 7, 1995.
28 Muir, p. 149.
29 HA, Jun. 15, 1944; SB, Apr 7 1963.
30 SB, May 24, 1944.
31 Potter, Nimitz, p. 303.
32 Ibid, p. 342.
33 Ibid, p. 343.
34 Huie, p. 11.
35 Ibid, p. 205.
36 Life Magazine, Collector's edition, Fall 1991, p. 53.
37 Ships' logs, NARA College Park, MD.
38 Potter, Nimitz, p. 390.
39 Ships' logs, NARA, College Park MD.
40 SB, Sept. 11, 1945, p. Al.

Chapter 29

1   Breemer, p. 17.
2   Potter, Nimitz, p. 380.
3   SB, Mar. 29, 1946.
4   US Navy Command Narrative, US Naval Base, Pearl Harbor, T.H. 1946.

5   HA, Oct. 16, 1946.
6   Wisniewski, Territorial Years, p. 109.
7   Fuchs, p. 409.
8   Alexander & Baldwin, Castle & Cooke, American Factors Ltd.,
     Theo. Davies & Co., C. Brewer & Co.
9   USCong 80:2, Senate Committee/Public Lands (Cordon Rpt) 1948.
10   USCong 86:1, 1956, p. 3461.
11   Russ, Republic, p. 376.
12   Daws, p. 387.
13   House UnAmerican Activities Committee.
14   International Longshoreman's and Warehouseman's Union.
15   Wisniewski, Territorial Years, p. 99-100.
16   Chapin, p. 236.
17   Day, p. 381.
18   POP, Feb. 1959, p. 11.
19   Wisniewski, Territorial Years, p. 114.
20   Ibid.
21   SB, Apr. 18, 1944, p. 2.
22   POP, Oct. 1944, p. 7.
23   Ibid, p. 8-9.
24   Wisniewski, Pearl Harbor, p. 55.
25   Swanborough & Bowers, p. 3.
26   Coulter, p. 36.
27   HSB, Sept. 18, 1951, p. 3.
28   Ibid.
29   Deck Logs, USS Iowa (BB61), NARA, College Park, MD.
30   Gordon, p. 20.
31   Ibid, p. 21.
32   Ibid, p. 22.
33   HA, Dec. 7, 1953, p A1.
34   Ibid.
35   SB, May 15, 1954, p. 12.
36   HA, May 19, 1955, p. B7.
37   POP, Nov. 1957, p. 99.
38   HA, Jul. 8, 1956, p. A 13.
39   PAT, Dec. 21, 1957.
40   Coulter, p. 36.
41   Wisniewski, Territorial Years, p. 95.
42   HVCB http://www.gohawaii.com/ p. 5.
43   POP, Aug. 1959, p. 38.
44   Jones, p. 52.
45   Coulter, p. 35.
46   Wisniewski, Territorial Years, p. 102.
47   Foster, p. 50.
48   USDI Brochure, Pu'uhonua o Honaunau.
49   Ibid

Chapter 30
1   SB, Nov. 20, 1960, p. Al.
2   Dodge, p. 8.
3   Polmar & Allen, p. 672-3.
4   COMSUBPAC, Personal Communication.
5   htip://www.cps.navy.mil.
6   SB, Apr. 11, 1961, p. 13.
7   SB, Feb. 13 1962, p. AI.
8   SB, Mar. 8, 1965, p. A4.
9   Love vol II, p. 487.
10   SB, Oct. 7, 1969, p. A1.
11   Patrol, Apr. 7, 1961, p. 7.
12   Ibid.
13   Wisniewski, Pearl Harbor, p. 56.
14   Lenihan, p. 176.
15   Ibid, p. 180.
16   National Survey of Historic Sites and Buildings,
     NPS Jul. 19, 1962, p C1, 2.
17   SB, Jun. 28, 1964, p A4.
18   HA, Sept. 13, 1968, p. A6.
19   Ship's Logs, NARA, College Park, MD.
20   Bailey & Farber, p. 4.
21   Ibid, p. 150.
22   Ibid, p. 151.
23   Ibid, p. 152.
24   Ibid, p. 158.
25   California History, Spring 1979, p. 62-75.
26   Zumwalt, My Father p. 117.
27   Polmar & Allen, p. 191.

Chapter 31
1   Rachel Carson, Oxford University Press, New York, 1951.
2   Rachel Carson, Houghton Mifflin Co., Boston, 1962.
3   HA, Mar. 27, 1970, p. B1.
4   HA, Sept. 17, 1970, p. B4.
5   Ibid.
6   SB May 15, 1996, p. A3.
7   HA, Sept. 17, 1970 p. B4.
8   Ibid.
9   HA, May 1, 1971, p. A2.
10   SB, Jul. 1, 1996, p. A2.
11   HA, Oct. 13, 1972, p. B9.
12   SB, Mar. 10, 1978, p. A5.
13   SB, Aug. 24, 1978, p. C9.
14   www.cpf.navy.mil/rimpac98/index.htm.
15   PACDIV Historic Preservation Plan, Feb. 1978 p. ES 2.
16   Ibid, p. ES 3.

17   NPS, Nat'l Survey of Historic Sites & Buildings, 1974 update, p. C 3.
18   NPS, National Survey of Historic Sites & Buildings, July 19, 1962.
19   Ibid, p. C-5.
20   SB, Sept. 17, 1974, p. D11.
21   HA, May 24, 1973, p. A1.
22   SB, May 24, 1973, p. A4.
23   SB, Sept. 17, 1973 p. D11.
24   Zumwalt, On Watch, p. 115.
25   Eller, p. ix.
26   Bosworth, p. 239.
27   USNIP, May 1972, p. 112- 125.
28   Breemer, p. 30.
29   SB, Feb. 22, 1970, p. F3.
30   HA, Sept. 19, 1975, p. A 10.
31   USNSY Modernization Study, June 18 1972.
32   SB, Feb. 17, 1981, p. A7.
33   HA, Oct. 17, 1989, p. A1.
34   SB, Nov. 9, 1982, p. A 17.
35   SB, Mar. 13, 1983, p. A5.
36   SB, Mar. 21, 1984, p. A1, A11.
37   HA, Jul. 17, 1986, p. A4.
38   HA, Feb. 3, 1975, p. 1.
39   SB, Mar. 6, 1972, p. B8.
40   SB, Mar. 25, 1972, p. A8

Chapter 32

1   Muir, p 120.
2   Breemer, p. 31.
3   HA, Jul. 7, 1984, p. A1, 6.
4   Ibid, p. A1.
5   HA, Jul. 19, 1984, p. A7.
6   Ibid, P A1, A4.
7   HA, May 13, 1989, p. A1.
8   HA, Sept. 14, 1984, p. A4.
9   SB, Oct. 5, 1984, p. A4.
10   HA, Oct. 28, 1989, p. A4.
11   Navy Dept., USS Arizona Memorial, May 1962.
12   SB, Aug. 25, 1973, p. 2.
13   SB, Dec. 10, 1973, p. C7.
14   Wisniewski, PH p. 64.
15   Lenihan, p. 173.
16   Wisniewski, PH, p. 173.
17   HA, Dec. 5, 1983 p. B1.
18   History of Bowfin, brochure.
19   HA, Dec. 9, 1987, p. A5.
20   SB, Dec. 7, 1991, p. 3.
21   HA, Dec. 7, 1995, p. Al.
22   SB, Aug. 8, 1984. p. A17,

23   SB, May 2, 1989, p. B 1.
24   HA, Oct. 13, 1982, p. D5.
25   HA, May 11, 1982, p. A2.
26   PACDIV Command Histories, Engineering Library,
      Pearl Harbor Naval Base.

Chapter 33

1   SB Mar. 22,1995 p. A-7.
2   SB, April 15, 1998, p. A 14.
3   Ibid.
4   Engineering News Record, Aug. 18, 1997, p. 34.
5   Ibid, p. 37.
6   HA April 15, 1998, p. A 8.
7   SB Jan. 11, 1996 p. A 14.
8   SB Nov. 29, 1996, p. A 3.
9   ENR Aug. 18, 1997, p. 34.
10   Patrol, June/July, 1997, p. 26.
11   HA April 16, 1998 p. A1
12   Fore and Aft, June/July, 1998, p. 9-10.
13   HA April 15, 1998 p. A1
14   HA April 13, 1998 p. A1.
15   Ibid p. A2.
16   Ibid p. A8.
17   OPNAVINST 3300.53.
18   HA Sept. 29, 1997, p. B 4.
19   HA Sept. 30, 1997, p. A 6.
20   Concept plan for Ford Island, Oct. 1996.
21   Ibid p. 2-5
22   Ford Island, A Navy Place. Facilities & Environment Dept. Pearl
      Harbor.
23   Personal communication, Jeff Dodge at PACDIV. Aug. 19, 1998.
24   Concept Plan for Ford Island, Oct. 1996.
25   NT, July 20, 1998, p. 20.
26   Ibid.
27   Holt, p. 14.
28   Coles, p. 64.
29   Coles, p. iii.
30   USNIP Aug. 1998, p. 56
31   Ibid, p. 57.
32   SB May 15, 1996, p. A3
33   SB July 1, 1996, p. A2
34   HA Sept. 20, 1994, p. A3.
35   HA Aug. 28, 1998, p. A4.
36   Pearl Harbor Naval Shipyard & IMF Strategic Plan, 1998-1999
37   LOG, April 24, 1997, p. 3.
38   Fore 'n Aft, Aug/Sep, 1998, p. 11.
39   HNN, May 8, 1998, p. 16.
40   Ibid

41   HNN, Apr. 1998.
42   HA Sept. 1, 1998, p. 1.
43   NT, May 18, 1998, p. 33.
44   HNN, May 8, 1998, p. A3.
45   SB Mar. 10, 1997, p. A3.
46   NT, Mar. 24, 1997, p. A1.
47   HNN, June 26, 1998, p. 7.
48   SB June 16, 1998 p. 1.
49   Ibid, p. A8.
50   SB June 17, 1998. Souvenir Edition, p. 1.
51   Ibid.
52   Sea Power, June 1998, p. 30.
53   HA Apr. 13, 1998, p B1.
54   Kaneohe Sun Press, Jun 26 - July 2, 1998. p. 18
55   HA June 14, 1998 p. A24.
56   HA June 4, 1998, p. B1.
57   HNN, June 26, 1998, p. 1.
58   Ford Island Plan.
59   HA Jun. 19, 1998 Special Report sec., p. 6.
60   SB Jun. 19, 1998, p. A8.
61   HA Mar. 26, 1991, p. A1.
62   Center Relay, FISC, Jun. 26, 1998, p. 6.
63   SB, Jun. 4, 1996, p. A1.
64   HNN, Jul. 3, 1998, p. A1; www.cpf.navy.mil/rimpac98/index.htm;
      Fore & Aft, Jun./Jul. 1998, P. 13.
65   Sea Power, Jul 1998; Pearl Harbor Naval Public Affairs Office,
      Aug. 17, 1998, p. 1.
66   LOG, May 21, 1998, p. 1.
67   PHNSY pamphlet, np.
68   www.hawaii.navy.mil, May 28, 1998, Admiral William Sutton,
      COMNAVBASE.
69   Captain John Shrewsbury, Chief/Staff COMNAVBASE,
      personal interview, Sept. 3, 1998.
70   HNN, Aug. 28, 1998, p. 1.
71   Patrol, Apr/May 1997; SB 652, Mar 11 1939.
72   LOG, Jan. 21, 1997, p. 1.
73   Ibid, Mar. 7, 1996, p. 1.
74   Ibid, Jan. 11, 1996, p. 2; Ibid, Feb 27 1997, p. 2.
75   Ibid, Mar. 21, 1996, p. 1.
76   HNN, Feb. 17, 2001. p. 1.
77   HNN, Apr. 15, 2001. p. 1.
78   NT, Aug. 10, 1998, p. 6.
79   Ibid, Jun. 22, 1998.
80   CINCPACFLT Today, P. 1.
81   NT, Jul. 13, 1998, p. 1.
82   LOG, Jan. 28, 1998, p. 7.
83   Preuher to Landauer and Landauer, Sept. 4, 1998.

Bibliography

Adler, Jacob & Robert Kamins. *The Fantastic Life of Walter Murray Gibson.* Honolulu: University of Hawaii Press, 1986.

Allen, Gardner W. *Our Navy and the Barbary Corsairs.* Boston: Houghton Mifflin, 1905.

Allen, Gwenfread. *Hawaii's War Years.* Honolulu: University of Hawaii Press, 1950.

American Navy in Cuba & Hawaii. Pictorial, Chicago: George M. Hill, Co., 1898.

Asler Ed & Gwynn Barrett. *Diaries of Walter Murray Gibson, 18861887.* Honolulu: University of Hawaii Press, 1973.

Bachisos, Marvin R. *Ships, USN, WWI, Korea Vietnam.* Bend, Oregon: Maverick Publications, 1978.

Baer, George W. *One Hundred Years of Sea Power.* Stanford: Stanford University Press, 1994.

Bailey, Beth & David Farber. *The First Strange Place: Race and Sex in WWII Hawaii.* Baltimore: Johns Hopkins Press, 1994.

Bailey, Paul. *Those Kings and Queens of Old Hawaii.* Los Angeles: Westernlore Books, 1975.

Barratt, Glynn. *The Russian Discovery of Hawaii.* Honolulu: Editions Ltd., 1987.

Barrere, Dorothy B. *Summary of Hawaiian History and Culture.* Typescript, National Park Service, Region 4, October 1961.
_____, Ancient Hawaiian Culture. Unpublished. Archives. Bishop Museum Library, Honolulu. 1967.

Bartholomew, C.A. *Mud, Muscle and Miracles.* Washington, D.C.: Natural History Center, 1990.

Beach, Edward L. *US Navy History: 200 Years.* New York: Henry Holt & Co., 1986.

Beechert, Edward D. *Crossroads of the Pacific.* Columbia: University South Carolina Press, 1991.

Bell, Roger. *Last Among Equals: Hawaiian Statehood and American Politics.* Honolulu: University of Hawaii Press, 1984.

Bingham, Hiram. *A Residence of Twenty One Years in the Sandwich Islands.* Rpt. Rutland, VT: Charles Tuttle Co., 1981.

Bird, Isabella. *Six Months in the Sandwich Islands.* Honolulu: University of Hawaii Press, 1964.

Bishop, Sereno Edward. *Reminiscences of Old Hawaii.* Honolulu: Hawaiian Gazette Co., 1916.
_____, *Correspondence with Reference to Pearl Harbor.* Honolulu: Hawaiian Gazette Co., 1892.

Blackman, William F. *The Making of Hawaii.* New York: AMS Press, 1977

Boll, Olivia. *History of the Hawaiian People.* Privately Printed, 1966.

Borg, Dorothy. *Two Ocean War Anthology.* New York: Columbia University Press, 1973.
_____& Shumpei Okamoto, eds. *Pearl Harbor as History.* New York: Columbia University Press, 1973.

Bosworth, Allan. *My Love Affair with the US Navy.* New York, Norton, 1969.
Bradford, James C. *Command Under Sail,* 1775-1880. Annapolis: Naval Institute Press, 1985.
Braisted, William Reynolds. United States Navy in the Pacific, *1897-1909.* Austin: University of Texas Press, 1958.
_____. *United States Navy in the Pacific 1909-1922.* Austin: University of Texas Press, 1971.
Breemer, Jan S. *U.S. Naval Developments.* Annapolis: Nautical and Aviation Publishing Co., 1983.
Broughton, William Robert. *A Voyage of Discovery to the North Pacific Ocean in the Years 1795-1798.* London, 1804.
Campbell, Archibald. *Voyage Around the World, 1806-1812.* Edinborough: Archibald Constable & Co., 1816.
Carr, Deryck. *History of the Pacific Islands.* Melbourne: MacMillan Co. of Australia, 1990.
Chapin, Helen Geraci. *Shaping History: The Role of Newspapers in Hawaii.* Honolulu: University of Hawaii Press, 1996.
Chickering, William H. *Within the Sound of the Waves.* New York: Harcourt Brace & Co., 1941.
Chinen, Jon J. *The Great Mahele. Honolulu:* University of Hawaii Press, 1958.
Clarke, Thurston. *Pearl Harbor Ghosts.* New York: William Morrow, 1991.
Cohen, Stan. *East Wind Rain.* Missoula: Pictorial Histories Publishing Co. 1987.
_____. *Images of the Spanish American War.* Missoula: Pictorial Histories Publishing Co., 1997.
_____. *Wings to the Orient. Missoula MT.* Pictoral Histories Publishing Co. 1985.
Coles, S.L. et al. *Biodiversity of Marine Communities in Pearl Harbor.* Honolulu: Bishop Museum Press, 1997.
Coletta, Paolo E. *United States Navy and Marine Corps Bases, Domestic.* Wesport, CN: Greenwood Press, 1985.
Coulter, John Wesley. *Pacific Dependencies of the United States.* New York: The MacMillan Co., 1957.
Craighill, E.S. *Ancient Hawaiian Civilization.* Rutland, VT: C.E. Tuttle Co., 1965.
Daws, Gavan. *Shoal of Time.* Honolulu: University of Hawaii Press, 1968
Day, Arthur Grove. *Hawaii and Its People.* New York: Meredith Press, 1968.
Delano, Amasa. *Narrative of Voyages and Travels.* Boston: E.G. House, 1818.
Denoon, E.D. *Cambridge History of Pacific Islanders.* Cambridge: Cambridge University Press, 1997.
Dibble, Sheldon. *A History of the Sandwich Islands.* Honolulu: T.H. Thrum, 1909.
Dodge, Jeffrey, AIA. *History of Quarters 'A'.* PACDIVNAVFACENGCOM, 1997.
Dole, Sanford. *Memoirs of the Hawaiian Revolution.* Honolulu: Honolulu Advertiser Publishing, Co., 1936.
Dorrance, John C. *The Pacific Islands and U.S. Security.* Westport, CT: Praeger Publishing Co., 1992.
Dulles, Foster Rhea. *America in the Pacific; A Century of Expansion.* Boston: Houghton Mifflin, 1932.
Dye, Bob, Ed. *Hawai'i Chronicles.* 2 vol. Honolulu: University of Hawaii Press. 1996, 1998.
Eller, Ernest McNeill. *Soviet Sea Challenge.* Chicago: Cowles Book Co., 1971.

Emmons, St. George F., USN. *The Navy of the United States from Commencement 1775-1853*. Washington: Gideon & Co., 1850.

Evans, Robley D., USN. *An Admiral's Log*. New York: D. Appleton & Co., 1910

Ewing, G. *Good Evening*. Honolulu: Honolulu Star Bulletin, 1943.

Falk, Edwin A. *From Perry to Pearl*. Garden City: Doubleday, 1943.

Feis, H. *The Road to Pearl Harbor*. Princeton: Institute for Advanced Study, 1950.

Fornander, Abraham. *An Account of the Polynesian Race*. 3 vol. Rutland, VT: C.E. Tuttle Co. 1969.

Foster, Nelson. *Bishop Museum and the Changing World of Hawaii*. Honolulu: Bishop Museum Press, 1993.

Fredman, L.E. *The U.S. Enters the Pacific*. London: Angus & Robertson, Ltd., n.d.

Fuchs, Lawrence. *Hawaii Pono: A Social History*. New York: Harcourt Brace & World, Inc., 1961.

Gast, Ross. *Letters and Journal of Don Francisco de Paulo Marin*. Agnes Conrad, Ed. Honolulu: University of Hawaii Press, 1975.

Gruppe, Henry. *The Frigates*. Alexandria, VA: Time Life Books, 1979.

Hagen, Kenneth. *American Gunboat Diplomacy*. New York: Greenwood Press, 1961.

Hart, Robert A. *Great White Fleet 1907-1909*. Boston: Little,

Hearn, Chester G. *George Washington's Schooners, First American Navy*. Annapolis: Naval Institute Press, 1995.

Hitch, Thomas Kemper. *Islands in Transition*. Honolulu: First Hawaiian Bank, 1992.

Hobbs, Jean. *Hawaii: A Pageant of the Soil*. Stanford: Stanford University Press, 1935.

Holt, John Dominis. *On Being Hawaiian*. Honolulu: Ku Pa'a Publishing Inc., 1964

Hooper, Paul F. *Elusive Destiny: The Internationalist Movement in Modem Hawaii*. Honolulu: University of Hawaii Press, 1980.

Hopkins, Jerry. *The Hula*. Hong Kong: Apa Productions, Ltd., 1982.

Horvat, William Joseph. *Above the Pacific*. Fallbrook, CA: Aero Publishers, 1966.

Howarth, Stephen. *To Shining Sea*. New York: Random House, 1991

Hoyt, Edwin. *Submarines at War*. New York: Stein & Day, 1983.

Huie, William B. *Can Do!* New York: E.P. Dutton, 1944.

Humble, Richard. *US. Fleet Carriers in World War H in Action*. Poole, England: Blandford Press, 1984.

Ii, John Papa. *Fragments of Hawaiian History*. Mary Pukui, Trans. Dorothy Barrere, Ed. Honolulu: Bishop Museum Press, 1963.

Joesting, Edward. *Hawaii: An Uncommon History*. New York: W.W. Norton & Co., Inc., 1972.

Johnson, Donald. *United States in the Pacific*. Westport, CT: Praeger Press, 1995.

Johnson, William L.C. *The West Loch Story*. Seattle: Westloch Publications, 1986.

Judd, Gerrit Parmele. *A Hawaiian Anthology*. New York: MacMillan, 1967.

Judd, Garrit P, IV. *Dr. Judd, Hawaii's Friend*. Honolulu: University of Hawaii Press, 1960.

Ka'anoi & Snakonberg. *The Hawaiian Name Book*. Honolulu: The Bess Press, 1988.

Kahn, David. The Codebreakers. New York: MacMillan Publishing Co., 1967.

Kamakau, Samuel M. Ruling Chiefs of Hawaii. Honolulu: Kamehameha Schools Press & Bishop Estate, 1992.

_____. *The People of Old*. Trans. Mary Kawena Pukui. Honolulu: Bishop Museum Press, 199 1.

Kame'eleihiwa, Lilikala. Native Lands and Foreign Desire. Honolulu: Bishop Museum Press, 1992.

Kanahele, George. *Waikiki From 100 BC to 1900 AD*. Honolulu: Queen Emma
    Foundations, 1995.
Kent, Harold Winfield. *Charles Reed Bishop, Man of Hawaii*. Palo Alto, Pacific Books,
    1965.
Knox, Dudley, *History of the US Navy*. New York: G. Putnam's Son, 1936.
Kotzebue, Otto von. *A Voyage Around the World in the Years 1823-1826*. London: Henry
    Colburn & Richard Bentley,1830
Kraus, Bob. *High Rise Honolulu*. New York: Coward-McCann, Inc. 1969.
Kuykendall, Ralph. *The Hawaiian Kingdom*. 3 vols. Honolulu:
    University of Hawaii Press, 1947.
_____. & A. Grove Day. Hawaii: A History. New York: Prentice Hall, 1948.
Kyselka, Will. *An Ocean in Mind*. Honolulu: University of Hawaii Press, 1987.
Langley, Harold. *Social Reforms in the USN*, 1798-1862. Urbana,IL:
    University Press of Illinois, 1967.
Langdon, Robert, ed. *Where the Whalers Went*. Canberra: Australian
    National University, 1984.
Lawson, R.L. *History of US Naval Air Power*. New York: The Military Press. 1918.
Ledyard, John. *Journal of Cook's Last Voyage*. Rpt. 1801 ed. Chicago: Quadrangle Books
    1963.
Lenihan, Daniel, ed. *Submerged Cultural Resources* study. Santa Fe:
    US Department of the Interior, 1990.
Lewis, C.L. *Our Navy in the Pacific and Far East Long Ago*. Annapolis: Naval Institute
    Press, 1943
Liliuokalani, *Hawaii's Story by Hawaii's Queen*. Rpt. 1898 ed. Tokyo:
    Charles Tuttle, 1961.
Linn, Brian McAllister. *Guardian of Empire*. Chapel Hill, NC:
    University of North Carolina Press, 1997.
Loomis, Albertine. *For Whom Are The Star's ?* Honolulu:
    University of Hawaii Press, 1976.
Lord, Walter. *A Day of Infamy*. New York: Bantam Books, 1956.
Love' Robert W., Jr. *History of the US Navy 1775-1941*. 2 vols.
    Harrisburg, PA: Stackpole Books, 1992
Lydgate, John M. *Ka-umu-alii, The Last King of Kauai*. Honolulu:
    Hawaiian Historical Society, 1915.
MacDonald, Gordon A., Agatin Abbott & Frank L. Peterson. *Volcanoes in the Sea*.
    Honolulu: University of Hawaii Press, 1970.
Macrae, James. *With Lord Byron at the Sandwich Islands in 1825*. Honolulu, 1922
Mahan, Alfred T. *From Sail to Steam*. New York: Da Capo Press, 1968.
_____. The Interest of America in Sea Power, Present and Future.
    New York: Little Brown & Co., 1890.
Mason, Theodore C. *Battleship Sailor*. Annapolis: Naval Institute Press, 1982.
Matson Navigation Co. *Matson, A Century of Service, 1882-1982*. San Francisco:
McAllister, J. Gilbert. *Archaeology of Oahu*. Honolulu: Bishop Museum Bulletin # 104,
    1933.
McComas, Terence. *Pearl Harbor Fact and Reference Book*. Honolulu: Mutual
    Publishing Co., 1991.
Miller, Nathan. *US Navy-Illustrated History*. Annapolis: American Heritage Publishing
    Co. & Naval Institute Press, 1977.

Millis, Walter. *This is Pearl!* Westport, CT: Greenwood Press, 1947.

Mintz, Frank Paul. *Revisionism and the Origins of Pearl Harbor.* Lanham, MD: University Press of America, 1985.

Morgan, William M. *"Strategic Factors in Hawaiian Annexation."* Diss. Claremont Graduate School, 1980.

Morison, Samuel Eliot. *History of United States Naval Operations in World War II.* 15 vols. Boston: Little Brown & Co. 1975

Morrell, William Parker. *Britain in the Pacific Islands.* Oxford: Oxford University Press, 1960.

Muir, Malcolm. *The Iowa Class Battleships.* Poole, England: Blandford Press, 1987.

Naval Shipyard Pearl Harbor. *And So It Was; A Brief History of Pearl Harbor and its Relationship to the Navy 1842-1941.* Pearl Harbor: 1941.

Navy Department. *Activities of the Bureau of Yards and Docks.* Washington: Government Printing Office, 1921

_____. *Building the Navy's Bases in World War II*, 1936-1946. Washington: Government Printing Office, 1946.

_____. *Civil War Chronology, 1861 - 1865.* Washington: Government Printing Office, 1971.

_____. *History of the Pacific Fleet.* www.history.navy.mil

_____. *Navy Chronology, World War II.* Washington, D.C.: Government Printing Office, 1955.

Nawahi, Joseph Kahooluhi. *Kukala a ka Hui Hawaii Aloha Aina. E malama I ka maluia.* Honolulu: Hui Aloha Aina, 1894.

Oden, Archibald. ED. *Navy Yearbook.* Washington: Government Printing Office, 1919.

Osborne, Thomas. *Empire Can Wait.* Kent, OH: Kent State University Press, 1981.

Palmer, Albert. *The Human Side of Hawaii.* Boston: The Pilgrim Press, 1924.

Pierce, Richard A. *Russia's Hawaiian Adventure, 1815-1817.* Berkeley: University of California Press, 1965.

Polmar, Norman & Thomas B. Allen. *Rickover.* New York: Simon & Schuster, 1982.

Ponko, Vincent. Jr. *Ships, Seas and Scientists.* Annapolis: Naval Institute Press, 1974.

Porter, Captain David. *Journal of a Cruise*, 1815. Annapolis: Naval Institute Press, 1986.

Porteus, Stanley. *Calabashes and Kings.* London: George G. Harrap & Co. Ltd., 1954.

Portlock, Nathaniel. *A Voyage Round the World, 1785-1788.* London: 1789.

Potter, E.B. *Bull Halsey.* Annapolis, Naval Institute Press, 1983.

_____. *Nimitz.* Annapolis: Naval Institute Press, 1976.

Potter, Norris W., Lawrence Kasdan, Dr. Ann Rayson. *The Hawaiian Monarchy.* Honolulu: The Bess Press Inc., 1983.

Prange, Gordon. At Dawn We Slept: *The Untold Story of Pearl Harbor.* New York: McGraw-Hill Co., 1981.

Pratt, Helen Gay. *In Hawaii.* New York: C. Scribner's & Sons. 1939.

_____. Hawaii, *Off Shore Territory.* New York: Charles Scribner's and Sons, 1944.

Price, A. Grenfell, Ed. *The Exploration of Captain James Cook in the Pacific as told by Selections of his own Journals 1768-1779.* New York: Dover Publications, 1971.

Pukui, Mary Kawena, Samuel Elbert, Esther T. Hookini. *Place Names of Hawaii.* Honolulu: University of Hawaii Press, 1974.

Rayson, Ann. *Modern Hawaiian History.* Honolulu: The Bess Press, 1984.

Reynolds, Lt. William. *Voyage to the Southern Ocean in 1838-1842.* Annapolis: Naval Institute Press, 1988.

Rigby, Barry. "American Expansion in the Pacific and Caribbean."
    Diss. University of Michigan, Ann Arbor, MI. 1978.
Roosevelt, F.D. *Personal Letters.* V. 1-4. New York: Duell, Sloan & Pearce, 1947.
Root, Eileen M. *Hawaiian Names/English Names.* Kailua, HI: Press Pacifica, 1987.
Russ, William Adam. *The Hawaiian Revolution (1893-1898).*
    Selingsgrove, PA: Susquehanna University Press, 1961.
_____. *The Hawaiian Republic (1894-1898).* Selingsgrove, PA:
    Susquehanna University Press, 1961.
Scofield, John. *Hail Columbia.* Portland: Oregon Historical Society, 1993.
Scott, Edward B. *Saga of the Sandwich Islands.* Tahoe City: Sierra
    Tahoe Publishing Co. Co., 1957.
Seager, Robert. Alfred Thayer Mahan, *The Man and His Letters.*
    Annapolis: Naval Institute Press, 1977.
Seiden, Allen. *Hawaii: The Royal Legacy.* Honolulu: Mutual
Smith, Bradford. *Yankees in Paradise.* Philadelphia: 1. B. Lippincott Co., 1966.
Smith' Stanley. *US Navy in World War II.* New York: William Morrow & Co., 1966.
Snowbarger, Willis Howard. "The Development of Pearl Harbor". Diss.
    University of California at Berkeley, Nov. 1950.
Solomons, Edward A. RAdm (ret). *Hawaii and the Navy 1820-1920.* Honolulu:
    Social Science Association, 1965.
Spence, Jonathan D. *God's Chinese Son.* New York: W.W. Norton & Co., 1966.
Stanton, William. *The Great United States Exploring Expedition.* Berkeley:
    University of California Press, 1975.
Sterling, Elspeth & Catherine C. Summers. *Sites of Oahu.*
    Honolulu: Bishop Museum Press, 1978.
Stevens, Sylvester D. *American Expansion in Hawaii 1842-1898.* New York:
    Russell & Russell, 1945.
Swanborough, Gordon & Peter M. Bowers. *United States Navy Aircraft Since 1911.*
    London: Putnam, 1968.
Tate, Merze. Hawaii: *Reciprocity or Annexation.* E. Lansing,
    Michigan State University Press, 1968.
Taylor, Albert Pierce. *Under Hawaiian Skies.* Honolulu: Advertiser Publishing Co., 1922.
Taylor, Leighton. *Sharks Of Hawaii.* Honolulu: University of Hawaii Press, 1993.
Toland, John. *Infamy: Pearl Harbor and Its Aftermath.* New York:
    Doubleday & Co., 1982.
Turnbull, Archibald. *History of United States Aviation.* New Haven:
    Yale University Press, 1949.
Twain, Mark. Letters from the Sandwich Islands. Stanford, CA:
    University of Stanford Press, 1938.
US Navy in Cuba and Hawaii. Pictorial. New York: Stackpole, 1898.
US Navy Shipyard. *And So It Was... Pearl Harbor,* Typescript.
Van Brackle, Joseph D. *Pearl Harbor from First Mention of "Pearl Lochs" to its Present
    Day Use.* Public Information Office, 14th naval District, Pearl Harbor, T.H.: 1955.
Vancouver, George. *Voyages of Discovery to the North Pacific and Round the World.* 3
    vols. London: G.G. & J. Robinson, 1798.
Weintraub, Stanley. *Long Day's Journey into War.* New York: Penguin Books, 1991.
Wilkes, Charles, USN. *Narrative of the US Exploring Expedition 1838-1841.*
    Philadelphia: Lee & Blanchard, 1845.

_____. *Voyage Round the World of the US Exploring Expedition*. Philadelphia: Geo. W. Orton, 1849.

Williams, Edith. *The Story of the Hawaiian Flag*. Honolulu: Edith Williams, 1963.

Wisniewski, Richard A. Hawaii: *The Territorial Years 1900-1959*. Honolulu: Pacific Basin Enterprises, 1989.

_____. *Pearl Harbor and the USS Arizona Memorial*. Honolulu: Pacific Basin Enterprises, Rev. Ed. 1986.

_____. *The Rise and Fall of the Hawaiian Kingdom*. Honolulu: Pacific Basin Enterprises, 1979.

Withington, Antoinette. *The Golden Cloak*. Honolulu: Hawaiiana Press, 1953.

Woodbury, David. *Builders for Battle*. New York: Doubleday & McClure, 1898.

Young, Lucien. *The Real Hawaii*. New York: Doubleday & McClure, 1898.

Zumwalt, Elmo Jr., USN. *My Father, My Son*. New York: Macmillan Publishing Co., 1986.

_____. *On Watch*. New York: Quadrangle/New York Times Book Co., 1976

Index

Symbols

14th Naval District
171, 183, 202, 208, 215, 253, 270, 291, 298, 305, 313

A

abdication 150, 151
Adams, John 35
Adams, John Quincy 69, 75
Adams, Samuel 23, 24, 42
Adamson, Thomas 114
Adler 130
Admiral Clarey Bridge 256, 339
Ahua point 254
Aiea Hospital 280
Akagi 245, 265, 276, 277
Ala Moana Assault Case 250
Alamagordo, New Mexico 287
Albert 90
Alden, John 85
Alexander and Baldwin 213
Alexander, Burton S. 116
Alfred 209
Algerine 25, 31, 65, 104
Aliiolani Hale 126
Aloha Oe 135, 158, 299
Aloha Week 300
American-Hawaiian Steamship Company 213
Annapolis 95
annexation 101,102, 103,104,107, 108,111,112, 115,116, 119,123, 124,
132, 138, 140, 143, 144, 145,147, 149, 151, 153, 155,156, 157, 158,
159, 161, 162,165,176, 178, 194
Anson, Lord 9, 59
Ariyoshi, George 324
Arizona Memorial Museum Association 329
Arthur 20
Atomic Energy Commission 316

B

Babbitt, Bruce 340
Bainbridge, William 34, 40
Balch, George 126
Bancroft, George 95
BANNER 282
Baranov, Alexander 66
Barber, Captain Henry 12, 20
Barbers Point 334
Barker, Albert 179
Barrere, Dorothy 85
Battleship Row 249
Bayonet Constitution 127
Beardslee, L.A. 154
Becket 73
Belknap, George E. 120
Belknap, William W. 116
Benard, R. 85
Beresford, Lord Charles 110, 111
Bering 66
Bigler, Epaminondas L. 184, 185
Bingham, Hiram 53, 56, 70, 71, 72, 73, 74, 76, 107
Bingham, Sibil 53
Bird, Horace 289
Bird, Isabella 125
Bishop, Bernice Pauahi 119, 120, 172
Bishop, Charles 119
Bishop Museum 189, 337
Bishop, Sereno Edwards 79
Bismarck, Otto von 130
Black Prince 23
Bloch, C.C. 270
Bloch, Claude C. 255
Blount, James H. 146, 147, 148, 158
Boki 58, 59, 61, 63, 71, 73, 76, 80
Bolt, John 28, 29
Bon Homme Richard 24
Boorda, Jeremy M. 349
Bouganville, Louis de 67
Boush, C.J. 208
Bradford, Royal 174
Brandt, Regina C. 261
Brannen, Sam 105
Briggs, Ralph 265

Britannia 20
Brown, Arthur 149
Brown, William 27, 28, 29
Browne, Herbert A. 315, 346
Bubonic Plague 173
Buchanan, Franklin 95
Bureau of Yards and Docks 88, 226
Bush, George 323, 324
Byron, Lord 59, 60, 61, 70, 72

C

Caetano, Juan 9
Calvinism 57
Camp H. M. Smith 299
Campbell, Archibald 21
canoes 1, 2, 11, 12, 15, 21, 43, 60, 259
Cape Horn 26, 37, 40, 44, 69, 104, 109, 154, 195, 197, 213
Carl Shurtz 212
carronades 39
Carter, George C. 181, 198
Carter, George R. 165
Carter, J.F. 185
Carter, Jimmy 323
Case #3 176
Castle and Cook 213
Castle, William 127
Catlin, Albertus W. 181, 182, 184, 185
Cayetano, Benjamin 328, 344
Centurian 9
Chadwick, Stephen 324
Chamberlain, Levi 13
Chambers, W.I. 201
Chandler, W.E. 126
Charlton, Richard 61, 76, 81, 88, 89, 92
Cherub 44
Chevron Oil Company 338
Chinese Exclusion Act 128
Chinese Exclusion act 155
Chow Ah Fo 176
Christie, Jonathan 114
Churchill, Winston 268, 274
Clarey, Bernard "Chick" 256, 327, 332, 333, 334, 339, 345 Clark,
George R. 208, 211
Clark, Harold M. 202, 214

Claudine 201
Clay, Henry 73
Cleghorn, A.V. 121
Clemins, Archie 332, 344
Clerke, Captain 12, 85
Cleveland, Grover 145, 148, 149
Coast Guard 25, 211, 214, 252, 253
Cochrane, Henry C. 114, 115
Colburn, John F. 201, 213
Cold War 297, 298, 303, 318, 323, 342, 346, 348
Coleman, James 28
College of Hawaii 189
Colley, B.F. 183
Columbia 26, 27, 81
Comete 68
Committee of Public Safety 144, 145
Committee of Safety 144
Congregationalists 52
Congress 69
Conners, Jeffrey 347
Constellation 33, 69, 91
Constitution of 1887 140
Construction Battalions 286
Continental Congress 23
Converse, G.A. 183
Convoy 71
Cook, Captain James 5, 9,10, 11,12, 13,14, 16, 22, 23, 25, 47,56,85, 99, 115, 141, 216, 336
Cook, Edwin 111, 112
Coolidge, Calvin 205
Coontz, Robert E. 206, 242, 244
Cooper, Alice B. 136
Coral Sea 274, 275, 277
Corney, Peter 12
Coronet 286
Coucal 305
Covington, George 347
Cowles, W.C. 225
Crilley, Frank W. 204, 205
Crowninshield, Benjamin 45, 69
CSA Alabama 109
CSA Shenandoah 109
Curtis, Joseph W. 95, 96, 186

D

D.S. Murray 121
Dallas, A.I. 93
Dalton, John 343
Dames, Thomas A. 332
Daniels, Josephus 200, 212, 224, 225, 228, 241
Davis, C.H. 169
Davis, Donald C. 305
Davis, Isaac 15, 16, 20, 51
Davis, Richard Harding 193
Decatur, Stephen 34, 36, 65
Delano, Amasa 10, 17, 21, 29
Denny, F.L. 182, 184
Department of Defense 338
Department of the Interior 315, 326
Dewey, George 156, 157, 170, 173
Dickerson, Mahlon 82
Dillingham, B.F. 135
Dillingham, Walter 157, 220, 225
Dillingham, Mason 332
Discovery 9, 11, 12, 16
Dobbin, James C. 104
Dole, James D. 215
Dole, Sanford 88,127, 145, 148, 149,153, 154, 155, 156, 157, 158,162,
163, 164, 165, 167, 190, 191, 201, 224
Dolphin 69, 70, 71, 73, 74
Dominis, John O. 138, 256
Dominis, Lydia 124, 137
Doolittle, James H. 273
Dorsey, James, Jr. 346
Doven, Charles A. 137
Dowell, J.S. 253
Downes, John 80, 81, 84
Downes, John 69, 80
Dowsett, lames 256
Doyle, R.M. 200
Dry-dock #1 217, 227, 254
Dry-dock #2 254
Dry-dock #3 254
Dube, M.J. 329
Dublin 91
Dunlap, Andrew 114
Dunne, J.J. 176
DuPont, Samuel F. 103

E

Earhart, Amelia 252
East wind rain 265
Ede, Alfred L. 203
Edison, Charles 257
Edwards, Ralph 325
Edwards, Thomas 71, 73, 74
Edwards, Webley 269
Eisenhower, Dwight D. 294, 305, 325
Eleanora 14, 15, 16
Ely, Eugene 201
Emma 110, 119, 120, 121, 122, 180
Emmons, Delos C. 268, 279
English, Robert S. 279
Enterprise 272, 273, 274, 275, 278
Environmental Protection Agency 311
Episcopalian 57
Ericsson, John 87
Essex 39, 40, 42
Estee, Morris M. 175
Evans, Robley 39, 174, 194, 195
Ewa 6, 7, 27, 28, 79, 85, 117, 135, 191, 281, 331
Ewa Beach 334
Explorer 129

F

F-4 203, 205
Fair American 15, 21
Fall, Albert B. 242
Farragut, David 40, 228
Farrin, James M. 305
Fasi, Frank 324
Federal Water Pollution Control Administration 312
Felt, Harry D. 305
filibusterers 105
Finch, William Bolton 63, 79, 80, 81, 84
FISC 249, 277, 348
Fish and Game Division 313
Fish, Hamilton 115
Fleet & Industrial Supply Center 249, 277
Fletcher, Frank J. 276, 278
Fletcher, W.B. 202
Flying Fish 83, 85

Ford Island 13, 48, 60, 61, 85, 180, 202, 206, 241, 243, 245, 249, 251, 252, 255, 256, 263, 266, 281, 295,304, 315, 324, 325, 326, 327, 331, 332, 333, 334, 335, 342, 345, 346
Ford Island - A Navy Place 335
Ford, Seth P. 256
Fords Island 48, 135, 136, 170, 173, 176
Forrestal, James 287
Fort Armstrong 186
Forward...From the Sea 348
Franklin, Benjamin 25
Frear, Walter F. 220
French, George 204
Freycinet, Louis de 67
Friendship 80
From the Sea 348
Fuchida, Mitsuo 265
Fukudome, Shigeru 262
Fuller, B.H. 185
Furer, Julius A. 204, 205
Furlong, W.R. 270, 271, 281
Furusho, Kouichi 341

G

Galapagos 40, 41, 42
Gamble, John Marshall 37, 40, 42, 43, 44, 47
Gamecock 105
Garfield, James 140
Gassendi 101
Gayler, Ernest R. 206
Gaylord 201
Geier 210, 211, 212
Geiger, Harold E. 202
General Board 173, 205
George, David 101
George III, King 16, 19
George IV, King 58
Gibson, Walter 129, 130
Gill, William F. 256
Gillette, C.S. 270
Globe 70
Goodrich, Caspar F. 154
Gore, John 9, 12
Grant, Ulysses S. 123

Gray, Robert 26, 27
Great White Fleet 194
Greenlet 305
Gregg, D.L. 111
Gresham, W.W. 146, 147, 148
Grogan, Leslie 264

H

Hagemeister, Captain 35, 36
Halawa gate 332
Halawa Gulch 223
Halawa Heights 298
Halawa Landing 324
Hale Ali'i 206
Halsey, William F. 196, 269, 272, 273, 274, 275, 278, 280, 282, 284, 285, 286, 287, 289
Hamilton, Paul 39
Hancock, John 23
Hanson Report 245
Harbottle, James 21, 44
Harding, Warren 242
Harllee, William C. 182, 184
Harris, Jeremy 344
Hart, Thomas 244
Hartwell, A.S. 150
Hawaii Calls 269
Hawaii Operation 262
Hawaii Ponoi 158
Hawaii Tourist Bureau 215
Hawaiian Dredging Company 198, 221, 226
Hawaiian Electric Company 312
Hawaiian Home Lands Recovery Act 340
Hawaiian League 127
Hawaiian National Guard 212
Hawaiian Navy 20, 131
Hawaiian Promotion Committee 215
Hayward, Thomas B. 323
Haywood, William 170, 171
HBMS Alert 39
HBMS Blonde 59, 70, 85, 169
HBMS Carysfort 88, 89
HBMS Clio 110

HBMS Greenwich 40, 42, 43
HBMS Seringapatam 40
HBMS Tenedos 120, 122
Helene 201
Hewahewa 51
Hickam Field 251
Hilbus, James 130
Hirohito 288
Hiroshima 287
Hiryu 245, 277
Historic Preservation Plan of 1978 315, 327
Hizen 210
HMS Achilles 253
Ho, Brian 314
Hoffman, Henry A. 318
hogging 32
Hokule'a 3, 300, 316
Hollingsworth, Alice Ho'ohokuokalani 268
Home Port Hawaii 324
Home Rule Party 164, 166, 190
Honolulu International Airport 316
Honolulu Rifles 127
Honouliuli Wildlife Refuge 331
Hooikaika 90
Hoover, Herbert 247
Hoover, John H. 287
Hope 48
Hopkins, Esek 24
Hopkins, W.E. 123
Horton, Jeter R. 184
Hospital Point 206, 249, 327
Hosyo 245
Houston Board 243
Houston, V.S. 208
Howard, Ava-Marie 347
Howell, John 29, 51, 138, 271
Howland Island 252, 253
Hull, Isaac 34, 65, 69, 74
Hull, Cordell 263
Humphreys, Joshua 32
Hunt, William H. 110
Hussey, Cyrus 70

I

Iaukea, C.P. 122
Ii, John 98, 177, 200
Ii, John Papa 85
Imperial Japanese Navy 245
Industrial Plant 244, 249
Inouye, Daniel 317, 324, 326, 336, 339, 342, 344
Inter-Island Steam Navigation Company 215
Intermediate Maintenance Facility 347
Intrepid 204
Iolani Palace 96, 116, 117, 122, 123, 126, 144, 149, 157, 158, 192, 251, 266, 300
Irons, John 329
Iroquois Point 261, 333
Irwin, William G. 177
Itasca 253
Iwo Jima 286

J

Jackal 27, 28
Jackson, George 129
Jajczay, Josef 119
Japan 245, 260, 269, 296
Japanese Naval General Staff 263
Jarrett, William 115
Jefferson, Thomas 25
Jensen, Martin 215
Johnson, Jay L. 349
Jones, John Coffin 61
Jones, John Coffin. 73
Jones, John Paul 23, 24, 25
Jones, Thomas ap Catesby 65, 74, 75, 76, 77, 80, 82, 87, 88, 92
Judd, A.F. 150
Judd, G.P. 89, 90, 95, 96, 99
Juicy Lucy II 311

K

Kaahumanu 49, 50, 51, 53, 58, 59, 62, 63, 71, 72, 73, 75, 76, 80
Ka'ahupahau 221, 222, 223, 224, 227
Kaai, Simon 121
Ka'akaukukui Reef 186
Kaeokulani 27, 28, 36
Kaga 245, 277
Kahai 6

Kahuna Kainani 227
Kahuna Kanakeawe 222
Kailua 48, 52
Kaimiloa 129, 130
Kaiulani 165
Kalakaua, David 119,120,121,122,123, 124,126, 127, 128, 129, 130, 131, 132, 135, 136, 137, 138, 140,141, 165, 300
Kalama 113, 114
Kalanianaole, Jonah 197
Kalanikupule 27, 28
Kalanimoku 20, 67, 72, 76
Kalaniopu'u 13, 14
Kalapapa 113
Kalauao 7, 28
Kalimoku 51
Kamamalu 58
Kamehameha 58
Kamehameha I 12,13, 14, 15, 16,18,19, 20, 21,22, 28, 35, 44, 47, 48, 49,50, 51,53,58,59, 62, 63, 67,72, 75,76, 84,101, 106,114,116, 122, 126, 133, 143,190, 192, 211, 255
Kamehameha II 49, 59, 62
Kamehameha III 62, 63, 76, 79, 80, 81, 82, 84, 88, 91, 92, 97,99, 101, 102,103,106,111,113
Kamehameha IV 106, 108, 110, 111, 119, 120, 256
Kamehameha V 115, 116, 118, 216
Kamikaze 285
Kanahele, George S. 105
kanaka 227
kanakas 17
Kaneoha, J.Y. 98
Kapiolani 126, 165
Kapole'i 334
kapu 5, 16, 53, 57
Kauikeaouli 59, 62, 72, 80, 88, 97, 101, 106
Kaumuali'i 35, 36, 47
Kawaiahao 92
Kawananaka, David 165
Ke awa lau o Pu'uloa 221
Ke Awa o Kau 27
Kealakekua 11, 13, 14, 20, 21
Kearney, Lawrence 91
Keaunui 6
Kekauluohi 84, 85
Kekuanaoa, M. 99

Kelso, Frank 337
Kendrick, John 14, 25, 26, 27, 28, 29, 31, 40
Kennedy, Edmund 81
Kennedy, John F. 305, 325
Keopuolani 51, 58
Kewalo Basin 325
KGMB 269
KGU 269
Kianapua'a 172
Kihune, Robert K.U. 345
Kilauea 121
Kimmel, Husband E. 255, 262, 263, 267, 271, 283
Kinau 63, 88, 106
Kinau Hale 122
King, Burger 329
King, Ernest J. 245, 262, 271, 286, 290
King, Martin Luther, Jr. 307
Kinkaid, Thomas C. 284
Knox, Frank 255, 271, 280
Knox, Henry 31
Knox, P.C. 176
Korean conflict 297
Koryu 245
Kotzebue, Otto von 67, 70
Ku 4, 13
Kuahua 60, 176, 177, 180, 201, 208, 244, 249, 261, 277
Kuahua Island 176
Kuakini 82
Kuehn, Otto 267

L

La Perouse, Jean 47, 67
La Place, Jean 81
La Poursuivante 101
Ladd Company 90
Lady Washington 14, 26, 27, 29, 48, 51
Langley, Samuel P. 169
LArtemise 81
Laulaunui 321
Laulaunui Island 305
Lay, William 70
Layton, Edwin T. 275
Leader, Miles T. 340
Leahy, William D. 286

Ledyard, John 9, 11, 26
Lehman, John 323
Lelia Bird 21
leprosy 113
Letters of Marque 25
Lexington 23, 242, 246, 251, 272, 274
Liberal Patriotic Party 164
Lifesaving Service 211
Lihia 58
Liholiho 49, 50, 51, 52, 58, 59, 62, 63, 75, 97, 106, 108,110, 111,120
Likelike 121
Liliuokalani 122, 124,128, 132,135,137, 138, 139,140, 141, 143, 144,
    145, 146, 147, 148, 149, 150, 151, 158, 162, 165, 195, 201, 224, 256
Locksun 212
Lockwood, Charles A. 279
LOG 282
London 71, 73
London, Jack 125, 136, 193
Long, John 169, 171, 173
Loughman, William F. 203
LST 353 283
Lualualei 247, 249, 261, 268, 315, 340
Luce, Stephen B. 110
Luke Field 202
Lunalilo 116, 117, 118, 119, 120
Lurline 216, 264, 299
Lyon, Henry 184

M

MacArthur, Arthur 181
MacArthur, Douglas 181, 272, 282, 284, 287, 289, 296
Macedonian 34, 39, 69
Macrae, James 59, 60, 61, 62
Mahan, Alfred T. 116, 143, 144, 209
Mahele 95, 97, 98, 99
Malden, C.R. 61, 70, 85, 169
Malolo 216
Manana 324
Marianas Turkey Shoot 284
Marin, Don Francisco 12, 48, 255
Marine Air Corps Station 281
Marine Barracks 181, 183, 186, 187, 198, 266, 271, 298, 315, 329
Marine Mammal Protection Act 337

Mariposa 216
Marquesas 1, 3, 40, 42, 67, 92
Marshall, J. F. B. 37, 42, 44, 69, 90, 91, 149
martial law 128, 145, 285
Massie Case 292
Masters, Bud 196
Matson Navigation Company 213, 216
Matsonia 216
Matsunaga, Spark 324, 325, 326
Maugham, Somerset 125
McCarthy, Charles J. 228
McCawley, Charles L. 184
McDonald, J.D. 244
McGinnis, Knefler 251
McKinley, William 153, 154, 157, 158, 161, 163, 164, 190, 191
Melville, Herman 125
Merry, J. F. 171,172, 173, 174, 175, 199, 200, 243
Merry Monarch 128, 137
Metcalf, Victor H. 185, 220
Metcalfe, Simon 14, 16
Metcalfe, Thomas 15
Meyer, George 197, 199
Midway 275, 276, 277
Mikasa 289
Miller, J.N. 1579 158
Mink, Patsy 312,317
missionaries 12, 51, 52, 53, 55, 56, 57, 58, 59, 60, 61, 62, 67, 68, 70, 71,
72, 73, 74, 75, 76, 79, 82, 84, 93, 97, 101, 103, 106, 112, 120, 140, 145, 153, 293
Missionary Boys 107, 140
Mitchell, William "Billy" 245, 246
Mitscher, Marc A. 283
Moknume'ume 13
Moku'ume'ume 7, 48, 222, 255
Monroe Doctrine 88, 132
Monroe, James 69
Moody, William H. 181
Moore, Charles B.T. 225
Morineau, Monsieur de 68
Mormon 57
Murfin, Orin S. 249, 253, 254
Musashi 250
Musick, Edward 252

N

Nagara 276
Nagasaki 288
Nagumo, Chuichi 263, 264, 272, 276, 277
Naniwa 154
National Historic Landmark 328, 331
National Park Service 306, 326
National Register of Historic Places 315
National Wildlife Refuge 316
Navajo 204
Naval Air Station 241, 243, 273, 281, 304, 340
Naval Base 132, 167, 174, 194, 213, 241, 244, 291, 292, 293, 297, 298, 304, 305, 306, 327, 334, 336, 340, 341, 346
Naval Club of the United States 295
Naval Coal Depot, Honolulu, T.H. 171
Naval Shipyard 249, 261, 307, 315, 320
Naval Station 36, 42, 124, 170, 172, 173, 174, 175, 177, 178,179, 180, 181, 182, 183, 184, 185, 186, 193, 197, 198, 199, 200, 201, 204, 206, 211, 225, 282, 298, 307, 315, 333, 347
Naval Supply Center 277, 312, 315, 329
Naval War College 110, 138, 143, 154
Navy Air Field 331
Navy Base 217, 301, 315, 329, 331, 340, 341
Navy League 328, 339, 342
Navy Square 335, 345
Navy Yard 32, 174, 176, 181, 186, 199, 227, 244, 266, 270, 271, 274, 278, 281, 282, 294
Nawiliwili Harbor 215
Neptune 35
Neva 35
Nevada 125
Newberry, Truman H. 184
Niblack, A.P. 183, 185
Niitaka, Mt 265
Nimitz, Chester W. 206, 226, 255, 271, 272, 273, 274, 275, 277,278, 279, 280, 281, 282, 284, 285, 286, 287, 289, 290, 340
Noble, Alfred 225
Noonan, Fred 252
Nordhoff, Charles 112
Nuku Hiva 40, 42
Nu'uanu 63, 125, 268

O

Oahu Railway 136, 170, 176, 177, 191, 200
Oahu Railway and Land Company 136, 171
Office of Naval Aeronautics 202, 214
Okinawa 286
OLD IRONSIDES 33
Oldendorf, Jesse B. 284
Olowalu 15
Ontario 69
Operation Olympic 286
Organic Act 176
Osborn, D.R. 257, 258
Outerbridge, William 265
Owen, Clarence S. 184

P

Pacific Air Detachment 256
Pacific Command 299
Pacific Fleet Command Center 319
Pacific Missile Range Facility 339
Pacific Squadron 65, 69, 74, 87, 88, 89, 92, 93, 97, 109, 110, 112,116,
123, 124, 137, 148, 151, 154, 158
Pacific Station 109, 138
Pacific War Memorial Commission 306
Pacific War Memorial Committee 325
Pan-American Airways 243, 253, 254
Pan-American clipper 252, 256
papists 68
Parke, Robert W. 149
Parker, Samuel 139
Patton, George 257
Paty, William 89
Paulding, Hiram 71, 256
Paulet, George 79, 88, 89, 90, 91, 92, 93
Paxton, Elmer 199
Peacock 34, 74, 81, 83
Pearl City peninsula 170, 256
Pearl Harbor Dry-dock #1 221
Pearl Harbor Memorial Trust 295
Pearl Harbor Yacht Club 256
Peirce, Henry 114, 115, 121, 123
Percival, John 69, 70, 71, 72, 73, 74, 75, 77, 83, 95, 256
Perry, Commodore Matthew 27, 111
Perry, Matthew 64, 82, 104

Pickett, H.K. 271
Pierce, Franklin 101, 111
Pi'ikoi, J. 99
Plan Orange 154, 197, 207, 262
Poindexter, Joseph B. 267
Poinsett, Joel 83
Poka 'Aliana 13
Polynesian Voyaging Society 316
Polynesians 1, 3, 336
Pond, Charles F. 175, 177, 183
Porpoise 83, 85 _
Porter, David 37, 39, 40, 41, 42, 43, 44, 65, 66, 69
Portlock, Nathaniel 12, 27
Potomac 80
Praise the Lord and Pass the Ammunition 271
Preble, Edward 34
Presbyterians 52
Presley, Elvis 325
Preston, William B. 103
Price, Kenton E. 298
Pries, Alfred 325
Prindle, F.C. 175
Provisional Government 144, 145, 146, 147, 148, 149, 164
Prueher, Joseph W. 344, 349
Public Works Center 315
Puget, Peter 19
Pukui, Mary Keawe 221
Punahawale 28
Punahou School 145
Puritans 57, 70
Puuloa 5, 6, 7, 12, 13, 17, 23, 28, 96, 131, 136, 159, 315, 334 _
Pu'uloa 199
Pu'uloa Naval Reservation 254
Pye, William S. 271

Q

Qualah Battoo 80
Quarry Point 205
Quarters A 206

R

Rabbit Island 13, 60, 61, 255
Radford, Arthur W. 295
Rainbow 5 262

Ramsey, Logan 265
Read, G.C. 81
Reagan, Ronald 323, 328
reciprocity 107,108,111,112,115,117,119,123,124,131,133,143,144
Red Cross Canteen 266
Red Hill 257, 259, 260, 295, 348
Reform Cabinet 127, 130, 137
Reform Party 136, 137, 139
regional maintenance 347
regionalization 347
Reimann, Robert T. 325
Relief 83, 209
Remember Pearl Harbor 271
Republic 149
Republic of Hawaii 149, 161, 162, 176, 201
Resolution 9, 11, 12, 13, 161
Retz, W.A. 325, 330
Revenue Cutter Service 25, 211
Richards, David Kanakeawe 222, 223, 224
Richards, William 98
Richardson, James O. 254, 255, 262
Rickover, Hyman 316, 317, 318
Ricord, John 98
RimPac 315, 342, 346
Rives, Jean 67, 68
Rochefort, Joseph 273, 274, 275, 279
Rodgers, John 214
Rodman Board 243
Roger B. Taney 252
Rogers, John 65, 109
Roman Catholic 57
Roosevelt, Franklin D. 225, 249, 254, 255, 262, 267, 273, 284, 285
Roosevelt, H.L. 184
Roosevelt, Theodore 143, 154, 165, 169, 174, 193, 194
Russell, J.H. 185, 186
Russian-American Company 66
Russo-Japanese War 193
Ryujo 278
Ryuzyo 245

S

Samoa 6, 129, 130, 132, 212
San Francisco Bridge Company 226
sandalwood 14, 15, 27, 48, 58, 62, 63, 66, 68, 76, 80

Sandwich, Earl of 10
Sandwich Islands 10, 19, 23, 25, 27, 35, 36, 44, 45, 69, 70, 73, 74,76,
79, 81, 84, 85, 86, 89, 91, 95, 103, 112, 116, 117, 125, 130
Sanford, H.R. 226
Saratoga 242, 246, 251, 272, 274, 275
Savo Sound 277
Scheffer, George 66, 67
Schofield, John M. 116, 117, 118, 124, 131
Sea Letters 25, 35
Sea Victory 343
Sea Bees 286
Seagull 83, 244
Serapis 25
Seringapatam 42, 43
Sessler, Warren 325
Sewall, Harold M. 190
Seward, William H. 111
shark goddess 170, 180, 195, 201, 217, 221, 223, 224, 227
Shearer, M.E. 185
Sheridan 182
Shoho 274
Shokaku 283
Shore Intermediate Maintenance Activity 347
Short, Walter C. 267, 283
Shrewsbury, John 336
Sir Andrew Hammond 42, 43, 44
Skerrett, Joseph S. 120
Smedley, Larry E. 329
Smith, A.G. 150
Smith, Francis 225
Smith, Holland M. 298
Smith, Kirk 319
Snark 136
Sokaku 245
Soryu 245, 277
Southard, Samuel 69, 79, 220
Soviet Union 318, 323, 346
Spanish-American War 154, 155, 156', 157, 170, 179
Spence, Floyd 348
Sprague, T.L. 285
Spruance, Raymond 275, 282, 283, 288, 290
Stark, Harold R. 255, 262, 263
State Historic Preservation Office 338
Stevens, John L. 144, 145, 146
Stevens, T.C. 124

Stevenson, Robert Louis 125
Stewart, A.J. 320
Stewart, Charles 34
Stoddart, Benjamin 35
Stratton, A. Clark 306
Submarine Base 205, 206, 244, 245, 251, 261, 271, 305, 315, 319, 347
Submarine Base Repair Department 347
Submarine Escape Training Tower 249, 305
Sutton, W.G. 330,340
Swanson, Charles 0. 316

T

Taft, William H. 190, 223
Tahiti 1, 3, 50, 62, 67, 92, 300, 316
Tai Sing Loo 329
Taiyo Maru 264
Tamoree, George 36
Tankan Bay 264
Tanner, Z. L. 170
Taussig, E. D. 171
Taylor, Albert P. 215
Teapot Dome 242
Territory 157
Territory of Hawaii 163, 181, 185, 186, 190, 200, 241, 250, 267, 268, 285, 306
Terry, S.W. 181, 182, 183, 184
Thaddeus 36, 52
Third Fleet 324
Thom, J.C. 208
Thomas, Robert E. 281
Thomas, Sir Richard 15, 25, 34, 74, 76, 82, 87, 89, 90, 91, 92, 93, 313
Thompson, Nainoa 3
Thorn, Johathan 36
Threat Condition Alpha 333
Thurston, L.A. 156, 158
Timberlake, Lewis 314
Tonquin 36
Tora, tora, tora 265
Traister, R.E. 320, 328
transpacific cable 193
Tromelin, Admiral de 101
Truman, Harry S. 296, 307, 318
Truxtun, Thomas 34
Truxtun, William 114, 115
Twain, Mark 125

U

Union 28
Union Jack 18, 92
United Nations 295, 305
United States Fleet 241, 254
United States Pacific Fleet 198, 271
University of Hawaii 58, 189, 303, 319, 321
Upshur, Abel 87, 88, 92, 93
Uranie 67
US Naval Institute 110
USCG Thetis 211
USS Adams 137
USS Alaska 126
USS Arizona 199, 251, 263, 270, 271, 281, 294, 295,298, 306,314, 325, 326, 328, 333, 335, 342, 345
USS Arkansas 223
USS Astoria 277
USS Beaver 205
USS Benicia 123
USS Bennington 169, 171
USS Birmingham 202
USS Boston 89, 90, 145
USS Bowfin 278, 327
USS California 116, 201, 224, 345
USS Capella 257
USS Carl Vinson 346
USS Cavalla 283
USS Charleston 137
USS Chicago 205
USS Colorado 253
USS Congress 97
USS Constitution 34, 36, 40, 74, 95, 345
USS Coronado 346
USS Cyane 63, 92, 96, 103
USS Delaware 220
USS Dolphin 69, 256
USS Dragon 313
USS Enterprise 81, 269
USS Essex 39
USS George Washington 304
USS Grayback 304
USS Grayling 271, 290
USS Greenville 346
USS Gudgeon 299

USS Helena 297
USS Hornet 40, 273
USS Houston 251
USS Independence 346
USS Iowa 278, 288, 289, 296
USS Iroquois 137, 180, 181, 185
USS Jamestown 114
USS John Adams 81
USS Lakawanna 112, 126
USS Langley 245
USS Lexington 245, 253, 269
USS Long Beach 304
USS Maine 154
USS Marion 154
USS Mars 307
USS Maryland 204
USS Menhaden 290
USS Midway 346
USS Mississippi 104, 111
USS Missouri 207, 282, 288, 289, 323, 328, 332, 333, 334, 335,336,
341, 342, 343, 344,345
USS Missouri Memorial Association 343
USS Mohican 157, 158
USS Monadnock 109
USS Monoghan 273
USS Nautilus 304
USS Navajo 257
USS Nero 171
USS Nevada 263, 327
USS New Jersey 278, 284,296
USS New Orleans 271
USS Oklahoma 243, 263, 328
USS Oregon 154
USS Pearl Harbor 346
USS Pennsylvania 202
USS Pensacola 123
USS Petrel 180, 198
USS Philadelphia 151, 154, 157, 158, 159, 169
USS Philippine Sea 296
USS Platte 257
USS Ponchatoula 313
USS Portsmouth 111, 120
USS Powhatan 109
USS R-1 244
USS Saratoga 246, 269

USS Sargo 304
USS South Dakota 203
USS St. Louis 208, 210
USS St. Marys 97, 111
USS Susquchanna 104, 111
USS Tuscarora 109, 120
USS United States 70, 92
USS Utah 270, 295, 327
USS Vandalia 105
USS Vanderbilt 109, 110
USS Vincennes 63, 79
USS Ward 262, 263, 265, 285
USS Wasp 278
USS West Virginia 203
USS Wisconsin 282
USS Wyoming 223

V

V-J Day 288
Vancouver, George 16, 17, 18, 19, 20, 21, 22, 27, 58, 76
Very, S.W. 88, 171, 182, 185, 186
Vietnam 305, 318
Vincennes 83, 85, 278
Vision, Presence, Power 348

W

Waialua Valley 265
Waikele Gulch 281
Waimano Home Road 324
Waimomi 5, 7, 23, 136, 159, 221, 251, 315
Waipio peninsula 79, 180, 201, 213
Waipio Point 327
Washington, George 23, 24, 31,.33, 35, 69, 72, 117, 118, 205
Watertown 222
Waverly 68
wayfinder 3
Weaver, Chase 329
Webster, Daniel 88, 91
Welch, L.F. 206
whaling 25, 40, 48, 56, 64, 69, 97, 109, 112
White, U.S. 175
Whiling, W.H. 173, 175
Whitney, Henry 119

Wilcox, Robert 136, 164
Wilhelmina 214
Wilkes, Charles 82, 83, 84, 85, 86, 95, 194
Willard Board 243
Willis, Albert S. 146, 147, 148
Wilson, Woodrow 242
Winship, Nathaniel 44
Women's Hawaiian Patriotic League 157
Woodman, T. 85
Woodruff, Simon 9
Woodward, Edwin T. 137
World War I 202, 205, 206, 209, 210, 212, 214, 215, 252
World War II 181, 206, 242, 263, 293, 295, 296, 300, 307,311,315, 319, 323, 327, 333, 334, 335, 336, 341, 342, 344
Wrenn, A.C. 184

Y

Yamamoto, Isoroku 262, 263, 264, 265, 268, 272, 277, 280
Yamato 250
Yarnell, Harry E. 246, 263
Yee, Roy 324
Yokota 338
Yokota, Clyde 338
Yorktown 87, 272, 274, 275, 276
Young, John 15, 16, 20, 21, 51, 58, 62, 84, 99
Young, Lucien 158

Z

Zacharias, E.M. 269
Zheng 341
Zuikaku 285
Zumwalt, Elmo R 309, 315, 317